M000208896

# THE OMAHA TRIBE

## Volume I

# THE
# OMAHA
# TRIBE

## VOLUME I

## ALICE C. FLETCHER
## AND
## FRANCIS LA FLESCHE

INTRODUCTION BY ROBIN RIDINGTON

UNIVERSITY OF NEBRASKA PRESS • LINCOLN AND LONDON

Introduction copyright © 1992 by the University of Nebraska Press
All rights reserved
Manufactured in the United States of America

First printing of this Bison Book edition: 1992

Library of Congress Cataloging-in-Publication Data
Fletcher, Alice C. (Alice Cunningham), 1838–1923.
The Omaha tribe / Alice C. Fletcher and Francis La Flesche; introduction
by Robin Ridington.—Bison book ed.
p.    cm.
"A Bison book."
Includes bibliographical references and index.
ISBN 0-8032-6876-9 (v. 1).—ISBN 0-8032-6877-7 (v. 2).—
ISBN 0-8032-6878-5 (set)
1. Omaha Indians. I. La Flesche, Francis, d. 1932. II. Title.
E99.O4F64     1992     91-42657
973'.04975—dc20       CIP

This Bison Book edition is reproduced from the Twenty-Seventh Annual
Report of the Bureau of American Ethnology to the Secretary of the
Smithsonian Institution, 1905–1906. It reproduces *in toto* the text and illustrations of the original work published by the Bureau of American
Ethnology in 1911. It omits from the appendix the list of original owners
of allotments on Omaha Reservation and the accompanying map. The
first volume includes Chapters I through VII; the second volume is comprised of Chapters VIII though XVI, the appendix, and the index.

# SUMMARY TABLE OF CONTENTS

## INTRODUCTION BY ROBIN RIDINGTON

In 1962 when I entered graduate school in anthropology at Harvard's Peabody Museum, the Sacred Pole of the Omaha tribe was on display in a glass case near the anthropology department office. I was drawn to visit there almost daily. The Pole reminded me that Native American history is physical as well as legendary. The Venerable Man, as he is called, spoke to me on matters of substance. He spoke to me by his very physical endurance through time, but he was also a mystery. I needed another source of information to explain what the Omahas meant when they called him their "Venerable Man."

During the course of my first year of study, I discovered a book that explained the Pole. The book, like the Pole, brought forward information from nineteenth-century Omaha life into my own time and place. I read it with amazement and wonder. I thought then and I am still of the opinion that *The Omaha Tribe* by Alice C. Fletcher and her Omaha coauthor, Francis La Flesche, is the single most important and comprehensive study ever written about a Native American tribe. If I had to choose one book to rescue from a pyre of burning ethnographies, it would probably be this one. Perhaps the University of Nebraska Press is doing just such a rescue in making this two-volume edition available.

*The Omaha Tribe* first appeared as the Twenty-Seventh Annual Report of the Bureau of American Ethnology. Although published in 1911, it was really the last in a series of great nineteenth-century ethnographies designed to document and interpret the Native presence in America. These books were giants in their quarto size, their handsome olive-green covers embossed with gold, and their splendid illustrations. They were also giants in the contribution they made to Native American ethnography and to American literature generally. The BAEs, as they have been referred to affectionately by generations of Native and non-Native scholars and readers, are distinctive in that they portray the Native American experience using information gained through intensive fieldwork. Their authors were no "armchair ethnographers." Long before Bronislaw Malinowski "invented" fieldwork and "discovered" the importance of myth and oral tradition in the 1920s, pioneer ethnographers like Frank Hamilton Cushing, James Owen Dorsey, Alice C. Fletcher, and James Mooney were engaged in the ethnographic enterprise in all its complexity and publishing their findings in the BAE Annual Reports. Although others like Prince Maximilian of Wied-Neuwied, Henry R. Schoolcraft, and Lewis Henry Morgan had previously written about Native Americans from personal experience, the BAE publications provided the first comprehensive outlet dedicated to ethnographic writing in America.

*The Omaha Tribe* is doubly important because it is the first major ethnography written jointly by an outside fieldworker (Fletcher) and a member of the tribe being described (La Flesche). Opposite Plate I, a portrait of La Flesche, the authors wrote:

> This joint work embodies the results of unusual opportunities to get close to the thoughts that underlie the ceremonies and customs of the Omaha tribe, and to give a fairly truthful picture of the people as they were during the early part of the last century, when most of the men on whose information this work is based were active participants in the life here described.

Their work together embodied a union of the complementary male and female forces that they identify as central "to the perpetuation of all living forms" (page 134). Their relationship was also personally complementary in that Fletcher adopted La Flesche as her son and they lived together for many years. They were aware that their surnames, meaning "arrow maker" and "the arrow," had some resonance with the roles they played as ethnographers of Omaha culture and history. As a complement to her European name, Fletcher had received the name Ma-she-ha-the—meaning "the motion of an eagle as he sweeps high in the air"—from Omaha elder Wajapa in 1881. In a passage later used on a plaque marking the place where her ashes were placed in a patio of the Art Museum at Santa Fe, Fletcher described how her contact with the Native American world had changed her. The plaque reads:

> Living with my Indian friends I found I was a stranger in my native land. As time when on, the outward aspect of nature remained the same, but a change was wrought in me. I learned to hear the echoes of a time

when every living thing even the sky had a voice. That voice devoutly heard by the ancient people of America I desired to make audible to others.[1]

Like "the arrow" and "the arrow maker," the Sacred Pole and the Twenty-Seventh Annual Report have deeply intertwined histories. Fletcher and La Flesche place the Sacred Pole at the very center of their book. La Flesche tells how he persuaded the Pole's last keeper, Yellow Smoke, to give the Venerable Man over to the safekeeping of the Peabody Museum. The "boy memory" La Flesche wrote describing the "ancient ceremonies of the Sacred Pole" (pages 245–51) is one of the first piece of narrative ethnographic writing by a Native American author, and still one of the very best.

Fletcher and La Flesche placed the Sacred Pole in the Peabody Museum for safekeeping in 1888. They placed the words and teachings of Yellow Smoke and other elders between the substantial olive-green covers of the Twenty-Seventh Annual Report in 1911. Both the book and the Sacred Pole are messengers from a different time. Both can be read as texts that carry meaning from one generation to another. The Venerable Man communicates in a language of philosophy and ceremony, a language familiar to the experience of Native American people. The book describes these ceremonies, both for non-Omahas and for Omahas who never experienced them directly. It provides what Alice Fletcher described as "a point of view . . . as from the center" (page 222). Both book and Pole speak to people from a time in the tribe's past when, in the words of the Sacred Legend, "a great council was being held to devise some means by which the bands of the tribe might be kept together and the tribe itself saved from extinction."

The Venerable Man was central to the tribe's ceremonies during their buffalo hunting days. In 1988, exactly a century after the Sacred Pole left Omaha hands, Omahas once again touched him. One of these was tribal chairman Doran Morris, Yellow Smoke's great-great-grandson according to Omaha kinship. A year later, the tribe successfully negotiated the Sacred Pole's return to their control. They welcomed him back as a returning elder at their annual pow-wow on July 20, 1989. Since then, the tribe has been successful in negotiating the return of other sacred objects described in *The Omaha Tribe*. One of these is the White Buffalo Hide, considered to be of equal status to the Sacred Pole and equally prominent in ceremonies related to the buffalo hunt.

The Sacred Pole's return to the Omahas is a challenge to them and also a challenge to anthropology, as is this Bison Book edition of the book. Anthropology has kept descriptions of Omaha ceremonial life bound within the pages of the Twenty-Seventh Annual Report. Now it must discover a language of interpretation that will release that information to the understanding of Omahas living today. Anthropology must provide a new reading of its old texts. The original one-volume edition of the Twenty-Seventh Annual Report is now an old book. Like the Sacred Pole, the book itself has become the survivor of a past way of life. This two-volume Bison edition, originally published in 1972 and now brought back into print, provides Omahas and non-Omahas alike with an opportunity to think about their traditions from a contemporary perspective. An appropriate companion to the newly returned sacred objects, this edition invites a new reading of old stories.

We now describe the BAE Annual Reports as "classics," but at the time of their publication they were original and inventive, even radical in their departure from early forms of armchair speculation and chauvinistic imperialism. The famous Englishman E. B. Tylor, often described as "the father of anthropology," ended his 1871 *Primitive Culture* with an exhortation that the "painful office of ethnography" is to "expose the remains of crude old culture which have passed into harmful superstition, and to mark those out for destruction."[2] How different that purpose is from the gentle and sympathetic statement by Fletcher and La Flesche that their purpose is "to get close to the thoughts that underlie the ceremonies and customs of the Omaha Tribe" (page 14). In the nineteenth century there was no canonical style of ethnographic writing. Each fieldworker had to invent the form that seemed best to suit his or her experience of the Native American world. Each BAE volume reflected a particular solution to the problem of genre. Each one gave voice to an original encounter between native and newcomer.

Fletcher and La Flesche were at liberty to use a variety of genres, while keeping throughout to a simple narrative voice. They wrote about the Omahas in a style of anthropology that came out of nineteenth-century experimentation, even though their book did not appear until 1911. They wrote in the style of a pioneering generation for whom there was no "correct" way of going about the task of documenting Native American experience or representing it to outsiders. They allowed themselves to be guided by Omaha categories rather than by those of an emergent academic discipline. They were educated by the task at hand, rather than by an academic institution.

An irony of their book's place in the history of anthropology is that it appeared just at the time when a revolution was taking place in the profession's culture and politics. According to Joan Mark, Alice Fletcher's biographer, Fletcher "found herself facing an unsympathetic generation of younger anthropologists, many of them connected with Columbia University, who were eager to assert themselves and disavow the mistakes of their elders." This new generation of self-important professional anthropologists was already predisposed to reject the long delayed work of Fletcher and La Flesche as "old fashioned." Mark cites a highly critical review by Robert Lowie in 1913, for instance, that "criticized them for classifying the material in accord with 'aboriginal' rather than 'scientific' logic."[3]

Lowie and others of his generation in the first decades of the twentieth century reversed the focus of anthropology from the world of Native Americans to that of the academy. They valued the university programs they were founding above an interest in the lives of aboriginal people. They did not admit, like Fletcher, to being changed by their experiences. In the years immediately following the publication of the Twenty-Seventh Annual Report, anthropologists became obsessed with a search for an "objectivity" that they envied in the physical sciences. As they began to train students and grant graduate degrees in anthropology, they rejected the philosophically sensitive work of authors like Fletcher and La Flesche as "subjective" and "unprofessional."

Anthropology has now come full circle. We can appreciate the language and interpretation of nineteenth-century writers like Fletcher and La Flesche. We have become aware that anthropological representation requires more than the repetition of ethnographic facts. We know that we construct the information we place upon the page in collaboration with the people who inform us. We recognize that ethnographic description is inherently interpretive. We realize that the ultimate ethnographic instrument is human, not mechanical. True objectivity requires understanding and interpretation. An ethnography that denies its own interpretive instrumentality risks becoming, itself, uncritically subjective. *The Omaha Tribe* resonates with a movement away from the "postmodernist pastiche" and toward a "neopremodernism."

*The Omaha Tribe* is remarkable because it resulted from the collaboration of a Native and non-Native ethnographer. It is remarkable because the Omaha tribe itself is remarkable in the beauty and cosmic symmetry of its fundamental forms. The book is remarkable for the wealth of songs, prayers, and ceremonies it documents. It is remarkable for a sometimes overwhelming abundance of ethnographic detail about clan names, place names, emblematic clan hair cuts given to children, vision quests, social organization, government, and history. As a balance to this detail, the book is remarkable for passages that are clear, beautiful, and philosophically interpretive. The chapter entitled "Tribal Organization," for instance, begins

with a statement of "fundamental religious ideals, cosmic in significance" that explain "how the visible universe came into being
and how it is maintained." The language is probably Fletcher's, but
the ideas come out of a deep engagement with Omaha thought she
shared with La Flesche. I have set the passage line for line, as in
poetry, to facilitate a fresh reading. It goes:

> An invisible and continuous life
> was believed to permeate all things,
> seen and unseen.
> This life manifests itself in two ways.
> First, by causing to move:
> All motion, all actions of mind or body,
> are because of this invisible life;
> Second, by causing permanency
> of structure and form,
> as in the rock, the physical features
> of the landscape, mountains, plains, streams,
> rivers, lakes, the animals and man.
> This invisible life
> is similar to the will power
> of which man is conscious
> within himself—
> a power by which things are brought to pass.
> Through this mysterious life and power
> All things are related to one another
> and to man, the seen to the unseen,
> the dead to the living,
> a fragment of anything
> to its entirety.
> This invisible life and power
> was called Wakon'da. (page 134)

A reissue of *The Omaha Tribe* invites a new reading. Nineteenth-
century reading habits were different from our own. This was the
age of Dickens rather than "Dallas," of letters rather than phone
calls, of newspapers and magazines rather than sound bites. Fletcher
and La Flesche felt perfectly comfortable inserting thirty pages of
detailed information about the related Ponca and Osage tribes before
even beginning to talk about the Omahas in Chapter Two. I prefer
to think of the book beginning with Plate 17 (opposite page 71), the
wonderful photograph of an Omaha woman and child outside their
tipi. You might want to save the history that follows for later and
move directly forward to the passage about Wakon'da (quote above)
that begins Chapter Four.

Following this passage, Fletcher and La Flesche describe a fundamental principle of complementarity that is a key to their interpretation of Omaha life. "The sun," they say, "was masculine, the moon feminine." Because of this, "day was male and night female. The union of these two forces was regarded as necessary to the perpetuation of all living forms, and to man's life by maintaining his food supply." All Omaha "religious rites and . . . social usages and organization," they say, are ways of "enforcing these cosmic and religious ideas." Thus, "the tribe was composed of two grand divisions, one representing Sky people or the Inshta'shunda; the other, the Earth people, of the Hon'gashenu" (pages 134–35). This "duality in the tribal organization" is a key to Omaha society as Fletcher and La Flesche read it. Duality is most obvious in the division of the great tribal circle, the Hu'thuga, into "Sky People" and "Earth People" during the summer buffalo hunt.

The reader might want to look at what the authors have to say about tribal government in Chapter Five. The idea of complementary opposites is particularly well illustrated by the two Sacred Pipes described on page 207. I would turn next to Chapter Six to discover the "point of view as from the center" that the Sacred Pole and its ceremonies revealed to Fletcher and La Flesche in September of 1888. The passage describing the Sacred Pole (page 217) through to the end of their description of the White Buffalo Hide ceremonies (page 308) is the most powerful and intense part of Volume One. Read it all with respect and attention. Here you will find stories within stories; narrative, adventure, time changes, genre shifts, clues to deeper levels of meaning, and powerful poetics. Chapters Six and Seven are really a book within a book, but references here connect forward and backward to every other part of the two volumes.

You may want to go back at some point to look at the fascinating description of the Omaha adolescent vision quest known as Non'zhinzhon, "to stand sleeping" in Chapter Three, "Rites Pertaining to the Individual." It is relevant to understanding the story of a vision quest in which the son of a chief discovered the Sacred Pole, so many years ago. You may also want to look ahead to pages 503–9 in Volume Two for the description of a complementary girl's visionary empowerment through the tattooing ceremony that gives her the Mark of Honor. The boy's power comes through the blessing of the night, what Fletcher and La Flesche called "the great mother force." The girl's power comes through the sun who "speaks" from the zenith point as his "symbol descends upon the maid with the promise of life-giving power" (page 504). *The Omaha Tribe* is a circle of stories that connect to one another in many ways. In your reading you will make them your own.

For many years, this wonderful book lay under the cloud of prejudice suggested by Lowie's remark that the authors classified the material "in accord with 'aboriginal' rather than 'scientific' logic." What to Lowie was a terrible error seems now to be a saving grace. It is certainly a saving grace to Native Americans tired of being subjects of experiments conducted by colonial oppressors. It is certainly a blessing to anthropologists newly sensitive to the issue of "ethnographic authority."[4] May it also be blessing to you, the reader of this new Bison edition. You can be sure that the book's authors respected the "mysterious life and power" through which "all things are related to one another and to man, the seen to the unseen, the dead to the living, a fragment of anything to its entirety." In the words of Omaha elder Clifford Wolf, Sr., reading this book may bring you "a blessing for a long time to come."

NOTES

1. Joan Mark, *A Stranger in Her Native Land: Alice Fletcher and the American Indians* (Lincoln: University of Nebraska Press, 1988), pp. 48, 335.

2. Edward B. Tylor, *Primitive Culture: Researches into the Development of Mythology, Philosophy, Religion, Language, Art and Custom* (London: J. Murray, 1871), p. 539. Reprinted as *The Origins of Culture*, Part I and II, with an introduction by Paul Radin (New York: Harper Torchbooks, 1958), p. 539.

3. Mark, pp. 337–38.

4. James Clifford, "On Ethnographic Authority," in *The Predicament of Culture: Twentieth-Century Ethnography, Literature, and Art* (Cambridge: Harvard University Press, 1988), pp. 21–54.

# BUREAU OF AMERICAN ETHNOLOGY

W. H. HOLMES, CHIEF

## RESEARCH WORK

Researches among the Indian tribes were conducted in accordance with the plan of operations approved by the Secretary June 5, 1905; these include investigations among the aborigines of Oregon, Colorado, New Mexico, Indian Territory, Oklahoma, Pennsylvania, and Florida, and, more especially, researches in the office of the Bureau and in various museums and libraries throughout the country. The scientific staff of the Bureau remains the same as during the previous year with the single exception that Mr. F. W. Hodge was transferred from the Secretary's office of the Smithsonian Institution to the Bureau, with the title of Ethnologist—a step which permits him to devote his entire time to the completion of the Handbook of the Indians.

Aside from his administrative duties, the chief was occupied with the completion and revision of papers for the Handbook of the Indians and in the preparation of a monographic work on the technology and art of the tribes. He also continued his duties as Honorary Curator of the Division of Prehistoric Archeology in the National Museum.

Mrs. M. C. Stevenson remained in the office during the early months of the year, reading the final proofs of her monograph on the Zuñi Indians, which issued from the press in December. In January she again entered the field, having selected the pueblo of Taos, New Mexico, as a suitable place for the continuation of her researches. In initiating her work in this pueblo Mrs. Stevenson encountered many difficulties, and her progress at first was slow; but later, owing largely to the very courteous cooperation of the Commissioner of Indian Affairs, her study of the history, language, and customs of the tribe was facilitated, and was progressing favorably at the close of the year.

During the early part of the year Mr. James Mooney was chiefly occupied, in collaboration with other members of the Bureau, with the Handbook of the Indians, which work was continued at intervals after he took the field. On September 19, 1905, he left Washington for western Oklahoma to continue researches among the Kiowa, Southern Cheyenne, and allied tribes, partly in fulfillment of the joint arrangement between the Bureau and the Field Museum of Natural History. His stay while with the Kiowa was chiefly at the agency at Anadarko, Oklahoma. Among the Cheyenne he made headquarters at Cantonment, Oklahoma, the central settlement of the most conservative element of the tribe. Mr. Mooney returned to Washington about the end of April, and resumed work on his report, giving much attention also to the Handbook of the Indians.

Dr. J. Walter Fewkes completed during the year his report on the aborigines of Porto Rico and neighboring islands. He prepared also an account of his field work in eastern Mexico, conducted under the joint auspices of the Smithsonian Institution and this Bureau during the winter of 1905–6. These papers were assigned to the Twenty-fifth Annual Report and were in type at the close of the year. Doctor Fewkes also made considerable progress in the preparation of a bulletin on the antiquities of the Little Colorado valley, Arizona.

During the year Dr. John R. Swanton completed and prepared for the press all of the Tlingit material, ethnological and mythological, collected by him during previous years; all of the ethnological and a portion of the mythological material has been accepted for introduction into the Twenty-sixth Annual Report. Doctor Swanton interested himself particularly also in the study of the linguistic stocks of Louisiana and southern Texas, many of which are either on the verge of extinction or are already extinct; and a grammar and dictionary of the Tunica language is well advanced, while a dictionary of the Natchez is in course of preparation.

Mr. J. N. B. Hewitt was engaged almost entirely in investigating and reporting on etymologies of terms and names and in elaborating and preparing important articles for the Handbook of the Indians, and also in reading proof of that important work conjointly with the other collaborators of the Office.

During the year Dr. Cyrus Thomas was engaged almost continuously on the Handbook of the Indians, assisting in final revision of the manuscript and in reading proof. During the first two or three months he assisted also in reading and correcting proofs of Bulletin 28, which treats of Mexican antiquities—a work for which his extensive researches regarding the glyphic writing of middle America especially fitted him.

The manuscript of the body of the Handbook of the Indians was transmitted to the Public Printer early in July. In view of the fact that numerous tribal and general articles were prepared by specialists not connected directly with the Bureau, it was deemed advisable to submit complete galley proofs of the Handbook to each as received. While this involved considerable delay in the proof reading, the corrections and suggestions received showed the wisdom of the plan. By the close of the year all the material was in type through the letter "N," and of this, 544 pages, to the article "Heraldry," have been finally printed.

The work on the Handbook of Languages, in charge of Dr. Franz Boas, honorary philologist of the Bureau, was continued during the year. The several sketches of American languages—sixteen in number—which are to form the body of this work are now practically complete, with the exception of those on the Eskimo and the Iroquois. Field work was conducted during the year by Edward Sapir among the Yakima of Oregon and by Frank J. Speck among the Yuchi in Indian Territory.

Mr. Stewart Culin, curator of ethnology in the Brooklyn Institute of Arts and Sciences, whose monograph on Indian Games forms the bulk of the Twenty-fourth Annual Report, was engaged during the year in reading the proofs of that work; but owing to his absence in the field for a protracted period the work was not completed at the close of the year.

The movement for the enactment by Congress of a law for the preservation of American antiquities, which was inaugurated during previous years, was continued by various individuals and institutions during the last year, and the perfected measure became a law in June. With the view of assisting the departments of the Government having charge of the public domain in the initiation of practical measures for the preservation of the antiquities of the Southwest, the Bureau has actively continued the compilation of a card catalogue of the archeological sites, especially the ruined pueblos and cliff-dwellings, and during the year has made much progress in the preparation of a series of bulletins to be devoted to the fuller presentation of all that is known regarding these antiquities. In promoting this work Mr. E. L. Hewett was commissioned to proceed to New Mexico for the purpose of making a survey of the ancient remains of the Jemez Plateau region, a large part of which is now included in the Jemez Forest Reserve. A preliminary report on this work was submitted immediately on Mr. Hewett's return to Washington, and later a paper was prepared in the form of an illustrated descriptive catalogue of the antiquities, to be published as Bulletin 32 of the Bureau series. In March Mr. Hewett was called on to represent the Bureau as a member of the Interior Department Survey of certain boundary lines in southern Colorado, the principal object being to determine the relation of the more important ruins of the Mesa Verde region to the boundaries of the proposed Mesa Verde park, a measure for the establishment of which was pending in Congress. Shortly after the receipt of Mr. Hewett's report this measure became a law. A leading object kept in view by Mr. Hewett on this expedition was the collection of data for the compilation of a bulletin on the antiquities of the Mesa Verde region, for the Bureau's bulletin series.

In February Dr. Aleš Hrdlička, of the National Museum, was commissioned to proceed to Osprey, on Sarasota bay,

Florida, for the purpose of examining several localities where fossil human bones, apparently indicating great age, have been discovered. The evidence obtained is adverse to the theory of the great antiquity of the remains, but the observations made by Doctor Hrdlička and Dr. T. Wayland Vaughan, who accompanied him as a representative of the Geological Survey, on the unusual activity of fossilizing agencies in the locality, are of extreme interest.

Dr. Walter Hough, of the National Museum, who has taken a prominent part in the investigation of the antiquities of the Southwest, has in preparation for the Bureau series a bulletin on the antiquities of the Upper Gila valley.

## PERMITS GRANTED FOR EXPLORATIONS ON PUBLIC LANDS

During the year applications for permits to conduct explorations on the public lands and reservations of the Southwest were acted on as follows:

(1) In September, 1905, the Southwest Society of the Archæological Institute of America applied for permission to conduct archeological explorations on Indian reservations and forest reserves in the Southwest, the work to begin in the spring of 1906. Later, permission to make a preliminary reconnaissance during the latter part of 1905 was asked. Recommended by the Bureau; granted by the Office of Indian Affairs and the Forest Service.

(2) In January, 1906, the request of the Bureau of American Ethnology for authority to prosecute ethnological researches in New Mexico, particularly at Taos, was favorably acted on by the Office of Indian Affairs.

(3) In April, 1906, the American Museum of Natural History, through Dr. Clark Wissler, Curator of Anthropology in that institution, requested permission to conduct explorations on Indian reservations in southern California. Recommended by the Bureau; granted by the Indian Office.

One application for a permit was denied, one was withdrawn, and one was pending at the close of the year.

## COLLECTIONS

The collections of archeological and ethnological specimens made during the year are more limited than heretofore, owing to the reduced amount of field work undertaken. The most important accession is the product of Mr. E. L. Hewett's explorations among the ancient ruins of the Jemez plateau. Other collections worthy of note are those made by Mr. Mooney in Oklahoma and by Doctor Hrdlička in Florida. All collections were transferred to the National Museum in accordance with established custom.

## STUDY OF INDIAN DELEGATIONS

The study of the Indian delegations visiting Washington during the year was continued, as heretofore. One hundred and forty-two portrait negatives were made and measurements and casts were obtained in a number of cases.

## EDITORIAL WORK

Mr. John P. Sanborn, jr., who was probationally appointed on April 6, 1905, Editor and Compiler, was permanently appointed October 6; but on October 19 he was, at his own request, indefinitely furloughed. On February 16, 1906, Mr. Joseph G. Gurley was probationally appointed Editor through certification by the Civil Service Commission. The Twenty-fifth and Twenty-sixth Annual Reports and Bulletins 31 and 32 were read and prepared for the press, and proof reading of the Twenty-third and Twenty-fourth Reports and of Bulletins 30, 31, and 32 further occupied the attention of the Editor, although Mr. Hodge and the various collaborators on Bulletin 30 (the Handbook of the Indians) assumed the main burden of the reading of that work.

## ILLUSTRATIONS

The illustration work, including photography, continued in charge of Mr. De Lancey Gill, who was assisted, as heretofore, by Mr. Henry Walther. The number of illustrations prepared for the reports was 852 and the whole number transmitted to the printer was 1,023.

## PUBLICATIONS

During the year the Twenty-fifth and Twenty-sixth Annual Reports were submitted to the Secretary and the Twenty-fifth was transmitted to the Public Printer, the Twenty-sixth being retained in the Bureau pending the completion of the two next preceding volumes. Bulletin 30 (part 1), submitted at the close of the preceding year, is in press, Bulletin 32 is in the bindery, and Bulletin 31 was transmitted to the printer toward the close of the year. The distribution of publications was continued as in former years. Bulletin 28 was published in October and Bulletin 29 and the Twenty-third Annual Report followed in December.

## LIBRARY

The library remained in charge of Miss Ella Leary, who completed the work of accessioning and cataloguing the books, pamphlets, and periodicals up to date. Owing to the crowded condition of the library, about 600 publications, chiefly periodicals, received by gift or through exchange, but not pertaining to the work of the Bureau, were transferred to the library of the National Museum. During the year there were received and recorded 306 volumes, 900 pamphlets, and the current issues of upward of 500 periodicals. One hundred and fifty volumes were bound at the Government Printing Office. The library now contains 12,858 bound volumes, 9,000 pamphlets, and a large number of periodicals which relate to anthropology and kindred topics.

## CLERICAL WORK

The clerical force of the Bureau consists of five regular employees: Mr. J. B. Clayton, head clerk; Miss Emilie R. Smedes and Miss May S. Clark, stenographers; Miss Ella Leary, clerk and acting librarian; and Mrs. Frances S. Nichols, typewriter. During the year Mr. William P. Bartel, messenger, was promoted to a clerkship and subsequently transferred to the Interstate Commerce Commission.

## PROPERTY

The property of the Bureau is comprised in seven classes: Office furniture and appliances; field outfits; linguistic and ethnological manuscripts, and other documents; photographs, drawings, paintings, and engravings; a working library; collections held temporarily by collaborators for use in research; and the undistributed residue of the editions of Bureau publications.

The additions to the property of the Bureau for the year include a typewriter and a few necessary articles of furniture.

## ACCOMPANYING PAPER

With this report appears a comprehensive monograph on the Omaha tribe, which, it is believed, constitutes an important contribution to North American ethnology, especially to our knowledge of the great Siouan group. This monograph is peculiarly fortunate in its authorship. For thirty years Miss Fletcher has been a close student of the Omaha, enjoying a measure of their friendship and confidence rarely accorded one of alien race, while Mr. La Flesche, a member of the tribe and the son of a former principal chief, has brought to the work a thorough grasp of the subject combined with an earnest desire to aid in the preservation and diffusion of information relating to his people.

The purpose and plan of the authors are thus succinctly stated:

This joint work embodies the results of unusual opportunities to get close to the thoughts that underlie the ceremonies and customs of the Omaha tribe, and to give a fairly truthful picture of the people as they were during the early part of the last century, when most of the men on whose information this work is based were active participants in the life here described. In the account here offered nothing has been borrowed from other observers; only original material gathered directly from the native people has been used.

The paper is rounded out by the inclusion of a final section dealing with the relations between the Omaha and the whites, in which are traced in outline from the beginning the ever-increasing encroachments of civilization and the gradual but inevitable molding of the weaker race to conform to the conditions imposed by the new order of things.

# THE OMAHA TRIBE

BY

## ALICE C. FLETCHER

HOLDER OF THE THAW FELLOWSHIP, PEABODY MUSEUM, HARVARD UNIVERSITY

AND

## FRANCIS LA FLESCHE

A MEMBER OF THE OMAHA TRIBE

# CONTENTS

## XIV

## XV

## XVI

# ILLUSTRATIONS

24

# PHONETIC GUIDE

All vowels have the continental values.

Superior $n$ ($^n$) gives a nasal modification to the vowel immediately preceding.

$x$ represents the rough sound of $h$ in the German *hoch*.

*th* has the sound of *th* in *the*.

ç has the sound of *th* in *thin*.

Every syllable ends in a vowel or in nasal $n$ ($^n$).

28

# FOREWORD

The following account of the Omaha tribe embodies the results of personal studies made while living among the people and revised from information gained through more or less constant intercourse throughout the last twenty-nine years. During this period the writer has received help and encouragement from the judicious criticisms of Prof. Frederic Ward Putnam, head of the Department of Anthropology of Harvard University, and the completion of the task undertaken has been made possible by means of the Thaw Fellowship. Objects once held in reverence by the Omaha tribe have been secured and deposited in the Peabody Museum for safe-keeping. Professor Putnam, curator of that institution, has permitted the free use of the Omaha material collected under its auspices and preserved there, for reproduction in the present volume.

At the time the writer went to live among the Omaha, to study their life and thought, the tribe had recently been forced to abandon hunting, owing to the sudden extinction of the buffalo herds. The old life, however, was almost as of yesterday, and remained a common memory among all the men and women. Many of the ancient customs were practised and much of the aboriginal life still lingered.

Contact with the white race was increasing daily and beginning to press on the people. The environment was changing rapidly, and the changes brought confusion of mind to the old people as well as to many in mature life. The beliefs of the fathers no longer applied to the conditions which confronted the people. All that they formerly had relied on as stable had been swept away. The buffalo, which they had been taught was given them as an inexhaustible food supply, had been destroyed by agencies new and strange. Even the wild grasses that had covered the prairies were changing. By the force of a power he could not understand, the Omaha found himself restricted in all his native pursuits. Great unrest and anxiety had come to the people through the Government's dealings with their kindred, the Ponca tribe, and fear haunted every Omaha fireside lest they, too, be driven from their homes and the graves of their fathers. The future was a dread to old and young. How pitiful was the trouble of mind everywhere manifest in the tribe can hardly be pictured, nor can the relief that came to the people when, in 1882, their lands were assured to them by act of Congress.

29

The story of their relations with the Government, of contact with the white race, of the overthrow of their ancient institutions, and of the final securing of their homes in individual holdings on their tribal lands, is briefly told in an appendix to this volume. To-day, towns with electric lights dot the prairies where the writer used to camp amid a sea of waving grass and flowers. Railroads cross and recross the gullied paths left by the departed game, and the plow has obliterated the broad westward trail along the ridge over which the tribe moved when starting out on the annual buffalo hunt. The past is overlaid by a thriving present. The old Omaha men and women sleep peacefully on the hills while their grandchildren farm beside their white neighbors, send their children to school, speak English, and keep bank accounts.

When these studies were begun nothing had been published on the Omaha tribe except short accounts by passing travelers or the comments of government officials. None of these writers had sought to penetrate below the external aspects of Indian life in search of the ideals or beliefs which animated the acts of the natives. In the account here offered nothing has been borrowed from other observers; only original material gathered directly from the native people has been used, and the writer has striven to make so far as possible the Omaha his own interpreter.

The following presentation of the customs, ceremonies, and beliefs of the Omaha is a joint work. For more than twenty-five years the writer has had as collaborator Mr. Francis La Flesche (pl. 1), the son of Joseph La Flesche, former principal chief of the tribe. In his boyhood Mr. La Flesche enjoyed the opportunity of witnessing some of the ceremonies herein described. Later these were explained to him by his father and by the old men who were the keepers of these ancient rites and rituals. Possessed of a good memory and having had awakened in his mind the desire to preserve in written form the history of his people as it was known to them, their music, the poetry of their rituals, and the meaning of their social and religious ceremonies, Mr. La Flesche early in his career determined to perfect himself in English and to gather the rapidly vanishing lore of the tribe, in order to carry out his cherished purpose.

This joint work embodies the results of unusual opportunities to get close to the thoughts that underlie the ceremonies and customs of the Omaha tribe, and to give a fairly truthful picture of the people as they were during the early part of the last century, when most of the men on whose information this work is based were active participants in the life here described—a life that has passed away, as have those who shared in it and made its history possible.

Mr. Edwin S. Tracy has given valuable assistance in transcribing some of the songs, particularly those of the Shell society. Several of

FRANCIS LA FLESCHE

the songs presented were transcribed and arranged for translation on the piano by the late Prof. John Comfort Fillmore, who for several years had carefully studied the music of the Omaha.

To enumerate all the Omaha men and women who have contributed of their knowledge and memory toward the making of this volume would be to catalogue the best part of the tribe. Unfortunately, but very few are now living to see the outcome of the assistance they rendered during the gathering of the material herein preserved for their descendants. A. C. F.

# THE OMAHA TRIBE

By Alice C. Fletcher and Francis La Flesche

## I

## LOCATION; LINGUISTIC RELATIONSHIPS

The people of the Omaha tribe live in the State of Nebraska, in Burt, Cuming, and Thurston counties, about 80 miles north of the city which bears their name.

The Omaha tribe has never been at war with the United States and is the only tribe now living in the State of Nebraska that was there when the white settlers entered the country.

In 1882 Congress passed an act under which every Omaha man, woman, and child received a certain number of acres of the land which the tribe selected as their reservation in 1854, when they ceded to the United States their extensive hunting grounds. The Omaha are dependent for their livelihood on their own exertions as farmers, mechanics, merchants, etc.; by the act of 1882, they were placed under the laws, civil and criminal, of the State of Nebraska. Their ancient tribal organization has ceased to exist, owing to changed environment, the extinction of the buffalo, and the immediate presence of the white man's civilization. Nothing remains intact of the ancient customs except the practice of exogamy between the kinship groups and the people still give their children names that belong to the gentes into which the children are born. A few of the societies exist but their influence is on the wane, although they are enjoyed because of their social character and the pleasure derived from their songs and dramatic dances, which revive the memory of the days when the Omaha were a distinct and independent people.

In June, 1884, the Omaha tribe numbered 1,179. In that month the allotment of lands to members of the tribe was completed. The people were divided as follows:

|  | Males. | Females. |
|---|---|---|
| Adults | 305 | 338 |
| Under 18 years | 259 | 277 |
| Total | 564 | 615 |

Excess of females over males, 51. Of these, 33 were adults and 18 were minors.

Number of families, 246.

Families having no children, 41.

Owing to the unwillingness of the people to speak of the dead, it was impracticable to attempt to get the exact number of children that had been born.

The following summary shows the proportion of the sexes at different stages of life:

|  | Males. | Females. |
|---|---|---|
| Under 3 years | 87 | 82 |
| Between 3 and 7 years | 69 | 82 |
| Between 7 and 17 years | 103 | 113 |
| Between 17 and 40 years | 192 | 232 |
| Between 40 and 55 years | 72 | 55 |
| Over 55 years | 41 | 51 |

The marked disproportion between the sexes of ages between 17 and 40 years may be due to the fact that during this stage of life all the men were exposed to the hazards of hunting and of war. As these avocations of the men did not cease until 1876, eight years before this census was taken, the influence of these duties on the length of life of the men is probably shown in the above table.

For many centuries before they became known to the white race through early travelers, traders, and colonists, the aboriginal peoples of North America north of Mexico had been passing and repassing one another from east to west or west to east, and from north to south or from south to north.[a] Many traces of these ancient movements had been overlaid by movements the outcome of which is shown by the map, and it is the task of the archeologist to disclose them and read their history. That the system of inland waterways and the extensive coast lines on two oceans have favored the spread of the culture of one region to another seems not improbable, viewed in the light of recent researches, while the accumulating evidence showing attrition between the various stocks indicated on the map in time will permit of generalizations touching the cultural development of the native peoples of this continent.

The Omaha tribe belongs to the Siouan linguistic stock. The map referred to represents the majority of this stock as having already moved westward beyond the Mississippi while some branches had advanced nearly to the eastern foothills of the Rocky mountains and north to the fifty-third parallel. There were also a few outlying Siouan communities—those who may have lagged behind—for example, the group dwelling on the eastern slope of the Appalachian mountains and spreading down toward the coastal plains of the Atlantic, and a group on the northern coast of the Gulf of Mexico that seem to have been cut off from that portion of their kindred who had pressed to the southwest. The story told by the map both explains and is explained

---

a Consult the Map of the Linguistic Families of American Indians north of Mexico (in the *Seventh Annual Report* and in *Bulletin 30*, part 1, of the Bureau of American Ethnology), which shows approximately the territories occupied by the several linguistic stocks when they became known to the whites.

by the traditions of many of the tribes belonging to this linguistic stock. All of these traditions speak of a movement from the east to the west, covering a long period of time. The primordial habitat of this stock lies hidden in the mystery that still enshrouds the beginnings of the ancient American race; it seems to have been situated, however, among the Appalachian mountains, and all their legends indicate that the people had knowledge of a large body of water in the vicinity of their early home. This water may have been the Atlantic ocean, for, as shown on the map, remnants of Siouan tribes survived near the mountains in the regions of Virginia, North Carolina, and South Carolina until after the coming of the white race.

In the extended westward migration of the Siouan stock groups seem to have broken off, some earlier than others, and to have made their way into localities where certain habits incident to their environment appear to have become fixed on them, and contact with other stocks during the migration to have influenced their culture. A group which kept together until within the last few hundred years seems to have been composed of the five closely cognate tribes now known as the Omaha, Ponca, Osage, Kansa, and Quapaw. Their languages as yet have hardly differentiated into distinct dialects. There are other groups of the Siouan stock which, from the evidence of their language, were probably similarly associated tribes. Some of these groups seem to have developed individual peculiarities of language which prevented them from coalescing with their kindred when in the course of wanderings they met. An instance in point is the meeting and journeying together of the Iowa and the Omaha without establishing tribal union. Although they belonged to the same linguistic stock, the Iowa tongue was practically unintelligible to the Omaha. The final parting of these tribes took place within the last two centuries.

The five cognate tribes, of which the Omaha is one, bear a strong resemblance to one another, not only in language but in tribal organization and religious rites. This account of the Omaha tribe with incorporated notes taken among their close cognates is presented in order to facilitate a comparative study not only of these tribes but of others of the Siouan stock, in the hope of thereby helping to solve some of the problems presented by this extensive linguistic group.

## Tribal Concept; the Name Omaha

*Uki'te*, the word for tribe, has a double import: As a verb, it means "to fight;" as a noun, it signifies "tribe." It seems probable that the noun has been derived from the verb; at least it throws light on the Omaha concept of what was an essential to the formation of a tribe. The verbal form signifies "to fight" against external foes, to take part in conflicts in which honor and fame can be won. Those who thus fought had to stand as one body against their assailants. The term *uki'te* is never applied to quarrels among members of the tribe in which fists and missiles are used; the words *niu^n*, *nage'*, *ki'na* are used to designate such contentions, from which the winner receives no renown. *Uki'te* alone in the Omaha tongue means "to fight" as men against men. The warriors of a tribe were the only bulwark against outside attacks; they had to be ever ready "to fight" (*uki'te*), to defend with their lives and safeguard by their valor those dependent on them. The word *uki'te*, as "tribe," explains the common obligation felt by the Omaha to defend, as a unit, the community, the tribe.

The descriptive name *Omaha* (*umo^n'ho^n*, "against the current" or "upstream") had been fixed on the people prior to 1541. In that year De Soto's party met the Quapaw tribe; *quapaw*, or *uga'xpa*, means "with the current" or "downstream," and is the complement of *umo^n'ho^n*, or *Omaha*. Both names are said by the tribes to refer to their parting company, the one going up and the other going down the river.

There are two versions of how this parting came about. One account says that—

The people were moving down the Uha'i ke river.[a] When they came to a wide river they made skin boats (see fig. 1) in which to cross the river. As they were crossing, a storm came up. The Omaha and Iowa got safely across, but the Quapaw drifted down the stream and were never seen again until within the last century. When the Iowa made their landing they camped in a sandy place. The strong wind blew the sand over the people and gave them a grayish appearance. From this circumstance they called themselves *Pa'xude*, "gray head," and the Omaha have known them by that name ever since. The Iowa accompanied the Omaha up the Mississippi to a stream spoken of as "Raccoon river"—probably the Des Moines, and the people followed this river to its headwaters, which brought them into the region of the Pipestone quarry.

The other version of the parting between the Omaha and the Quapaw is that—

When the wide river was reached the people made a rope of grape vines. They fastened one end on the eastern bank and the other end was taken by strong swimmers and carried across the river and fastened to the western bank. The people crossed the river by clinging to the grapevine. When about half their number were across, including the Iowa and Omaha, the rope broke, leaving the rest of the people behind. Those who were left were the Quapaw. This crossing was made on a foggy morning, and those left behind, believing that their companions who had crossed had followed the river downward on the western side, themselves turned downstream on the eastern side, and so the two groups lost sight of each other.

If an Omaha were accosted by a stranger and asked to what tribe he belonged, or were the same question to be asked him in the dark, when recognition was impossible, he would reply, *Umo^n'ho^n bthi^n ha*, "I am an Omaha." Should he be asked "Who are you?" he would say:

---

[a] *Uha'i ke*, "the river down which they came;" the name is still applied by the Omaha to the Ohio

"I am [giving his name] the son or the nephew of So-and-so," mentioning the name.

If a group of Omaha should be asked to what tribe they belonged, they would reply, "We are Omaha." If they were asked, "Who are you?" the one making answer would say, "I am the son or nephew of So-and-so, and these are the sons of So-and-so."

If young men were playing a game in which there were two parties or sides, as in ball, and one of the players should be asked, "To which side do you belong?" he would say, *The'giha bthi$^n$ ha*, "I belong to this

FIG. 1.  Skin boat or " bull-boat."

side or party." *The'giha* means "on this side," and the word can be used only as a designation of a side or party in a game. It has no tribal significance whatever, nor has it ever been used to indicate the Omaha people or their place of abode.

### THE FIVE COGNATE TRIBES—EVIDENCE OF FORMER UNITY

Traditions common to the Omaha, Ponca, Osage, Kansa, and Quapaw tribes state that they were once one people. Their language bears witness to the truth of this tradition and the similarity of their tribal organization offers equally strong testimony. It would seem that the parent organization had so impressed itself upon the mode of life and thought of the people that when groups branched off and organized themselves as distinct tribes they preserved the familiar characteristic features; for all of these cognate tribes have certain features in common. All are divided into kinship groups which practise exogamy and trace descent through the father only. Each group or gens has its own name and a set of personal names, one of which is bestowed on each child born within the gens. These personal names refer either to the symbol which belongs to and marks the kinship group or to the rites allied to the symbol, which were the especial charge of the gens.

According to traditions preserved among the Omaha, Ponca, Osage, Kansa, and Quapaw tribes, their severance from the parent organization of which they once formed a part, as well as their later partings from one another, did not occur through any concerted action; they were the result of accident, as in the case already cited of the Omaha and the Quapaw, or of strifes fomented by ambitious chiefs, or of circumstances incident to following the game. A tradition of the Wazha'zhe or Osage tells that they broke away from the Ponca because of a quarrel over game. The Wazha'zhe gens of the Ponca have a like story, which says "The parting was due to a quarrel about game. Those who left us became lost but we hear of them now as a large tribe bearing our name, Wazha'zhe."

Tradition indicates also that when, for some reason or other, a group broke off, not all of the members belonged to one gens but to several gentes of the parent organization, and when this group organized as a distinct tribe, those of gentile kindred retained their identity in name and the practice of a common rite, and formed a gens in the new tribe. These traditions are corroborated by conditions which obtain in all of these cognate tribes.

For instance, among the Omaha, Osage, Kansa, and Quapaw a turtle group is found as a subgens in each tribe, and in each instance its members are the keepers of the turtle rites of the tribe.

Again, among the Omaha, Osage, Kansa, and Quapaw the Kansa, or Wind people, form a gens in each tribe, and in each of the tribes are the keepers of rites pertaining to the wind.

Among the Omaha, Osage, Kansa, and Quapaw tribes there is in each a gens similar to the Mon'thinkagaxe ("earth makers").

A Nu'xe, or Ice gens, is found in the Ponca tribe, and the name is borne also by a subgens in each the Osage, Kansa, and Quapaw tribes.

There is a tradition that the Ponca were once a gens in the Omaha tribe and broke away in a body, and that when they became a tribe

the subdivisions of the Ponca gens became the gentes of the Ponca
tribe. This may possibly be true. It would seem, however, that
in earlier days some, at least, of the Ponca had accompanied the
Osage, Kansa, and Quapaw groups when they separated from the
parent organization, and when these groups became distinct tribes
the Ponca kindred appear to have combined to form a Ponca gens,
for we find a gens of that name in each· of the cognate tribes just
mentioned.

Another class of evidence which has relation to the former union of
these tribes is found in personal names, some of which refer to ceremonies no longer observed in the tribe in which the names exist but
still practised in some of the cognate tribes—a fact which indicates
apparently that the rite was once known and observed by the tribe
in which the personal name is now found. For instance, in the
Washe'to$^n$ subgens of the I$^n$shta'çu$^n$da gens of the Omaha tribe is
the name Ushu'demo$^n$thi$^n$, meaning "he who walks in the mist" or
"in the dust raised by the wind." This name has no significance
taken merely as an Omaha name, but its meaning becomes apparent
when we turn to the cognate Osage. In that tribe there is a gens
called Mo$^n$so'tsemo$^n$i$^n$, meaning "they who walk concealed by the
mist or dust." The word refers to a rite in the keeping of this gens,
a rite that pertained to war. When a war party was about to make
an attack or was forced to retreat, it was the office of this gens to
perform the rite, which had the effect of causing a mist to rise or a
strong wind to blow up a cloud of dust in which the warriors could
walk concealed from their enemies. Again, the Omaha personal
name Uzu'gaxe, meaning "to clear the pathway," finds its explanation in the office of the Osage gens of the same name, whose duty it
was to find a way across or around any natural obstacle that lay
in the path of a war party, as a safe place to ford a dangerous river
or a pathway over or around a cliff.

Instances similar to those cited above could be multiplied, all
going to show that rites and customs lost in one tribe have frequently
been preserved in another of these cognates. It is probable that
were all the rites and customs of these tribes brought together and a
comparative study made of them, much of the ancestral organization from which these cognates took their rise might be discovered
and light thrown on the question, Why certain forms, religious and
secular, were lost and others retained and developed; also, as to
which of these were original with the people, which were adopted,
and of the latter from what culture they were taken.

In all the traditions that touch on the common source from which
these cognates have come no reference to the name of the parent
or common organization is to be found. Ponca, Kansa, Wazha'zhe

(Osage) are old terms the meanings of which are lost; these occur as names of gentes in the cognate tribes, and three of the five cognates bear them as tribal names. It is to be noted that the descriptive names Omaha and Quapaw do not appear in any of these tribes as terms denoting kinship groups. Among the names used to denominate kinship groups we find one occurring frequently and always used to designate a group that holds important offices in the tribe. The same term also appears in the designation of tribal divisions which are more comprehensive than the gens. This name is *Hon'ga*, meaning "leader." In the Kansa tribe there are gentes called the Great Hon'ga, the Small Hon'ga, and the Separate Hon'ga. In the Quapaw are two gentes having this name, the Great and the Small Hon'ga. In the Omaha the term is applied to one of the two grand divisions of the tribe, the Hon'gashenu, Hon'ga people, and one of the gentes in this division bears the name Hon'ga. In the Osage, one of the five divisions of the tribe is called Hon'ga. Within this division there is also a Hon'ga gens. Another of the divisions of the Osage is called Hon'ga utanatsi, Separate Hon'ga. The following Osage tradition tells who the Hon'ga utanatsi were and how they came to be a part of the Osage organization:

> The Osage in their wanderings on the hunt came across a tribe whose language was the same as their own. This strange people called themselves Hon'ga. The Osage made peace with them and invited them to join and become a part of the Osage tribe. The Hon'ga tribe consented, and it is their descendants who are known to-day as the Hon'ga utanatsi.

The term Hon'ga utanatsi may be roughly translated as "the Separate Hon'ga," but the words *utana tsi* imply something more than merely "separate;" they explain why this group had to be so designated. The strange Hon'ga whom the Osage met and invited to become a part of their tribe would not give up their own name Hon'ga, and as the Osage were themselves called Hon'ga people, explanatory words had to be added to the name Hon'ga in order to identify and at the same time to distinguish the newcomers from the rest of the tribe. These explanatory words were *utana tsi*, by itself ("separate"). Hence the group in the Osage tribe called Hon'ga utanatsi.

The name of the Hon'ga utanatsi gens of the Kansa tribe has the same meaning, and indicates that the Kansa people, as did the Osage, claimed Hon'ga as their common name.

There is a tradition preserved among the Ponca that in the past they and the other cognate tribes knew the Omaha by the name Hon'ga. An incident is related that explains the meaning of a name given to a small stream in northern Nebraska, Hon'ga she'nonwatha-i ke (or Hon'gawa'xthi i ke), "where the Hon'ga were slaughtered." On this creek a battle is said to have taken place in which the Omaha met with a disastrous defeat from an unknown enemy, which decimated the tribe. The tradition concerning the name of this stream is known to both Omaha and Ponca, and in both tribes the tradition is that the name Ho$^n$'ga, as here used, referred to the Omaha. The Omaha name for the month of January was Ho$^n$'ga umu'bthi, meaning "the drifting of the snow into the lodges of the Ho$^n$'ga," that is, of the tribe.

From these traditions and the use of the term Ho$^n$'ga as applied to divisions and gentes in the Omaha, Osage, Kansa, and Quapaw tribes, together with the fact that these tribes either claimed for themselves this name or were known to one another by it, it seems not improbable that Ho$^n$'ga may have been the name by which the people called themselves when they were living together as one community or tribe. The general meaning of Ho$^n$'ga ("leader") is not unlike that belonging to names by which other Indian tribes designate themselves, i. e., "the men," "the people," etc. The term Ho$^n$'ga is sometimes combined with another word to form the title of an officer, as Nudo$^n$ Ho$^n$'ga, "war leader" or "captain."

The following data concerning the gentes, personal names, and other features of the Omaha cognate tribes are taken from original notes made by the writers.

### THE PONCA TRIBE[a]

*Po$^n$'ca* is an old word, the meaning of which is lost. It occurs as the name of a gens or subdivision of a gens in the Osage, Kansa, and Quapaw tribes, but not in the Omaha, a fact which may have significance because of the tradition that the Ponca constituted a gens of the Omaha before the separation of the tribes. As the Omaha retained at the parting possession of the sacred tribal objects, their rituals and ceremonies, the Ponca were everward after spoken of as "Orphans."

There are seven gentes in the Ponca tribe, namely: Waça'be, Thi'xida, Ni'kapashna, Po$^n$'caxti, Washa'be, Wazha'zhe, Nu'xe. These camped in the order indicated in the diagram (fig. 2), beginning on the southern side of the eastern entrance of the tribal circle, to which

---

[a] The Ponca tribe is now divided. One part is living in northern Oklahoma on lands purchased by the Government from the Cherokee in 1883, which were allotted in severalty to the tribe some ten years later. The other part lives in northern Nebraska on the Niobrara river. Their land was given them in 1881, and some years later was allotted to them under the Severalty act. Already these two parts are spoken of by different designations. Those in Oklahoma are "the hot-country Ponca;" those in Nebraska, "the cold-country Ponca." Relations between the Ponca and the United States were officially opened by a treaty made in 1817 "to reestablish peace and friendship as before the war of 1812." In 1825 another treaty was made by which only American citizens were to be allowed to reside among the tribe as traders, and the tribe agreed to delegate the punishment of offenders to the United States Government. In 1858 the Ponca ceded their hunting grounds to the United States, reserving, however, a certain tract for their own use. In 1865 the Government, by treaty, reconfirmed this tract. In 1877 the tribe was forcibly removed to the then Indian Territory (now Oklahoma). See note, p. 51.

the Ponca give the name *hu'thuga*, the word used by the Omaha also to designate their tribal circle.

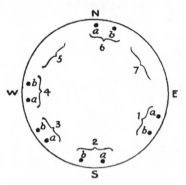

FIG. 2. Diagram of Ponca *hu'thuga*.

1. WAÇA'BE. Black bear. Subgentes: (a) Waça'be; tabu, fat of the black bear. (b) Hi'çada (stretched, referring to the stretch of the legs in running); tabu, birds. 2. THI'XIDA. Meaning lost. Subgentes: (a) Thi'xida; tabu, blood. (b) Ingthon'çinçnedewetǐ (*ingthon'çinçnede*, puma; *wetǐ*, to dwell in); tabu, blue (or green) paint. 3. NI'KAPASHNA. A man's skull. Subgentes: (a) Taha'ton itazhi (*ta*, deer; *ha*, skin; *ton*, possess; *i'tazhi*, do not touch); tabu, deer. (b) Teçin'de itazhi (*te*, buffalo; *çin'de*, tail; *itazhi*, do not touch); tabu, buffalo tail. 4. PON'CAXTI. Real or original Ponca. Subgentes: (a) Pon'caxti; (b) Monkon' (mystery or medicine); one tabu, buffalo head. 5. WASHA'BE. A dark object, as seen against the horizon; tabu, skin of buffalo calf. 6. WAZHA'ZHE. An old term. Subgentes: (a) Wazha'zhe (real Wazha'zhe); name said to refer to the snake after shedding old skin and again in full power. (b) Wazha'zhexude (gray Wazha'zhe); refers to the grayish appearance of the snake's cast-off skin; one tabu, snakes. 7. NU'XE. Ice; tabu, male buffalo.

## RITES AND CUSTOMS OF THE GENTES

### 1. WAÇA'BE GENS

To the Hi'çada subgens of the Waça'be gens belonged the keeping of the ritual songs sung at the ceremony held when the first thunder was heard in the spring. This subgens, whose tabu was birds, was spoken of as the Eagle group of the gens, and the people were supposed to be connected with thunder. At death they went to the thunder villages, and their voices would be heard in the thunder-storms. They were forbidden to climb trees, as by so doing they would be going upward, thus anticipating their deaths and therefore shortening their lives. In the legend (see p. 48) the people of this gens were said to wear wreaths of cedar; in all the cognate tribes cedar was associated with thunder rites (note the Ni'ka wakondagi of the Osage (p. 60); the Cedar Pole of the Omaha (p. 229); the association of the bear and the eagle in the Tha'tada gens of the Omaha (p.159); also the connection of thunder with war and of the eagle with war and thunder. The position of the Waça'be gens in the Ponca tribal circle was similar to that of the We'zhinshte gens in the Omaha tribal circle, which was also associated with thunder.

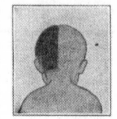

FIG. 3. Cut of hair, Waça'be gens (Ponca).

It was a custom in the Ponca tribe for each gens to have its peculiar manner of marking arrows, so there should be no dispute in hunting as to the gens to which a fatal arrow belonged. This mark, however, did not exclude or interfere with a man's private mark. The arrow of the Waça'be had the shaft red about one-half the length of the feathers.

The symbolic cut of the children's hair consisted in closely cropping one side of the head and leaving the other side untouched to the neck (fig. 3.)

### 2. THI'XIDA GENS

It is said that the Pawnee call all the Ponca by the name Thi'xida. To this gens belonged a pack used in testing the truth of warriors when they were accorded war honors. Formerly there were two of these packs, but one was buried some twenty years ago with its keeper, Ton'deamonthin. The other, near the close of the last century, was kept by Shu'degaxe. The ceremony of conferring honors was similar to the Omaha Wate'giçtu (p. 434). To this gens belonged the right to preside at the election of chiefs.

The members of the subgens Ingthon'çinçnedeweti painted the peace pipe (that used in the Wa'wan ceremony, p. 376) on one side of their tents and the puma on the other. The tabu, green or blue paint, was used on these pipes. *Du* was the word for green; *du çabe*, blue; *çabe* means black; the words indicate that the two colors were regarded as the same, one being merely a darker shade than the other. The skin of the puma was used to cover or wrap up these pipes. The name of the sub-division (meaning "to dwell with the puma") refers to the covering of the peace pipes; these and the puma were represented in the tent decoration and helped to interpret the name of the subgens— "those who dwell with the covered pipes that give

FIG. 4.  Cut of hair, Thi'xida gens (Ponca).

peace." The arrow shafts of this gens were painted black where the feathers were fastened, and the sinew was painted red to represent the tabu of the gens, blood.

The symbolic cut of the child's hair consisted in leaving only a roach running from the forehead to the nape of the neck. This roach was trimmed by notching it like a saw. A small tuft of hair was left on each side of the roach (fig. 4). This notched roach is similar to the cut of hair of a buffalo gens in the Oto tribe (also of the Siouan stock), and but for the notching is like that of a buffalo gens of the Omaha. These resemblances suggest that the tabu of the gens may refer to the blood of the slain buffalo.

The people of this gens were said to have the power to cure pain in the head, in the following manner: The sufferer brought a bow and arrow to the Thi'xida, who wet the arrow with saliva, set it on the bow string, pointed it at the sick man's head four times, then rubbed the head with the arrow, and so effected a cure of the pain.

### 3. NI'KAPASHNA GENS

The name Ni'kapashna ("skull") is said to refer to the exposure of
the bone by the process of scalping. This gens had charge of the
war pipes and directed the council of war. To them belonged also
the supervision of all hunting of the deer.

When a member of the subdivision Taha'ton itazhi died, moccasins
made from the skin of the deer (which was tabu to the living) were
put on his feet that he might not "lose his way," but go on safely
and "be recognized by his own people" in the spirit world.

The symbolic cut of the child's hair consisted
in removing all the hair except a fringe around
the head, as shown in figure 5.

Fig. 5. Cut of hair, Ni'kapashna gens (Ponca).

### 4. PON'CAXTI GENS

The Pon'caxti (*xti*, "original," or "real")
camped in the rear part of the tribal circle, facing the opening. This gens and its subdivision,
the Monkon', had charge of the principal pipes,
one of which was the chief's pipe that was used
for conjuring. In this gens was preserved the tradition of the
finding of the Omaha Sacred Pole; it was a man of the Monkon' subgens who in the race was the first to reach the Pole (p. 218).

There were only two ceremonies during which the Ponca tribe was
required to camp in the order shown on the diagram, when, as it was
said, "the people must make the *hu'thuga* complete." These ceremonies were the Feast of Soldiers, which generally took place while
the tribe was on the buffalo hunt, and Turning the Child. At the
latter ceremony the lock was cut from the boy's head and a name
which belonged to its gens was given to the child. The Monkon' subdivision had the direction of both of these ceremonies. The ceremony
connected with the child took place in the spring. A tent was pitched
in front of the Monkon' subdivision and set toward the center of the
tribal circle, "made complete" for this ceremony. The tent was
dedicated—"made holy"—a stone placed in the center near the fire
and sweet grass laid on it. It was the duty of the mothers to bring
their children to the old man to whom belonged the hereditary right
to perform the ceremony of Turning the Child. After the child had
entered the tent he took it by the hand, led it to the center of the
tent, and stood it on the stone, facing the east; then he lifted the child
by the shoulders, turned it to the south, and let its feet rest on the stone.
In the same manner he again lifted the child, turned it to the west,
and then rested its feet on the stone. Once more he lifted it, as before,
causing it to face the north, and set its feet on the stone; finally he
lifted it back, with its face to the east. " The Turning of the Child,"
the old informant said, "brought the child face to face with the life-

giving winds of the four directions," while "the stone represented long life." The child's baby name was then "thrown away," and a name from the gens to which its father belonged was publicly announced and bestowed upon it. All children were "turned" but only boys had the lock of hair severed from the crown of the head, the lock being laid away in a pack kept by the old man who performed the rite. The boy was then taken home and the father cut his hair in the symbolic manner of his gens. (See Omaha rite of Turning the Child, p. 117.)

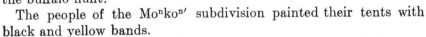

(For an account of the Feast of the Soldier and its ritual, see pp. 309–311.)

This gens had duties also in connection with the buffalo hunt.

Fig. 6. Cut of hair, Poⁿ'-caxti gens (Ponca).

The people of the Moⁿkoⁿ' subdivision painted their tents with black and yellow bands.

The symbolic cut of the child's hair consisted in leaving only a tuft on the forehead, one at the nape of the neck, and one on each side of the head (fig. 6).

#### 5. WASHA'BE GENS

The name of this gens, Washa'be, was the same as the name of the ceremonial staff used by the Omaha leader of the annual tribal buffalo hunt, and also of that subdivision of the Omaha Hoⁿ'ga gens which had charge of the tent containing the White Buffalo Hide, of its ritual, and of that of the maize (see p. 261). The Ponca gens, like the Omaha Washa'be subdivision, had duties connected with the tribal buffalo hunt, and was associated with the Moⁿkoⁿ' subdivision of the Poⁿ'caxti gens in regulating the people at that time and appointing officers to maintain order on the hunt. There were no ceremonies in the Ponca tribe relative to the planting or the care of maize. The Ponca are said to have depended for food principally on hunting, and to have obtained their maize more by barter than by cultivation.

Fig. 7. Cut of hair, Wa-sha'be gens (Ponca).

The symbolic cut of the child's hair consisted in leaving only a tuft on the forehead and one at the nape of the neck (fig. 7).

#### 6. WAZHA'ZHE GENS

The name Osage is a corruption of the native term *wazha'zhe.* Whether or not in the tabu and customs of this gens the Ponca have conserved something of the early rites of the Wazha'zhe, or Osage, people (rites connected with the snake) can be determined only by more careful research than it has been possible for the writers to make.

A member of this gens must not touch or kill a snake, and care had to be exercised always to enter the tent by the door, otherwise snakes would go in and do harm. Mothers in this gens were very particular to impress on their children the importance of entering the tent by the door and little children were watched lest one should creep under the tent cover and so bring harm to itself or the inmates.

A man harboring a grudge against a person could bring about the punishment of that individual by dropping inside the offender's tent a figure of a snake cut out of rawhide. Shortly afterward the man would be bitten by a snake. A drawing made of the snake to be cut out showed it to be a rattlesnake.

When any one in the tribe chanced to be bitten by a snake, he sent at once for a member of the Wazha'zhe gens, who on arriving at the tent quickly dug a hole beside the fire with a stick, and then sucked the wound so as to draw out the blood and prevent any serious trouble

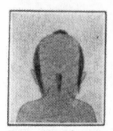

FIG. 8. Cut of hair, Wa-
zha'zhe gens (Ponca).

from the injury. The purpose in digging the hole could not be learned from the writer's informant.

When on the tribal hunt, the women gathered the bones of the buffalo and boiled them to extract the marrow for future use. If a person wished to tease a woman so employed, he would catch up with a stick and throw away some of the scum from the pot. This act would prevent any more marrow from leaving the bones, and the only way to undo the mischief was to send for a Wazha'zhe, who on arriving removed by means of a stick some of the fat from the boiling bones. The marrow would then come out freely at once and the woman would be able to secure an ample supply of tallow. "That is the mystery of my people," said the old informant, with a sly smile, in response to inquiries on the subject.

It is said that the Wazha'zhe were a warlike and quarrelsome people, and that at the organization of the tribe a peace pipe was given into their keeping. By accepting this trust they committed themselves to more peaceful and orderly conduct in the tribe. It is still a matter of dispute within the gens as to which of the two subdivisions the custody of the peace pipe originally belonged, whether to the "real" or to the "gray" Wazha'zhe.

The office of tribal herald was in this gens.

The symbolic cut of the hair consisted in leaving a lock on the forehead, one at the back of the head, and one over each ear (fig. 8).

### 7. NU'XE GENS

The name of this gens, Nu'xe ("ice"), found also in the Osage tribe, refers to the hail. The Osage gens of this name is closely associated with the Buffalo-bull people, and in this connection it is to be noted that the tabu of the Ponca Nu'xe gens is the male buffalo. The Osage have a tradition that the Ponca were once a part of their tribe, but that very long ago the people became separated on the buffalo hunt, and the Ponca never came back. It will be noted that the Osage have a Ponca gens and the Ponca a Wazha'zhe gens, that there is a Waça'be gens in each tribe, also a Hi'çada gens, which in each tribe had rites referring to thunder; all of these resemblances are probably the result of movements which took place long before the Ponca and the Omaha were as closely associated as at a later period, prior to finally becoming distinct tribes.

## LEGENDARY ACCOUNTS [a]

### THE PEACE PIPES

The people came across a great water on rafts—logs tied together—and pitched their tents on the shore. While there they thought to make themselves *u'shkon*, limits or bounds within which to move, and regulations by which their actions were to be governed. They cleared a space of grass and weeds so that they could see one another's faces, and sat down, and there was no obstruction between them.

While they were deliberating they heard the hooting of an owl in the timber near by, and the leader, who had called the people together, said, "That bird is to take part in our action; he calls to us, offering his aid." Immediately afterward they heard the cry of the woodpecker and his knocking against the trees, and the leader said, "That bird calls and offers his aid; he will take part in our action."

The leader then addressed the man he had appointed to act as servant, and said, "Go to the woods and get an ash sapling." The servant went out and returned with a sapling having a rough bark. "This is not what we want," said the leader. "Go again, and get a sapling that has a smooth bark, bluish in color at the joint" (where a branch comes). The servant went out, and returned with a sapling of the kind described.

When the leader took up the ash sapling, an eagle came and soared above where the council sat. He dropped a downy feather; it fell, and balanced itself in the center of the cleared space. This was the white eagle. The leader said, "This is not what we want;" so the white eagle passed on.

Then the bald eagle came swooping down as though making an attack upon its prey, balanced itself on its wings directly over the cleared space, uttering fierce cries, and dropped one of its downy feathers, which stood on the ground as the other eagle's feather had done. The leader said, "This is not what we want;" and the bald eagle passed on.

Then came the spotted eagle and soared over the council and dropped its feather, which stood as the others had done. The leader said, "This is not what we want;" and the spotted eagle passed on.

The eagle with the fantail (imperial eagle, *Aquila heliaca* Savigny) then came, and soared over the people. It dropped a downy feather which stood upright in the center of the cleared space. The leader said, "This is what we want." The feathers of this eagle were those used in making the peace pipes, together with the other birds (the owl and the woodpecker) and the animals, making in all nine kinds of articles. These pipes were to be used in establishing friendly relations with other tribes.[b]

---

[a] Obtained from chiefs and other prominent Ponca.

[b] This account of the Ponca introduction to the Wa'wan pipes should be compared with the Omaha account of receiving these pipes from the Arikara (p. 74) and the Omaha ceremony (p. 376). The nine articles are as follows: Owl feathers, eagle feathers, woodpecker, rabbit, deer, ash tree, paint, cat-tail, and sinew.

## THE ORGANIZATION OF THE TRIBE

When the peace pipes were made (those for "establishing friendly relations with other tribes"), seven other pipes were made for the keeping of peace within the tribe. These pipes were also for use to prevent bloodshed. If one man should kill another, in such a case the chiefs were to take a pipe to the aggrieved relatives and offer it to them. If they refused, the pipe was to be again offered them; if the pipe was offered and refused four successive times, then the chiefs said to them, "You must now take the consequences; we will do nothing, and you can not ask to see the pipes," meaning that if trouble should come to any of them because of their acts taken in revenge they could not appeal for help or mercy.

When these seven pipes were finished they were taken to be distributed among the different bands of the tribe.

The first band to which the pipe bearers came was the Waça'be. They were found to be engaged in a ceremony that did not pertain to peace, but rather to the taking of life. The Hi'çada sat in a tent with red-hot stones, and had on their heads wreaths of cedar branches. The pipe bearers passed them by, and even to this day they are reminded of this occurrence by the other bands saying, "You are no people; you have no peace pipe!"

The next band the pipe bearers came to was the Thi'xida. To them a pipe was given, and they were to have charge of the council which elected chiefs.

Next they came to the Ni'kapashna, and to them a pipe was given, and they were to have the management of the council of war and also the direction of the people when they went to hunt the deer, so that order might be preserved in the pursuit of that game.

The Pon'caxti and the Monkon' were reached next, and a pipe was given them.

The Washa'be were next, and a pipe was given them. This band, together with the Monkon', were given charge of the tribal buffalo hunt—the direction of the journey, the making of the camps, and the preservation of order. From these two bands the two principal chiefs must come.

When the pipe bearers reached the Wazha'zhe the latter were divided, and there were trouble and murder between the factions. So, instead of giving them a flat-stemmed pipe, they gave them one with a round stem, ornamented. Because of the feud there was carelessness, and to this day there is a dispute as to the division to which the pipe for the maintenance of peace was presented.

When the pipe bearers reached the Nu'xe, they gave them a pipe and an office in the buffalo hunt.

Each band had its pipe, but there was one pipe which was to belong to the chiefs. This could be filled only by the leading chiefs, and was to be used to punish people who made trouble in the tribe. It was placed in charge of the Monkon' band.

When a man was to be punished, all the chiefs gathered together and this pipe was filled by the leader and smoked by all the chiefs present. Then each chief put his mind on the offender as the leader took the pipe to clean it. He poured some of the tobacco ashes on the ground, and said, "This shall rankle in the calves of the man's legs." Then he twirled the cleaning stick in the pipe and took out a little more ashes, and, putting them on the earth, said, "This shall be for the base of the sinews, and he shall start with pain" (in the back). A third time he twirled the cleaning stick, put more ashes on the earth, and said, "This is for the spine, at the base of the head." A fourth time he twirled the cleaning stick in the pipe, poured out the ashes, put them on the ground, and said, "This is for the crown of his head." This act finished the man, who died soon after.

STANDING  BUFFALO

WHITE EAGLE (XITHA'ÇKA)

## THE WAZHA'ZHE GENS

Standing Buffalo (pl. 2), of the Wazha'zhe gens, told the following story some ten years ago:

When I was a boy I often asked my mother where my people came from, but she would not tell me, until one day she said, "I will give you the story as it has been handed down from generation to generation.

"In the real beginning Wako$^n$'da made the Wazha'zhe—men, women, and children. After they were made he said 'Go!' So the people took all they had, carried their children, and started toward the setting sun. They traveled until they came to a great water. Seeing they could go no farther, they halted. Again Wako$^n$'da said 'Go!' And once more they started, and wondered what would happen to them. As they were about to step into the water there appeared from under the water rocks. These projected just above the surface, and there were others barely covered with water. Upon these stones the people walked, stepping from stone to stone until they came to land. When they stood on dry land the wind blew, the water became violent and threw the rocks upon the land, and they became great cliffs. Therefore when men enter the sweat lodge they thank the stones for preserving their lives and ask for a continuation of their help that their lives may be prolonged. Here on the shore the people dwelt; but again Wako$^n$'da said 'Go!' And again they started and traveled on until they came to a people whose appearance was like their own; but not knowing whether they were friends or foes, the people rushed at each other for combat. In the midst of the confusion Wako$^n$'da said, 'Stand still!' The people obeyed. They questioned each other, found they spoke the same language, and became friends.

"Wako$^n$'da gave the people a bow, a dog, and a grain of corn. The people made other bows like the one given them and learned to use them for killing wild animals for food and to make clothing out of their skins. The dogs gave increase and were used as burden bearers and for hunting. The corn they planted, and when it grew they found it good to eat, and they continued to plant it.

"The people traveled on and came to a lake. There the Omaha found a Sacred Tree and took it with them. The people (Ponca) went on and came to a river now called Nishu'de (the Missouri). They traveled along its banks until they came to a place where they could step over the water. From there they went across the land and came to a river now called Nibtha'çka (the Platte). This river they followed, and it led them back to the Missouri.

"Again they went up this river until they came to a river now called Niobrara, where we live to-day."

The latter part of this legend, which deals with the Ponca movements after the Omaha found the Sacred Tree, has been obtained from a number of old men. All follow the general outline given by Standing Buffalo, while some preserve details omitted by him, as the meeting with the Padouca (Comanche), the obtaining of horses, etc., which are given elsewhere. (See p. 78.)

### HOW WHITE EAGLE BECAME A CHIEF

The following account of how White Eagle (pl. 3) came to be a chief was given by him ten years or more ago and was introductory to the information he then imparted to the writers. He regarded the story as important, for it served to make clear his tribal status and therefore, he thought, to give weight to his statements concerning the Ponca tribe. The story is repeated here as throwing light on Ponca customs during the eighteenth century:

A chief by the name of Zhi<sup>n</sup>ga'gahige (Little Chief), of the Washa'be band, had a son who went on the warpath. The father sat in his tent weeping because he had heard that his son was killed, for the young man did not return. As he wept he thought of various persons in the tribe whom he might call on to avenge the death of his son. As he cast about, he recalled a young man who belonged to a poor family and had no notable relations. The young man's name was Waça'bezhi<sup>n</sup>ga (Little Bear). The chief remembered that this young man dressed and painted himself in a peculiar manner, and thought that he did so that he might act in accordance with a dream, and therefore it was probable that he possessed more than ordinary power and courage. So the chief said to himself, "I will call on him and see what he can do."

Then the chief called together all the other chiefs of the tribe, and when they were assembled he sent for Little Bear. On the arrival of the young man the chief addressed him, saying, "My son went on the warpath and has never returned. I do not know where his bones lie. I have only heard he has been killed. I wish you to go and find the land where he was killed. If you return successful four times, then I shall resign my place in your favor."

Little Bear accepted the offer. He had a sacred headdress that had on it a ball of human hair; he obtained the hair in this manner: Whenever men and women of his acquaintance combed their hair and any of the hair fell out, Little Bear asked to have the combings given to him. By and by he accumulated enough hair to make his peculiar headdress. This was a close-fitting skull cap of skin; on the front part was fastened the ball of human hair; on the back part were tied a downy eagle feather and one of the sharp-pointed feathers from the wing of that bird. He had another sacred article, a buffalo horn, which he fastened at his belt.

Little Bear called a few warriors together and asked them to go with him, and they consented. Putting on his headdress and buffalo horn, he and his companions started. They met a party of Sioux, hunting. One of the Sioux made a charge at Little Bear, who fell over a bluff. The Sioux stood above him and shot arrows at him; one struck the headdress and the other the buffalo horn. After he had shot these two arrows the Sioux turned and fled. Little Bear, who was uninjured, climbed up the bluff, and, seeing the Sioux, drew his bow and shot the man through the head. Besides this scalp Little Bear and his party captured some ponies. On the return of the party Little Bear gave his share of the booty to the chief who had lost his son.

Little Bear went on three other expeditions and always returned successful, and each time he gave his share of the spoils to the chief. When Little Bear came back the fourth time the chief kept his word and resigned his office in favor of the young man.

Little Bear was my grandfather. When he died he was succeeded by his eldest son, Two Bulls. At his death his brother, We'gaçapi (pl. 4),[a] who was my father, became chief, and I succeeded him.

---

[a] An old Ponca, speaking of We'gaçapi, said: "He was a successful man, and had a pack which had descended to him. He always carried it in war. Both he and the original owner of the pack are said to have had dreams of wolves." We'gaçapi had the honor of having some of his brave deeds preserved in song by the Hethu'shka society, and the song is known to members of the society in both the Ponca and Omaha tribes.

WE'GAÇAPI

STANDING BEAR

RECENT HISTORY; PERSONAL NAMES

The following list of Ponca names was taken in November, 1874, while the entire tribe was living on the Niobrara river.[a]

The total population of the tribe at that time was 733, divided as follows:[b]

|  | Full bloods. | Mixed bloods. |  | Full bloods. | Mixed bloods. |
|---|---|---|---|---|---|
| Men | 172 | 32 | Girls | 129 | 45 |
| Women | 164 | 21 | Families | 185 | 32 |
| Boys | 135 | 35 |  |  |  |

The people dwelt in three villages. The village at the United States agency contained 89 families and 377 persons. The village called Hubtho$^{n\prime}$ ("those who smell of fish") had 46 families and 144 persons. "Point" village had 82 families and 248 persons.

There were eight chiefs, each of whom had his "band." These bands were probably composed of persons from the gens or subgens to which the chief belonged.

|  | Families. | Persons. |
|---|---|---|
| White Eagle's band (Waça′be, Hi′çada subgens) | 26 | 89 |
| Big Soldier's band (Waça′be, Hi′çada subgens) | 31 | 97 |
| Traveling Buffalo's band (Thi′xida) | 23 | 72 |
| Black Crow's band (Ni′kapashna) | 28 | 90 |
| Over the Land's band (Po$^{n\prime}$caxti and Mo$^{n}$ko$^{n\prime}$) | 21 | 73 |
| Woodpecker's band (Washa′be) | 27 | 75 |
| Standing Bear's band (Wazha′zhe) | 20 | 82 |
| Big-hoofed Buffalo's band (Nu′xe) | 9 | 22 |

---

[a] In 1858 the Ponca ceded their hunting grounds to the United States, and reserved for their home the land about their old village sites on the Niobrara river  They were never at war with the Government or the white race. Their reservation was reconfirmed to them by the Government in 1865. In 1868 a large reservation was granted to the Sioux, in which the Ponca reservation on the Niobrara was included. The Ponca tribe was ignorant of this official transfer of its land. In 1877 the Ponca, without any warning, were informed they must move to the Indian Territory, and the eight chiefs were conducted there by an official and told to select a new reservation  The reason for leaving their old home was not explained to the protesting chiefs or to the people. The chiefs who went with the official refused to select a home in "the strange land." They begged to be allowed to go back. Being refused, they left the official, and, in the winter, with but a few dollars and a blanket each, started home, walking 500 miles in forty days. When they reached the Niobrara the United States Indian agent summoned the military and on the 1st of May the entire tribe was forcibly removed to the Indian Territory. The change from a cool climate to a warm and humid one caused suffering. Within a year one-third of the people were dead and nearly all the survivors were sick or disabled. A son of Chief Standing Bear (pl. 5) died. The father could not bury him away from his ancestors, so taking the bones, he and his immediate following turned from "the hot country," and in January, 1879, started to walk back  They reached the Omaha reservation in May, destitute, and asked the loan of land and seed, which was granted. As they were about to put in a crop, soldiers appeared with orders to arrest Standing Bear and his party and take them back. They were obliged to obey. On their way north they camped near Omaha city. Their story was made known, the citizens became interested, lawyers offered help, and a writ of habeas corpus was secured. The United States denied the prisoners' right to sue out a writ, because "an Indian was not a person within the meaning of the law." The case came before Judge Dundy, who decided that "An Indian is a person within the meaning of the law," and that there was no authority under the laws of the United States forcibly to remove the prisoners to the Indian Territory, and ordered their release. In the winter Standing Bear visited the principal cities of the East, repeating the story of his people. The United States Senate ordered an investigation of the Ponca removal, when all the facts were brought out. Those Ponca who chose to remain in Oklahoma were given good lands. Their old home on the Niobrara was restored to Standing Bear and his followers and lost property was paid for  In September, 1908, Standing Bear died and was buried with his fathers. By his sufferings and courage he was instrumental in putting an end to enforced Indian removals.

[b] Data furnished by Office of Commissioner of Indian Affairs.

## PERSONAL NAMES[a]

### WAÇA'BE GENS, HI'ÇADA SUBGENS

#### White Eagle's band

##### Male.

Çi'ha—Soles (O.: Te'pa, Tha'tada, Tapa').

Çithe'dezhi$^n$ga—Little heel (O., I$^n$shta'çu$^n$da).

De'mo$^n$thi$^n$—Talks walking.

Gahi'ge zhi$^n$ga—Little chief (O.: I$^n$ke'çabe, Ko$^n$'çe).

Gaku'wi$^n$xe—Whirled by the wind.

Gamo$^{n'}$xpi—Wind strikes the clouds (O.: Wazhi$^n$'ga, Tha'tada).

Gashta'gabi—Beaten into submission.

Ha'nugahi—Nettle weed.

Ke'to$^n$ga—Big turtle (O.: Wazhi$^n$'ga, Tha'tada).

Mi'xazhi$^n$ga—Duck.

Mo$^n$chu'nita—Grizzly bear's ears.

Mo$^n$chu'wathihi—Stampedes the grizzly bear.

Mo$^n$chu'zhi$^n$ga—Little grizzly bear.

Mo$^n$e'gahi—Arrow chief (O., I$^n$ke'çabe).

Mo$^{n'}$sho$^n$zhide—Red feather.

Mo$^{n'}$tega—New arrow.

Ni'çtumo$^n$thi$^n$—Walking backward (O.: Xu'ka, Tha'tada).

Nishu'dezho$^n$—Missouri River timber.

Niwa'i—Gives water.

No$^{n'}$pabi—One who is feared (O.: Waça'be, Tha'tada).

Nudo$^{n'}$ho$^n$ga—Leader (O., Ho$^n$'ga).

Nudo$^{n'}$mo$^n$thi$^n$—Warrior walking.

O$^n$'po$^n$çabe—Black Elk.

Pe'degahi—Fire chief (O.: Wazhi$^n$'ga, Tha'tada).

Sho$^n$to$^n$ga—Gray wolf.

Shu'degaxe—Smoke maker (pl. 6).

Shui'na—Meaning uncertain (O.: Waça'be, Tha'tada).

Shuka'mo$^n$thi$^n$—Walking in groups (O., Ho$^n$'ga).

Teço$^{n'}$—White buffalo (O.: Wazhi$^n$'ga, Tha'tada).

Tenu'gaçabe—Black bull.

Thi'o$^n$bagigthe—Lightning passing (O., I$^n$shta'çu$^n$da).

Thi'o$^n$batigthe—Sudden lightning (O., I$^n$shta'çu$^n$da).

Tide'gigthe—Passes by with a roar.

Ti'uthio$^n$ba—Lightning flashes in the tent (O., I$^n$shta'çu$^n$da).

Wahu'to$^n$the—Gun.

Wai$^n$gabtha—Spreads robe.

Wazhi'dathi$^n$—Has red medicine.

Xitha'çka—White eagle (O., Tapa').

##### Female

Mi'gasho$^n$thi$^n$—Traveling sun (O., I$^n$ke'çabe).

Mi'texi—Sacred moon (O., Mo$^{n'}$thi$^n$kagaxe).

#### Big Soldier's band

##### Male

Agi'chidato$^n$ga—Big soldier.

A'hi$^n$çka—White wings (O.: Te'pa, Tha'tada).

A'shkano$^n$ge—Short runner.

A'xewo$^n$—Covered with frost.

Gahi'ge—Chief (O.: I$^n$ke'çabe, Te'pa, Tha'tada), plate 7.

He'xude—Gray horns (O., Teçi$^{n'}$de).

I'kuhabi—He who causes fear

I$^n$shta'duba—Four eyes (O.: Waça'be, Tha'tada).

Ki'shtawagu—Said to be a Pawnee name (O., Mo$^{n'}$thi$^n$kagaxe).

Mo$^n$'hi$^n$gahi—Knife chief.

Mo$^n$'thumo$^n$çe—Metal or iron chief.

Nini'ba—Pipe (O., Te'pa, Tha'tada).

No$^n$ba'mo$^n$thi$^n$—Two walking (O.: Wazhi$^n$'ga, Tha'tada).

No$^{n'}$gemo$^n$thi$^n$—Travels running (O., Mo$^{n'}$thi$^n$kagaxe).

Nudo$^{n'}$axa—Cries for war.

Paho$^{n'}$gamo$^n$thi$^n$—Walking first (O., I$^n$ke'çabe).

Shage'duba—Four hoofs (O., Tapa').

Shu'kabi—Bunch of clouds.

Tato$^{n'}$gapa—Bull head.

Tenu'gaçka—White bull.

Te'thiti—Buffalo rib (O.: Waça'be, Tha'tada).

Thi'tiaxa—Cries for rib.

U'ho$^n$zhi$^n$ga—Little cook (O., I$^n$shta'çu$^n$da).

Uzho$^n$'ge—Road.

Waça'bezhi$^n$ga—Little black bear (O.: Waça'be, Tha'tada).

---

[a] This list is necessarily incomplete. Names found in tribes other than the Ponca are followed by the names of the respective tribes, accompanied by those of the gentes where known, in parentheses. (O.=Omaha.)

SMOKE-MAKER (SHU'DEGAXE)

GAHI'GE

Wako$^n$dagi—Monster.
Wazhi$^n$ga—Bird (O.: Wazhi$^n$ga, Tha'tada).
Wazhi$^n$gaçabe—Blackbird (O., Mo$^n$thi$^n$kagaxe).
Wazhi$^n$gagahi—Bird chief (O.: Wazhi$^n$ga, Tha'tada).
We'zhno$^n$wathe—He who causes fog.
Zha'beçka—White beaver.
Zhi$^n$gapezhi—Bad little one.
Zho$^n$xude—Gray wood.

### Female

A'o$^n$wi$^n$—Meaning uncertain (O., Ho$^n$ga).
Mi'tena—Meaning uncertain (O., Ho$^n$ga).
Mi'waço$^n$—White moon (O., Ho$^n$ga).
No$^n$çe'i$^n$çe—Meaning uncertain (O., We'zhi$^n$shte).
Teço$^n$dabe—White buffalo (O., Ho$^n$ga).
Teço$^n$wi$^n$—White buffalo woman (O., Ho$^n$ga).
To$^n$i$^n$gthihe—Sudden appearing of new moon (O., I$^n$ke'çabe).
Zho$^n$i'wathe—To carry wood (O., We'zhi$^n$shte).

### THI'XIDA GENS

#### Traveling Buffalo's band

##### Male

Gaku'wi$^n$xe—Soaring eagle (O.: Te'pa, Tha'tada).
Ha'shimo$^n$thi$^n$—Walking last in a file (O., I$^n$shta'çu$^n$da).
He'shathage—Branching horns (O., I$^n$shta'çu$^n$da).
Hewo$^n$zhi$^n$tha—One horn (Dakota).
Hezha'ta—Forked horns (O., Tapa').
Hezhi$^n$ga—Little horn.
Ka'xeno$^n$ba—Two crows (O., Ho$^n$ga).
Keba'ha—Turtle showing himself (O., Tapa').
Ma'azhi$^n$ga—Little cottonwood (O.: Wazhi$^n$ga, Tha'tada).
Mixa'çka—White swan (O., Mo$^n$thi$^n$kagaxe).
Mo$^n$a'zhi$^n$ga—Little bank (O., I$^n$gthe'zhide).
Mo$^n$chu'çka—White bear.
Mo$^n$shi'ahamo$^n$thi$^n$—Moving above (O., I$^n$shta'çu$^n$da).
No$^n$be'thiku—Cramped hand.
O$^n$'po$^n$to$^n$ga—Big Elk (O., We'zhi$^n$shte).

Pa'thi$^n$no$^n$pazhi$^n$—Fears not Pawnee (O.: Waça'be, Tha'tada).
Sha'geçka—White claws (O., Tha'tada).
Sha'geshuga—Thick claws.
Sha'nugahi—Meaning uncertain (O., I$^n$gthe'zhide).
Shathu'—Gurgle (water).
Tato$^n$ga—Great male deer (old name) (O., Tapa').
Tato$^n$gano$^n$zhi$^n$—Standing bull.
Tenu'gano$^n$ba—Two buffalo bulls (O., Tapa').
Tenu'gazhi$^n$ga—Little bull (O., Teçi$^n$de).
U'do$^n$—Good.
Uga'sho$^n$to$^n$—The traveler or wanderer (O., Teçi$^n$de).
Waba'hizhi$^n$ga—The little grazer (O., Ko$^n$çe).
Waça'beto$^n$ge—Big black bear (O., Mo$^n$thi$^n$kagaxe).
Wada'thi$^n$ge—Refers to chief (O., I$^n$ke'çabe).
Wami'—Blood (O., Ko$^n$çe).
Wano$^n$xe—Ghost.
Washi'chuçabe—Black man (Sioux).
Washi$^n$nuka—Wet fat, or fresh fat.
Washi'shka—Shell (O., Mo$^n$thi$^n$kagaxe).
Washu'she—Brave (O., I$^n$ke'çabe).
Wazhi$^n$çka—Wisdom (O., I$^n$shta'çu$^n$da).
Wazhi$^n$gaçi—Yellow bird.
Wazhi$^n$wathe—He who provokes anger.
Xitha'çka—White eagle (O., Tapa').

##### Female

Mi'gasho$^n$thi$^n$—Traveling moon (O., I$^n$ke'çabe).
Mi'gthedo$^n$wi$^n$—Moon hawk woman (O., I$^n$ke'çabe).
Mi'gthito$^n$i$^n$—Return of new moon (O., I$^n$shta'çu$^n$da).
Mi'o$^n$bathi$^n$—Moon moving by day (O., I$^n$shta'çu$^n$da).
Mi'tena—Meaning uncertain (O., Ho$^n$ga).
Nazhe'gito$^n$—Meaning uncertain (O., Ho$^n$ga).
No$^n$çe'i$^n$çe—Meaning uncertain (O., We'zhi$^n$shte).
To$^n$'ithi$^n$—New moon moving (O., Ho$^n$ga).
Wate'wi$^n$—May refer to the stream Wate (O., Tha'tada).
We'to$^n$na—Meaning uncertain (O., I$^n$shta'çu$^n$da).

## NI'KAPASHNA GENS
### Black Crow's band
#### Male

A'kidagahigi—Chief who watches (O., Tapa').

Çikon xega—Brown ankles (O., In ke'çabe).

Gahi'gewashushe—Brave chief.

Gahi'gezhin ga—Little chief (O., Kon 'çe).

Gthedon 'non zhin—Standing hawk (O.: Wazhin 'ga, Tha'tada).

Gthedon 'xude—Gray hawk (O.: Wazhin 'ga, Tha'tada).

He'çithin ke—New yellow horn (O., We'zhin shte).

Hethi'shizhe—Crooked horn.

Hin 'xega—Brown hair (Omaha).

Hu'ton tigthe—Cries out in the distance.

I'bahon bi—He is known (O., In shta'çun da).

In chun 'gaçka—White weasel (O., Tapa').

Kaxe'çabe—Black crow (O., Tapa'), plate 8.

Ke'zhin ga—Little turtle (O.: Ke'in, Tha'tada).

Mika'—Raccoon.

Mixabaku—Bent goose (O.: Ke'in, Tha'tada).

Mon chu'dathin—Crazy bear.

Mon 'geutin—Strikes the breast.

Mon hin 'thin ge—No knife (O., We'zhin shte).

Mon non 'uton—Paws the earth.

Mon 'shkaaxa—Cries for crawfish (O.: Waça'be, Tha'tada).

Mon sho n 'çka—White feather (O., In gthe'zhide).

Non ba'aton—Treads on two.

Non 'getithe—Passes by running.

Non ka'tu—Blue-back (O., In gthe'zhide).

Nudon 'gina—Returns from war.

Shon 'gehin çabe—Black horse.

Taton 'gamon thin—Big deer walking (O., Tapa').

Ta'xtiçka—White deer.

Waçe'zhide—Red paint.

Wanon 'pazhi—Without fear (O., In gthe'zhide).

Zhin ga'un ça—Little runner.

#### Female

Gthedon 'shtewin—Hawk woman (O., Tapa').

Mi'gthedon 'win—Moon hawk woman (O. In ke'çabe).

Mon 'shadethin—One moving on high (O., In shta'çun da).

Ton 'in gina—New moon coming (O., In shta'çun da).

## PON 'CAXTI GENS
### Over the Land's band
#### Male

Çin 'deçka—White tail (Omaha).

Çin 'dedon ka—Blunt tail (O., We'zhin shte).

Çithin 'ge—No feet.

Ezhno n 'non zhin—Stands alone.

Gthedon ' texi—Sacred hawk.

Hon 'gazhin ga—Little Hon 'ga (O., Hon 'ga).

In ke'ton ga—Big shoulder (O., In shta'çun da).

In shta'pede—Fire eyes (O., In ke'çabe).

Keon 'hazhi—Turtle that flees not (O.: Waça'be, Tha'tada).

Kigtha'zhon zhon—Shakes himself (O., Teçin 'de).

Mika'xage—Crying raccoon (O., Tapa').

Mon ka'ta—On the land (old name, now used among the Dakota).

Mon kon 'ton ga—Big medicine.

Mon zhon 'ibahon—Knows the land.

Non 'gethia—Not able to run (O., Teçin 'de).

Nuga'—Male (O., In ke'çabe).

Nuga'xte—Original male (O., We'zhin shte).

On 'pon zhin ga—Little elk (O., We'zhin shte).

Shenon 'zhin—Stands there.

Te'mon thin—Buffalo walking (O., In gthe'zhide).

Tenu'gawakega—Sick bull.

Thae'gethabi—One who is loved (O., Tapa').

The'baxon—Broken jaw.

The'dewathe—Looks back.

Thihie'non—Frightens the game.

Une'gthon xe—Seeks poison.

Waba'hizi—Yellow grazer (O., Mon 'thin kagaxe).

Wagi'on—Thunder bird (Dakota).

Washko n 'zhin ga—Little strength.

Wa'xanon zhin—Standing in advance (O., Tapa').

Xitha'gahige—Eagle chief (O., Tapa').

Xitha'gaxe—Eagle maker (O., Tapa').

Zhin ga'nudon—Little warrior.

BLACK CROW (KAXE'ÇABE)

BIG GOOSE

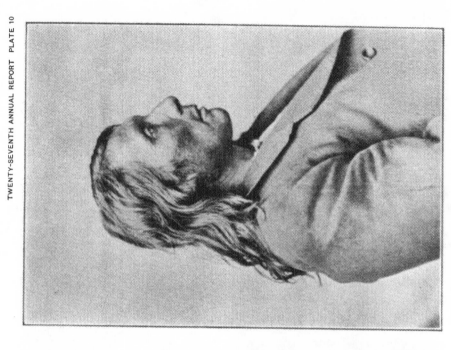

BUFFALO CHIP

*Female*

Açe'to$^n$ga—Meaning uncertain (O., Ko$^n$'çe).

Gthedon'wi$^n$texe—Sacred hawk woman (O., Tapa').

Mi'ako$^n$da—Sacred moon (O., Teçi$^n$'de).

Mi'bthiwi$^n$—Meaning uncertain (O., Tha'tada).

Mi'mo$^n$shihathi$^n$—Moon moving on high (O., Tha'tada).

Mi'tena—Meaning uncertain (O., Ho$^n$'ga).

Mi'waço$^n$—White moon (O., Ho$^n$'ga).

Po$^n$ca'ço$^n$—White Ponca (O., Mo$^n$'thi$^n$kagaxe).

Zho$^n$'i$^n$wathe—To carry wood (O., We'zhi$^n$shte).

WASHA'BE GENS

*Woodpecker's band*

*Male*

A'gahamo$^n$thi$^n$ — Walks outside (O.: Xu'ka, Tha'tada).

Çi$^n$'deçabe—Black tail.

E'tho$^n$tho$^n$be—To appear repeatedly (O., Ho$^n$'ga).

Hexa'gaçabe—Black elk.

Hexa'gamo$^n$thi$^n$—Standing elk (O., Mo$^n$'thi$^n$kagaxe).

Hi$^n$çi'zhi$^n$ga—Little yellow hair (O., Teçi$^n$'de).

Hu'hazhi—Meaning uncertain (O., Tapa').

I$^n$shta'çabe—Black eyes (O., Teçi$^n$'de).

I$^n$shta'dathi$^n$—Crazy eyes.

I$^n$shta'duba—Four eyes (O., Waça'be, Tha'tada).

Ko$^n$'çeto$^n$ga—Big Kansa.

Ma'çito$^n$—Lone cedar tree.

Mi'kaçixthaha—Lean coyote.

Mi'xato$^n$ga—Big goose (pl. 9).

Mo$^n$'çedo$^n$—Meaning uncertain (O., I$^n$gthe'zhide).

Mo$^n$chu'çi$^n$dethi$^n$ge—Bob-tailed bear.

Mo$^n$ga'azhi—Not afraid of arrows (O., Mo$^n$'thi$^n$kagaxe).

Mo$^n$'gazhi$^n$ga—Little skunk.

No$^n$'ço$^n$dazhi—Does not dodge (O., Tapa').

No$^n$'kaçka—White back.

No$^n$zhi$^n$'mo$^n$thi$^n$—Rain travels (O., Mo$^n$'thi$^n$kagaxe).

Nudo$^n$'ho$^n$ga—Leader (O., Ho$^n$'ga).

Paçi'duba—Four buffaloes—very old name (O., Ko$^n$'çe; Osage).

Sha'ge—Hoofs.

Sho$^n$'geçabe—Black horse (O., Tapa').

Te'çehi$^n$çabe—Black hair on belly of buffalo (O., Tapa').

Te'nuga—Buffalo bull (O., Ho$^n$'ga).

Tezhe'bate—Buffalo chip (pl. 10).

Te'zhi$^n$ga—Little buffalo (O., I$^n$gthe'zhide).

Thigthi'çemo$^n$thi$^n$—Zigzag lightning walking (O., I$^n$shta'çu$^n$da).

Tishi'muxa—Spreading tent poles (O., I$^n$gthe'zhide).

Uga'sho$^n$zhi$^n$ga—Little traveler (O., Mo$^n$'thi$^n$kagaxe).

Ugtha'atigthe—He who shouts (victory name).

Uho$^n$'no$^n$ba—Two cooks (O.: Wazhi$^n$'ga, Tha'tada).

Uho$^n$'zhi$^n$ga—Little cook (O., I$^n$shta'çu$^n$da).

Wahaxi—Yellow skin (O., I$^n$shta'çu$^n$da).

Waho$^n$'thi$^n$ge—Orphan (O. Teçi$^n$'de).

Wa'ino$^n$zhi$^n$—Standing over them (O., I$^n$gthe'zhide).

Wapa'de—One who cuts the carcass (O., Tapa').

Washko$^n$'mo$^n$thi$^n$—Walking strength (O.: Wazhi$^n$'ga, Tha'tada).

Zhi$^n$ga'gahige—Little chief (O., Tapa').

Zhi$^n$ga'washushe—Little brave.

*Female*

Gthedo$^n$'wi$^n$texi—Sacred hawk woman (O., I$^n$ke'çabe).

Mi'gthedo$^n$wi$^n$—Moon hawk woman (O., I$^n$ke'çabe).

Migthi'to$^n$i$^n$ — New moon. (O., I$^n$ke'çabe).

Mi'tena—Meaning uncertain (O., Ho$^n$'ga).

Mi'waçon—White moon (O., Ho$^n$'ga).

Mo$^n$sha'dethi$^n$—Moving on high (O., I$^n$shta'çu$^n$da).

Po$^n$'caço$^n$—Pale Ponca. (O., Mo$^n$'thi$^n$kagaxe).

Po$^n$'cawi$^n$—Ponca woman (O., Mo$^n$'thi$^n$kagaxe).

Wihe'to$^n$ga—Big little sister (O., We'zhi$^n$shte).

### WAZHA'ZHE GENS

*Standing Bear's band*

#### Male

A'gahawashushe—Distinguished for bravery (O.: Waça'be, Tha'tada).

A'thiude—Abandoned (O., I<sup>n</sup>shta'çu<sup>n</sup>da).

Bachi'zhithe—To rush through obstacles (O., Tapa').

Çigthe'no<sup>n</sup>pabi—One whose footprints are feared (O., Mo<sup>n</sup>'thi<sup>n</sup>kagaxe).

Da'do<sup>n</sup>thi<sup>n</sup>ge—Has nothing (O., Ko<sup>n</sup>'çe).

Gaçu'be—Meaning uncertain (O., Ho<sup>n</sup>'ga).

Gahi'gezhi<sup>n</sup>ga—Little chief (O., I<sup>n</sup>ke'çabe).

Gakuwi<sup>n</sup>xe—Eagle soaring (O.: Te'pa, Tha'tada).

Hexa'ga—Rough horns (O., Tapa').

Ho<sup>n</sup>'gashenu—Ho<sup>n</sup>'ga man (O., I<sup>n</sup>shta'çu<sup>n</sup>da).

I<sup>n</sup>de'xaga—Rough face.

Ki'mo<sup>n</sup>ho<sup>n</sup>—Facing the wind (O., I<sup>n</sup>shta'çu<sup>n</sup>da).

Ko<sup>n</sup>'çeho<sup>n</sup>ga—Kansa leader (O., Mo<sup>n</sup>'thi<sup>n</sup>kagaxe).

Maci'kide—Shooting cedar (O., I<sup>n</sup>shta'çu<sup>n</sup>da).

Mo<sup>n</sup>chu'duba—Four bears, grizzly.

Mo<sup>n</sup>chu'kino<sup>n</sup>pabi—The bear who is feared.

Mo<sup>n</sup>chu'no<sup>n</sup>zhi<sup>n</sup>—Standing bear.

Mo<sup>n</sup>chu'to<sup>n</sup>ga—Big bear.

Mo<sup>n</sup>shti<sup>n</sup>'çka—White rabbit (O.: Wazhi<sup>n</sup>'ga, Tha'tada).

Ni'juba—Little water.

No<sup>n</sup>'kahega—Brown back (O., Tapa').

No<sup>n</sup>o<sup>n</sup>'bi—One who is heard (O., Teçi<sup>n</sup>'de).

No<sup>n</sup>pe'wathe—One who is feared (O.: Wazhi<sup>n</sup>'ga, Tha'tada).

No<sup>n</sup>xi'dethi<sup>n</sup>ge—The incorrigible.

Nushia'hagino<sup>n</sup>—Returns bending low.

Pethi'shage—Curly brows.

Sho<sup>n</sup>'gehi<sup>n</sup>çi—Yellow horse.

Tade'umo<sup>n</sup>thi<sup>n</sup>—Walking wind (O., Ko<sup>n</sup>'çe).

Tai'hi<sup>n</sup>to<sup>n</sup>ga—Big mane.

Tato<sup>n</sup>'gano<sup>n</sup>zhi<sup>n</sup>zhi<sup>n</sup>ga—Little standing bull.

Tato<sup>n</sup>'gashkade—Buffalo playing (O., Teçi<sup>n</sup>'de).

Tenu'gazhi<sup>n</sup>ga—Little buffalo bull (O., Teçi<sup>n</sup>'de).

The'çeçabe—Black tongue (O., I<sup>n</sup>ke'çabe).

Uçu'gaxe—To make paths (O., I<sup>n</sup>shta'çu<sup>n</sup>da).

Uzha'ta—Confluence.

Waa<sup>n</sup>'—To sing (O., I<sup>n</sup>gthe'zhide).

Waba'açe—He puts to flight (O., I<sup>n</sup>shta'çu<sup>n</sup>da).

Wabahi'zhi<sup>n</sup>ga—Little nibbles (O., Ko<sup>n</sup>'çe).

Wagi'asha—Meaning lost (O., I<sup>n</sup>shta'çu<sup>n</sup>da).

Wako<sup>n</sup>'da—Power (O., Mo<sup>n</sup>'thi<sup>n</sup>kagaxe).

Wano<sup>n</sup>'shezhi<sup>n</sup>ga—Little soldier (O., I<sup>n</sup>shta'çu<sup>n</sup>da).

Washko<sup>n</sup>'hi—Strong (O., I<sup>n</sup>shta'çu<sup>n</sup>da).

Washu'she—Brave (O., I<sup>n</sup>ke'çabe).

Wa'thidaxe—Sound of claws tearing (O.: Wazhi<sup>n</sup>'ga, Tha'tada).

Wathi'xekashi—He who pursues long.

Waxpe'sha—Old name, meaning lost (O., Tapa').

Wazhe'thi<sup>n</sup>ge—Without gratitude (O., I<sup>n</sup>shta'çu<sup>n</sup>da).

We'ç'a—Snake (O., I<sup>n</sup>shta'çu<sup>n</sup>da).

We'ç'aho<sup>n</sup>ga—Snake leader (O., Tapa').

We'ç'ato<sup>n</sup>ga—Big snake (pl. 11).

We'ç'azhi<sup>n</sup>ga—Little snake (O., I<sup>n</sup>shta'çu<sup>n</sup>da).

Xitha'nika—Eagle person (O., Tapa').

Xitha'zhi<sup>n</sup>ga—Little eagle (O.: Te'pa, Tha'tada).

#### Female

Açe'xube—Sacred paint (O., We'zhi<sup>n</sup>shte).

Mi'tena—Meaning uncertain (O., Ho<sup>n</sup>'ga).

No<sup>n</sup>çe'i<sup>n</sup>çe—Meaning uncertain (O., We'zhi<sup>n</sup>shte).

No<sup>n</sup>zhe'gito<sup>n</sup>—Meaning uncertain (O., Mo<sup>n</sup>'thi<sup>n</sup>kagaxe).

Ta'çabewi<sup>n</sup>—Black deer woman (O., We'zhi<sup>n</sup>shte).

Te'ço<sup>n</sup>wi<sup>n</sup>—White buffalo woman (O., Teçi<sup>n</sup>'de).

To<sup>n</sup>'i<sup>n</sup>gthihe—New moon soaring (O., I<sup>n</sup>ke'çabe).

Umo<sup>n</sup>'ho<sup>n</sup>wau—Omaha woman.

Wihe'to<sup>n</sup>ga—Big little sister (O., We'zhi<sup>n</sup>shte).

BIG SNAKE

OSAGE CHIEF

OSAGE CHIEF

NU'XE GENS

*Big-hoofed buffalo's band*

Male

Btho$^n$'ti—Scent borne by wind (O., We'-zhi$^n$shte).

Çi$^n$'dethiho$^n$—Lifting the tail (O., Te-çi$^n$'de).

Du'bamo$^n$thi$^n$—Four walking (O., I$^n$ke'-çabe).

I$^n$sha'gemo$^n$thi$^n$—Old man walking (O., I$^n$shta'çu$^n$da).

I$^n$shta'baçude—Shedding hair about the eyes (O., Ho$^n$'ga).

No$^n$'gethia—Not able to run (O., Teçi$^n$'de).

Nu'xezhi$^n$ga—Little ice.

Pahe'agthi$^n$—Sits on hill.

Pude'tha—Meaning unknown (O., I$^n$ke'-çabe).

Sha'beno$^n$zhi$^n$—Stands dark (O., Ho$^n$'ga).

Sho$^n$ge'çka—White horse (O., Mo$^n$'thi$^n$-kagaxe).

Tenu'gagahi—Male buffalo chief (O.: Wazhi$^n$'ga, Tha'tada).

Tenu'gashageto$^n$ga—Big-hoofed bull.

Thae'go$^n$—Pitiful.

Uho$^n$'gemo$^n$thi$^n$—Walking at end of file (O., I$^n$gthe'zhide).

Uho$^n$'geno$^n$zhi$^n$—Standing at end of file (O., I$^n$gthe'zhide).

Uki'pato$^n$—Rolling himself (O., I$^n$gthe'zhide).

U'shkadazhi—Undaunted (O., Mo$^n$'thi$^n$-kagaxe).

Uthi'xide—Looking about (O., I$^n$ke'-çabe).

Uzhna'gaxe—To make clear (refers to buffalo wallows) (O., Teçi$^n$'de).

Waça'apa—Meaning uncertain (O.: Waça'be, Tha'tada).

Waça'bezhi$^n$ga—Little black bear (O.: Waça'be, Tha'tada).

*Female*

Mi'mite—Meaning uncertain (O., I$^n$ke'-çabe).

We'to$^n$na—Meaning uncertain (O., I$^n$ke'-çabe).

## THE OSAGE, OR WAZHA'ZHE, TRIBE [a]

### Recent History; Organization

The Osage tribe is composed of five kinship groups, each of which is made up of a number of subgroups. Of these latter many have a group attached that acts as *sho'ka*—servant or attendant at a given ceremony. Of the five kinship groups two always camp on the northern side of the eastern opening of the tribal circle. The other three remain on the opposite side of the circle, but change their relative positions. The tribe, therefore, has two grand divisions, that on the northern side being composed of two kinship groups and that on the southern side of three kinship groups.

[a] The Osage now live in the northern part of Oklahoma, on the Arkansas river. This locality was not their home when they were first met by the white race. They were then dwelling on the western side of the Mississippi, both north and south of the Missouri, including the Ozark Mountain region, the name Ozark being a corruption of the native term Wazha'zhe. The territory occupied by the Osage, lying, as it did, adjacent to the Mississippi river, was very soon needed by the white people who were pressing westward. The Osage made a number of cessions to the United States, the earliest in 1808, when they parted with territory on the Mississippi. In 1818 they gave up their claim to land on the Arkansas and Verdigris rivers. In 1825 they ceded all their lands in Missouri and Arkansas. Further cessions were made in 1839 and 1865. Finally, in 1871 and 1872 lands were purchased from the Cherokee in the then Indian Territory, and on these lands the Osage are living to-day. The payments for lands ceded by them in Missouri and Kansas were placed in the United States Treasury at interest, yielding the Osage a considerable sum per capita and relieving the people from urgent necessity to labor in order to obtain food and clothing—a condition not altogether favorable to the best development of a naturally strong and promising tribe. (Pictures of Osage chiefs are shown in pls. 12, 13, 15.)

Owing to the shifting of the positions of the three groups forming the southern side, there were three arrangements of the tribal circle (see figs. 9–11), which was called *tsi'-uthuga*. This is the same as the Omaha *hu'thuga*, with the dialectic difference in pronunciation. Moreover, the Osage circle was symbolically oriented, as was the case with the Omaha, the actual opening being in the direction the tribe was moving. The marked similarity in the form of camping and in the fundamental ideas representing the tribal organization seems to show that the two tribes are organized on the same plan. (See p. 138.)

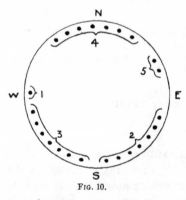

Fig. 9.

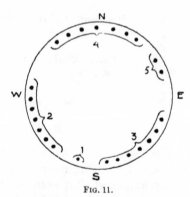

FIG. 10.                    FIG. 11.

FIG. 9. Diagram of Osage *hu'thuga*—usual order. 1. HO<sup>N</sup>'GA UTANATSI (pp. 58–59). 2. WAZHA'ZHE (p. 59). Subgroups: (*a*) Wazha'zheçka; (*b*) Ke'k'i<sup>n</sup>; (*c*) Mike'estetse; (*d*) Wa'tsetsi; (*e*) Uzu'gaxe; (*f*) Tathi'hi; (*g*) Hu zhoigara. 3. HO<sup>N</sup>'GA (p. 60). Subgroups: (*a*) Waça'beto<sup>n</sup>; (*b*) I<sup>n</sup>gro<sup>n</sup>'ga zhoigara; (*c*) Opxo<sup>n</sup>; (*d*) Mo<sup>n</sup>'i<sup>n</sup>kagaxa; (*e*) Po<sup>n</sup>'ca washtage; (*f*) Xi'tha; (*g*) I'batsetatse. 4. TSI'ZHU (p. 60). Subgroups: (*a*) Tsi'zhu wano<sup>n</sup>; (*b*) Si<sup>n</sup>'tsagre; (*c*) Pe'to<sup>n</sup>to<sup>n</sup>ga zhoigara; (*d*) Tseto'ga i<sup>n</sup>tse; (*e*) Mi'k'i<sup>n</sup> wano<sup>n</sup>; (*f*) Ho<sup>n</sup> zhoigara; (*g*) Tsi'zhu uthuhage. 5. NI'KA WAKO<sup>N</sup>DAGI or GRON'I<sup>N</sup> (p. 60–61). Subgroups: (*a*) Xo<sup>n</sup>'tsewatse; (*b*) Nu'xe.

FIG. 10. Diagram of Osage *hu'thuga*—hunting order. 2. WAZHA'ZHE. 3. HO<sup>N</sup>'GA. 1. HO<sup>N</sup>'GA UTANATSI. 4. TSI'ZHU. 5. NI'KA WAKO<sup>N</sup>DAGI or GRON'I<sup>N</sup>. The dots represent the same order of subgroups as given in figure 9.

FIG. 11. Diagram of Osage *hu'thuga*—sacred order. 3. HO<sup>N</sup>'GA. 1. HO<sup>N</sup>'GA UTANATSI. 2. WAZHA'ZHE. 4. TSI'ZHU. 5. NI'KA WAKO<sup>N</sup>DAGI or GRON'I<sup>N</sup>  The dots represent the order of the subgroups, which is the same as in figure 9.

KINSHIP GROUPS [a]

1. Ho<sup>n</sup>'ga utanatsi ⎫
2. Wazha'zhe            ⎬ Comprising southern half of *hu'thuga*.
3. Ho<sup>n</sup>'ga              ⎭

5. Ni'ka wako<sup>n</sup>dagi or Groni<sup>n</sup> ⎫
4. Tsi'zhu                         ⎬ Comprising northern half.
                                  ⎭

---

[a] The information here given relative to the names, duties, and positions of the kinship groups was furnished by the following men, members of the tribe: Sho<sup>n</sup>'to<sup>n</sup>çabe, Wazha'zhewadai<sup>n</sup>ga, Washi<sup>n</sup>'ha (pl. 14), and Big Heart.

WASHIᴺHA  (OSAGE)

### 1. HOⁿGA UTANATSI (THE SEPARATE HOⁿGA) GROUP

The meaning and significance of this name have been already explained. (See p. 40.) The Hoⁿ'ga utanatsi are spoken of as "Instructor of rites."

*Subdivision:* Moⁿ'hiⁿçi ("stone knife").[a] This group was *sho'ka*, or servant, to the Hoⁿ'ga utanatsi. This office was an honorable one, being that of intermediary between the officials in charge of a ceremony and the people who took part in it.

### 2. WAZHA'ZHE GROUP

This is an old and untranslatable term. The group was divided into seven subgroups, each with its distinctive name and attendant *sho'ka* group, but all having a right to the general name Wazha'zhe.

#### Subgroups

(*a*) Wazha'zhe çka ("the white" or "pure Wazha'zhe"); *çka* is the Osage equivalent of the Omaha *xti*, meaning "original," "unmixed." This group is the keeper of the seven pipes for making peace within the tribe. Iⁿgroⁿ'ga ni moⁿtse ("puma in the water") is the name of the Sho'ka subdivision.

(*b*) Ke'k'iⁿ ("great turtle").

Pak'a zhoigara (*pak'a*, mystery; *zhoigara*, those who are with, i. e., the group whose rites pertain to), Sho'ka subdivision.

(*c*) Mike'estetse, the cat-tail (*Typha latifolia*).

Ka'xewahuça, the loud-voiced crow,[b] Sho'ka subdivision.

(*d*) Wa'tsetsi. It is said that a comet fell from the morning star and came to join the council of this subgroup. Xutha'paçoⁿ zhoigara (*xutha'paçoⁿ*, the bald eagle), Sho'ka subdivision.

(*e*) Uzu'gaxe[b] (*uzu'*, straight; *gaxe*, to make—they who make the path straight). It was the duty of this subgroup to make clear the way of a war party; to find a safe way around any obstruction. The scouts of the war parties were taken from this group.

Moⁿso'tsemoⁿiⁿ (*moⁿ*, land; *so'tse*, smoke; *moⁿiⁿ*, to walk—they who walk in smoke, fog, or dust), the Sho'ka subdivision, was called on to cause a fog, or a wind to raise the dust in order to conceal the movements of a war party.

(*f*) Tathi'hi, white-tail deer.

Watsi'tsazhiⁿga zhoigara (*watsi'tsazhiⁿga*, small animals), subdivision.

---

a Articles of utility in the past, although they may have passed out of daily use among the people, are frequently conserved in sacred rites. For example, the stone knife was the only kind of knife that could be used ceremonially and its name appears as a personal name among the Omaha families that had hereditary duties connected with rites that belonged to the Iⁿshta'çuⁿda and We'zhiⁿshte gentes.

b The name of this subdivision appears as a personal name in the Omaha tribe.

(g) Hu zhoigara (*hu*, fish). Eno$^n$'mi$^n$tse to$^n$ (*eno$^n$*, they alone; *mi$^n$tse*, bow; *to$^n$*, to have or possess—they alone possess the bow), Sho'ka subdivision. These were known as the bow makers.

### 3. HO$^N$'GA (LEADER) GROUP

This kinship group was divided into seven subgroups, as follows:

(a) Waça'be to$^n$ (*waça'be*, bear; *to$^n$*, to possess).

Waça'be çka ("white" or "original bear"), Sho'ka subdivision.

(b) I$^n$gro$^n$'ga zhoigara (*i$^n$gro$^n$'ga*, puma).

Hi$^n$wa'xaga zhoigara (*hi$^n$wa'xaga*, porcupine), Sho'ka subdivision.

(c) O'pxo$^n$, elk. Tahe'shabe zhoigara (*tahe'shabe*, male elk with dark horns), Sho'ka subdivision.

(d) Mo$^n$'i$^n$kagaxe (*mo$^n$i$^n$ka*, earth; *gaxe*, to make—earth-makers).

(e) Po$^n$'ca washtage (*washtage*, peace). This subgroup had the office of peacemakers.

(f) Xitha ("white eagle").

(g) Ho$^n$'gashi$^n$ga ("little Ho$^n$'ga"). I'batsetatse (*ibatse*, coming together; *tatse*, the wind—associated by rites pertaining to the wind), Sho'ka subdivision. The office of herald was in this group.

### 4. TSI'ZHU (HOUSEHOLD) GROUP

This kinship group also had seven subgroups:

(a) Tsi'zhu wano$^n$ (*wano$^n$*, the oldest; age implies wisdom), or Wako$^n$'da no$^n$pabi (*wako$^n$'da*, gods; *no$^n$pabi*, afraid of).

Waba'xi, Sho'ka subdivision.

(b) Si$^n$'tsagre ("wearing the wolf's tail on the scalp lock").

Sho$^n$'ke zhoigara (*sho$^n$'ke*, wolf), Sho'ka subdivision.

(c) Pe'to$^n$ to$^n$ga zhoigara (*pe'to$^n$*, crane; *to$^n$ga*, big).

(d) Tseto'ga i$^n$tse (*tseto'ga*, buffalo bull; *i$^n$tse*, face). It is said that Waba'xi went in search of game. He found a buffalo, pointed his finger at its face, and killed it; Wako$^n$'da reproved him for the act. Because of this deed his people were called Buffalo-face people.

Tsea'ko$^n$, Sho'ka subdivision.

(e) Mi'k'i$^n$ wano$^n$ (*mi*, sun; *k'i$^n$*, to carry; *wano$^n$*, the oldest). Tsi'zhu washtage (*washtage*, peaceful), division. This division made peace. Red-eagle people.

(f) Ho$^n$ zhoigara (*ho$^n$*, night).

Ta'pa zhoigara (*ta'pa*, the name of the Pleiades), Sho'ka subdivision.

(g) Tsi'zhu uthuhage (*uthuhage*, the last). The last household refers to the end of the line of the group.

### 5. NI'KA WAKO$^N$DAGI OR GRONI$^N$ GROUP

This kinship group had three subgroups. (Derivation of name: *Ni'ka*, people; *wako$^n$dagi* refers to the thunder—the Thunder people).

(a) Xo$^n$'tsewatse (*xo$^n$tse*, cedar; *watse*, to touch, as the striking of an enemy). The name refers to the cedar tree upon which the thunder rested as it descended.

This subgroup acts as sho'ka in the rites of the Thunder people.

(b) Nu'xe, ice. This is the name of a people from the upper world. When one came down he was asked, "What are you?" He answered, "I am Nu'xe," ice or hail.

Sub-Shoka group, Tseto'ga zhoigara (*tseto'ga*, buffalo bull).

The two divisions of the Osage tribe were called the Tsi'zhu and the Hon'ga. The Tsi'zhu was composed of two kinship groups and occupied the northern side of the tribal circle viewed as having the opening at the east. The position of the Osage Thunder group was similar to that occupied by the Omaha Inshta'çunda, whose name and rites referred to thunder, and the Tsi'zhu division seems in a measure to correspond to the ideas symbolized by the northern half of the Omaha tribal circle. (See p. 138.)

The Hon'ga division was composed of three kinship groups. Those given in the diagram on page 58 show that their positions with relation to one another changed during tribal rites and ceremonies, but remained stable in comparison with the Tsi'zhu division. The similarity between the position and the duties devolving on this southern half of the oriented Osage tribal circle and those of the corresponding division of the Omaha suggests a strong probability that both organizations had a common pattern or origin.

While the Ponca tribe does not present the picture of a closely organized body, the similarity in the position of the Nu'xe gens of the Ponca as compared with that of the Nu'xe group of the Osage seems to indicate the perpetuation of some idea or belief common to the two tribes.

### ADOPTION CEREMONY

The ceremony of adoption into the Osage tribe throws light on the functions and symbolism of the Osage groups. It was described by old chiefs as follows:

When a war party took a captive, anyone who had lost a child or who was without children could adopt the captive to fill the vacant place. After the ceremony the person became an Osage in all respects as one born in the tribe and was subject to the duties and requirements of the family into which he entered by a kind of new birth.

When a captive was held for the purpose of adoption, the captor sent an invitation to the leading men of the Tsi'zhu washtage, who were peacemakers, and also to the chiefs of the Ingron'ga, who had charge of war rites. Food was prepared and set before these leaders, when the host, in a solemn speech, set forth his desire to adopt the captive. Thereupon these leaders sent for the leading men who were versed in the rituals of the groups which were to take part in the ceremony. These were the Nu'xe, ice; the O'pxon, elk; the I'batse, wind; the Wa'tsetsi, water; and the Hon'ga, who were the leaders of the tribal hunt. When all were assembled the captive was brought and placed in the back part of the lodge opposite the entrance, the seat of the stranger. Then the ritual used at the initiation and naming of a child born in the tribe was given. This ritual recounts the creation and history of the tribe and the four stages of man's life. At the close the captive was led to the chief of the Tsi'zhu washtage, who passed him on to the Iⁿgroⁿʹga, whose place was on the south side of the tribal circle. By this act the captive symbolically traversed the tribal circle, passing from those on the north, who made peace, to those on the south, who had charge of war—the act indicating that he was to share in all that concerned the tribe.

Then the chief of the Iⁿgroⁿʹga took a sharp-pointed flint knife and made a quick stroke on the end of the captive's nose, causing the blood to flow. The chief of the Tsiʹzhu washtage wiped away the blood. Then the chief of the Waʹtsetsi brought water, and the chief of the Hoⁿʹga food (corn or meat), and these were administered to the captive by the chief of the Tsiʹzhu washtage, who then took the sacred pipe, filled it, and placed on it fronds of cedar brought by the Iʹbatse. The pipe was lit and ceremonially smoked by the captive. Then the chief of the Nuʹxe brought buffalo fat and anointed the body of the captive, after which the chief of the Oʹpxoⁿ painted two black stripes across the face from the left eyebrow to the lower part of the right cheek. This done, the chief of the Tsiʹzhu washtage announced the name, Niʹwathe ("made to live"), and the captive became the child of the man who adopted him.

The letting of blood symbolized that the captive lost the blood and kinship of the tribe into which he had been born. All trace of his former birth was removed by the washing away of the blood by the Waʹtsetsi. He was then given food by those who led the tribe in the hunt when the food supply was obtained. The new blood made by the Osage food was thus made Osage blood.

This symbolic act was confirmed and sanctified by the smoking of the pipe, the aromatic cedar being provided by the Iʹbatse. Finally, the anointing of the body by the Nuʹxe (who, together with the Buffalo people, controlled the planting of the corn) brought the captive entirely within the rites and avocations of the tribe. The black stripes put on by the Oʹpxoⁿ were in recognition of the Thunder as the god of war and the captive's future duties as a warrior of the tribe. The giving of the name Niʹwathe explained and closed the ceremony.

It was further explained that the drama "means to represent the death of the captive not only to the people of his birth but to his past life, and his rebirth into the family of the Osage who saved him and "made" him " to live" by adopting him."

At the close of the ceremony all the chiefs who had taken part in the rites partook of the feast which the man who adopted the captive had provided for the occasion. Not long after, the name Niʹwathe was dropped and the adopted child without further ceremony was given a name belonging to the father's group.

### LEGENDARY ACCOUNTS

#### THE PRESENT TRIBAL ORGANIZATION

##### (Given by Black Dog, pl. 15.)

The Wazhaʹzhe kinship group had seven pipes. These were used to make peace within the tribe. If a quarrel occurred, one of these pipes was sent by the hand of the shoʹka, and the difficulty was settled peaceably.

When the Wazhaʹzhe met the Hoⁿʹga, they were united by means of one of these peace pipes. After they were united they met the Hoⁿʹga utanatsi, who had a pipe of their own; but peace was made, and the Hoⁿʹga utanatsi united with the Wazhaʹzhe and the Hoⁿʹga. Later these three met and united with the Tsiʹzhu.

According to Big Heart and others, each of the five groups had its own traditions, and one did not interfere with another.

BLACK DOG AND OTHER OSAGE CHIEFS

Black Dog (Shǫⁿ'toⁿqȧbe) appears on the extreme left

## WAZHA′ZHE GROUP

Way beyond (an expression similar to "once upon a time") a part of the Wazha′zhe lived in the sky. They desired to know their origin, the source from which they came into existence. They went to the sun. He told them that they were his children. Then they wandered still farther and came to the moon. She told them that she gave birth to them, and that the sun was their father. She told them that they must leave their present abode and go down to the earth and dwell there. They came to the earth, but found it covered with water. They could not return to the place they had left, so they wept, but no answer came to them from anywhere. They floated about in the air, seeking in every direction for help from some god; but they found none. The animals were with them, and of all these the elk was the finest and most stately, and inspired all the creatures with confidence; so they appealed to the elk for help. He dropped into the water and began to sink. Then he called to the winds and the winds came from all quarters and blew until the waters went upward as in a mist. Before that time the winds traveled only in two directions, from north to south and then back from south to north; but when the elk called they came from the east, the north, the west, and the south, and met at a central point,[a] and carried the water upward.

At first rocks only were exposed, and the people traveled on the rocky places that produced no plants, and there was nothing to eat. Then the waters began to go down until the soft earth was exposed. When this happened the elk in his joy rolled over and over on the soft earth, and all his loose hairs clung to the soil. The hairs grew, and from them sprang beans, corn, potatoes, and wild turnips, and then all the grasses and trees.

The people went over the land, and in their wanderings came across human footprints, and followed them. They came upon people who called themselves Wazha′-zhe. The Ho[n]′ga and the Elk[b] affiliated with them, and together they traveled in search of food. In these wanderings they came across the Ho[n]′ga utanatsi. The Wazha′zhe had a pipe. This they filled and presented to the Ho[n]′ga, who accepted it, and thus the Ho[n]′ga utanatsi were incorporated with the three affiliated bands. Then they came upon the Tsi′zhu, and they were taken in, with their seven bands.

## HO[N]′GA GROUP

The Ho[n]′ga came down from above, and found the earth covered with water. They flew in every direction seeking for gods to call upon who would render them help and drive away the water; but they found none. Then the elk came and with his loud voice shouted to the four quarters. The four winds came in response to his call, and they blew upon the water and it ascended, leaving rocks visible. The rocks gave but a limited space for the people to stand on. The muskrat was sent down into the water and was drowned. Then the loon was sent, but he also was drowned. Next the beaver was sent down, and was drowned. Then the crawfish dived into the waters, and when he came up there was some mud adhering to his claws, but he was so exhausted that he died. From this mud the land was formed.

## WA′TSETSI GROUP

The stars are believed to be the children of the sun and moon. The people of the Wa′tsetsi[c] are said to have been stars that came down to the earth like meteors and became people.

---

[a] Note the name I′batsetatse ("winds coming together") of the Sho′ka subdivision of (g) of the Ho[n]′ga group (p. 60).

[b] The O′pxo[n], or Elk, is (c) of the Ho[n]′ga group. Note the use of the term Ho[n]′ga in this legend as the name of a people, in connection with what has already been pointed out on pp. 40–41.

[c] The Wa′tsetsi subgroup (d) of the Wazha′zhe group, p. 59.

### THE WATER PEOPLE

There are people who came from under the water. They lived in the water weeds that hang down, are green in color, and have leaves on the stem. The people who lived in water dwelt in shells which protected them from the water, keeping the water out and serving as houses.

There were creatures who lived under the earth, as the cougar, the bear, the buffalo, and the elk. These creatures came up out of the ground. The land creatures and those that lived in shells came to the earth, and the star people came down; all three came together, intermarried, and from these unions sprang the people of to-day.

The men of the Hon'ga division cut the hair so that there should be five bunches in rows running from front to back.

The men of the Tsi'zhu division wore the hair in three bunches—one just above the forehead, one at the top of the head, and one at the nape of the neck.

### Personal Names

The following Osage names were obtained in 1896:

#### TSI'ZHU WASHTAGE (PEACEMAKERS' HOUSEHOLD)

*Male*

A'huzhine—Little wings.
Blo'gahike—All the chiefs.
Bpabaxon—Cut head. Refers to war. Cutting off the head.
Dhon'tsewahi—Bone heart (O., Tapa').
Dton'wongaxe—Village maker (O., Mon'thinkagaxe).
Dton'wonihi—Refers to war. The warriors cause the villagers to stampede.
Gahi'geste—Tall chief (O., Inke'çabe).
Gahi'gkewadainga—Chief's power to control the people (O., Mon'thinkagaxe).
Gka'washinka—Little horse.
Gkon'sanonbawahri—Kills two Kansa. War name.
Gkon'sawatainga—*Gkon'sa*, Kansa; *watainga*, eccentric (old word).
Gredon'shinka—Little hawk (O., Tha'tada).
Grezhe'ruse—War name. Captures spotted horses.
Haxu'mizhe—Woman's name. Ropes.
Howa'saope—War name. Goes on the warpath after mourning.
Hua'shutse—Red eagle.
Inshta' monze—*Inshta'*, eye; *monze*, protruding like breasts (O., We'zhinshte).
Mon'hogrin monkasabpe—Sitting by the bank. Refers to a village site.
Mon'kasabe—Black breast. Refers to the elk.
Mon'zenonopin—Iron necklace.
Mon'zhakita—(*Monzha*, land; *kita*, watches—watches over the land). Refers to the wind (O., Kon'çe).
Mon'zhakuta—(*Kuta*, shoots; guards or shoots over the land). Refers to the wind (O., Kansa).
Ni'wathe—Made to live. (See Adoption ceremony, p. 61.)
Nonbe'ze—Yellow claws. Refers to the eagle.
Opxonshibpe—Elk entrails.
Ota'non—Space between two objects. Refers to warriors passing between the tents.
Othu'hawae—Envious.
Pahu'çka—White hair. Refers to white buffalo (O., Hon'ga and Tapa').
Pasu'—Hail.
Ponhon'gregahre—War name. One who strikes the enemy first.
Sa'pekie—Paints himself black.

To$^n$wo$^n$gaxe—Village-maker (O., Mo$^n'$thi$^n$kagaxe).

Tsesi$^n'$eno$^n$pe—Buffalo-tail necklace.

Tsi$'$zhuho$^n$ka (2)—Ho$^n'$ga household. Leader name.

Tsi$'$zhuni$^n$kashi$^n$ka—Little Ho$^n'$ga household.

Tsi$'$zhushi$^n$ka—Little household.

Tsi$'$zhutsage—Old man of the Tsi$'$zhu gens.

Tso$'$he—Puckery taste. Nickname.

Uki$'$sa—Deserted (as an empty village or house) (O., I$^n$shta$'$çu$^n$da).

Wako$^n'$daokie—Talks to Wako$^n'$da (an old Omaha name—Mo$^n'$thi$^n$kagaxe).

Wathigro$^n$ringe (2)—No mind (O., Mo$^n'$thi$^n$kagaxe).

Watsa$'$no$^n$zhi$^n$—War name. One who grasps the enemy.

Wazhi$^n'$bpizhi—A$'$nger.

Wazhi$^n'$gasabpe—Blackbird (O., Mo$^n'$thi$^n$kagaxe).

Wazhi$^n'$hotse—Gray bird. Refers to hawk (O., Tapa$'$).

Wazhi$^n'$sabpe—Cautious mind.

### Female

Mi$'$tai$^n$ga—Coming, or new moon (O.).

Mi$'$tai$^n$gashi$^n$ka—Little new moon.

### SI$^N$TSAGRE

### Male

Ba$'$zo$^n$tsie—War name. Going into the midst; attacking a village.

Bpa$'$htato$^n$i$^n$—Big head. Refers to buffalo head.

Bpa$'$ri$^n$wawexta—War name. Attacking the Pawnee.

Do$^n$he$'$mo$^n$i$^n$—Good walker.

Gahi$'$gashi—Not a chief.

Gka$'$wasabpeagthi$^n$—One who rides a black horse.

Gko$^n'$segaxri—War name. One who kills a Kansa.

Gko$^n'$sekibpa—War name. Meeting the Kansa.

Gredo$^n'$mo$^n$i$^n$—Walking hawk (O., I$^n$ke$'$çabe).

Ho$'$moni$^n$—Howler.

$'$Ione$'$go$^n$—War name. Refers to the success of the warrior. Success comes as though seeking the man.

Hutha$'$watoni$^n$te—War name. The light of the eagle soaring on high.

I$^n'$dokawadai$^n$ga—War name. Refers to taking trophies.

Mo$^n'$zeuno$^n$zhi$^n$—Iron shirt (Ponca).

Ni$'$gka$'$sabegaxri—War name. One who kills a black man.

Ni$'$kano$^n$tsewa—War name. One who kills the enemy.

Ni$'$koibro$^n$—Smelling a human being (O., Tha$'$tada).

Otha$'$hamo$^n$i$^n$—War name. Follower; one who follows the leader.

Sho$^n$gkeihi—War name. Refers to the barking of dogs when the warriors approach.

Tha$'$bthi$^n$waxri—Kills three.

Tsewa$'$hu—Buffalo bone.

Wa$'$bisu$^n$tse—War name. A warrior presses an enemy to the ground.

Wa$'$dashtae—War name. Refers to setting fire to the grass to scare out the enemy.

Wadoh$'$kie—War name. Refers to taking the scalp.

Waho$^n'$gashi—Mischievous. Nickname.

Wa$'$i$^n$no$^n$zhi$^n$—War name. Holding the captive.

Waki$'$ashke—Refers to hunting and packing the buffalo meat.

Watse$'$wahe—War name.

Waxri$'$—Stingy. Nickname.

Wazha$'$kibpa—War name. Refers to meeting a Wazha$'$zhe.

We$'$i$^n$gaxe—Refers to hunting. Making a pack strap.

MI'K'I$^N$ WANO$^N$

*Male*

Be'ga'xazhi (pl. 12)—War name. One who can not be outstripped. Refers to running.

Bpahi'thagthi$^n$—Good hair.

Ho'thagthi$^n$—Good voice.

Migk'i$^{n'}$wadai$^n$ga—Eccentric sun carrier.

FIG. 12. Kansa chief.

Mi'hiçe—Yellow hair. Refers to buffalo calf.

Mio'tamo$^{ni n}$—Straight sun or moon.

Shi$^n$niça—Refers to intercepting the game.

We'to$^n$mo$^{n i n}$—War name. Refers to the women singing *weto$^n$* songs.

### THE KANSA TRIBE [a]

The name Kansa is an old term. As the rites pertaining to the winds belong to the Kansa gens in the several cognate tribes, it may be that the word had some reference to the wind.

#### GENTES

The following list of gentes is not complete, nor has it been possible to obtain satisfactory information as to the location of each gens in the tribal circle, owing to the disintegration of the tribe and the breaking up of their ancient customs and ceremonies. The information obtained goes to

[a] Of the Kansa tribe fewer than 300 are now living; these are in northern Oklahoma. Their lands adjoin those of the Osage. They, too, have been pushed from the place where they were dwelling when the white people first came into their vicinity. They were then northwest of the Osage, in the region along the river which bears their name. They began ceding land to the United States in 1825. Further relinquishments were made in 1846, and again in 1859 and 1862. In 1872 their present reservation was purchased from the Osage. While the Kansa have not been so reduced as the Quapaw, they have failed to maintain fully their old tribal organization; though much has lapsed from the memory of the people owing to disuse of former customs and rites, considerable knowledge of the ancient tribal life still might possibly be recovered. (Portraits of Kansa chiefs are shown in pl. 16 and fig. 12.)

KANSA  CHIEF

show that their former organization was similar to that of the other cognates, that the tribe was composed of two great divisions, and that the names of Kansa gentes are to be found in the Osage, Ponca, Omaha, and Quapaw tribes.  The names obtained and verified are:

1. Mo$^n$i$^n$$'$ka ("earth").  This name corresponds to Mo$^n$$'$i$^n$kagaxe of the Osage tribe, and to Mo$^n$$'$thi$^n$kagaxe of the Omaha tribe, both of which mean "earth makers."

2. Wazha$'$zhe.  This name occurs as the name of the Osage tribe and of one of the large kinship groups in that tribe; also as the name of a gens in the Ponca tribe.

3. Ponca.  This name occurs as the name of a gens in the Osage and Ponca tribes.

4. Kansa.  There is a Kansa gens in the Omaha tribe.

5. Wazhi$^n$$'$ga inikashikithe (*wazhi$^n$$'$-ga*, bird; *inikashikithe* corresponds to the Omaha *i$'$nikashiga*, and means that with which they make themselves a people—that is, by observing a common rite they make themselves one people).  (See Wazhi$^n$$'$ga subgens of the Tha$'$tada, p. 160.)  Birds figure in the rites of all the cognates, and are tabu in those gentes practising rites which pertain to certain birds.

6. Te inikashikithe (*te*, buffalo).  Buffalo rites occur in all the five cognates.

7. O$'$pxo$^n$ inikashikithe (*o$'$pxo$^n$*, elk).  Gentes bearing the name of the elk occur in the Osage and Quapaw tribes, and in the Omaha the elk is tabu to the We$'$zhi$^n$shte gens.

8. Ho$^n$ (night).  This name occurs in the Osage tribe as the name of a group.

9. Ho$^n$$'$gashi$^n$ga ("little Ho$^n$$'$ga").  This name occurs in the Osage and Quapaw tribes, and the name Ho$^n$$'$ga in the Omaha and Osage tribes.

Fig. 13.  Quapaw man.

10. Ho$^n$$'$gato$^n$ga ("big Ho$^n$$'$ga").  This name is found also in the Quapaw.

11. Tsedu$'$ga ("buffalo bull").  This occurs also in the Osage tribe.

12. Tsi$'$zhu washtage (*washtage*, docile, peaceable).  Tsi$'$zhu is the name of a large group of the Osage, and Tsi$'$zhu washtage of the peacemakers of that group.

### THE QUAPAW TRIBE[a]

The origin of the word *quapaw* has already been explained (see p. 36).

---

[a] The remnant of the Quapaw tribe (hardly a hundred in number) are living in the northern part of Oklahoma.  (See figs. 13, 14.)  When first met by the white people they were living south of the Osage. The Quapaw came into contact with the French and Spanish traders of the sixteenth century, being in the line of march of these early traders from the South.  With the stimulus given to immigration and settlement after the Louisiana Purchase, their lands were soon wanted.  In 1818 they ceded to the United States their country lying between the Arkansas, Canadian, and Red rivers, receiving a tract for themselves south of the Arkansas and Washita rivers.  This reservation they relinquished in 1824, retiring to a smaller tract in the vicinity of their present home.  Their vicissitudes have been such as to shatter their tribal life, so that it is now difficult to obtain accurate information concerning their ancient organization.  Only fragments can be gathered here and there, to be pieced together by knowledge gained from those cognates who have been more fortunate in preserving their old tribal form and rites.

GENTES

It has been difficult to obtain definite information concerning the gentes of the tribe. The people have become so disintegrated that questions are usually met with a weary shake of the head as the answer comes, "All is gone; gone long ago!" A fragmentary list of gentes has been secured. Some of the following may be subgentes. There were two divisions in the tribe, but how the following groups were divided between these it has been thus far impossible to learn.

1. Hon'gaton ga—Big Hon'ga.
2. Hon'gazhin ga—Little Hon'ga.
3. Wazhin'ga inikashiha (*wazhin ga*, bird; *inikashiha*, meaning with which they make themselves a people, i. e., by the rite of which the bird is the symbol).
4. Te'nikashiha (*te*, buffalo).
5. On'pon inikashiha (*on'pon*, elk).
6. Hu'inikashiha (*hu*, fish).
7. Ke'nikashiha (*ke*, turtle).
8. Nan'pan ta—deer.
9. Wa'sa inikashiha (*wasa*, black bear).
10. Mon chu' inikashiha (*mon chu*, grizzly bear).
11. Miha'ke nikashiha (*miha'ke*, star).
12. Pe'ton inikashiha (*peton*, crane).
13. Mi'inikashiha (*mi*, sun).
14. Wakon'ta inikashiha—Thunder.

FIG. 14. Quapaw woman.

The foregoing brief account of the four tribes that are close cognates of the Omaha has been given for the following reasons:

First, to indicate some of the peculiarities of tribal organization which, while common to all, are remarkably developed among the Omaha, as will be apparent from the following detailed account of that tribe.

Second, to suggest the importance of careful study of such a cognate group as likely to throw light on the manner in which tribes have come to be built up into separate organizations and to bear on the reason why each shows different phases of development.

In the Omaha and the four cognates there appear to be certain stable characteristics which indicate a common ideal of organization, as the two divisions of the tribal circle and the functions pertaining to each; the ceremonies connected with warfare and the awarding of war honors. There seems to be also a common type of religious ceremonial for the recognition of those cosmic forces which were believed to affect directly the life of man, as the rites attending the naming of children and the class of names given, and the customs relating to birth and to death. These resemblances between the tribes will become clearer as the story of the Omaha tribe is told and discussion is had of customs among the cognates which seem to be similar in purpose even when they differ in details, the differences being as suggestive as the similarities.[a]

---

[a] Since the foregoing brief account of the Osage tribe was written an ethnological study of that tribe has been undertaken by Mr. Francis La Flesche for the Bureau of American Ethnology. It is expected that, as a result of this investigation, additional light will be thrown on the relationship between the ribes of the cognate group to which the Osage and the Omaha belong.

## II

## ENVIRONMENT; RESULTANT INFLUENCES

### Omaha Sacred Legend

#### EARLY HABITAT AND CONDITIONS

The Omaha do not claim to have been born in the region they now occupy. On the contrary, their traditions, like those of their cognates, place their early home in the East, "near a great body of water." This account of their ancient environment had become blended with the idea of a physical birth, as was explained by Shu'-denaçi when he repeated the fragmentary Legend, at the time the Sacred Pole was turned over to the writers to be deposited for safe-keeping in the Peabody Museum of Harvard University. This Legend was in the custody of those who had charge of that cere-monial object and was considered sacred.

The Legend says:

In the beginning the people were in water. They opened their eyes but they could see nothing. From that we get the child name in the Hon'ga gens, Nia'di inshtagabtha, "eyes open in the water." As the people came out of the water they beheld the day, so we have the child name Ke'tha gaxe, "to make (or behold) the clear sky." As they came forth from the water they were naked and without shame. But after many days passed they desired covering. They took the fiber of weeds and grass and wove it about their loins for covering.

It is noteworthy, when taken in connection with the traditions and usages already mentioned as associated with the name Hon'ga, (p. 40) that the personal names which refer to the birth of the people are preserved in the Hon'ga gens.

The Legend continues:

The people dwelt near a large body of water, in a wooded country where there was game. The men hunted the deer with clubs; they did not know the use of the bow. The people wandered about the shores of the great water and were poor and cold. And the people thought, What shall we do to help ourselves? They began chipping stones; they found a bluish stone that was easily flaked and chipped and they made knives and arrowheads [sic] out of it. They had now knives and arrows [sic], but they suffered from the cold and the people thought, What shall we do? A man found an elm root that was very dry and dug a hole in it and put a stick in and rubbed it. Then smoke came. He smelled it. Then the people smelled it and came near; others helped him to rub. At last a spark came; they blew this into a flame and so fire came to warm the people and to cook their food. After this the people built grass houses; they cut the grass with the shoulder blade of a deer. Now the people had

70

TIPIS

fire and ate their meat roasted; but they tired of roast meat, and the people thought, How shall we have our meat cooked differently? A man found a bunch of clay that stuck well together; then he brought sand to mix with it; then he molded it as a vessel. Then he gathered grass and made a heap; he put the clay vessel into the midst of the grass, set it on fire, and made the clay vessel hard. Then, after a time, he put water into the vessel and it held water. This was good. So he put water into the vessel and then meat into it and put the vessel over the fire and the people had boiled meat to eat.

Their grass coverings would fuzz and drop off. It was difficult to gather and keep these coverings. The people were dissatisfied and again the people thought, What can we do to have something different to wear? Heretofore they had been throwing away the hides they had taken from the game. So they took their stone knives to scrape down the hides and make them thin; they rubbed the hides with grass and with their hands to make them soft and then used the hides for clothing. Now they had clothing and were comfortable.

The women had to break the dry wood to keep up the fires; the men had some consideration for the women and sought plans for their relief. So they made the stone ax with a groove, and put a handle on the ax and fastened it with rawhide. This was used. But they wanted something better for breaking the wood. So they made wedges of stone. [These were of the same shape as the iron wedges used for splitting logs, explained the old narrator.]

The grass shelter became unsatisfactory and the people thought, How shall we better ourselves? So they substituted bark for grass as a covering for their dwellings.

The comfort derived from their skin clothing seems to have suggested the idea of trying the experiment of covering their dwellings with skins, for the Legend says:

The people determined to put skins on the poles of their dwellings. They tried the deerskins, but they were too small. They tried the elk, but both deer and elk skins became hard and unmanageable under the influence of the sun and rain. So they abandoned the use of the skins and returned to bark as a covering for their houses.

There is no mention made in this Legend, or in any known tradition, as to when or where the people met the buffalo; but there is an indirect reference to the animal in this Legend from which it would seem that the meeting with the buffalo must have taken place after they had left the wooded region where they could obtain elm bark for the covering of their houses, and that the need of a portable shelter started the idea among the people of experimenting again with a skin covering for their tents, for the Legend says:

Until they had the buffalo the people could not have good tents. They took one of the leg bones of the deer, splintered it, and made it sharp for an awl and with sinew sewed the buffalo skin and made comfortable tent covers. (Pl. 17.)

From this Legend and other traditions both the buffalo and the maize seem to have come into the life of the people while they were still in their eastern habitat. The story of finding the maize is told as follows in this Legend:

Then a man in wandering about found some kernels, blue, red, and white. He thought he had secured something of great value, so he concealed them in a mound. One day he thought he would go to see if they were safe. When he came to the mound he found it covered with stalks having ears bearing kernels of these colors. He took an ear of each kind and gave the rest to the people to experiment with. They tried it for food, found it good, and have ever since called it their life. As soon as the people found the corn good, they thought to make mounds like that in which the kernels had been hid. So they took the shoulder blade of the elk and built mounds like the first and buried the corn in them. So the corn grew and the people had abundant food.

In their wanderings the people reached the forests where the birch trees grow and where there were great lakes. Here they made birch-bark canoes and traveled in them about the shores of the lakes. A man in his wanderings discovered two young animals and carried them home. He fed them and they grew large and were docile. He discovered that these animals would carry burdens, so a harness was fixed on them to which poles were fastened and they became the burden bearers. Before this every burden had to be carried on the back. The people bred the dogs and they were a help to the people.

## WESTERN MOVEMENTS

The western movement of the people is not definitely traced in any of their traditions, nor is there any account of the separations of kindred which from time to time must have taken place. By inference, there must have been considerable warfare, as the making of peace with enemies is referred to. The tribe seem to have lingered long in the northern territory now covered by the States of Minnesota, North Dakota, South Dakota, and Iowa, and between the Mississippi and Missouri rivers; their claims to portions of this territory were acknowledged in the last century when they joined in the treaty made at Prairie du Chien in 1830, at which time they relinquished all their rights to this land to the United States. Six years later they made a like relinquishment of their claims east of the Missouri river in the States of Missouri and Iowa. Tradition is silent as to their movements from the Lake region south to the Ohio river, where it is said they parted from the Quapaw, as already told.

A period of considerably more than three hundred years must have elapsed between the time of parting from the Quapaw on the banks of the Mississippi, at the mouth of the Ohio, and the date of the Omaha's first cession to the United States, mentioned above. After the separation from the Quapaw it is not probable that the Omaha were ever again as far south as the Ohio river or as far east as Lake Michigan.

Tradition says that the Omaha after parting from the Quapaw followed the Mika'to$^n$ ke river (the Des Moines) to its headwaters, and wandered northeast. One day about thirty years ago the old men were talking of these early movements of the tribe when Shu'denaçi said, "I think that we could trace the sites of the old Omaha villages of the time the tribe went up the Mi'kato$^n$ ke". The question, How could the sites be identified? elicited the reply: "By the circles of stones which were left when the people abandoned a village." It was the custom to place stones around the bottom of the tent cover to hold it firmly on the ground; when the tent was taken down the stones were left where they had been used.   Some of the old men said that they had seen such traces of deserted village sites east of the Missouri in the region where the tribe is said once to have lived. Dakota tradition tells of their meeting the Omaha near the Blue Earth and Minnesota rivers.   That the Omaha dwelt for a considerable time in the forest region seems to be borne out by both legends and rites, which show the influence of the woods. The Sacred Pole was cut while the people were dwelling in the wooded country, as all the traditions of the cutting seem to indicate. When that occurred the Ponca were still with the Omaha, and their legends are similar to those of the latter touching the finding and cutting of the Pole.   The tree from which it was cut is said to have stood near a lake, and the suggestion has been made that the place was Lake Andes, in Choteau county, South Dakota; but this iden-tification has not been accepted by the best tribal authorities and traditions do not favor placing the act in the vicinity of this lake.

It was prior to the cutting of the Sacred Pole that the Omaha organ-ized themselves into their present order.   The inauguration of the rites connected with the Sacred Pole seems to have been for the purpose of conserving that order; and it was after these rites had been instituted that the Omaha reached the vicinity of the Big Sioux, where on the banks of a small stream that flows in from the north-east they built a village.   It was while they were living here that a disastrous battle took place (tradition does not say with whom), and as a result this village seems to have been abandoned, after the dead had been gathered and buried in a great mound, around which a stone wall was built.   In the middle of the last century this wall was still to be seen.   Tradition says, "In this battle the Sacred Pole came near being captured."

It was while the Omaha were in the vicinity of the upper Mississippi that they came into contact with the Cheyenne.   The Legend says, "We made peace with the Cheyenne.   At that time the Ponca were with us, and the Iowa and Oto joined in the peace."   The old narrator added: "The Osage say they were with us, too; but it is not so told by our people."   This overture of peace may have been made in conse-quence of the Omaha having invaded the Cheyenne territory in the northern movement.   According to Dakota traditions the Cheyenne were in possession of the upper Mississippi country when the Dakota arrived there.   It may be difficult to determine whether or not at this time the Dakota as distinct tribes had come into contact with the Omaha and the Ponca.

While in this region experiences disruptive in character must have visited the people—possibly the defection of the Ponca—which finally resulted in their complete separation.   At any rate, something happened which caused the Omaha to take steps toward a closer organization of the people. The Legend says:

At this place [where peace with the Cheyenne had been made] we formed a government. The people said, "Let us appoint men who shall preserve order." Accordingly they selected men, the wisest, the most thoughtful, generous, and kind, and they consulted together and agreed upon a council of seven who should govern the people.

Then follows the account of the organization of the tribe in its present order and the story of finding and cutting the Sacred Pole. Both of these narratives will be given later on.

After the great battle on the Big Sioux the Omaha seem to have turned slightly southward, but to have remained in the main on the east side of the Missouri, although war parties apparently reached the river and even crossed to the farther side, where they met and fought the Arikara, who were dwelling where the Omaha live to-day. Traditions are definite in stating that "the Arikara were first encountered on the west side of the Missouri."

About the time of these events the Omaha seem to have returned to the Big Sioux and to have built a village where the river makes a loop, at a point where a small stream enters from a canyon which, the Omaha story says, has "two cliffs, like pinnacles, standing at its entrance, through which the wind rushes with such violence as to disturb the water." When they built this village, according to the Legend, the Omaha were living in bark houses (pl. 18). They had met and fought the Arikara, but had not yet adopted the earth lodge. The continued forays of the Omaha made the Arikara seek peace and it was in this village at the mouth of the canyon that peace was made among the Arikara, the Cheyenne, the Omaha, the Ponca, the Iowa, and the Oto, and sought to be confirmed through the ceremony now known among the Omaha as the Wa'wan (see p. 376)—the same ceremony as the Pawnee Hako.[a]

In view of the part this ceremony has played in the life of the Omaha and its cognate tribes, it is fitting to call attention to the extent of territory throughout which it was observed before and during the seventeenth century. The early French travelers found it among the Caddo group in the country now known as Texas, Louisiana, and Arkansas, while Marquette met with it among the tribes living on the Mississippi when he entered that stream from the Wisconsin river. The Omaha Legend shows that it was known to the Arikara on the Missouri river and was probably introduced by them to the Omaha, Ponca, Iowa, Oto, and Cheyenne at the village on the Big Sioux river. The Cheyenne seem to have lost the rite in the course of their western movement, but it has ever since been practised by the other tribes who took part in this peacemaking. A rite which was both recognized and revered throughout so extensive a

---

[a] See Hako, in the *Twenty-second Annual Report of the Bureau of American Ethnology*, pt. II.

BARK HOUSES

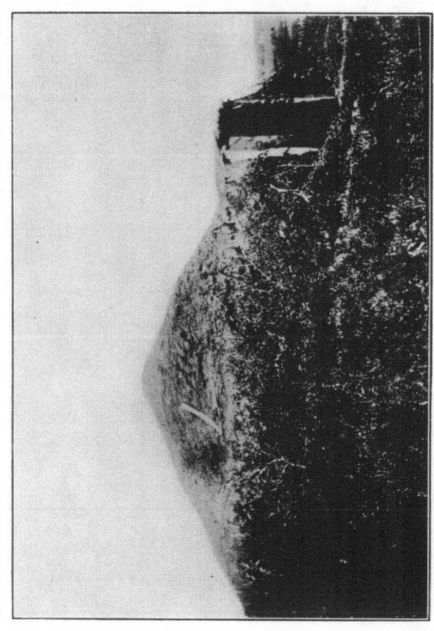

EARTH LODGE

territory, occupied by so many tribes, must have been instrumental in modifying the customs of the peoples practising it, in extending the use of certain symbols, and in bringing about some measure of unity in the forms of religious beliefs.

<h2 style="text-align:center">CONTACT WITH THE ARIKARA</h2>

Traditions are more explicit concerning contact with the Arikara than with any other tribe. Both Omaha and Ponca legends give evidence of the influence exerted on the people by this tribe. When the Missouri river was reached by the Omaha, they found the Arikara there, cultivating the maize and living in villages composed of earth lodges—evidently a peaceful, sedentary folk. Omaha war parties from the east side of the river harassed the Arikara, who were living on the west side. The Arikara sought to obtain peace through the influence of the Wa'wan ceremony, as already related, but Omaha war parties seem finally to have driven them from their homes and to have forced them northward up the Missouri river. The tradition that the Arikara were driven away from the land the Omaha now own is confirmed by a Ponca story that refers to the sale of the Omaha lands to the United States Government in the middle of the last century; at that time an Arikara said to a Ponca: "Had my people known that these lands were valuable, they would have contested the right of the Omaha to make the sale, for the Arikara were the first to occupy the land, a proof of which is to be seen in the remains of our earth lodges and village sites on the bluffs of the Missouri." These earth circles have often been seen by the writers on the Omaha reservation, and the traditions of the Omaha declare them to be the remains of the earth lodges occupied by the Arikara when they dwelt in this region. Both Omaha and Ponca traditions say that the tribes were together when they met and drove the Arikara northward. It was from the Arikara that the Omaha and Ponca learned to make and use earth lodges. According to the Omaha Legend: "It was the women who saved the life of the people. They built the sod houses; they made them by their labor. The work was divided. Men cut the poles and fixed the frame and tied the opening for the smoke hole; the women brought the willows and sod and finished the building."

In this connection it is interesting to note that while the Omaha adopted the earth lodge (pl. 19) they did so from a purely practical point of view, as affording them a better permanent dwelling than tents, and were probably ignorant of the symbolic character of the structure. With the tribe from which it was taken this lodge represented certain religious ideas. Rituals attended the cutting of the trees for its structure and the planting of the four posts that inclosed the space about the central fire. The Omaha did not observe any of these ceremonies nor did they use the prescribed number of posts. They set up about the fireplace six, seven, or eight posts as suited their convenience, for the sole purpose of supporting the roof, these posts possessing no ceremonial importance or other significance. The Omaha built the earth lodge only for village use; the tipi, or tent, was still the habitation when on the buffalo hunt. There is a tradition that the tribe received the maize from the Arikara but it is questionable if this was the first knowledge the Omaha had of the plant. It may be that in their northward migrations the people passed out of the corn belt into environments not favorable to its cultivation, so that its general use was partially discontinued; but nothing definite is known, although there are indications favorable to this conjecture. If there was any hiatus in the cultivation of the maize among the Omaha, as the following story might suggest, there is nothing to indicate that the tribe has not constantly cultivated it since the time the Missouri was reached. This story, preserved among the Omaha but credited to the Arikara, tells how the latter found the maize and how the former received it from them:

The Arikara were the first to find the maize. A young man went out hunting. He came to a high hill, and, looking down upon a valley, he saw a buffalo bull standing in the middle of a bottom land lying between two rivers where they conjoined. As the young man surveyed the country to find a safe way of approaching the buffalo he was impressed with the beauty of the landscape. The banks of the two rivers were low and well timbered. He observed that the buffalo stood facing the north; he saw that he could not approach the animal from any side within bow shot. He thought that the only way to get a chance to shoot the buffalo would be to wait until the animal moved close to the banks of one of the rivers, or to the hills where there were ravines and shrubs. So the young man waited. The sun went down before the buffalo moved; the young man went home disappointed. Nearly all night the hunter lay awake brooding over his disappointment, for food had become scarce and the buffalo would have given a good supply. Before dawn the young man arose and hurried to the scene of the buffalo to see if he could find the animal somewhere near the place, if it had moved. Just as he reached the summit of the hill, where he was the day before, the sun arose, and he saw that the buffalo was still in the same spot. But he noticed that it was now facing the east. Again the young man waited for the animal to move, but again the sun went down and the buffalo remained standing in the same spot. The hunter went home and passed another night of unrest. He started out again before dawn and came to the top of the hill just as the sun arose, and saw the buffalo still standing in the same place, but it had turned around to face the south. The young man waited until dark for the buffalo to move, and had to go again to his home disappointed, where he passed another sleepless night. The hunter's desire to secure the game was not unmixed with some curiosity to know why the buffalo should so persistently remain in that one spot without eating or drinking or lying down to rest. With this curiosity working in his mind, he arose for the fourth time before dawn, and hastened to the hill to see if the buffalo was still standing in the same place. It was again daylight when he came to the hill, and there stood the buffalo exactly in the same place, but it had turned around to face the west. Being now determined to know what the animal would do, the young man settled down to watch as he had done the three days before. He thought that the animal was acting in this manner under the influence of an unseen power for some mysterious purpose, and that he, as well as the buffalo, was controlled by the same influence. Darkness came upon him again with the animal still standing in the same position. The hunter returned to his home and lay awake all night, wondering what would come of this strange experience. He arose before dawn and again hurried to the mysterious scene. As he reached the summit of the hill the light of day spread over the land. The buffalo had gone. But in the spot where it had been standing there stood something like a small bush. The young man approached the place with a feeling of curiosity and disappointment. He came to the object that from the distance appeared like a small bush and saw that it was a strange plant. He looked upon the ground and saw the tracks of the buffalo, and followed them as they had turned from the north to the east and to the south and to the west, and in the center there was but one buffalo track, and out of that had sprung this strange plant. He examined the ground near this plant to find where the buffalo had left the place, but there were no other footprints besides those near the plant. The hunter hurried home and told of his strange experience to the chiefs and the prominent men of his people. The men, led by the hunter, proceeded to the place of the buffalo and examined the ground, and found that what he had told them was true. They saw the tracks of the buffalo where he had turned and stood, but could find no tracks of his coming to the place or leaving it. While all of these men believed that this plant was given to the people in this mysterious manner by Wako${}^{n}$da, they were not sure how it was to be used. The people knew of other plants that were used for food, and the season for their ripening, and, believing that the fruit of this strange plant would ripen at its own proper time, they arranged to guard and protect it carefully, awaiting the time of its ripening.

The plant blossomed, but from their knowledge of other plants they knew that the blossom of the plant was but the flower and not the fruit. When they were watching the blossom to develop into fruit, as they expected it would, a new growth appeared from the joints of the plant. Their attention was now diverted from the blossom to this growth. It grew larger and larger, until there appeared at the top something that looked like hair. This, in the course of time, turned from pale green to a dark brown, and after much discussion the people believed that this growth was the fruit of the plant and that it had ripened. Up to this time no one had dared to approach within touch of the plant. Although the people were anxious to know the use to which the plant could be put or for which it was intended, no one dared to touch it. As the people were assembled around the plant undetermined as to the manner of examining it, a youth stepped forward and spoke:

"Everyone knows how my life from my childhood has been worse than worthless, that my life among you has been more for evil than for good. Since no one would regret, should any evil befall me, let me be the first to touch this plant and taste of its fruit so that you may know of its qualities whether they be good or bad." The people having given their assent, the youth stepped boldly forward and placed his right hand on the blossoms of the plant, and brought his hand with a downward motion to the root of the plant as though blessing it. He then grasped the fruit and, turning to the people, said: "It is solid, it is ripe." He then parted the husks at the top very gently and, again turning to the people, he said: "The fruit is red." He took a few of the grains, showed them to the people, then ate of them, and replaced the husks. The youth suffered no ill effects, and the people became convinced that this plant was given them for food. In the fall, when the prairie grass had turned brown, the stalk and the leaves of this plant turned brown also. The fruit was plucked and put carefully away. In the following spring the kernels were divided among the people, four to each family. The people removed to the spot where the strange apparition had taken place, and there they built their bark huts along the banks of the two rivers. As the hills began to take on a green tinge from the new prairie grass, the people planted the kernels of this strange plant, having first built little mounds like the one out of which the first stalk grew. To the great joy of the people the kernels sprouted and grew into strong and healthy plants. Through the summer they grew, and developed, and the fruit ripened as did that of the first stock. The fruit was gathered and eaten, and was found to be good. In gathering the fruit the people discovered that there were various colors—some ears were white and others were blue and some were yellow.

The next season the people reaped a rich harvest of this new plant. In the fall of the year these people, the Arikara, sent invitations to a number of different tribes to come and spend the winter with them. Six tribes came, and among them were the Omaha. The Arikara were very generous in the distribution of the fruit of this new plant among their guests, and in this manner a knowledge of the plant spread to the Omaha.

The composition of this story presents points of interest. The importance and the mysterious power of the great game, the buffalo, reflect the thought of the hunting tribe; with it is blended the equally mysterious gift of the maize, so sacred to the tiller of the ground, for the buffalo and the maize represented the principal food supply of the people. The scene of the marvelous occurrence is placed in a hilly country where flowed rivers and yet the prairie seems to have been near at hand, for the story tells of the observation of the people that "in the fall, when the prairie turned brown, the stalk and leaves of this plant turned brown also," and that they timed the planting of the kernels the following spring by the upspringing of "the new prairie grass." Then we are told that "when the people removed to the spot, where the strange occurrence had taken place, they built their 'bark huts' along the banks of the two rivers."

The bark hut (see pl. 18) is a type of dwelling belonging to a forest people. The Omaha used to live in such houses, as is told in the ancient Legend here so often quoted, and in other Omaha traditions. The people seem well aware that they once lived in bark houses like those in use among the Winnebago at the present day. The Arikara were not a forest people, and did not use the bark hut. The presence of these details illustrates how a story takes on coloring and becomes modified in passing from a people of one culture to a people of another. That the cultivation of the maize was long known and practised by the Arikara is evident from their rites, traditions, and customs when they were first known historically; but that the Omaha gained their first knowledge of the plant from them is very doubtful.

### SEPARATION OF PONCA FROM OMAHA; FINDING OF HORSES

The Ponca were the last of the cognates to form a tribe by themselves. They were with the Omaha at the peace ceremony with the Arikara and other tribes, but their departure seems to have taken place not far from that time and on or near the Missouri river.

According to Ponca traditions already given, the people followed this stream northward to a place where "they could step over the water," and thence they seem to have turned southward. As they were going "across the land," they hunted buffalo far toward the Rocky mountains, and on one of their hunts they encountered the Padouca (Comanche). The following tradition tells of this meeting and its results:

At that time the Ponca had no animals but dogs to help them to carry burdens. Wherever they went they had to go on foot, but the people were strong and fleet; they could run a great distance and not be weary. While they were off hunting buffalo they first met the Padouca, and afterward had many battles with them. The Padouca were mounted on strange animals. At first the Ponca thought the men and animals were one creature, but they learned better after a while. The Padouca had bows made from elk horn. They were not very long, nor were they strong. To make these bows the horn was boiled until it was soft. While in this condition it was scraped down, then spliced and bound together with sinew and glue. Their arrows were tipped with bone. But the weapon the Padouca depended on in fighting was a stone battle-ax. Its long handle was a sapling bound with rawhide to which a grooved stone ax head, pointed at both ends, was bound by bands of rawhide. This weapon made them terrible fighters at close quarters. The weakness of their bows and arrows reduced the value of their horses in battle save as a means to bring them rapidly up to their enemies, where they could bring their battle-axes into play. If their foes were armed with strong bows and arrows, the Padouca would suffer before they came to close range. To protect their horses from arrows they made a covering for the horses' breasts and sides, to prevent an arrow taking effect at ordinary range. This covering (armor) was made of thick rawhide cut in round pieces and made to overlap like the scales of a fish. Over the surface was sand held on by glue. This covering made the Ponca arrows glance off and do no damage. The Padouca protected their own bodies by long shields of rawhide. Some of them had breastplates made like those on their horses. When the Ponca found out that the terrible creature they first encountered was a man on the back of an animal, they called the animal *kawa*, a name in use by the Osage to-day to designate the horse. The Ponca noticed the smell of the horse, and the odor would apprise them of the approach of the Padouca. When a man perceived the smell, he would run and tell the herald, who would at once go about the camp, and cry: "The wind tells us the kawa are coming!" So the Ponca would make ready to defend themselves. The Ponca had many battles with the Padouca. The Ponca did not know the use of the horses, so they killed them as well as the men. Nor could they find out where were the Padouca villages, for when the two tribes met, the Padouca always moved in an opposite direction from the location of their dwellings. So the Ponca could not discover where the Padouca lived.

One day the two tribes had a great battle. The people fought all day long. Sometimes the Ponca were driven, sometimes the Padouca, until at last a Ponca shot a Padouca in the eye, and he dropped from his horse. Then the battle ceased. After the death of this man one of the Padouca came toward the Ponca and motioned that one of the Ponca should come toward him.. Then the Padouca said in plain Ponca: "Who are you? What do you call yourselves?" The Ponca replied: "We call ourselves Ponca; but you speak our language well; are you of our tribe?" The Padouca said: "No; we are Padouca. I speak your language as a gift from a Ponca spirit. As I lay one day on a Ponca grave after one of our battles with you a man rose from the grave and spoke to me, so I know your language."

Then it was agreed to make peace. Visits were exchanged, the Ponca bartered their bows and arrows for horses, and found out the whereabouts of the Padouca village.

The Padouca taught the Ponca how to ride and to put burdens on the horses. When the Ponca had learned how to use horses they renewed war with the Padouca and attacked them in their village. The Padouca met the Ponca outside their village but, being driven, jumped into the stockade which surrounded the village and fought from behind the barricade. The Ponca made such continual war on the Padouca and stole so many of their horses that the Padouca abandoned their village and departed we know not where. After that the Ponca followed the Platte river east and returned to the Missouri, bringing the horses back with them.

That is how the Ponca first had horses, and we have had them ever since.

There is no definite tradition among the Omaha as to the tribe from which they first obtained horses. The Legend already quoted says:

It happened that a man in his wanderings discovered two animals. At first he thought they were elk, but they did not look like elk. Then he thought they were deer, but they were larger than deer. He did not know what they were, although he saw many. When the man showed himself the animals did not run away, but circled around him. He was troubled, and, fearing them, he tried to get away, but the animals kept about him; he edged off and finally reached the village. The people were curious; they saw that the animals were gentle and could be led. Some of the men tried to mount them, but fell off, for they did not know how to ride. The people found the animals could bear burdens and be led by a string. There were two, male and female; they multiplied; and thus horses came among the Omaha. The people loved the horses, and when they died the people wailed. So dogs were no longer the sole bearers of the people's burdens.

There are traditions which say that "horses came from the Southwest."

Traditions concerning the movements of the Omaha when in the vicinity of the Missouri river are somewhat more definite but they are still vague.

In 1695 Le Sueur places the Omaha near the Missouri river, where the Iowa had joined them.[a] As he was about to establish his trading post on the Blue Earth, Le Sueur sent runners to recall the Iowa that they might build a village near the fort, as these Indians were "industrious and accustomed to cultivate the earth." The trader hoped thus to procure provisions for his post as well as workers for the mines.[b] De l'Isle's map (1703) places the Omaha near the mouth of the Big Sioux. About 1737 a trading post was established near the southern end of Lake Winnipeg, where the Omaha are said to have traded;[c] they have a tradition that "long ago they visited a great lake to the far north and traded there with white men." This post may have been Fort La Reine. It appears on Jeffery's map of 1762.[d] Carver, who traveled in 1766, says that "to this place the Mahahs, who inhabit a country 250 miles southwest, come also to trade with them; and bring great quantities of Indian corn, to ex-

a *Minnesota Historical Collections*, I, 328, 332.
b Neill's The History of Minnesota, etc., 164, Philadelphia, 1858.
c Ibid., 186.
d Ibid., 300.

change for knives, tomahawks, and other articles."[a] The Omaha knowledge of this northern country would seem to have been traditional, and may have been connected with their earlier sojourn in the wooded region of the north.

### MEETING WITH THE WHITE MEN [b]

From the Sacred Legend already quoted, in which epochal events of the tribe are mentioned, it appears that the first meeting with the white race was in the northern region near the lakes, where the Omaha used birch-bark canoes. The Legend says:

One day the people discovered white objects on the waters, and they knew not what to make of them. The white objects floated toward the shores. The people were frightened. They abandoned their canoes, ran to the woods, climbed the trees, and watched. The white objects reached the shore, and men were seen getting out of them. The Indians watched the strange men, but did not speak or go near them. For several days they watched; then the strangers entered into the white objects and floated off. They left, however, a man—a leader, the Indians thought. He was in a starving condition. Seeing this, the Indians approached him, extending toward him a stalk of maize having ears on it, and bade him eat and live. He did eat, and expressed his gratitude by signs. The Indians kept this man, treating him kindly, until his companions returned. Thus the white people became acquainted with the Omaha by means of one whom the latter had befriended. In return the white people gave the Indians implements of iron. It was in this way that we gained iron among us.

From the story of this encounter and the fact that the Omaha are known historically to have traded at a fort near Lake Winnipeg, it is probable that the incident cited in the legend refers to some reconnoitering party of white adventurers, possibly of the Hudson Bay Company, one of whose number remained behind, and was later picked up or joined by the rest of the party.

The Omaha had come into contact with the French prior to 1724. At that time, in order to prevent the eastward spread of Spanish influence, a trading post was established on the Missouri river. The French then counted on the friendship of the Omaha, Osage, Iowa, Oto, and Pawnee, and were instrumental in bringing about peace between these tribes and the Padouca at a council called by M. de Bourgmont, commandant of Fort Orleans, which was held on one of the western tributaries of the Kansas river.

The following tradition may refer to an occurrence not long prior to this council:

"The Omaha were camped in the timber, and one day a man heard pounding in the woods. He went to see what caused the strange noise and returned to the camp in great fright. He said he

---

[a] Carver's Three Years' Travel Through the Interior Parts of North-America, etc., 69, Philadelphia, 1796.
[b] The Appendix to this volume deals with the more recent history of the Omaha in their relations with the whites.

had seen some sort of a beast, his face covered with hair and his skin the color of the inner layer of the corn husk." This inner husk is called *wa'xo^nha*, and the Omaha name for white man, *wa'xe*, is probably a corruption of this term.

The tradition continues as follows: "This was not the first meeting of the Omaha with the white race, but the earlier encounter had been forgotten by the people." This statement probably refers to the meeting described in the Sacred Legend, as already quoted. The "*wa'xe* built houses out of logs, and traded with the people." The old men of the tribe used to declare that these early traders were French.

## INFLUENCE OF TRADERS

Contact with the traders had a disturbing influence on the politics of the tribe. The traders lent aid to those chiefs and leading men who favored schemes for barter, and these Indians used the favors shown them to enhance their own importance in the tribe. The following narrative, compiled from stories told by old men of the tribe, illustrates this state of affairs:

The great-grandfather of a chief who was living twenty-five years ago visited the trading post at St. Louis, and on his return assumed an air of importance, saying that he had been made a great chief by the white men. He began to appoint "soldiers" and ambitious men sought his favor. He made Blackbird a "soldier" and took him to St. Louis. [This was the Blackbird the apocryphal story of whose burial on horseback on the bluffs of the Missouri is told by Lewis and Clark.] Blackbird was a handsome man and the white people made much of him, showing him more attention than they did his companion. When Blackbird returned to the tribe he declared he had been made a chief by the white people. Blackbird was an ambitious man, who loved power and was unscrupulous as to how he obtained it. The traders found him a pliant tool. They fostered his ambitions, supplied him with goods and reaped a harvest in trade. From them he learned the use of poisons, particularly arsenic. If an Indian opposed him or stood in the way of his designs, sickness and death overtook the man and Blackbird would claim that he had lost his life through supernatural agencies as a punishment for attempting to thwart his chief. Because of these occurrences Blackbird was feared. He exercised considerable power and adopted the airs of a despot. Before he died, however, the secret of his poisonings became known and the fact led to the loss of much of his power. The romantic picture of his interment on horseback must be credited to grateful traders, as must also be the bestowal of his name on the hills and creek where later the Omaha built a village when they

BLACKBIRD HILLS, NEBRASKA

moved to their present reservation. It is a fact that horses were frequently strangled at funerals and their bodies left near the burial mound, which was always on a hill or at some elevation, but they were never buried alive or interred with the body. It is one of the humors of Indian history that a relic hunter should have picked up

FIG. 15. Big Elk.

a horse's skull on one of the Blackbird hills and preserved it in a museum in memory of this fanciful entombment.

The "Blackbird hills" (pl. 20) are not known to the Omaha by that name, but as Onʹpontonga xaithon ("where Big Elk is buried"). Big Elk (fig. 15) died in 1853. He was the third of his name, a member of the We'zhinshte gens, and a leading chief of the tribe. According to tradition, all three, named Big Elk, were men of ability, brave and prudent chiefs. The last of the name was a man of considerable foresight and what may be termed an advanced thinker. He took part in some of the early treaties of his tribe and visited Washington before his death. On his return from this visit he called the tribe together and made the following address, which is here given as it was told more than twenty-five years ago:

My chiefs, braves, and young men, I have just returned from a visit to a far-off country toward the rising sun, and have seen many strange things. I bring to you news which it saddens my heart to think of. There is a coming flood which will soon reach us, and I advise you to prepare for it. Soon the animals which Wako$^{n}$'da has given us for sustenance will disappear beneath this flood to return no more, and it will be very hard for you. Look at me; you see I am advanced in age; I am near the grave. I can no longer think for you and lead you as in my younger days. You must think for yourselves what will be best for your welfare. I tell you this that you may be prepared for the coming change. You may not know my meaning. Many of you are old, as I am, and by the time the change comes we may be lying peacefully in our graves; but these young men will remain to suffer. Speak kindly to one another; do what you can to help each other, even in the troubles with the coming tide. Now, my people, this is all I have to say. Bear these words in mind, and when the time comes think of what I have said.

One day, in 1883, during the allotment of the land in severalty to the Omaha tribe, as a large group of the Indians were gathered about the allotting agent watching the surveyor and talking of the location of allotments, there stood on a hill near by an old Indian. In a loud voice he recited this speech of Big Elk. At its close he paused, then shouted: "Friends, the flood has come!" and disappeared.

To the best of his understanding Big Elk tried to face his people toward civilization. At the same time he was politic and kept the tribe well in hand. Instances of his eloquent and courtly speech have been preserved in official proceedings with the Government and these betray a dignity and heartiness that accord with the following incident: The son who Big Elk hoped would succeed him died in the prime of young manhood and the father grieved sadly for his child. The death occurred while the tribe was on the Elkhorn river. The body was wrapped in skins, and, accompanied by near relatives, was carried across the prairies more than a hundred miles, to be laid on the hills near the village of his ancestors. A year afterward, when the tribe was on its annual hunt, Big Elk was riding with the people when his eyes rested on a spirited horse—the best one he owned. Suddenly the memory of his son came to him; he seemed to see the youth, and murmured: "He would have had that horse and all of the best I had—but he needs no gift of mine!" Just then he saw an old man whose fortune had always been hard and who had never owned a horse. Big Elk beckoned him to come near, and said: "Friend, the horse my son would have ridden shall be yours; take him and mount." As the old man raised his arms in thanks the chief turned and rode off alone.

The interference of the traders, and later of Government officials, in tribal affairs, caused two classes of chiefs to be recognized— those whose office was due to white influence and those who were chiefs according to tribal right and custom. The first were designated "paper chiefs," because they usually had some written document setting forth their claim to the office; the second class were known simply as "chiefs." This conflict in authority as to the making of chiefs was a potent factor in the disintegration of the ancient tribal life.

## The Omaha Country

### VILLAGES ON THE MISSOURI

Traditions are somewhat vague as to Omaha villages on the Missouri river. While in this region the people seem to have suffered from wars and also from lack of food. Near the mouth of the White river, South Dakota, the tribe once found a flock of snowbirds, which brought so much relief to the hungry people that the village they erected at that place was known as "Where the snowbirds came." They seem to have stayed in this village for a considerable time, but were finally driven away by wars. There is no mention of any village being built on their southward movements until after they had passed the Niobrara river. On Bow creek, Nebraska, near where the present town of St. James stands, a village of earth lodges was erected, and here the people remained until a tragedy occurred which caused a separation in the tribe and an abandonment of this village by all the people. The site was known and pointed out in the last century as the place where stood the Ton'won̄pezhi, "Bad Village."

The following is the story of how this village came to be abandoned and received the name of "Bad Village." It is a story that used frequently to be told and is probably historical and suggests how separations may have come about in the more remote past.

In the Teçin̄'de gens lived a man and his wife with their three sons and one daughter. Although the man was not a chief, he was respected and honored by the people because of his bravery and hospitality. His daughter was sought in marriage by many men in the tribe. There was one whom she preferred, and to whom she gave her word to be his wife. This fact was not known to her parents, who promised her to a warrior long past his youth. Against her will she was taken to the warrior's dwelling with the usual ceremonies in such marriages. The girl determined in her own mind never to be his wife. She did not cry or struggle when they took her, but acted well her part at the wedding feast, and none knew her purpose. When the feast was over and the sun had set, she slipped away in the dark and was gone. At once a search was started, which was kept up by the disappointed old warrior and his relatives for several days, but without success. The girl's mother grieved over the loss of her daughter, but the father was silent. It was noticed that a certain young man was also missing, and it was thought that the two were probably together. After the girl had been gone some time, a boy rushed to the father's house one morning, as the family were eating their meal, and said: "Your daughter is found! The old man has stripped her of her clothing and is flogging her to death. Hurry, if you would see her alive!" The father turned to his sons and said: "Go, see if there is truth in this." The eldest refused, the second son bowed his head and sat still. The youngest arose, seized his bow, put on his quiver, and went out. The village had gathered to the scene. As the brother approached, he heard his sister's cries of anguish. Pushing his way through the crowd he shouted words of indignation to those who had not tried to rescue the girl, and, drawing his bow, shot the angry old man. The relatives of the dead man and those who sympathized with his exercise of marital rights ran for their bows and fought those who sided with the young rescuer. A battle ensued; fathers fought sons and brothers contended with brothers. All day the two sides contested and many were slain before night put an end to the conflict. The next day those who had fought with the brother left the village with him and traveled eastward, while their opponents picked up their belongings, turned their back on their homes and moved toward the south. There was no wailing nor any outward sign of mourning. Silently the living separated, and the village was left with the unburied dead. * * *

"A new generation had grown up," this strange story continues, "when a war party traveling east beyond the Missouri river encountered a village where the people spoke the Omaha language. Abandoning their warlike intents, the Omaha warriors entered the village peaceably, persuaded their new-found relatives to return with them, and so the Omaha people were once more united." The village where the reunion took place was near one then occupied by the Iowa, not far from the site of the present town of Ponca City.

The attacks of the Dakota tribes forced the Iowa to leave that part of the country and they moved southward as far as the river Platte and never again built a town near the Omaha tribe. The Omaha were driven by the Dakota from their village at the same time as the Iowa and finally settled on a stream that flows in a northerly direction into the Missouri, which they named Ton'wonni, or Village creek, from the village they built on its wooded banks. This village was erected near a rock containing a hole or depression in which the fork-tailed kites used to nest, and the site was known as In'be zhunka monshonde te, "the fork-tailed kites' hole." The village itself, built in the last quarter of the eighteenth century, was called Ton'wontonga, "large village." The stream on which it was situated is now called Omaha creek. It was here that the smallpox and cholera reached the people and nearly destroyed them.

The traditions concerning the effects of the scourge of smallpox vividly portray the terror and desperation of the people. It is said that when the enfeebled survivors saw the disfigured appearance of their children and companions they resolved to put an end to their existence, since both comeliness and vigor were gone. They did not know that new-born children would not inherit their parents' disfiguration, and that in time the tribe would again be as they were of old, strong and well-looking. Being determined to die, they proposed to die fighting their enemies, therefore the tribe—men, women, and children—moved out as a great tribal war party to find their foes and meet a valiant death. The Cheyenne had been harrying the people, so the strange war party started for the Cheyenne country.

The story of this war party runs as follows:

On their way they encountered the Ponca tribe returning from a successful buffalo hunt, well supplied with meat and pelts. The Omaha chiefs sent messengers to the Ponca, explaining that their people were going against the Cheyenne, but they were in need and asked for food. The Ponca drove the Omaha messengers away and shot at them. This angered the Omaha and they prepared to fight the Ponca. In the battle that followed it was observed that one of the fiercest warriors on the Ponca side was an Omaha, who was known to have married a Ponca woman. This warrior was the nephew of a prominent man of the Omaha tribe, and therefore his capture, rather than his death, was sought. At last he was taken and word was sent to his uncle, who was fighting in another part of the field, that his nephew was captured, and he was asked, "What shall be done?" "Hold him until I come," was the reply. When the uncle arrived at the place of capture he saw his nephew standing with an Omaha warrior on each side holding his arms. The uncle raised his spear and plunged it through the body of the man who had fought against his kindred.

The Ponca were driven from their camp and lost possession of their meat and camp equipage. Then the Ponca sought to make peace, and dispatched a man to the Omaha with the tribal pipe. As he approached, the Omaha chief called out, "Who is he?" When he was told, he replied: "The man is a man of blood." So the pipe was refused and the man driven back, but not killed. A second man was sent. He came toward the Omaha with the pipe extended in his left hand and his right hand raised in supplication. Again the chief asked: "Who is he?" When told, he replied: "He is a man of peace." The pipe was received and the fighting ceased. The food of the Ponca was divided between the two tribes, and the Omaha moved on.

The story goes on to recount the desperate fighting with the Cheyenne, the Pawnee, and the Oto. At last those that remained of the Omaha returned to their village on Omaha creek. Here Lewis and Clark met the people at the beginning of the nineteenth century, and it was from the bluffs near this site in 1836 that the tribe saw the little steamboat *Antelope* puff its way up the Missouri. As the boat seemed to move of itself, they called it *mondeʹwaxube*, "mystery boat"—a term that has lost its early significance, and has become the common Omaha name for all steamboats.

Forays of the Dakota grew to be more and more frequent, and later the Ponca joined them in these attacks. The Omaha lost many of their horses, and life became so unsafe that the people abandoned this village and moved southwest in the first quarter of the last century. At this period the Omaha were harassed on the north by the Dakota and Ponca and on the south and west by the Oto and Pawnee. Peace was made from time to time, and as frequently broken; consequently the village on Omaha creek was never again steadily occupied, although the people frequently brougnt their dead from their camps to the southward and westward to be buried where their fathers had dwelt.

The country through which the tribe was accustomed to hunt covered a range of several hundred miles north and south and east and west. Its topography was well known to the Omaha, not only the general direction of the rivers and their numerous branches, but the turns and twists of the streams and the valleys, also the number of days or camps required to go from one point to another; short cuts were known by which time could be saved, an important consideration in a journey for which food and shelter had to be transported. It was not unusual for directions as to a certain route to be supplemented by a rude map of the country to be traversed, traced on the ground with a finger or a stick, on which were indicated the trails, streams, and fords, and perhaps other details, as the locations of trees, springs, or creeks, affording suitable places to make camps, and of stretches where water or wood would have to be carried. These maps were always oriented, so that one could follow the course laid down, by the sun during the day or at night by the north star. All the large rivers known to the Omaha flow in a southerly direction; their tributaries running northward were said to "flow backward."

The accompanying map (pl. 21) shows the country known to the Omaha tribe; the Omaha and Ponca names of the streams which flow through territory once claimed by the Omaha as their hunting grounds are given below. Much of this region was disputed by other tribes, who coveted the "sand hills" to the westward, where game was plentiful. The Omaha villages lay near the Missouri, not farther west than the Elkhorn; but the hunting grounds claimed by the tribe extended on the east from the Missouri to the Raccoon or Des Moines river, and on the west to the country of the Padouca, whose most easterly village, in the forks of the Dismal river, was known to the Omaha. The Pawnee in their northeastern migration encroached on the country watered by the Loup. They moved down the Platte to that river and built their villages there. In the battles which ensued the Pawnee villages were destroyed, but only to be rebuilt. Peace was made between the two tribes, and soon broken. Wars were followed by alliances against other enemies.[a] Meanwhile the Pawnee continued to encroach and finally obtained a foothold, but the ancient hunting right of the Omaha on the land was recognized by the Pawnee, for when the two tribes hunted together north of the Platte, as they frequently did in the first half of the last century, the Omaha led, and Omaha officers controlled all persons taking part

---

[a] The map indicates the places where well-known battles took place during contentions for controi of this territory. Minor battle fields are not marked; only those are indicated in which the number slain on both sides left a deep impression on the memory of the people.

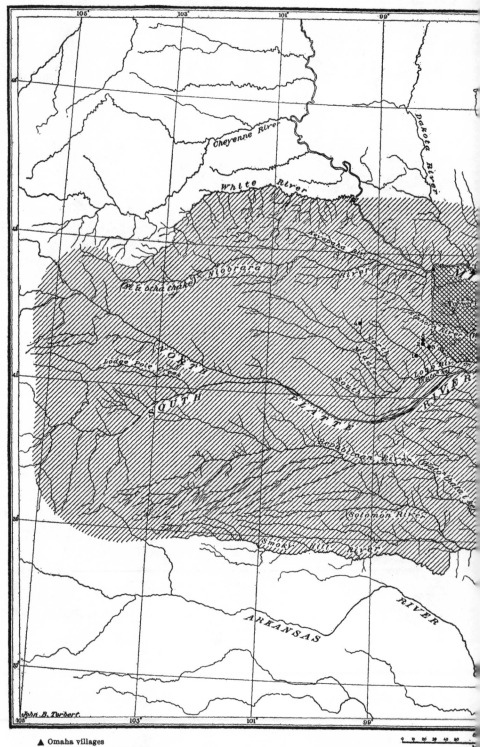

▲ Omaha villages
● Principal Indian battlefields

COUNTRY KNOW

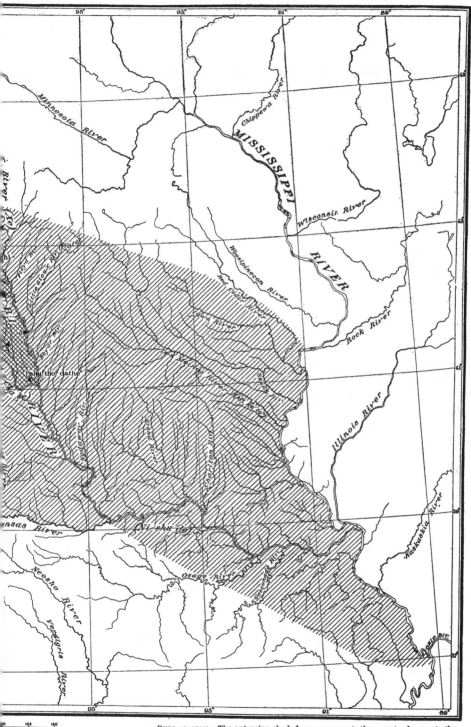

**O THE OMAHA**

EXPLANATION.—The extensive shaded area represents the country known to the Omaha; the included area of darker shading (cross hatched), the country occupied by the Omaha; and the small rectangle bounded on the east by the Missouri River, the Omaha reservation

in the hunt. When, however, the two tribes hunted together south of the Platte, the Pawnee led, and the Omaha hunters accepted the control of the Pawnee directors of the hunt.

The territory lying west of Shell creek and northward to the mouth of the Niobrara continued to be a disputed hunting ground among the Cheyenne, Dakota, Pawnee, Omaha, and Ponca until nearly 1857, when the region was finally ceded to the United States. In the treaty of cession the Pawnee claim was recognized and payments for the land were made to that tribe.

The country east of the Missouri was practically abandoned by the Omaha in the eighteenth century; their villages were then west of that river and the tribal hunts were conducted to the westward, but small parties sought elk and deer east of the Missouri up to the middle of the last century. The Omaha rights to the land east of that river were recognized in the treaties made in 1830, 1836, and 1854, when that territory was ceded to the United States.

### STREAMS KNOWN TO THE OMAHA[a]

*The Elkhorn and its tributaries*

| | | |
|---|---|---|
| Wate′ | Meaning unknown | Elkhorn river. |
| Umo$^n$ho$^n$ waa i te | Where the Omaha planted | Bell creek. |
| Logan hi te | Where Logan came (to trade). | Hyde creek. |
| Ti′ha xa i ke | Where the tent skins were cached (at a time when the Omaha went to fight the Pawnee). | Maple creek. |
| To$^{n}$′wo$^n$zh$^n$iga | The little village | Clark creek. |
| Taçpo$^n$′hi bate ke | Thorn-apple creek | Lower Logan, including Middle creek. |
| Uki′pato$^n$ tenuga t'ethe te | Where Uki′pato$^n$ killed a buffalo bull. | Pebble creek. |
| or | | |
| Pa′tithihu izhi$^n$ge xa i te | Where the son of Pa′tithihu is buried. | |
| Niu′thite te | The ford (buffalo hunting trail crossed here). | Camings creek. |
| Zha′uzhi ke | Weed creek | Plum creek. |
| Mo$^n$ko$^n$′ninida ke | Sweet-flag creek | Rock creek. |
| Mo$^n$thi$^n$′xudetibe te | Prairie-dog creek | Humbug creek. |
| Mo$^n$xu′ de anatushi kitha i te. | Where there was an explosion of gunpowder. | No name on maps; probably dry run. |
| Ni′shkube te | Deep water | Taylor creek. |
| Uhe′çaa i te | Noisy-ford creek (so called because the dangerous condition of the ford caused excitement in crossing). | Union creek, branch of Taylor. |

---

[a] To the Omaha ear euphony demands that in composite terms but one accent be used, that given in the first word.

On'pon monthinka thata i te. Elk lick.................... Dry run, first branch of Taylor.

Mi'xa uçaa i te............ The lake that resounds with the cackling of geese. Lake west of Taylor creek, south of Elkhorn.

E'zhon winax'çhi te ........ One elm tree............... Dry run near town of Stanton, north of Elkhorn.

Umon'eçabe wae te ........ Where Umon'eçabe planted. Dry run near Bursting Powder creek.

Utha'dawon te ............ Old name, Echo creek...... North fork of Elkhorn.

Monhon'hon te............. Miry creek.................. Willow creek, branch of north fork of Elkhorn.

Hubthu'ga waçi i te ..... Where they fished for trout.. Battle creek.

Monkon'ninida ke........... Sweet-flag lake............ Lake near town of Warren, above Battle creek.

Hide'thinge te............. No-outlet creek............ Creek east of town of Oakdale, north of Elkhorn.

Ni'shkube te............. Deep water................. Creek near Oakdale, south of Elkhorn.

Te'thishka i te............ Where the pack of the Sacred Buffalo Hide was untied or opened. Upper Logan creek, branch of Logan.

### The Platte and its tributaries

Ni btha'çka ke .......... Flat river................. Platte river.

Tashnon'ge uzhi ke...... Ash creek................. Shell creek.

Keton'ke.................. Turtle creek............... Silver creek.

Pon'xe ton ke............ Artichoke creek.......... Wood river.

Niçki'the ke............. Salt creek................. Salt creek.

Mon'shewakude uzhon ke. Where Mon'shewakude lies (was buried). Wahoo creek.

Mon'çeguhe uzhon ke..... Where Mon'çeguhe lies (was buried). Rock creek.

Pa'thin tiuthixthige thon.. The Old Pawnee village (Pitahawirat). This was the village attacked by Wa'baçka. (See story, p. 406.)

### The Loup and its tributaries

Nuton' ke................ Plenty potato river......... Loup river.

Uki'thaçonde ke........... Hugging closely (to the Loup). Looking-glass creek.

Zha'beton ke............. Plenty beaver creek........ Beaver creek.

Monga'shude te........... Dust creek................. Council creek.

Nibtha'çkazhinga ke...... Little Nibtha'çka........... Cedar creek.

Monga'nade ke............ Miry creek................. Timber creek.

Pa'thinton'wonzhinga ...... Little Pawnee village....... Horse creek.

Pa'thinmonhonton'won ...... Skidi village............... Cottonwood creek.

Ni'shkube te............. Deep water................. Spring creek.

Ma'çi uthuthaha te........ Cedar river................ North Loup.

Niçni'te ................... Cold water................. Calamus river.

Pehin'xewathe wathigthon te. Where Pehin'xewathe prophesied. Oak creek.

| | | |
|---|---|---|
| Zha'betihe te.............. | The beaver village......... | No name on maps. |
| Shko$^n$'shko$^n$tithe uzho$^n$ke.. | In which Shko$^n$'shko$^n$tithe lies (is buried). | Middle Loup. |
| No$^n$'ebubatigtha i te....... | Where a hand was hung up.. | Mud creek. |
| Te ni u'baaçai ke........... | Where a herd of buffalo were driven into the water. | Clear creek. |
| Pa'do$^n$ka no$^n$ça gaxa i ke.. | Where the Padouca built breastworks. | Dismal river. |
| Ka$^n$'çezhi$^n$ga ano$^n$zhi$^n$ te.. | Where Kan'çezhi$^n$ga stood on a hill. | North Loup, west of Calamus river. |

### Omaha Creek and its tributaries

| | | |
|---|---|---|
| To$^n$'wo$^n$ni ke............ | Village creek (a village was built on this creek by the Omaha). | Omaha creek. |
| Waçe'ço$^n$ te.............. | White-clay creek........... | First branch of Omaha creek, near town of Homer (no name on maps). |
| Ki'bano$^n$ githa i te...... | Where they raced......... | Second branch of Omaha creek (no name on maps). |
| Nithato$^n$' i te.............. | Where they drink water (there is a spring at the head where the people stop to drink). | Third branch of Omaha creek (no name on maps). |

### Blackbird Creeks

| | | |
|---|---|---|
| Xa'tha thethe te.......... | Running backward........ | South Blackbird (flows into the Missouri). |
| Wako$^n$'dagi pezhi te..... | The bad Wako$^n$'dagi....... | North Blackbird (flows into the Missouri). |

### The Missouri and its tributaries

| | | |
|---|---|---|
| Nishu'de ke ............... | Turbid water .............. | Missouri. |
| Umo$^n$'ho$^n$ waa i ke........ | Where the Omaha farmed... | Big Papillion. |
| Shao$^n$'petho$^n$ba waxthi i te. | Where they (Omaha and Oto) killed 7 Sioux. | Branch of the Papilion. |
| Uhe'ato$^n$ te................ | The bridge creek.......... | Creek between Homer and Jackson, Nebraska (no name on maps). |
| Ta'gehite ................. | The walnut creek.......... | Elk creek. |
| Waçe'ço$^n$ te.............. | White-clay creek........... | Branch of Elk (no name on maps). |
| Ma'xude waa i te.......... | Where the Iowa farmed..... | Ayoway creek. |
| Sho$^n$'to$^n$ga wabaaça i te ... | Where the people were frightened by gray wolves. | Branch of Ayoway creek. |
| Thi'xeshpo$^n$ ugthe te..... | Soft-willow creek........... | Nameless creek having no outlet south of Floyds river; flows into small lake, Iowa. |
| Wako$^n$'daxuti te........... | Meaning uncertain......... | Floyds river. |
| Xe..................... | Buried.................... | Big Sioux, Iowa. |

| | | |
|---|---|---|
| To$^n$wo$^n$ni ke | Village creek | Bow creek, Nebraska. |
| Ni'ugashude te | Turbid river | White river. |
| Wate' | Meaning unknown | Little Sioux, Iowa. |
| Ni'xebe te | Shallow water | Bayer creek, Iowa. |
| Di'xe ut'a i te | Where many died of the smallpox. | Creek running by Council Bluffs, Iowa (no name on maps). |
| Waçe'ço$^n$ thiça i te | Where they take white clay. | Vermilion creek, South Dakota. |

### The Ponca and its tributaries

| | | |
|---|---|---|
| Ni'uthit'e te | Death river [called so because many Ponca died there.] | Ponca river. |
| Ho$^n$ga waxthi i ke | Where the Ho$^n$ga people were massacred. | First creek to the north (no name on maps). |
| Piça'bahehe ugthe te | (Creek) running through the sand hills. | Second creek to the north (no name on maps). |
| Pahe'zho$^n$ weç'a thaxta i te. | Where Pahe'zho$^n$ was bitten by a snake. | First creek to the south (no name on maps). |
| Mo$^n$thi$^n$'ka shno$^n$ te | Bare earth (so called because of the bare hill near the creek.) | Second creek to the south (no name on maps). |
| Po$^n$'ka sheno$^n$ watha i thuto$^n$ thethe te. | Creek running straight on, where Ponca were massacred. | North fork of Ponca (no name on maps). |
| E'zho$^n$ to$^n$ga niuthuthaç'i$^n$te. | Large elm trees with stream running among them. | South fork of Ponca (no name on maps). |

### Keyabaha and its tributaries

| | | |
|---|---|---|
| Xe'i$^n$ azhi ke | Cedar Ridge creek (so called from a ridge covered with cedar.) | Keyabaha. |
| Mo$^n$'gauti te | Skunk creek | Spring creek. |
| Ko$^n$'de uzhiha te | The plum-bag creek | Burton creek. |
| I$^n$'e uzhi wachishka te | Rock creek | Creek next to Burton, west (no name on maps). |
| Tax'ti wachishka te | Deer creek | Creek next to Rock creek, west (no name on maps). |

### The Verdigris and its tributaries

| | | |
|---|---|---|
| Waçe'tupezhi te | The bad green-clay creek | Verdigris. |
| Waçe'tupezhi hide uzhi$^n$ga te. | The little Waçe tupezhi, branch of Big Verdigris near its mouth. | First branch of Verdigris from the mouth on east (no name on maps). |
| Ma'çi uzhi te | Cedar creek | Creek down which railroad runs (no name on maps); second branch of Verdigris on the east. |
| Mo$^n$chu'to$^n$ga t'etha i te | Where Big Grizzly Bear was killed. (A man by this name tried to take a horse from some men and was killed by them on this creek.) | First branch of Verdigris on west side (no name on maps). |

| | | |
|---|---|---|
| Pa'thiⁿ nadathiⁿ te........ | Where a Pawnee was crazed by heat. (A Ponca invited a Pawnee to a sweat lodge when the Ponca were camped on this creek. The Pawnee, not being able to endure the heat, fled without his clothes and was not heard of again.) | Third branch of Verdigris on east (no name on maps). |
| Hethi'shizhe gahi uhoⁿte. | Where Hethi'shizhe made a feast to the chiefs. | Second branch of Verdigris on west side (no name on maps). |
| Zha'be uti i te............ | Where there is a beaver village, or dam. | Third branch of Verdigris on west side (no name on maps). |
| Wani'tawaxa hi te........ | Where Wani'tawaxa came. (An Omaha by this name visited the Ponca at this place.) | Fourth branch of Verdigris on east side (no name on maps). |

*The Niobrara and branches from the Verdigris on south side*

| | | |
|---|---|---|
| Ni'ubthatha ke.......... | Wide river................. | Niobrara river. |
| Wa'bakihe t'e te............ | Where Wa'bakihe died. | First creek from Verdigris (no name on maps). |
| Tenu'gaçabe wae te........ | Where Black Buffalo Bull planted. | Second creek from Verdigris (no name on maps). |
| Mi'zhiⁿga shiⁿnuda ikinai te. | Where a girl was bitten to death by a dog. | Third creek from Verdigris (no name on maps). |
| Ubi'çka izhuⁿge t'e te..... | Where Ubi'çka's daughter died. | Fourth creek from Verdigris (no name on maps). |
| She'hi toⁿ te............... | Thorn-apple creek.......... | Fifth creek from Verdigris (no name on maps). |
| Wau' waxthi i te.......... | Where some women were killed by a war party. | Sixth creek from Verdigris (no name on maps). |
| Shaoⁿ'pa awachi i te....... | Where a dance was held over the head of a Sioux. | Seventh creek from Verdigris (no name on maps). |
| Ma'ah wiⁿthoⁿthoⁿ te...... | Creek of the scattering cottonwood trees. | Eighth creek from Verdigris (no name on maps). |
| Uⁿ'zhiⁿga hi te............ | Hazelnut creek............. | Ninth creek from Verdigris (no name on maps). |
| Moⁿa' ithitiⁿ thoⁿ.......... | The crooked-cliff creek..... | Tenth creek from Verdigris (no name on maps). |
| Piça' çka te................ | White-sand creek........... | Eleventh creek from Verdigris (no name on maps). |
| Gube'hi te................. | Hackberry creek........... | Twelfth creek from Verdigris, first w. of Keyabaha. |
| Uhe'atoⁿ te................. | The bridge creek. (At this creek a bridge would be built of tent poles and skins, the creek not being fordable.) | Ash creek. (?) |
| Tenu'ga t'e tha i te........ | Where Buffalo Bull was killed. | Long Pine. (?) |

Wachi'shka çnede te....... The long creek. (So called Plum Creek. (?)
because of its length. At
the head is a small lake
and an old Padouca (Co-
manche) village site.
Here also was found a
meteorite (?) which gave
the name In'e thiho
i thoⁿ, "place where
they lifted a stone."
The young men lifted
the stone to test their
strength.)

Muⁿchu' uti te............. Bear creek. (There used to Fairfield creek. (?)
be many grizzlies at this
place. There were cedar
trees along this creek.)

Çiⁿ'de kinoⁿçnįⁿda i te..... Horse-tail creek. (The ap- Small creek (no name on
proaches to the ford were maps).
so steep that in going
down the horses trod on
one another's tails.)

Ni'xue te.................. The roaring waters......... Schlegels  c r e e k . ( ? )
(There was a fort here.)

Ni' biçe te................ The dry creek. (The peo- Gordons creek.
ple had to dig wells when
they camped here.)

Çiçi'ka wabahi i te......... Where they gathered tur- Snake river.
keys. (Many turkeys
were found here, starved
to death, and men gath-
ered them to pluck the
feathers to feather their
arrows.)

Iⁿ'e ikitiⁿ i te.............. Where they fought with peb- Small creek on north side
bles. (When camped at of Niobrara, a short dis-
this creek the boys fought tance above Fairfield.
one another, using pebbles
as missiles.)

Pahe'nude te ............. Where there is a ridge with a Creek on north side of Nio-
hole through it. brara, nearly opposite
Horse-tail creek.

### The Republican river

Watoⁿ'thata i ke........... Where they ate squash ..... Republican river.
Niwa'xube ke............. Holy river ............... Solomon river, Kansas.

Paheshu'de ke ............. Smoky hill ............... Smoky Hill river.

Uha'i ke ................. The river down which they Ohio river.
came.

Mika'toⁿ .................. Plenty of raccoons......... Des Moines river.

## THE VILLAGE

### SITE

The site for a village was always chosen near a running stream convenient to timber and generally not far from hills, from which an outlook over the country could be obtained. A watch was commonly stationed on these hills to detect the stealthy approach of enemies and to keep an eye on the horses pastured near by, although these were usually herded by boys during the day and brought into the village at night, where each family had a corral built near its lodge for safety. The bottom lands were the planting places; each family selected its plot, and as long as the land was cultivated its occupancy was respected. Corn, beans, squash, and melons were raised in considerable quantities, and while these products were sometimes traded, they were usually stored for winter use.

Occasionally a man would take a fancy to some locality and determine to live there. He would be joined by his kindred, who would erect their lodges near his and cultivate gardens. Such outlying little settlements were a temptation to marauding war parties, and if an attack was made by a large party of enemies, capture and death were sure to follow; any degree of safety was secured only through untiring vigilance.

### DWELLINGS

The earth lodge and the tipi (tent) were the only types of dwelling used by the Omaha during the last few centuries.

The tipi (pl. 17 and fig. 16) was a conical tent. Formerly the cover was made of 9 to 12 buffalo skins tanned on both sides. To cut and sew this cover so that it would fit well and be shapely when stretched over the circular framework of poles required skilful workmanship, the result of training and of accurate measurements. The cover was cut semicircular. To the straight edges, which were to form the front of the tent, were added at the top triangular flaps. These were to be adjusted by poles according to the direction from which the wind blew, so as to guide the smoke from the central fire out of the tent. These smoke-flaps were called *ti'hugabthi$^n$tha* (from *ti*, "tent or house;" *hugabthi$^n$tha*, "to twist"). At intervals from about 3 feet above the bottom up to the smoke-flaps holes were made and worked in the straight edges. Through these holes pins (sticks) about 8 inches long, well shaped and often ornamented, were thrust to fasten the tent together, when the two edges lapped in front or were laced together with a thong. This front lap of the tent was called *ti'mo$^n$thuhe* (from *ti*, "tent"; *mo$^n$thuhe*, "breast"). The term refers to the part of the hide forming the lap. The tent poles were 14 to 16 feet long. Straight young cedar poles were preferred. The bark was removed and the poles were rubbed smooth.  The setting up of a tent was always a woman's task.  She first took four poles, laid them together on the ground, and then tied them firmly with a thong about 3 feet from one end.  She then raised the poles and spread their free ends apart and thrust them firmly into the ground.  These four tied poles formed the true framework of the tent.  Other poles— 10 to 20 in number, according to the size of the tent—were arranged in a circle, one end pressed well into the ground, the other end laid in the forks made by the tied ends of the four poles.  There was a definite order in setting up the poles so that they would lock one another, and when they were all in place they constituted an elastic but firm

FIG. 16.  Típi.

frame, which could resist a fairly heavy wind.  There was no name for the fundamental four poles, nor for any other pole except the one at the back, to which the tent cover was tied.  This pole was called *teçin'deugashke*, "the one to which the buffalo tail was tied."  The name tells that the back part of the tent cover was a whole hide, the tail indicating the center line.  When the poles were all set, this back pole was laid on the ground and the tent cover brought. This had been folded so as to be ready to be tied and opened.  The front edges had been rolled or folded over and over back to the line indicating the middle of the cover; on this line thongs had been sewed at the top and bottom of the cover; the cover was laid on the ground

EARTH LODGE—FRAMEWORK AND STRUCTURE

in such manner that this back line was parallel to the pole, which was then securely tied to the cover by the thongs. When this was done, the pole and the folded tent cover were grasped firmly together, lifted, and set in place. Then, if there were two women doing the work, one took one fold of the cover and the other the other fold, and each walked with her side around the framework of poles. The two straight edges were then lapped over each other and the wooden pins were put in or the thong was threaded. Each of the lower ends of the straight edges had a loop sewed to it, and through both loops a stake was thrust into the ground. The oval opening formed the door, which was called *tizhe'be*. Over this opening a skin was hung. A stick fastened across from one foreleg to the other, and another stick running from one hindleg to the other, held this covering taut, so that it could be easily tipped to one side when a person stooped to enter the oval door opening. It was always an interesting sight to watch the rapid and precise movements of the women and their deftness in setting up a tent. On a journey, no matter how dark the evening might be when the tent was pitched the opening was generally so arranged as to face the east. In the village, or in a camping place likely to be used for some time, a band of willow withes was bound around the frame of poles about midway their height to give additional stability.

The earth lodge (pls. 19, 22) was a circular dwelling, having walls about 8 feet high and a dome-shaped roof, with a central opening for the escape of smoke and the admission of light. The task of building an earth lodge was shared by men and women. The marking out of the site and the cutting of the heavy logs were done by the men. When the location was chosen, a stick was thrust in the spot where the fireplace was to be, one end of a rawhide rope was fastened to the stick and a circle 20 to 60 feet in diameter was drawn on the earth to mark where the wall was to be erected. The sod within the circle was removed, the ground excavated about a foot in depth, and the earth thrown around the circle like an embankment. Small crotched posts about 10 feet high were set 8 or 10 feet apart and 1½ feet within the circle, and on these were laid beams. Outside this frame split posts were set close together, having one end braced against the bottom of the bank and the other end leaning against the beams, thus forming a wall of timber. The opening generally, though not always, faced the east. Midway between the central fireplace and the wall were planted 4 to 8 large crotched posts about 10 feet in height, on which heavy beams rested, these serving to support the roof. This was made of long, slender, tapering trees stripped of their bark. These were tied at their large ends with cords (made from the inner bark of the linden) to the beams at the top of the stockade and at the middle to those resting in the crotches of the large posts forming the

inner circle about the fireplace. The slender ends were cut so as
to form the circular opening for the smoke, the edges being woven
together with elm twine, so as to be firm. Outside the woodwork of
the walls and roof, branches of willow were laid crosswise and bound
tight to each slab and pole. Over the willows a heavy thatch of
coarse grass was arranged so as to shed water. On the grass was
placed a thick coating of sod. The sods were cut to lap and be laid
like shingles. Finally they were tamped with earth and made
impervious to rain. The entrance way, 6 to 10 feet long, projected
from the door and was built in the same manner as the lodge and
formed a part of it. A curtain of skin hung at the inner and one at
the outer door of this entrance way. Much labor was expended on
the floor of the lodge. The loose earth was carefully removed and the
ground then tamped. It was next flooded with water, after which
dried grass was spread over it and set on fire. Then the ground was
tamped once again. This wetting and heating was repeated two or
three times, until the floor became hard and level and could be easily
swept and kept clean. Brooms were made of brush or twigs tied
together. Couches were arranged around the wall in the spaces
between the posts of the framework. These were provided with
skins and pillows and served as seats by day and as beds by night.
In the building of an earth lodge the cutting and putting on of the

sods was always done by women, and as this
part of the task had to be accomplished
rapidly to prevent the drying out of the
sods, which must hold well together, kindred
helped one another. The erection of this
class of dwelling required considerable labor,
hence only the industrious and thrifty possessed these lodges.

Near each dwelling, generally to the left
of the entrance, the cache (fig. 17) was built.
This consisted of a hole in the ground about
8 feet deep, rounded at the bottom and

FIG. 17.   Common form of cache.

sides, provided with a neck just large enough to admit the body of a
person. The whole was lined with split posts, to which was tied
an inner lining of bunches of dried grass. The opening was protected by grass, over which sod was placed. In these caches the
winter supply of food was stored; the shelled corn was put into skin
bags, long strings of corn on the cob were made by braiding the
outer husks, while the jerked meat was packed in parfleche cases.
Pelts, regalia, and extra clothing were generally kept in the cache;
but these were laid in ornamented parfleche cases, never used but
for this purpose.

PART OF OMAHA VILLAGE (ABOUT 1860)

When the people left the village for the summer buffalo hunt, all cumbersome household articles—as the mortars and pestles, extra hides, etc.—were placed in the caches and the openings carefully concealed. The cases containing gala clothing and regalia were taken along, as these garments were needed at the great tribal ceremonies which took place during that period.

In a village in which the entire tribe lived the lodges and tents were not arranged about a central open space nor were they set so the people could live in the order of their gentes, an order observed when they were on the hunt and during their tribal ceremonies. Yet each family knew to what gens it belonged, observed its rites, and obeyed strictly the rule of exogamy. To the outward appearance a village presented a motley group of tribesmen. The dwellings and their adjacent corrals were huddled together; the passageways between the lodges were narrow and tortuous. There was little of the picturesque. The grass and weeds that grew over the earth lodges while the people were off on their summer buffalo hunt were all cut away when the tribe returned. So, except for the decorations on the skin tents, there was nothing to relieve the dun-colored aspect. (Pl. 23.)

The village was never wholly deserted, even when most of the tribe left for the annual buffalo hunt; for the sick, the infirm, and the very poor were forced to remain behind. This class of stay-at-homes were called *he'begthi$^n$*, "those who sit half-way." Usually a sprinkling of able-bodied men remained with their old or sick relatives, and these served as a guard, to defend the village in case of an attack. Occasionally a young man or two would remain in the village in order to be near a sweetheart who had to stay at home and help care for the sick in her family.

### HISTORIC VILLAGES AND PLACES

*To$^{n'}$wo$^n$pezhi*, Bad Village. This name, bestowed on an old village built by the Omaha in their migration down the Missouri river, owes its origin to a tragedy which for a number of years caused a division in the tribe. (See p. 85.) This village was located on East Bow creek, in the northeast part of township 32, range 2 east of the sixth principal meridian, Cedar county, Nebraska.

*To$^{n'}$wo$^n$to$^n$gatho$^n$*, Large Village. This town was on Omaha creek in Dakota county, Nebraska, about half a mile north of the present town of Homer; it was built in the eighteenth century, and the people were found here by Lewis and Clark in 1805.

*Tenu'gano$^n$pewathe shko$^n$thaitho$^n$*, "The place where the camp of Tenu'gano$^n$pewathe (father of Kaxe'no$^n$ba) was attacked" in 1840 by an unknown tribe and a number were killed on both sides. The fight took place on Cedar creek, Albion county, Nebraska, in township 19, range 8 west of the sixth principal meridian.

*Ezhno$^{n\prime}$zhuwagthe shko$^{n}$thaitho$^{n}$*, "The place where Ezhno$^{n\prime}$zhuwagthe was attacked." This battle between a part of the Omaha and one of the Sioux tribes was fought in the same year (1840) on Beaver creek, in the southeastern part of township 21, range 7 west of the sixth principal meridian, Boone county, Nebraska.

*To$^{n\prime}$wo$^{n}$zhi$^{n}$ga*, The Little Village. This was the name of the village built by the Omaha on Elkhorn river, near Clark creek, in Dodge county, Nebraska, in the spring of 1841, the tribe having moved there from the Missouri river on account of attacks by the Sioux. There were few earth lodges, as the village was occupied for only two years, after which the people went back to their old village on Omaha creek, Dakota county, Nebraska.

*Pahu$^{\prime}$tho$^{n}$datho$^{n}$*, "The hill rising in the center of a plain." This village on Papilion creek, about 8 miles west of the present town of Bellevue, was built in 1847. The tribe lived there until they sold their lands to the United States Government in 1854; two years later they moved to their present reservation some 80 miles northward.

*To$^{n\prime}$wo$^{n}$gaxe shko$^{n}$thaitho$^{n}$*, "The place where To$^{n\prime}$wo$^{n}$gaxe was attacked." The assault on the Omaha camp here referred to was made by the Yankton and Santee on December 12, 1846. At the time of the attack the camp, composed mostly of old men, women, and children, was on the Missouri river near the northeast corner of township 21, range 11 east of the sixth principal meridian, Burt county, Nebraska. To$^{n\prime}$wo$^{n}$gaxe, or Village Maker, was the only chief present at the time of the attack. From this fact the place took its name. All the other chiefs were on a buffalo hunt, with most of the men of the tribe, who knew nothing of the attack until they returned. More than 80 persons were slain.

*U$^{\prime}$ho$^{n}$to$^{n}$ga t$^{\prime}$ethaitho$^{n}$*, "Where U$^{\prime}$ho$^{n}$to$^{n}$ga was killed," in township 24, range 17 west of the sixth principal meridian, Loup county, Nebraska. U$^{\prime}$ho$^{n}$to$^{n}$ga, or Big Cook, a prominent Omaha, was one of the warriors killed in a battle fought at this place with the Oglala and other Sioux tribes in 1852.

*Thugina gaxthiitho$^{n}$*, "The place where Thugina (Logan Fontenelle) was slain." Logan Fontenelle (fig. 18), a prominent half breed of the Omaha tribe, while hunting alone was killed by the Oglala Sioux in the summer of 1855. The Sioux made a charge on the Omaha camp when the Omaha were moving. Some of the Sioux warriors came on Logan in a ravine where he had dismounted to pick gooseberries. When he discovered the Sioux he sprang on his horse and made for the ford to rejoin his tribe, who were on the opposite side of the stream, but he was overtaken and killed before he reached the ford. This account of his death was given by Kaxe$^{\prime}$no$^{n}$ba, or Two Crows, who went in search of Logan immediately after the fight, and traced the course of his flight from the gooseberry bush to the spot where the body was found. This fight took place on Beaver creek, in the northern part of township 21, range 7 west of the sixth principal meridian, Boone county, Nebraska.

FIG. 18. Logan Fontenelle.

*Wanon'kuge shkontha i thon* (for portrait of Wanon'kuge, see fig. 44), "Where Wanon'kuge was attacked." This battle, between a part of the Omaha and the Oglala Sioux, took place in August, 1859. A number of lives were lost in the battle, the attacking party of Sioux suffering greater loss than the Omaha. Two Omaha, a woman and a child, were taken captive. The child was returned, and the woman, after many adventures, found her way back to her people. This fight was on Beaver creek, in township 20, range 6 west of the sixth principal meridian, Boone county, Nebraska.

The following names were given by the Omaha to the cities and towns named below:

*Pahi' zhide tonwon*,   St. Louis.
Hair   red   town   (Referring to the color of Governor Clark's hair.)

*We'ç'a çabe thitha i thon*,  Leavenworth.
Snake   black   they take   the (place)

*Umon'hon tonwon*, Omaha City.
Omaha   town

*Shaon' tonwon*, Sioux City.
Sioux   town

*Zhon muça i   thon*,  Fremont.
Pole   they planted   the place

*Uzha'ta thon*,     Columbus.
Forks   the (of the Platte and the Loup)

*Ni çkithe*, Lincoln (Salt town, because situated near the stream to which the people went to gather salt).

## TRIBES KNOWN TO THE OMAHA

The following are the Omaha names for the tribes that are known to them.

Of their own linguistic stock they know the following:

Ponca, Pon'ca.
Quapaw, Uga'xpa.   The name means "downstream."
Osage, Wazha'zhe.
Kaw or Kansa, Kon'çe.

Iowa, Ma'xude.  Ma'xude is a corruption of Pa'xude, meaning "gray head," the name by which the Iowa call themselves.

Oto, Wathu'tada.  This is not the name by which the Oto speak of themselves.

Missouri, Niu'tachi.  The name means "those who came floating down dead."

Winnebago, Hu'tunga.

Mandan, Mawa'dani.

Crows, Ka'xe niashiga (from ka'xe, "crow;" ni'ashiga, "people").

Yankton, Ihon'tonwin.[a]  An Omaha version of the Yanktons' own name.

Santee, Incon'ati.[a]  The name means "those who dwell on the white rocks."

Oglala, Ubtha'tha.[a]

Of tribes belonging to other linguistic stocks the Omaha have names for the following:

Pawnee, Pa'thin.

Arikara, Pa'thinpiça.  The name means "sand Pawnee."

Caddo, Pa'thinwaçabe.  This name means "black Pawnee."

Wichita are known as Wichita.

Cheyenne, Shahi'etha.

Blackfeet, Çi'çabe.  The Omaha name means "blackfeet."

Sauk, Ça'ge.

Arapaho } Maxpi'ato ("blue clouds").
Kiowa

Comanche, Pa'dunka (Padouca).

Kickapoo, Hi'gabu.

Potawatomie, Wahi'uthaxa.  This name is a corruption of the Oto name for this tribe, Woraxa.

Bannock, Ba'niki.  The Omaha name is probably a modification of Bannock.

Nez Perces, Pegaçunde.  This tribe was known through the Ponca.  The name given them means "braids on the forehead."

That the Omaha have a name for the Arikara and one which indicates a knowledge of their relationship to the Pawnee, and yet have none for the northern Sioux tribes who belong to their own linguistic stock, is an interesting point, particularly when taken in connection with the influence exercised on the tribe by the Arikara, mentioned on p. 75.  There is no name for the Chippewa group, yet it is not improbable that the tribes long ago came more or less into contact.  The similarity between the "Shell society" of the Omaha and the "Grand Medicine" of the Chippewa suggests some communication, direct or indirect, though all knowledge of how the Shell society was introduced has been lost.  Nor do the Omaha seem to know anything of the tribes of the Muskhogean or Iroquoian stock to the south and east; nor of those belonging to the Shoshonean and Athapascan stocks to the west and southwest.  They knew of the Rocky Mountains, which they called Pahe'monshi, meaning "high hills" or "mountains."  Yet they seem never to have come into contact with the tribes living so far to the west.  The Black Hills of South Dakota were familiar to them, and were known as Pahe'çabe, the word meaning literally "black hills."

---

[a] This is one of the three distinctive names by which the bands of the Dakota are known.  There is a general name for all persons speaking that language, Shaun'—possibly a corruption of Sioux.

The Ponca names for the above tribes were similar to the Omaha names, with few exceptions. The Crows were called by two names, Hu'patitha and Ko$^n$xe' wichasha$^n$. The names given by Ponca to the Yankton and the Santee were identical with those used by the Omaha, but they had distinct names for the following bands of Sioux:

Lower Brulé, Ku'dawichasha.  Lower people.
Rosebud Brulé, Sha'u$^n$ixti.  Real or Pure Sioux.
Oglala, Pine Ridge Sioux, Sicho$^{n'}$xu.  Burnt leg.

The Ponca have names for the following tribes for which the Omaha have none:

Cherokee, Che'thuki.  Probably a corruption of Cherokee.
Ni'kathate, Tonkawa.

It is probable that the Ponca gained knowledge of these two tribes while in the Indian Territory, and that their posession of distinctive names for the bands of the Sioux is to be accounted for by their living near the people and fighting both for and against them during the last century.

## FAUNA AND FLORA KNOWN TO THE OMAHA

### ANIMALS

#### Animals (general term), Wani'ta

[The asterisk (*) indicates those used for food]

* Antelope, Tachu'ge.
* Badger, Xu'ga.
Bat, Dide'shi.
* Bear, black, Waça'be.
* Bear, grizzly, Mo$^n$chu'.
* Beaver, Zha'be.
* Buffalo, Te.
Cat, domestic, I$^n$gthu$^{n'}$ga.
* Cat, wild, I$^n$gthu$^{n'}$ga.
* Cattle, domestic, Te'çka.
* Chipmunk, Tashni'ga.
Cougar, I$^n$gthu$^n$çi$^{n'}$çnede (long-tailed cat).
Coyote, Mi'kaçi.
* Deer, Ta'xti.
* Dog, Shi$^{n'}$nuda.
Donkey (see Mule), Nita'to$^n$ga nushiaha (big ears low).
Elephant, Tiba'xia tha (push over a house—refers to its strength).
* Elk, O$^{n'}$po$^n$.
Ermine, I$^n$chu$^{n'}$gaçka (white mouse).
Fox, a small variety, Mo$^n$thi$^{n'}$kasheha.
Fox, gray, Ma'zho$^n$ha.
Fox, red, Ti'ko$^n$xude.
Frog, Te'bia.
Goat, He'çakiba.
Gopher, Mo$^n$thi$^{n'}$ga.
* Hog, Ku'kuçi.

Horse, Sho$^n$/ge.

Lion, Wani'ta waxa (greater animal).

Lizard, Wagthishka heduba (four-legged bug).

Lynx, I$^n$gthu$^n$/ga hi$^n$ shkube (furry wild cat).

Mice, I$^n$chu$^n$/ga.

Mice that live in dry bones, Tepauti (*tepa*, buffalo skull; *ute*, to live in).

Mice that store food, I$^n$chu$^n$/ga waxema (mice that cache).

Mink, Tushi$^n$/ge.

Mole, No$^n$be'xawi$^n$ (hands turned backward).

Monkey, Ishti$^n$/thi$^n$ke (a mythical, mischievous, capricious being, representing the wind. Because of its acts in the myths its name was transferred to the monkey when the Omaha first saw that animal.)

Mule (*see* Donkey), Nita to$^n$/ga (big ears).

* Musk rat, Çi$^n$/nedewagithe.

* Opossum, I$^n$shti$^n$/pa.

Otter, Nuzhno$^n$/.

Porcupine, Ba'hi$^n$.

Prairie dog, Monthi$^n$/xude.

* Rabbit, Mo$^n$shti$^n$/ge.

* Rabbit, jack, Mo$^n$shti$^n$/çka (white rabbit).

* Raccoon, Mika',

* Rat, I$^n$cho$^n$/to$^n$ga (big mouse).

* Sheep, domestic, Tax'tiçka.

* Sheep, Rocky Mountain, Pashto$^n$/ga.

* Skunk, Mo$^n$/ga.

Snail, Niha'.

Snake, We'ç'a.

Snake, black, We'ç'a çabe (black snake).

Snake, bull, Nitha'xupa (water sucker).

Snake, garter, We'ç'anideka.

Snake, moccasin, She'ki.

Snake, rattle, Çathu'.

* Squirrel, ground, He'xthi$^n$.

* Squirrel, tree, Ci$^n$/ga.

Toad, Iko$^n$/git'e (his grandmother is dead).

Tortoise, Ke'gtheçe (striped turtle).

*Turtle, Ke.

* Turtle, diamond-back (terrapin), Keha'mo$^n$zhide (red-breast turtle.)

* Turtle, snapping, Ke' to$^n$ga (big turtle).

* Turtle, soft-shell, Ke ha'be bedo$^n$ (flexible-shell turtle).

Weasel, I$^n$/chu$^n$gaçi (yellow mouse).

Wolf, gray, Sho$^n$/to$^n$ga.

## BIRDS

### Bird (general term), Wazhi$^n$/ga

[The asterisk (*) indicates those used for food]

American bittern, Mo$^n$/xata.wado$^n$be (looks up at the sky).

* Bee martin, or king bird, Wati'duka.

Belted kingfisher, No$^n$xi'de shkuni$^n$.

* Blackbird, Mo$^n$gthi'xta.

Blue-bird, Wazhi$^n$/tu (blue bird).

Blue jay, I$^n$cho$^n$g'agiudu$^n$ (fond of mice).

* Crane, Pe'to$^n$.

Crow, Ka'xe.

\* Curlew, Ki'ko$^n$çi.

\* Curlew, long-billed (*Numenius longirostris*), Ki'kato$^n$ga (big curlew).

\* Dove, Thi'ta.

\* Dove, Carolina or common, Thitato$^n$ga (big dove).

\* Duck, Mi'xazhi$^n$ga (little goose).

Duck, blue-winged teal (*Querquedula discors*), A'hi$^n$ hide tu, (blue wing); also Mi'xa wagtho$^n$xe, "betrayer duck," so called because it betrayed the water monster in the myth of Ha'xegi.

\* Duck, mallard, green head (*Anas boschas*), Pa'hitu (green neck).

\* Duck, wood, summer duck, bridal duck (*Aix spousa*), Mi'xa zhi$^n$ga xage egu$^n$ (the crying duck).

Eagle, Xitha'.

Eagle, bald, Paçu$^{n\prime}$ (whitish head).

Eagle, golden (*Aquila chrysaetus*), Xitha' çka (white eagle).

Eagle, gray sea, Xitha' gthezhe (spotted eagle).

Flicker, Tho$^{n\prime}$çiga.

\* Goose, Mi'xa.

\* Goose, American white-footed, Canadian goose, Mi'xa to$^n$ga (big goose).

\* Goose, lesser snow (*Chen hyperborea*), Kiçnu$^{n\prime}$.

Gull, Ne'tha.

Hawk, American sparrow, Gthedo$^{n\prime}$.

Hawk, night, Te'ubixo$^n$ (the buffalo inflator).

Hawk, red shoulder, Gtho$^n$shka'.

Hawk, red tail, I$^{n\prime}$beçiga (yellow tail).

Hawk, swallow-tailed or fork-tailed kite, I$^{n\prime}$be zho$^n$ka (forked tail).

Hawk, white tail, Gtho$^n$shka' xithaego$^n$ (hawk like an eagle).

Humming bird, Wati'ninika wazhi$^n$ga (butterfly bird).

\* Lark, pallid horned, Ma'çi çka.

Magpie, American, Wazhi$^{n\prime}$be çnede (long-tail bird).

\* Meadow lark, Ta'tithi$^n$ge.

Owl, Pa'nuhu.

Owl, barred, Wapu'gahahada.

Owl, horned, Pa'nuhu heto$^n$ ego$^n$ (owl having horns).

Owl, screech, Ne' thazhibe.

Owl, snowy, I$^{n\prime}$chu$^n$çu$^n$ (now white).

Pelican, American white, Bthe'xe.

\* Prairie hen or chicken lesser, Shu.

\* Quail (bobwhite), U'shiwathe (one who fools (people)).

\* Robin, Pa'thi$^n$ wazhi$^n$ga (Pawnee bird).

\* Snipe, To$^{n\prime}$i$^n$.

Swallow, Nishku'shku.

\*Swan, American white, Mi'xaço$^n$ (white goose).

Thrush, Taçka'çka.

\* Turkey, Çiçi'ka.

Turkey vulture, He'ga.

Whippoorwill, Ha'kugthi.

\* Woodcock, American (*Philohela minor*), Pa'xthega (freckled head).

Woodpecker, hairy, Zho$^{n\prime}$panini.

Woodpecker, pileated, ivory bill, Wazhi$^{n\prime}$gapa (bird head).[a]

Woodpecker, red-headed, Tu'çka or Mu'xpa.

Wren, Kixaxaja (laughing bird).

---

[a] The head of this bird is used on the tribal and the Wa'wa$^n$ pipes.

## INSECTS

Insects, bugs, etc. (general term), Wagthi'shka

Ants, Zho$^n$'gthishka (wood bugs—no varieties distinguished).
Bee, Kigtho$^n$'xe.
Beetle, Wagthi'shka (the general name for bugs).
Butterfly, Wati'nini ka.
Caterpillar, Wagthi'shka (general term for bugs).
Fly, Ho$^n$'t'ega.
Grasshopper, Xtho$^n$xtho$^n$'shka.
Lightning-bug, Wana'xo$^n$xo$^n$.
Locust, Watha'çae (noisy bug).
Mosquito, Naho$^n$ga.
Spider, Uki'gthiçke (weaving itself—no name for varieties).
Worm, angle, Mo$^n$thi$^n$'ka shibe (ground intestine).   No general term for worms; all are called Wagthi'shka, the name applied also to beetles and bugs.

## FISH

Fish (general term), Huhu

[The asterisk (*) indicates those used for food]

* Buffalo fish, Hui'buta (round mouth).
Catfish, Tu'çe.
Crawfish and lobster, Mo$^n$'shka.
Eels, no name; they are not eaten.
* Garfish, Hupa'çiçnede (long-nose fish).
Leech, Kicna'.
Mussels, clams, oysters, Ti'haba.
* Pickerel, Hugthe'zhe (spotted fish).
* Trout, Hubthu'ga (round fish).

## TREES

Tree, or bush (general term), Xtha'be; wood, felled trees (general term), Zho$^n$.   The names below are given according to their customary use.   The terminal syllable *hi* means "stalk," as the stalk of the corn, the trunk of the tree, the vine of the potato.
Apple tree, She' hi.
Ash, Tazhno$^n$'ge.
Box elder, Zha'beta zho$^n$ (beaver wood).
Buffalo berry tree, Wazhi'de hi.
Cedar, red, Ma'çi.
Cherry tree, No$^n$'pa hi.
Coffee-bean tree, No$^n$'tita hi.
Cottonwood, Mah'ah.
Elm, E'zho$^n$.
Hackberry tree, Gube' hi.
Hazel, O$^n$'zhi$^n$ga hi.
Hickory, No$^n$'çi.
Ironwood, He'tazho$^n$ta.
Linden, Hi$^n$'de hi.
Maple, We'nashabethe hi (black dye tree).
Mulberry, Zho$^n$çi, (yellow wood).
Oak, red, Bu'de hi, and No$^n$ bo$^n$ naxthi$^n$, "flame" (favorite firewood).

Oak, white, Tosh′ka hi.
Osage orange, Zho$^n$çi (yellow wood).
Plum tree, Ko$^n$de hi.
Red haw, thorn apple tree, Taçpo$^{n′}$ hi.
Spruce, Ma′çi.
Walnut, black, Ta′ge hi.
Willow, Thi′xe.
Willow, diamond, Thi′xe kibtho$^n$btho$^n$xe (gnarled willow).
Willow, hard, Thi′xe çagi (hard willow).
Willow, soft, Thi′xe ushpo$^n$ (soft willow).

## THE HUMAN BODY AS KNOWN TO THE OMAHA

Head (not including face), No$^n$shki′.
Head (including face), Pa.
Brain, We′thixthi.
Side of head from ear up, No$^n$tha′de.
Ear, Nita′.
Helix, Nitabaxu′ke (*baxu′ke*, ridge).
Lobe, Nitaushto$^{n′}$ga (*ushto$^{n′}$ga*, soft).
Ear (inner part or organ of hearing), No$^n$xi′de.
Top of head, Taxpi′.
Back of head, Tai′.
Face, I$^n$de′.
Forehead, Pe.
Temples, No$^n$tha′deho$^n$ho$^n$ (*ho$^n$ho$^n$*, to throb).
Center of forehead, Peuta′no$^n$ (*utano$^n$*, between).
Eyebrow, I$^n$shta′no$^n$xixe.
Depression between eyebrows, Pau′çkida.
Eye, I$^n$shta.
White of the eye, Inshta′uçka tho$^n$.
Pupil, I$^n$shta′ usha betho$^n$.
Socket, I$^n$shta′ugtho$^n$ (*ugtho$^n$*, to put into a hollow place).
Eyelid, I$^n$shta′ha (*ha*, skin).
Upper lid, I$^n$shta′ha igabizhe (*igabizhe*, to wink with).
Eyelashes, I$^n$shta′thehi$^n$.
Hair of head (human), No$^n$zhi′ha *or* Pahi′.
Hair on forehead, Pehi$^{n′}$.
Hair on body (human or animal), Hi$^n$.
Nose, Pa.
Bridge of nose, Paxi′xe.
Tip of nose, Pashi′zhe.
Nostrils, Pa′xthuge (*xthuge*, hole).
Wing of nose, Pauga′dazhe (*uga′dazhe*, base).
Septum, Paushto$^{n′}$ga (*shto$^{n′}$ga*, soft).
Cheek, The′xo$^n$de.
Cheekbone, I$^n$de′no$^n$hi$^n$.
Mouth, I.
Lips, I′ha.
Corners of mouth, I′thede.
Jaw, The′ba.
Joint of jaw, The′baugthe.

Teeth, Hi.

Molars, Hiu′to<sup>n</sup>ga.

Gums, Hizhu′.

Tongue, The′çe.

Tip of tongue, Theçe′paçi (*paçi′*, tip).

Base of tongue, Theçe′hide (*hide*, base).

Ridge above teeth and roof of mouth, Ko<sup>n</sup>btha′de.

Chin, I′ki.

Double chin, The′bazhu.

Neck, Pa′hi.

Chords at side of neck, Nu′deko<sup>n</sup>.

Hollow at base of neck in front, The′shkaxthuah.

Two chords at the back of neck, Tai′ko<sup>n</sup>.

Hollow at nape of neck, Taiu′gthe.

Throat, Nu′de.

Adam's apple, Nu′de tashe (*tashe*, lump).

Windpipe, Nu′dexixibe.

Pharynx, We′no<sup>n</sup>bthe.

Body, Zhu′ga.

Breast, Mo<sup>n′</sup>ge.

Mamma, Mo<sup>n</sup>çe′.

Nipples, Mo<sup>n</sup>çe′pa.

Collar bone, Mo<sup>n′</sup>ge wahi (*mo<sup>n′</sup>ge*, breast; *wahi*, bone).

Sternum, Temo<sup>n′</sup>hin.

Ribs, Thi′ti.

Short ribs, Thi′tiusha′gthe.

Epigastric region, Mo<sup>n</sup>hi<sup>n′</sup>be.

Lumbar region, Thie.

Hypogastric region, Tapu′ *or* Washna′.

Umbilical region, Ni′xa.

Navel, The′tasho<sup>n</sup>.

Waist, Te′çe.

Spine, No<sup>n′</sup>xahi.

Coccyx, Çi<sup>n′</sup>de ita (*çi<sup>n′</sup>de*, tail; *ita*, end).

Back, No<sup>n′</sup>ka.

Muscles on side of spine, lower end, Taki<sup>n′</sup>de.

Sinew beneath these muscles, Teno<sup>n′</sup>kako<sup>n</sup>.

Fleshy bunch on back below neck, A′baku.

Shoulder, I<sup>n</sup>ke′de.

Shoulder blade, Waba′ço<sup>n</sup>.

Arm, A.

Upper arm, Auto<sup>n′</sup>ga (*uto<sup>n′</sup>ga*, large part).

Lower arm, Au′çni.

Muscles on front of upper arm, A′ko<sup>n</sup>ta.

Muscles on back upper arm, A′zhuhi.

Armpit, Nuçi′.

Elbow, Açtu′hi.

Wrist, No<sup>n</sup>be′usho<sup>n</sup>sho<sup>n</sup> (*usho<sup>n</sup>sho<sup>n</sup>*, pliable).

Hand, No<sup>n</sup>be′.

Palm of hand, No<sup>n</sup>be′utho<sup>n</sup>da (*utho<sup>n</sup>da*, center).

Fingers, No<sup>n</sup>be′hi *or* Uça′be.

Thumb, No<sup>n</sup>be′hi uto<sup>n</sup>ga (*uto<sup>n</sup>ga*, big).

Index finger, No<sup>n</sup>be′hi  weabaçu (*weabaçu*, to point with).

Middle finger, No$^n$be'hiuthiço$^n$ (*utheço$^n$*, middle).

Finger next to little one, No$^n$be'hi  uzhi$^n$ga  uthuato$^n$ (*uthuato$^n$*, next to one).

Little finger, No$^n$be'hi  uzhi$^n$ga (*uzhi$^n$ga*, little).

Tip of finger, No$^n$be'hi  itaxe.

Nails, Sha'ge.  The same word is applied to claws and hoofs.

Knuckles, No$^n$be'usho$^n$sho$^n$.

Contents of body, the internal organs, U'gaxectha.

Heart, No$^n$de.

Lungs, Tha'xi.

Liver, Pi.

Gall, Pizi'.

Kidney, Tea'ço$^n$taçi.

Bladder, Ne'xe.

Intestines, Shi'be.

Small intestine, Shi'be  uzhi$^n$ga.

Large intestine, Shi'be  uto$^n$ga.

Layer of fat covering stomach and internal organs, Hu'xthabe.

Groin, Iti'washko$^n$.

Hips, Çi$^n$de'hi.

Hip joint, Zhega'ugthe; also U'gaho$^n$, where the cut is made in butchering.

Body between hip joint and ribs, "ticklish place," Shtashta'de.

Legs, Zhi'be *or* Hi.

Upper leg, thigh, Zhega'uto$^n$ga..

Inner, flat part of thigh, Ke'go$^n$.

Upper part of thigh, Çiçu'.

Flat part of thigh near buttock, Zhega' ubthaçka.

Buttock, Ni'de.

Knee, whole of knee, Shino$^{n\prime}$de.

Kneejoint, Hiü'kite.

Kneecap, Shino$^{n\prime}$dewashko$^n$.

End of fibula, Hia'xte.

Shin, No$^{n\prime}$xpehi.

Calf of leg, Hiuça'gi.

Ankles, Çiko$^{n\prime}$.

Ankle bones, Çita'xe.

Feet, Çi.

Soles, Çiha'to$^n$.

Instep, top, Çiu'no$^n$xixe.

Instep, hollow below, Çiu'no$^n$çkida.

Tendon achilles, Hi'ko$^n$.

Heel, Çithe'de.

Toes, Çipa'hi.

Great toe, Çipa'hi  uto$^n$ga.

Next (second) toe, Çipa'hi  uto$^n$ga  uthuato$^n$ (*uthuato$^n$*, next to).

Middle toe, Çipa'hi  uthiço$^n$ (*uthiço$^n$*, middle).

Next toe, Çipa'hi  uazhi$^n$ga  uthuato$^n$.

Little toe, Çipa'hi  uzhi$^n$ga (*uzhi$^n$ga*, little).

Bones, Wahi'.

Skin, Ha *or* Xi$^n$ha'.

Marrow, Wazhi'be.

Veins, Ko$^n$.

Skull devoid of flesh, Ni'kapa.

## MISCELLANEOUS TERMS USED BY THE OMAHA

### NATURAL OBJECTS AND PHENOMENA

Sky, Mo$^n$'xe.

Sun, Mi.

Moon, Nio$^n$'ba.

Stars, Mika'e.

North Star, Mika'emo$^n$thi$^n$azhi (*mikae*, star; *mo$^n$thi$^n$*, walk or move; *azhi*, not).

Pleiades.   This constellation bore the ancient name of Tapa' (deer's head), but this term, which had a religious significance, was not commonly used, the popular name being Mixaçi'zhi$^n$ga (little duck's foot).

Great Bear, Wa'baha, the litter.

The Morning or Evening Star, Mika'eto$^n$ga (big star).

Meteor, Mika'e uxpathe (stars fall).

Clouds, Mo$^n$xpi'.

Rain, No$^n$zhi$^n$'.

Mist, Shu'de mo$^n$ho$^n$ (smoke on the earth).

Hail, Ma'çi.

Snow, Ma.

Thunder, I$^n$gthu$^n$'huto$^n$ (*huto$^n$*, to cry; *i$^n$gthu$^n$* implies the idea of a creature similar to a bird).

Lightning, Thio$^n$'ba.

Rainbow, Tushni'ge.

Light, Ugo$^n$'ba.

Darkness, Uga'ho$^n$no$^n$paçe.

Night, Ho$^n$.

Day, O$^n$'ba.

Dawn, O$^n$'ba ço$^n$tihe (day lies pale).

Morning, Ho$^n$e'go$^n$che.

Noon, Mi'thumo$^n$shi (sun high).

Dusk, I$^n$de'ho$^n$no$^n$paçe (face hidden in darkness).

Evening, Pa'çe.

Water, Ni.

Ice, Nu'xe.

Wind, Tade'.

Fire, Pe'de.

Smoke, Shu'de.

Charcoal, No$^n$xthe'.

Ashes, Mo$^n$xu'de (gray earth).

Heat, Na'kade.

Cold, U'çni.

Earth, To$^n$'de.

Land, Mo$^n$zho$^n$.

Lake, Ne'uthesho$^n$.

River, Ni.

Creek, Wachi'shka.

### TASTE

Sweet, Çki'the.

Salt,
Sour,  } Ç'a'the.
Acid,

Stringent, T'u'xe.

Bitter, Pa.

Taste of nuts, $\left.\right\}$ No$^n$be.
Taste of fat,

Salt, the article, Niçki'the (sweet water).

## COLORS

White, Çka.
Pale, Ço$^n$.
Black, Ça'be.
Green, Tu.
Blue, Tu ça'be.
Yellow, Çi.
Red, Zhi'de.
Gray or Brown, Xu'de.

### POINTS OF THE COMPASS

North, Uçni'atathisho$^n$ (*uçni*, cold; *áta*, there; *thisho$^n$*, toward)—toward the cold.

East, Miuia'tathisho$^n$ (*mi*, sun; *ui*, it comes; *ata*, there; *thisho$^n$*, toward)—toward the coming of the sun.

South, Mo$^n$shtea'tathisho$^n$ (*mo$^n$shte*, heat; *ata*, there; *thisho$^n$*, toward)—toward the heat.

West, Mi'itheatathisho$^n$ (*mi*, sun; *ithe*, gone; *ata*, there; *thisho$^n$*, toward)—toward where the sun has gone.

Up (as when the pipes are pointed upward), Mo$^{n'}$xata (*mo$^n$xa*, sky; *ta, ata*, there).

Down (as when the pipes are pointed downward), To$^{n'}$deata (*to$^n$de*, earth; *ata*, there).

### DIVISIONS OF TIME

January, Ho$^{n'}$ga umubthi ike: When the snow drifts into the tents of the Ho$^{n'}$ga.
February, Mi'xa agthi ike: The moon when geese come home (come back).
March, Pe'nishka mieta ike: The little frog moon.
April, Miu'o$^n$thi$^n$ge ke: The moon in which nothing happens.
May, Mi waa' ike: The moon in which they (the tribe) plant.
June, Tenu'gamigauna ike: The buffalo bulls hunt the cows.
July, Tehu'ta$^n$ ike: When the buffalo bellow.
August, U$^{n'}$po$^n$huta$^n$ ike: When the elk bellow.
September, Ta'xte ma$^n$no$^n$xa ike: When the deer paw the earth.
October, Ta'xti kithixa ike: When the deer rut.
November, Ta'xte hebaxo$^{n'}$ ike: When the deer shed the antlers.
December, Waça'be zhi$^n$ga i'da ike: When the little black bears are born.

The Oto and Iowa tribes use the same names for the months except for January, which is called "the raccoon month."

The general name for month was "a moon."

The night, or sleeping time, marked the division of days, so a journey might be spoken of as having taken so many "sleeps." In like manner the year was spoken of as "a winter." The sun indicated the time of day: Sunrise, mi'etho$^n$be (*mi*, sun; *etho$^n$be*, to come out); sunset, mi'ethe (*mi*, sun; *ithe*, gone). A motion toward the zenith meant noon (mi'tho$^n$ mo$^n$shi—*mi*, sun; *tho$^n$*, round; *mo$^n$shi*, on high); midway between the zenith and the west, afternoon; and midway toward the east, forenoon. There were no smaller divisions of time among the Omaha.

## WEATHER SIGNS

The storm which usually precedes the coming of the new moon was called Mia'non_xthe, "the hiding of the moon" (the act of the storm).

Early in the month of February there is usually a severe storm, often a blizzard. This storm was called Mi'xa ikinon_xthe agthi ike, "the geese come home hidden by the storm." It is said that soon after this storm a few geese are seen, which are shortly followed by the flocks.

A ring around the moon is a sign of rain.

When the horns of the moon are turned upward, it is a sign that cold weather is coming.

When the fireflies swarm it will rain during the night.

When birds sing in the early morning the day will be clear.

A mist in the morning portends a hot day.

After a long rain, when the horses prick up their ears and play, it is known that the rain is over.

White spots on the nails betoken the approach of spring. If they come in summer it is because summer is here; if in winter, they indicate that spring will surely come, no matter how long or cold the season.

To break a moccasin string is a sign that summer is coming.

## SUMMARY

From the evidence afforded by the native names of animals and trees it would seem that the physical environment of the Omaha has not greatly varied in the course of the last few centuries; during that period the tribe does not appear to have experienced conditions that prevail in the extreme north or far to the southward, or that are peculiar to the region west of the Rocky Mountains. This seemingly persistent character of the Omaha surroundings made possible the development of the tribe along lines that led to substantial rather than to striking results.

During this period both the peaceful and the warlike relations of the Omaha were for the most part with tribes to which they were more or less closely related linguistically, tribes which presumably had many ideas and customs in common. There was, therefore, little in this contact likely to deflect the Omaha from their natural course of development. To this, however, their relations with the Arikara constituted an exception. This tribe belongs to the Caddoan, a southwestern stock, different from the Omaha in mental characteristics and in culture. From the Arikara the Omaha adopted the use of the earth lodge; it may be that contact with this tribe stimulated a general revival of the cultivation of the maize; and the knowledge of the Wawan ceremony was probably derived from the same source. While the Arikara exercised on the Omaha a somewhat stimulating influence, the contact does not seem to have had any vital effect on the development of the latter's tribal organization and government.

The character of the environmental conditions noted above seems reflected in the Sacred Legend, which preserves in fragmentary form the story of the people.   The value of this Legend is psychic rather than historic, for little is told in it that is definite as to movements or localities; it is singularly free from the mythic element; it contains no marvels, but reveals the mental atmosphere through which the people beheld their past achievements, and constitutes a narrative remarkably true to what seems to be the Omaha character, religious, thoughtful, and practical rather than imaginative and emotional.

The Omaha depended on their powers of observation and thought as the means by which they could better the conditions of their daily life and, as will be seen later, they utilized their observation of nature in forming their ethical code.   The character of the people is indicated in their names for living forms and for natural phenomena; these show how the Omaha looked on their environment and differentiated what they saw and experienced.   The influence of hunting is detected in the familiarity displayed with the anatomy of the larger animals, a knowledge which, as has been seen, the Omaha applied to the human form.   Some of the terms, as those designating parts of the human face, the corners of the mouth, the depression on the forehead, indicate close observation.   In color perception the Omaha seem to be of somewhat limited capacity, as is true also of the sensation of taste, but there is a noteworthy appreciation of the gradation of light in the coming and the going of the day.   The names of the months and of the points of the compass are not fanciful or symbolic but express the results of practical observations or experiences. All the names bear out the sober-minded, self-contained character indicated in the Sacred Legend and add to its value in helping toward an understanding of the tribe.

The map of the Omaha country (pl. 21) presents the region with which the people have been familiar from the sixteenth century to the present, and such historic data have been given as may throw light on the movements of the tribe during that period.   The steady westward advance of the white settlements from their beginnings on the Atlantic coast, together with the consequent contentions with the tribes native to that region, pressed the eastern tribes back on their western neighbors, creating disturbances whose effects traveled westward and were felt by all the people dwelling on and beyond the Lakes and the Mississippi, forcing many tribes through influences they did not understand or recognize to move westward.   The Omaha could not escape the effect of this general disturbance, although they did not become embroiled in wars between the Indians and the white people dwelling to the eastward of them.

The Omaha did not come into contact with the white people as early as did some of their cognates. They do not seem to have felt the influence of the Spanish from the southwest, although late indirect effects were transmitted through the Comanche and the Pawnee. French influence did not reach the Omaha from the south, but came from the north through Canadian traders. The French were the first white men to become personally known to the Omaha, but they did not reach the tribe until well into the eighteenth century. The English followed the French and exerted a more powerful and disturbing influence on the social life of the people. Finally the American came and remained.

A general view of the Omaha environment during recent centuries makes apparent certain limitations, and it can hardly be questioned that these limitations must have exercised an influence not only on the direction but also on the manner in which the people evolved their social and religious life. Indeed the Omaha seem to have been exempt to a remarkable degree from strong foreign control and to have developed their tribal organization in comparative isolation. Consequently they were able to preserve their type, a circumstance which adds to the value and interest of the tribe as a study.

# III

## RITES PERTAINING TO THE INDIVIDUAL

### INTRODUCTION OF THE OMAHA CHILD TO THE COSMOS

When a child was born it was not regarded as a member of its gens or of the tribe but simply as a living being coming forth into the universe, whose advent must be ceremonially announced in order to assure it an accepted place among the already existing forms. This ceremonial announcement took the form of an expression of the Omaha belief in the oneness of the universe through the bond of a common life-power that pervaded all things in nature animate and inanimate.

Although in the Teçin'de and Inshta'çunda gentes the custom survived of placing on the child, the fourth day after birth, certain symbols pertaining to the peculiar rites of those gentes, these acts did not serve the purpose of introducing the child into the teeming life of the universe. This ceremony of introduction took place on the eighth day after birth. Unfortunately the full details of the ceremony have been lost through the death of the priests who had charge of it. The hereditary right to perform the ceremony belonged in the Washe'ton subgens of the Inshta'çunda gens. (See meaning of the term *Washe'-ton*, p. 186.)

On the appointed day the priest was sent for. When he arrived he took his place at the door of the tent in which the child lay and raising his right hand to the sky, palm outward, he intoned the following in a loud, ringing voice:

Ho! Ye Sun, Moon, Stars, all ye that move in the heavens,
  I bid you hear me!
Into your midst has come a new life.
  Consent ye, I implore!
Make its path smooth, that it may reach the brow of the first hill!

Ho! Ye Winds, Clouds, Rain, Mist, all ye that move in the air,
  I bid you hear me!
Into your midst has come a new life.
  Consent ye, I implore!
Make its path smooth, that it may reach the brow of the second hill!

Ho! Ye Hills, Valleys, Rivers, Lakes, Trees, Grasses, all ye of the earth,
  I bid you hear me!

115

Into your midst has come a new life.
Consent ye, I implore!
Make its path smooth, that it may reach the brow of the third hill!
Ho!  Ye Birds, great and small, that fly in the air,
Ho!  Ye Animals, great and small, that dwell in the forest,
Ho!  Ye insects that creep among the grasses and burrow in the ground—
I bid you hear me!
Into your midst has come a new life.
Consent ye, I implore!
Make its path smooth, that it may reach the brow of the fourth hill!

Ho!  All ye of the heavens, all ye of the air, all ye of the earth:
I bid you all to hear me!
Into your midst has come a new life.
Consent ye, consent ye all, I implore!
Make its path smooth—then shall it travel beyond the four hills!

This ritual was a supplication to the powers of the heavens, the air, and the earth for the safety of the child from birth to old age. In it the life of the infant is pictured as about to travel a rugged road stretching over four hills, marking the stages of infancy, youth, manhood, and old age.

The ceremony which finds oral expression in this ritual voices in no uncertain manner the Omaha belief in man's relation to the visible powers of the heavens and in the interdependence of all forms of life.  The appeal bears evidence of its antiquity, breathing of a time antedating established rites and ceremonies.  It expresses the emotions of the human soul, touched with the love of offspring, alone with the might of nature, and companioned only by the living creatures whose friendliness must be sought if life is to be secure on its journey.

The cognate tribes[a] had ceremonies similar in purport although differing in details.  Among the Omaha no further ceremony took place in reference to the child in its relation to the cosmos, to its gens, or to the tribe, until it was able to walk.  When the period arrived at which the child could walk steadily by itself, the time was at hand when it must be introduced into the tribe.  This was done ceremonially.

---

[a] Among the Osage, on the birth of a child "a man who had talked with the gods" was sent for.  On his arrival he recited to the infant the story of the Creation and of the animals that move on the earth. Then, after placing the tip of his finger on the mother's nipple, he pressed that finger on the lips of the child, after which he passed his hands over the body of the child.  Then the infant was allowed to take nourishment.  Later, when the child desired to drink water the same or a like man was sent for.  Again the ritual of the Creation was recited, and the beginning of water was told.  The man then dipped the tip of his finger into water and laid it on the lips of the child and passed his hands over its body from head to foot.  After this ceremony the child could be given water to drink.  When the child reached the age when it needed or desired solid food, the same man or one of his class was again sent for.  Once more the Creation story was recited and the gift of corn and other food was recounted.  At the close the man placed the tip of his finger upon the food prepared for the child and then laid this finger on the lips of the child, after which he passed his hands over its body.  This ceremony prepared the child to receive solid food.  Fees were given to the man who performed these rites.

## Introduction of the Child into the Tribe

### Ceremony of Turning the Child

The name of this ceremony was Thiku'wi$^n$xe (*thi*, a prefix indicating action by the hand; *ku'wi$^n$xe*, "to turn"). Although the child is not mentioned, it is understoed as being referred to. The translation of the term, therefore, would be "turning the child."

All children, both boys and girls, passed through this ceremony, which is a survival of that class of ceremonies belonging to the lowest, or oldest, stratum of tribal rites; it is directly related to the cosmic forces—the wind, the earth, and the fire. Through this ceremony all the children who had reached the period when they could move about unaided, could direct their own steps, were symbolically "sent into the midst of the winds"—that element essential to life and health; their feet were set upon the stone—emblem of long life upon the earth and of the wisdom derived from age; while the "flames," typical of the life-giving power, were invoked to give their aid toward insuring the capacity for a long, fruitful, and successful life within the tribe. Through this ceremony the child passed out of that stage in its life wherein it was hardly distinguished from all other living forms into its place as distinctively a human being, a member of its birth gens, and through this to a recognized place in the tribe. As it went forth its baby name was thrown away, its feet were clad in new moccasins made after the manner of the tribe, and its *ni'kie* name (see p. 136) was proclaimed to all nature and to the assembled people.

The significance of the new moccasins put on the child will appear more clearly by the light of the following custom, still observed in families in which all the old traditions of the tribe are conserved: When moccasins are made for a little baby, a small hole is cut in the sole of one. This is done in order that "if a messenger from the spirit world should come and say to the child, 'I have come for you,' the child could answer, 'I can not go on a journey—my moccasins are worn out!'" A similar custom obtains in the Oto tribe. A little hole is cut in the first pair of moccasins made for a child. When the relatives come to see the little one they examine the moccasins, and, seeing the hole, they say: "Why, he (or she) has worn out his moccasins; he has traveled over the earth!" This is an indirect prayer that the child may live long. The new (whole) moccasins put on the child at the close of the ceremony of introducing it into the tribe constitute an assurance that it is prepared for the journey of life and that the journey will be a long one.

The ceremony of Turning the Child took place in the springtime, after the first thunders had been heard. When the grass was well up and the birds were singing, "particularly the meadow lark," the tribal herald proclaimed that the time for these ceremonies had come. A tent was set up for the purpose, made *xube*, or sacred, and the keeper of these rites, who belonged to the Washe'to$^n$ subgens of the I$^n$shta'çu$^n$da gens, made himself ready and entered the tent. Meanwhile the parents whose children had arrived at the proper age, that is, could walk steadily unassisted, took their little ones and proceeded to the Sacred Tent. The only requisite for the child was a pair of new moccasins, but large fees were given to the priest for his services.

Only parts of the ritual belonging to this ceremony have been obtained. Those whose prerogative it was to conduct the rites are all dead, and with them knowledge of much of the ceremony passed away. The preservation of the fragments here given came about thus: An old and trusted friend of Joseph La Flesche, a former principal chief of the tribe, was greatly interested when a boy, in the tribal rites. One of his near kinsmen was a priest of this rite. When the Sacred Tent was set up this boy more than once succeeded in secreting himself behind packs within and from his hiding place was able to observe what took place. Having a retentive memory and a quick ear for song, he was able to learn and remember the six songs here given. Subsequent inquiries have added somewhat to the knowledge secured from this informant, although, so far as the writers have been able to ascertain, no one seems ever to have obtained quite so close an inside view of the entire ceremony as this inquisitive boy. Of course no one who had passed through the ceremony could accurately remember it, as the child was generally only 3 or 4 years of age at the time it had a part in the rite.

The tent was always a large one, set facing the east, and open at the entrance, so that the bystanders, who kept at a respectful distance, could see something of what was going on within. As the ceremony was one of tribal interest, many flocked to the Sacred Tent to watch the proceedings. In the center was a fire. On the east of the fire was placed a stone. There was also a ball of grass, placed at the west of the fire-place near its edge. It was the mother who led the child to the tent. At the door she paused, and addressed the priest within, saying: "Venerable man! I desire my child to wear moccasins." Then she dropped the hand of the child, and the little one, carrying his new moccasins, entered the tent alone. He was met by the priest, who advanced to the door to receive the gifts brought by the mother as fees. Here she again addressed him, saying: "I desire my child to walk long upon the earth; I desire him to be content with the light of many days. We seek your protection; we hold to you for strength." The priest replied, addressing the child: "You shall reach the fourth hill sighing; you shall be bowed over; you shall have wrinkles; your staff shall bend under your weight. I speak to you that you may be strong." Laying his hand on the shoulder of the child, he added: "What you have brought me shall not be lost to you; you shall live long and enjoy many possessions; your eyes shall be satisfied with many good things." Then, moving with the child toward the fireplace in the center of the lodge, and speaking in the capacity of the Thunder, whose priest he was, he uttered these words: "I am a powerful being; I breathe from my lips over you." Then he began to sing the Invocation addressed to the Winds:

Du - ba ha ti non - zhin ga     She - non - zhin  ga........

Du - ba - ha   ti........................     non  zhin   ga.........

She  non- zhin   ga......     She  non-zhin   ga......     In   In

Duba ha ti nonzhin ga she nonzhin ga
Duba ha ti nonzhin ga
She nonzhin ga!  She nonzhin ga
In In

Literal translation: *Duba*, four; *ha* signifies that the number four refers to groups; *ti*, from *ati*, come ye; *nonzhin*, stand; *a*, from *iga*, word of command given to a number; *she*, from *shethu*, a definite place near by; *ga*, a command, and end of the sentence; *In*, the rolling thunder. The "four" refers to the four winds, to which the invocation is addressed by the Thunder priest.

*Free translation*

Ye four, come hither and stand, near shall ye stand
In four groups shall ye stand
Here shall ye stand, in this place stand
(The Thunder rolls)

The music of this invocation is in the five-toned scale. The voice dwells on the words *ti*, "come," and *she*, "near in this place." The roll of the Thunder is given in the relative minor.

At the close of this ritual song the priest faces the child to the east, lifting it by the shoulders; its feet are allowed to rest upon the stone. He then turns the child completely around, from left to right. If by any chance the child should struggle or move so as to turn from right to left the onlookers set up a cry of alarm. It was considered very disastrous to turn ever so little in the wrong way, so the priest was most careful to prevent any accident. When the child had been turned, its feet rested on the stone as it faced the south. The priest then lifted it by the arms, turned it, and set its feet on the stone as it faced the west; then he again lifted the child, turned it, and set its feet on the stone as it faced the north. Lastly the child was lifted to its feet and placed on the stone as it again faced the east. During this action the following ritual song was sung:

She gakuwi$^n$xe akithe tha
She gakuwi$^n$xe akithe tha
Baxu duba ha te tade duba ha te
Tade baço$^n$ the akithe tha
Tade duba ha te
I$^n$ I$^n$

Literal translation: *She*, from *shethi$^n$*, going yonder, implies a person speaking; *ga*, to strike by the wind; *kuwi$^n$xe*, to whirl; *tha*, oratorical end of the sentence; *baxu*, ridge or hill; *duba*, four; *ha*, groups; *te*, descriptive suffix indicating standing; *baço$^n$*, in the midst; *the*, goes (third person); *akithe*, I cause him; *tha*, end of sentence; *tade*, winds; *duba*, four; *ha*, groups; *te*, standing; *I$^n$*, rolling of the Thunder.

### Free translation

Turned by the winds goes the one I send yonder;
Yonder he goes who is whirled by the winds;
Goes, where the four hills of life and the four winds are standing;
There, in the midst of the winds do I send him,
Into the midst of the winds, standing there.
(The Thunder rolls)

The winds invoked by the priest stand in four groups, and receive the child, which is whirled by them, and by them enabled "to face in every direction." This action symbolizes that the winds will come and strengthen him as hereafter he shall traverse the earth and meet the vicissitudes he must encounter as he passes over the four hills and completes the circuit of a long life. It was believed that this ceremony exercised a marked influence on the child, and enabled it to grow in strength and in the ability to practise self-control.

The priest now put the new moccasins on the feet of the child, as the following ritual song was sung. Toward its close the child was lifted, set on its feet, and made to take four steps typical of its entrance into a long life.

Shethu te thon ie winthake
Shethu te thon ie winthake
Hede winthake nonzhin ga
Ie te winthake
Shethu te thon ie winthake
Hede winthake nonzhinga
In In.

Literal translation: *Shethu,* a place near, also a time; *te* refers to action or occurrence, in this instance to the ceremony; *thon,* round place, refers both to the lodge and to the *hu'thuga; ie,* words, declaration; *winthake,* truth (to you) (*winke,* truth; *tha,* to you); *hede,* in consequence of, therefore, because (old term); *nonzhin,* arise, stand; *ga,* the sign of command; *in,* the rolling of thunder.

### Free translation

Here unto you has been spoken the truth;
Because of this truth you shall stand.
Here, declared is the truth.
Here in this place has been shown you the truth.
Therefore, arise! go forth in its strength!
(The thunder rolls)

The *ni'kie* name of the child was now announced, after which the priest cried aloud: "Ye hills, ye grass, ye trees, ye creeping things both great and small, I bid you hear! This child has thrown away its baby name. Ho!" (a call to take notice).

The priest next instructed the child as to the tabu it must observe, and what would be the penalty for disobedience. If the child was a girl, she now passed out of the tent and rejoined her mother.

Up to this point the ceremony of introducing the child into the tribe was the same for male and female; but in the case of boys there was a supplemental rite which pertained to them as future warriors.

### CONSECRATION OF THE BOY TO THUNDER

This ceremony was called We'bashna, meaning "to cut the hair." According to traditions, this specialized ceremony belonged to the period in the growth of the political development of the tribe when efforts were being made to hold the tribe more firmly together by checking the independence of the warriors and placing them under control—efforts that finally resulted in the placing of the rites of war in charge of the We'zhi$^n$shte gens.

In the ceremony of cutting the hair the priest in charge gathered a tuft from the crown of the boy's head, tied it, then cut it off and laid it away in a parfleche case, which was kept as a sacred repository, singing as he cut the lock a ritual song explanatory of the action. The severing of the lock was an act that implied the consecration of the life of the boy to Thunder, the symbol of the power that controlled the life and death of the warrior—for every man had to be a warrior in order to defend the home and the tribe. The ritual song which followed the cutting of the lock indicated the acceptance of the offering made; that is, the life of the warrior henceforth was under the control of the Thunder to prolong or to cut short at will.

The Washe'to$^n$ subgens, which had charge of this rite of the consecration of the boy to the Thunder as the god of war, camped at the end of the I$^n$shta'çu$^n$da division, and formed the northern side of the entrance into the hu'thuga when the opening faced the east; while the We'zhi$^n$shte gens, which had charge of the rites pertaining to war, including the bestowal of honors, formed the southern side of the entrance. Thus the "door," through which all must pass who would enter the hu'thuga (see p. 138), was guarded on each side by gentes having charge of rites pertaining to Thunder, as the god of war, the power that could not only hold in check enemies from without, but which met each man child at his entrance into the tribe and controlled him even to the hour of his death.

In a community beginning to crystallize into organized social relations the sphere of the warrior would naturally rise above that of the mere fighter; and when the belief of the people concerning nature is taken into consideration it is not surprising that the movement toward social organization should tend to place the warriors—the men of power—in close relation to those natural manifestations of power seen in the fury of the storm and heard in the rolling of the thunder. Moreover, in the efforts toward political unification such rites as those which were connected with the Thunder would conduce to the welding of the people by the inculcation of a common dependence upon a powerful god and the sign of consecration to him would be put upon the head of every male member of the tribe.

The priest took the boy to the space west of the fire; there, facing the east, he cut a lock of hair from the crown of the boy's head, as he sang the following ritual song:

Tigonha monshia ta ha
Shabe tithe nonzhia ha
Tigonha monshia ta ha
Shabe tithe nonzhia shethu aha
Tigonha monshia ta ha
Shabe tithe nonzhia
Tigonha monshia ta ha
Shabe tithe nonzhia ha shethu aha
Tigonha monshia ta ha
Shabe tithe nonzhia ha

Literal translation: *Tigonha*, grandfather—a form of respect used when addressing the person of power; *monshia*, far above, on high; *ta*, from *shiata*, there, used to express an indefinite place; *ha*, end of sentence; *shabe*, dark, like a shadow; *tithe*, passing before one; *nonzhia*, human hair; *shethu*, there in your direction, as toward the one addressed; *aha*, in the midst of.

*Free translation*

Grandfather! far above on high,
The hair like a shadow passes before you.
Grandfather! far above on high,
Dark like a shadow the hair sweeps before you into the midst of your realm.
Grandfather! there above, on high,
Dark like a shadow the hair passes before you.
Grandfather! dwelling afar on high,
Like a dark shadow the hair sweeps before you into the midst of your realm.
Grandfather! far above on high,
The hair like a shadow passes before you.

From this ritual song we learn that the lock laid away in the sacred case in care of the Thunder priest symbolically was sent to the Thunder god dwelling "far above on high," who was ceremonially addressed as "Grandfather"—the term of highest respect in the language. The hair of a person was popularly believed to have a vital connection with the life of the body, so that anyone becoming possessed of a lock of hair might work his will on the individual from whom it came. In ceremonial expressions of grief the throwing of locks of hair upon the dead was indicative of the vital loss sustained. In the light of customs that obtained among the people the hair, under certain conditions, might be said to typify life. Because of the belief in the continuity of life a part could stand for the whole, so in this rite by the cutting off of a lock of the boy's hair and giving it to the Thunder the life of the child was given into the keeping of the god. It is to be noted that later, when the hair was suffered to grow on the boy's head, a lock on the crown of the head was parted in a circle from the rest of the hair and kept constantly distinct and neatly braided. Upon this lock the war honors of the warrior were worn, and it was this lock that was cut from the head of a slain enemy and formed the central object in the triumph ceremonies, for the reason that it preeminently represented the life of the man who had been slain in battle.

In the next ritual song the Thunder god speaks and proclaims his acceptance of the consecration of the life through the lock of hair and also declares his control over the life of the warrior.

(Sung in octaves)

She-thu pi-tho$^n$- di he    Ni- ka wi$^n$ go$^n$ - ke a - the

She- thu pi- tho$^n$ - di    Ni- ka - wi$^n$ go$^n$    ke a-the

She-thu pi-tho$^n$ - di he    Ni-ka-wi$^n$ sha-be    ke a - the he

She thu pi-tho$^n$ di    Ni - ka - wi$^n$ go$^n$ - ke a - the

She-thu pi-tho$^n$ - di he    Ni-ka- wi$^n$ zhi-de    ke a - the he

She- thu pi - tho$^n$ - di    Ni - ka - wi$^n$ go$^n$ - ke a- the

Shethu pi tho$^n$di he
Nika wi$^n$ go$^n$ke athe
Shethu pi tho$^n$di
Nika wi$^n$ go$^n$ke athe
Shethu pi tho$^n$di he
Nika wi$^n$ shabe ke athe he
Shethu pi tho$^n$di
Nika wi$^n$ go$^n$ke athe
Shethu pi tho$^n$di he
Nika wi$^n$  zhide ke athe he
Shethu pi tho$^n$di
Nika wi$^n$ go$^n$ke athe

Literal translation: *Shethu,* there; *pi,* I have been; *tho$^n$di,* when; *he,* end of the sentence and vowel prolongation; *nika,* man; *wi$^n$,* a or one; *go$^n$ke,* a peculiar exclamatory expression indicating the action of coming suddenly on a fearful or startling object; *athe,* I cause, used only in reference to inanimate things and intended here to convey the idea that man has no power to act independently of the gods; *shabe*, dark, like a shadow; *ke* indicates that the object is long and is lying down; *zhide*, red.

*Free translation*

What time I will, then only then,
A man lies dead, a gruesome thing.
What time I will, then suddenly
A man lies dead, a gruesome thing.
What time I will, then, only then,
Like a shadow dark the man shall lie.
What time I will, then suddenly
A man lies dead, a gruesome thing.
What time I will, then, only then,
Reddened and stark a man lies dead.
What time I will, then suddenly
A man lies dead, a gruesome thing.

The word *shabe*, dark like a shadow, is used in the preceding song to describe the lock of hair that was cut from the child's head as a symbol that his life was offered to the god; in this song the same word, *shabe*, is applied to the man who, "like a shadow dark," "shall lie" when his life has been taken by the god. The use of this word bears out the meaning of the rite that accompanied the preceding song, that by the giving of the lock of hair the life of the person was given to the god. This song shows that the god intends to do as he wills with that life. There are other songs used in the tribe which iterate this belief that a man dies only when the gods decree.

The music is in the five-tone scale, and the phrase which carries the assertion of the god rises and dwells on the tonic, a movement rare in Omaha songs, the general trend being from higher to lower tones.

The imperfect account of this ritual makes it impossible to state whether or not the six songs here given were all that belonged to this ceremony. It is also uncertain whether or not the invocation to the winds was sung before the turning of every child; it may have been sung only once, at the opening of the general ceremony, there being indications that such was the case. It is probable that the song given below was also sung but once, at the close of the general ceremony, but it has been impossible to obtain accurate information on this point. Only one point is certain—that the following was the final song of the ceremony:

(Sung in octaves)

Ku-the goⁿ di iⁿ-gi-be   he   nax   thiⁿ ba   nax thiⁿ ba   ha

Pe- de zhi-de na-ka - de......   nax   thiⁿ ba   nax thiⁿ ba   ha !

Ku - the   goⁿ - di   iⁿ - gi be   he   nax   thiⁿ   ba

nax   thiⁿ   ba   ha !   Pe - de   zhi - de   na - ka   de.........

nax   thiⁿ ha   nax thiⁿ ba   ha !   Ku-the goⁿ-di   iⁿ - gi be.........he

Kuthe goⁿ di iⁿgi be he
Naxthiⁿ ba naxthiⁿ ba ha
Pede zhide nakade
Naxthiⁿ ba naxthiⁿ ba ha
Kuthe goⁿ di iⁿgi be he
Naxthiⁿ ba naxthiⁿ ba ha
Pede zhide nakade·
Naxthiⁿ ba naxthiⁿ ba ha
Kuthe goⁿ di iⁿgi be he

Literal translation: *Kuthe*, hasten; *goⁿ*, suddenly; *di*, here, hither; *iⁿgi*, to ask help, assistance; *be*, sign of the plural; *naxthiⁿ*, flame; *ba*, sign of the plural; *ha*, the end of the sentence; *pede*, fire; *zhide*, red; *nakade*, hot.

*Free translation*

Come hither, haste to help me,
Ye flames, ye flames, O come!
O red-hot fire, hasten!
O haste, ye flames, to come.
Come speedily to help me,
Ye flames, ye flames, O come!
O red-hot fire, hasten!
O haste, ye flames, to come!
Come hither, haste, to help me!

As this song was sung the ball of grass to which reference has already been made was held aloft and then hurled to the ground, where it mysteriously burst into flames, which were regarded as symbolizing the lightning.

In this closing song there is a return to the cosmic forces which were appealed to and represented in the ceremony of Turning the Child. In early times before this ceremony had been arranged so as to include the rite of consecrating the boy to the Thunder god, the song which appears on the preceding page was sung probably soon after, if not immediately at the conclusion of, the third song given in this account.

At the conclusion of this tribal ceremony, when the child reached its home the father cut the hair of his son after the symbolic manner of his gens;[a] the hair was thus worn until the second dentition. Then the hair was allowed to grow, and the scalp lock, the sign of the warrior to which reference has already been made was parted off and kept carefully braided, no matter how frowzy and tangled the rest of the hair might be.

## CEREMONIAL INTRODUCTION TO INDIVIDUAL LIFE AND TO THE SUPERNATURAL

The next stage in the life of the Omaha youth was marked by the rite known by the name of Non'zhinzhon. The literal meaning of the word is "to stand sleeping;" it here implies that during the rite the person stands as if oblivious of the outward world and conscious only of what transpires within himself, his own mind. This rite took place at puberty, when the mind of the child had "become white." This characterization was drawn from the passing of night into day. It should be remembered that in native symbolism night is the mother of day; so the mind of the new-born child is dark, like the night of its birth; gradually it begins to discern and remember things as objects seen in the early dawn; finally it is able to remember and observe discriminatingly; then its mind is said to be "white," as with the clear light of day. At the period when the youth is at the verge of his conscious individual life, is "old enough to know sorrow," it was considered time that through the rite Non'zhinzhon he should enter into personal relations with the mysterious power that permeates and controls all nature as well as his own existence.

In the Sacred Legend, which recounts briefly the history of the people and from which quotations have been made, the origin of this rite is thus given:

The people felt themselves weak and poor. Then the old men gathered together and said: "Let us make our children cry to Wakon'da that he may give us strength." So all the parents took their children who were old enough to pray in earnest, put soft clay on their faces, and sent them forth to lonely places. The old men said to the youths: "You shall go forth to cry to Wakon'da. When on the hills you shall not ask for any particular thing. The answer may not come to you as you expect;

---

[a] The various styles of cutting the child's hair to symbolize the tabu of his gens are shown with the account given of the gentes (pp. 144-188).

whatever is good, that may Wako$^{n\prime}$da give." Four days upon the hills shall the youths pray, crying. When they stop, they shall wipe their tears with the palms of their hands and lift their wet hands to the sky, then lay them to the earth. This was the people's first appeal to Wako$^{n\prime}$da.

The closing statement as to "the first appeal" should not be taken literally, for the rite thus said to have been introduced is too complex, and embodies beliefs that must have required a long time for formulation into the dramatic forms observed in this rite.

The old men, when explaining the rite, said "It must be observed by all youths. After the first time, the youth could repeat the rite until he was old enough to marry and had children; by that time his life was fixed, and he prayed no more unless he was a priest, then he would continue to fast and pray." "In the No$^{n\prime}$zhi$^{n}$zho$^{n}$," it was further explained, "the appeal was to Wako$^{n}$'da, the great power. There were other powers—the sun, the stars, the moon, the earth— but these were lesser; the prayer was not to them." The old men added: "The appeal was for help throughout life. As the youth goes forth to fast he thinks of a happy life, good health, success in hunting; in war he desires to secure spoils and escape the enemy; if he should be attacked that the weapons of his adversaries might fail to injure him. Such were the thoughts and hopes of the youth when he entered upon this fast, although he was forbidden to ask for any special favor." The rite No$^{n\prime}$zhi$^{n}$zho$^{n}$ was observed in the spring; never in the summer or winter. The meaning of putting clay on the head has been explained in different ways. Some have said it symbolized humility; others that it referred to the soft clay or mud brought up by the diving animals, out of which the earth was created. In the opinion of the writers the latter seems the more probable explanation.

In preparation the youth was taught the following prayer, which was to be sung during the ordeal of the fast. It was known to every youth in the tribe, no matter what his gens.[a] This prayer must be accepted, therefore, as voicing a fundamental belief of the entire Omaha tribe. The music is in keeping with the words, being unmistakably an earnest invocation.

---

[a] Every male was obliged to pass through the rite of No$^{n}$'zhi$^{n}$zho$^{n}$ when he reached the proper age; whether he should continue to practise the rite was left to his personal choice. The No$^{n\prime}$zhi$^{n}$zho$^{n}$ was not obligatory on girls or women but they sometimes went through the fast, for the rite was open to them

### OMAHA PRAYER[a]

Harmonized by John C. Fillmore for interpretation on the piano

Wakoⁿda thethu wahpathiⁿ atoⁿhe
Wakoⁿda thethu wahpathiⁿ atoⁿhe

Literal translation: *Wakoⁿda*, the permeating life of nature and of man, the great mysterious power; *thethu*, here; *wahpathiⁿ*, poor, needy; *atoⁿhe*, he stands, and I am he—a form of expression used to indicate humility. *Wakoⁿda!* here, needy, he stands, and I am he.

This prayer was called *Wakoⁿ'da gikoⁿ* (*gigikoⁿ*, "to weep from loss," as that of kindred, the prefix *gi* indicating possession; *gikoⁿ*, therefore, is to weep from the want of something not possessed, from conscious insufficiency and the desire for something that could bring happiness or prosperity). This prayer and the aspect of the suppliant, standing alone in the solitary place, with clay on his head, tears falling from his eyes, and his hands lifted in supplication, were based on anthropomorphic ideas concerning Wakoⁿ'da. The Omaha conceived that the appeal from one so young and untried, who showed poverty and the need of help, could not fail to move the power thus appealed to, even as a man so importuned would render the aid that was asked. The words of the prayer set forth the belief that Wakoⁿ'da was able to understand and to respond to the one who thus voiced his consciousness of dependence and his craving for help from a power higher than himself.

---

[a] The upper line gives the aria as sung; the two lines below translate the aria; so that when played on an instrument like the piano the meaning and feeling of the song become intelligible to us. This translation has the approval of the Indians.

Four days and nights the youth was to fast and pray provided he was physically able to bear so long a strain. No matter how hungry he became, he was forbidden to use the bow and arrows put into his hands by his father when he left his home for this solitary test of endurance. When he fell into a sleep or a trance, if he saw or heard anything, that thing was to become a special medium through which the youth could receive supernatural aid. Generally with the sight of the thing came an accompanying cadence. This cadence was the song or call by which the man might summon aid in his time of need. The form, animate or inanimate, which appeared to the man was drawn toward him, it was believed, by the feeling of pity. The term used to express this impelling of the form to the man was *i'thaethe*, meaning "to have compassion on." If the youth at this time saw a buffalo, it would be said: *Te i'thaethe*, "the buffalo had compassion on him;" if he heard the thunder: *I$^n$gthu$^{n'}$ ithaethe*, "the thunder had compassion." The vision, with its sacred call or song, was the one thing that the Omaha held as his own, incapable of loss so long as life and memory lasted. It was his personal connection with the vast universe, by which he could strengthen his spirit and his physical powers. He never gave the details of his vision to anyone, nor was it even casually spoken of; it was too sacred for ordinary speech.

When going forth to fast, the youth went silently and unobserved. No one accosted him or gave him counsel or direction. He passed through his experience alone, and alone he returned to his father's lodge. No one asked him of his absence, or even mentioned the fact that he had been away. For four days he must rest, eat little, and speak little. After that period he might go to an old and worthy man who was known to have had a similar vision. After eating and smoking with the old man, when they were quite alone it was permitted the youth to mention that he had had a vision like that of his host, of beast, or bird, or whatever it might have been. Should he speak of his vision before the expiration of the four days, it would be the same as lost to him. After the youth had spoken to the old man it became his duty to travel until he should meet the animal or bird seen in his vision, when he had to slay it, and preserve either the whole or a part of its body. This trophy became the visible sign of his vision and the most sacred of his possessions. He might wear it on his scalp lock or elsewhere on his person during sacred festivals, when going to war, or on some other important occasions. This article has been spoken of by some writers as the man's "personal totem." When the vision came in the form of a cloud or the sound of the thunder, these were symbolized by certain objects or were typified in designs painted on the man or on his belongings.

Some visions were regarded as "lucky," as giving special and helpful advantages to the man. Hawks were "lucky"—they helped to success and prowess in war. Bears, being slow and clumsy, were "not so good," although possessing great recuperative power. The elk was fleet. Snakes were "not good," etc. To dream of the moon might bring a great calamity. It is said that the moon would appear to a man having in one hand a burden strap, in the other a bow and arrows, and the man would be bidden to make a choice. When he reached for the bow, the moon would cross its hands and try to force the strap on the man. If he awaked before he took the strap, or if he succeeded in capturing the bow, he escaped the penalty of the dream. If, on the other hand, he failed and the strap came into his hand, he was doomed to forfeit his manhood and become like a woman. He must speak as a woman, pursue her avocations, adopt her dress, and sometimes become subject to gross actions. It is said that there have been those who, having dreamed of the moon and having had the burden strap forced on them, have tried to conceal their ill luck for a time, but that few have succeeded. Instances are known in which the unfortunate dreamer, even with the help of his parents, could not ward off the evil influence of the dream, and resorted to suicide as the only means of escape.

The following stories of Osage men who through dreams became as women were given by Black Dog in 1898:

Men who become as women are called Mixu'ga (mi, "moon"; xu'ga, "to instruct"—"instructed by the moon"). The young men who go to fast sometimes remain out many days. This is done to secure dreams or visions which will support them in manly enterprises, in war or in hunting—that is, give them strength. But sometimes it happens that a young man has dreams or sees visions which make him imagine that he is a woman. From that time he takes upon himself the dress and occupations of a woman. He lets his hair grow, parts it in the middle, and wears braids. From days beyond the memory of man the Osage men shaved the head, leaving a roach on the top. Only the women wore the hair long and parted it in the middle. Now many of the Osage men wear the hair long and parted in the middle, in imitation of the Ponca, who, I think, took the fashion from the Sioux.

Once a young man went to fast, and was gone many days. He started home, not having had any dreams or visions, and on his way home he met a matronly woman who addressed him as "daughter." She said to the young man: "You are my daughter, and you shall be as I am. I give to you this hoe. With it you shall cultivate the ground, raise corn, beans, and squash, and you shall be skillful in braiding buffalo hair and in embroidering moccasins, leggings, and robes." In speaking to the woman the young man discovered that he had been unconsciously using the feminine terminals of speech. He tried to recover himself and use the speech of man, but he failed. On his return to his people he dressed himself as a woman, and took upon himself the avocations of a woman.

A young man went to fast, and was gone many days. On his way home he came to an earth lodge and entered. There were four men in the lodge, who greeted him very cordially and assigned to him the usual place of a guest. The young man looked about the lodge and saw hung upon the posts bows and arrows, shields and spears. Food was prepared for him, and he ate with the strangers. When he had finished his visit he thanked these people and started to go out. As he was about to pass the doorway he was halted and his attention was directed to two objects which hung one on each side of the door. One was a spear and the other a battle-ax. The young man was told to take his choice. He was long in choosing. The battle-ax is considered the manliest of weapons. This the young man remembered, and he finally chose that weapon, took it down, and departed.   On his way to his village he planned in his mind war excursions, and thought how he would conduct himself in battles. When he was nearing the village he desired to look once more at his battle-ax.   He did so, and, and, behold, it had turned into a hoe!   When he arrived home he became as a woman.

There was a young man who had been out to fast many times.   He had dreams which he thought were the kind that would make of him a man of valor.   He went on the warpath and took with him a number of followers.   They found the enemy, defeated them, and returned with many trophies.   On the way home he got up a dance one night in honor of his victory.   As he was dancing, brandishing his weapons and praising himself, an owl hooted near-by in the woods, and after each hooting the owl would say: "The leader is a *mixu'ga!*"   The people listened in amazement, and at last the leader cried: "I have done that which a *mixu'ga* could never do!"   However, on reaching his home the young leader dressed as a woman and spoke as a woman. He married and had children.   He was successful as a warrior, but when about to go to war he discarded his woman's clothing and dressed himself as a man.

Among the Omaha, as well as their cognates, there were societies whose membership was made up of men who had had visions of the same object. It has already been mentioned that the object seen in the vision was said to have had compassion on the man when it appeared to him. It was also thought that because the same form could come to certain men and be seen by them there was something in common in the nature of these men—that a sort of brotherhood existed among them. Out of this belief societies grew up based on the members having had similar visions, and the ceremonies of these societies, quasi religious in character, dealt with the special gifts vouchsafed by Wakon'da through the particular form or the animal. The article which was the symbol of a man's dream, as a feather from a bird, a tuft of hair from an animal, or a black stone or translucent pebble representing the thunder or the water, was never an object of worship. It was a memento of the vision, a sort of credential that served to connect its possessor with the potentiality of the species or class represented by the form seen in the vision, through which the man's strength or faculties could be reenforced by virtue of the continuity of life throughout the universe because of the ever-present power of Wakon'da.

In the sequence of rites just detailed, which began at birth with the announcement to all created things that a new life had come into their midst, and later, when the child had acquired ability to move about of its own volition, its feet were set in the path of life, and it entered into membership in the tribe, are represented progressive steps in the life of the individual from a mere living form to a being with a recognized place. The entrance into manhood required a voluntary effort by which, through the rite of fasting and prayer, the man came into direct and personal relations with the supernatural and realized within himself the forceful power of the union of the seen with the unseen.

# IV

# TRIBAL ORGANIZATION

## BASIC PRINCIPLES

The tribal organization of the Omaha was based on certain fundamental religious ideas, cosmic in significance; these had reference to conceptions as to how the visible universe came into being and how it is maintained.

An invisible and continuous life was believed to permeate all things, seen and unseen. This life manifests itself in two ways: First, by causing to move—all motion, all actions of mind or body are because of this invisible life; second, by causing permanency of structure and form, as in the rock, the physical features of the landscape, mountains, plains, streams, rivers, lakes, the animals and man. This invisible life was also conceived of as being similar to the will power of which man is conscious within himself—a power by which things are brought to pass. Through this mysterious life and power all things are related to one another and to man, the seen to the unseen, the dead to the living, a fragment of anything to its entirety. This invisible life and power was called Wakon'da (see p. 597). While it was a vague entity, yet there was an anthropomorphic coloring to the conception, as is shown in the prayers offered and the manner in which appeals for compassion and help were made, also in the ethical quality attributed to certain natural phenomena—the regularity of night following day, of summer winter (these were recognized as emphasizing truthfulness as a dependable quality and set forth for man's guidance)—and in the approval by Wakon'da of certain ethical actions on the part of mankind.

Human conditions were projected upon nature, and male and female forces recognized. The Above was regarded as masculine, the Below feminine; so the sky was father, the earth, mother. The heavenly bodies were conceived of as having sex; the sun was masculine, the moon feminine, consequently day was male and night female. The union of these two forces was regarded as necessary to the perpetuation of all living forms, and to man's life by maintaining his food supply. This order or method for the continuation of life was believed to have been arranged by Wakon'da and had to be obeyed if the race was to continue to exist. In order to keep this belief alive in the minds of the people, it was symbolized in religious rites and in social usages and organization.    Consonant with this manner of enforcing these cosmic and religious ideas, the tribe was composed of two grand divisions, one representing the Sky people, or the I$^n$shta'çu$^n$da; the other, the Earth people, or the Ho$^n$'gashenu.    Within each of these divisions there were five gentes.    While each gens had its designation, its rites, its place, its tabu and its personal names, all these distinctive marks were subordinate to the two grand divisions and membership in the gens became merged in membership in one of these divisions, the I$^n$shta'çu$^n$da or the Ho$^n$'gashenu.

These divisions were not phratries, as they were not based on ties of blood but on mythic ideas as to how creation came about and how life must be continued on the earth.    Myths relate that human beings were born of a union between the Sky people and the Earth people; and, in accordance with this belief, the union of the Sky people and the Earth people was conceived to be necessary to the existence of the tribe.    There was a teaching preserved among the old men that the division of the tribe into I$^n$shta'çu$^n$da and Ho$^n$'gashenu was for marital purposes—a teaching which bears out the mythic symbolism of these two divisions.    It is possible that this symbolic arrangement throws light on the force which made possible the artificial practice of exogamy.    In this connection it is interesting to note that of the marriages in existence among the Omaha twenty-five years ago, a good majority represented the union between members of gentes belonging to the two rather than to one of these grand divisions.    And it is also important that, amid the wreckage of the ancient tribal organization at the present time, the practice of exogamy is still observed.    In short, all the conditions seem to show that the custom is based on fundamental religious ideas.

The duality in the tribal organization was further represented by two principal chiefs, one standing for the I$^n$shta'çu$^n$da and the other for the Ho$^n$'gashenu.    There were also two tribal pipes, which were always kept together and were never separated in any ceremonial use.    Both had flat stems; one was ornamented with porcupine-quill work, and had fastened on it the head of a pileated woodpecker, with the upper mandible turned back over the crest of the bird.    The stem of the other pipe was plain, but had bound in a row along its length seven woodpeckers' heads, the mandibles turned back as just described.    It is not improbable that these pipes pertained to the fundamental ideas on which the two grand divisions of the tribe were based; but which pipe belonged to the Sky people and was masculine, and which to the Earth people and was feminine, the writers have been unable to learn.

The gens [a] was called in the Omaha tongue, _to$^n$'wo$^n$gtho$^n$_, "village." The same term was applied to the village in which all the tribe dwelt.

---

[a] This term is used to indicate that the kinship group traced descent in the paternal rather than the maternal line.

When the Omaha visited the towns and cities of the white people, they applied to these settlements the same designation. St. Louis and Washington were spoken of as $to^n{}'wo^ngtho^n$. To distinguish the village signifying the gens, from the village in which the tribe dwelt the name of the stream on which the latter was situated was mentioned. When the gens was spoken of, to the term $to^n{}'wo^ngtho^n$ was added $uba'no^n$, which means a group of a kind in a given place. While the idea of relationship is not directly stated, the word $uba'no^n$ added to the term for "village" is understood to indicate a village of people who are kindred, of one kind, between whom marriage is prohibited.

The question "To what gens do you belong?" put into Omaha and literally translated, would be, "In which of the various (many) villag's (of the tribe) are you there (have you a place)?" If the questioner belonged to the Omaha or the Ponca tribe, he would know the names of the gentes, so the reply would be: "Tapa', there I am;" that is, "I belong to the Tapa' gens." But if the question were asked by a stranger, a member of a different tribe, to whom the names of the Omaha gentes were unknown, then the reply would indicate the symbol of the religious rite (the tabu) of the gens of the person questioned, and he might say: "I am a buffalo person" or an "elk person." The reply would not be understood to mean that the man thought of himself as a buffalo or an elk, or as descended from one, but as belonging to a group which had charge of rites in which that animal was used as a symbol. The rites thus spoken of were designated as Ni'kie,[a] and in them all the people had a claim, although those who officiated at a rite were confined to the particular gens which had charge of the rite.

It was the duty of a gens having charge of a Ni'kie rite to take care of the symbols and paraphernalia of the rite, and act as its priests, so to speak; but the claim to take part in the ceremony was not confined to the gens having charge of the rite, for the people of the tribe had a voice in it and a share in its benefits.

Each gens had its distinctive name. Some of the names, as has been already pointed out, occur in more than one of the tribes that are close cognates of the Omaha. These duplicated names may have been names of gentes in the parent organization, and when the Omaha and their cognates organized as distinct tribes the remnants of the former gens may have clung together and kept their old rites and name. An Omaha gens, however, was not a simple but a com-

---

[a] *Ni'kie* is compounded from *ni'k* (from *ni'kashiga*, "people"; *ie*, "words or speech"). From *ni'kashiga* is also derived *ni'kagahi*, "chief" (*ga'he*, "thrown upon")—literally, "those upon whom the people are thrown" or "who carry the people." *Ni'kie* signifies a declaration by the people or their chiefs of consent to a certain proposition.

posite group, made up of subgentes or subdivisions which were some-
times called $to^{n\prime}wo^{n}gtho^{n}$ $zhi^{n}ga$, "little villages," or $to^{n\prime}wo^{n}gtho^{n}$ $uga'\c{c}ne$,
$uga'\c{c}ne$ meaning "that which is split," and implying that the subdivision
had been split off, although it still kept with the main body.     Each of
the subgentes had its name, its rite, which was of the Ni'kie class,
its set of personal names, its tabu, and its place when the gens camped
with the tribe in ceremonial order.     A subdivision differed from a subgens in not having a distinctive rite, although it had a particular office
in the rite belonging to the gens.     A subdivision might have its tabu,
which would refer to its duties in the rite, and its set of personal
names, but it was bound to the gens by a common rite and observed
the tabu of the gens.     The number of subgentes or subdivisions in a
gens does not seem to have been uniform.     The common bond between the subgentes of a gens was that of kinship, traced solely
through the father.     Marriage between the members of the subgentes
or subdivisions of a gens was forbidden.     When a person was asked
where he belonged, he did not give the name of the subgens into
which he was born, but the name of the gens of which his birth group
was a part.     If more definite information was desired, then he would
give the name of his subgens or subdivision.     The gens was regarded
as paramount to the subgentes or to the subdivisions, as it contained
them all, even as the tribe embraced all the gentes and stood as one
body.

There were ten gentes in the tribe.     The meaning of the Omaha
word for tribe, $uki'te$, has already been discussed (p. 35).     This word
is distinct in meaning from $hu'thuga$, the term used to designate the
form or order in which the tribal organization ceremonially camped,
in which each one of the villages, or gens, had its definite place.
$Hu'thuga$ is an old term and carries the idea of a dwelling.     The
order of camping expressed by $hu'thuga$ was used when the tribe
was away from its village on the annual buffalo hunt.     This hunt
was a serious occasion, when all the people united in a common effort
to secure a supply of meat and pelts, food and clothing, for themselves and for their children; therefore it was initiated and conducted
with religious ceremonies.     The people were placed under the control of men who through elaborate and sacred rites were appointed
for the direction of the hunt, and to these appointed men all persons,
including the chiefs, had to render obedience.     It was while on this
hunt that the great tribal ceremonies took place, at which time the
people camped according to their gentes in the form known as
$hu'thuga$.

This form was circular, with an opening to the east, which
represented the door of a dwelling.     "Through it," the old men
said, "the people went forth in quest of the game, and through it

they returned with their supply of food, as one enters the door of one's home. The warriors passed hence to defend the tribe from its foes, and here they were welcomed when they came back." The entrance was therefore the door through which one entered into the dwelling place of the tribe, in which each gens had its place as had each member of the family within the lodge. There are indications that the *hu'thuga* embodies the idea of the union of the forces represented in the fundamental concept upon which the two grand divisions of the tribe were based. The opening or door of the *hu'thuga* was always symbolically to the east, and the five gentes which composed the I\[n\]shta'çu\[n\]da division (Sky people) always, theoretically, formed the northern half, while the five gentes that formed the Ho\[n\]'gashenu division (Earth people) in theory made the southern half. The literal fact is that the opening was actually toward the east only when the tribal ceremonies took place; at all other times it faced the direction toward which the tribe happened to be traveling, but the order of the gentes was always as it would have been had opening faced the east. This was effected by turning the tribal circle as on a hinge placed opposite the eastern opening, so that no matter in which direction the opening actually was, the I\[n\]shta'çu\[n\]da and Ho\[n\]'gashenu divisions were always as they would have been had opening faced the east. This interesting fact, of the carrying out of a symbolism in the manner of pitching the tents of the tribe on the wide unbroken prairie, indicates how deeply rooted in the minds of the people was the importance of the fundamental ideas represented in the *hu'thuga*—the two grand divisions and the orientation of the dwelling. In view of these and kindred ideas connected with the *hu'thuga*, it seems probable that in this form we are dealing with a symbol rather than with an arrangement for convenience and safety, as has been stated by some writers. That the idea of safety was involved in the form of the *hu'thuga* is probably true, but the dependence for safety was placed in the help to be derived through the recognition of cosmic forces and religious observances rather than in an advantageous arrangement of tents made in order to protect ponies and camp equipage.

When an orator addressed the people of the tribe he did not say: *Ho! Omaha!* but *Ho! I\[n\]shta'çu\[n\]da, Ho\[n\]'gashenu ti agtho\[n\]'kaho\[n\]! Ti agtho\[n\]'kaho\[n\]* means "both sides of the house." This was the only form of speech by which the people of the tribe could be addressed collectively. It bears out the meaning of the *hu'thuga* as given by the old men.

The *hu'thuga* regarded as the dwelling of the entire tribe presented the type that was to be reproduced in the dwelling of each member of the tribe, wherein were to be united the masculine and feminine forces drawn from two distinct groups or regions, a union symbolized in the *hu'thuga* by the union of the Earth people and the Sky people. The rending of the natural family by exogamy seems to have been demanded in order to typify what was believed to be a cosmic regulation.     In this way it became possible to interweave the split parts so

FIG. 19.  Family group.  The parents represent both sides of the *hu thuga*.

as to bind together by the natural tie of kinship the different gentes composing the tribe.  This tie came through the mothers in the tribe. Descent in the gens was traced solely through the father.  The fathers held the gens together and distinct from every other gens.

Through the father the child inherited his name, his place, and his share in the rites of his gens; but it was through his mother that his kinship relations were extended beyond his birth gens and that he thus became conscious of being a part of a great kinship community. (Fig. 19.)

The Ponca tribe does not present a clear picture of those ideas which seem to have been fundamental to the tribal organization of their kindred, the Omaha; and yet these ideas appear to have been present in the mind of the people when they organized as a distinct tribe. This imperfect form may have given rise to the custom of the Omaha of designating the Ponca as "orphans."

The Ponca camped in a circle with the opening to the east when the gentes were in ceremonial order, and gave to this form the same name as that used by the Omaha, *hu'thuga* (see p. 42). Each gens of the Ponca had its *ni'kie* rites and its *ni'kie* names; the latter were bestowed during ceremonies similar to those observed among the Omaha.

In the Ponca tribal circle the gentes seem to be grouped according to their duties: Those to the south, or left, of the eastern opening, were charged with the care of rites connected with the Thunder and with warfare. The next group to the left administered the rites and ceremonies which pertained to the government of the people and to the securing of food and clothing by means of the annual hunt. The group to the north, or right of the entrance, controlled the rites relating to ice or hail (both of which are symbolically connected with the upper world) and to the serpent, generally symbolic of the lightning. In this order, as in a shattered mirror, one can discern the outlines of the symbolic picture which the Omaha organization also so distinctly presents. From the Ponca tribe taken by itself it would be difficult to discern the presence of those ideas which we have seen definitely expressed in the Omaha tribe; but turning from the contemplation of the Omaha to that of the Ponca, one is able to recognize these ideas in the fragmentary order which obtained among the latter.

The Ponca as well as the Omaha regarded all life and the preservation of all forms as the result of the union of the sky and the earth forces, and believed the combining of these two opposite and differentiated cosmic powers symbolically set forth to man a law he must obey, a course he must follow, if he would secure the continuation of his own life and the perpetuation of his tribe—a law which made exogamy a practical expression of this belief.

In the Osage tribe, which seems to be an agglomeration, we find the same ideas fundamental to the tribal organization, but certain conditions have tended to modify their expression.

The Osage were divided into two great divisions. One of these was composed of three kinship groups which shifted their relative positions in accordance with the rite or duties to be performed. The other division was made up of two kinship groups which never changed their positions with respect to each other or to the other division of the tribal circle (see p. 58). These two unchangeable groups camped on the north, or to the right of the eastern entrance. They represented the ideas which were symbolized in the Omaha Inshta'çunda half, the Sky people; while the other three, which camped to the left of the eastern entrance, in both position and duties resembled the Hon'gashenu division of the Omaha tribe, and were the Earth people, on whom devolved the care of the material welfare of the tribe. Here, again, we find the tribal order standing for the union of sky and earth, the masculine and feminine forces from whose union all living things arise.

The Kansa and Quapaw tribes also were divided into two parts each, and from the fragmentary information obtainable they seem to have embodied the same ideas as those found among their kindred tribes; so that it would appear to be fairly well established that the ideas and beliefs which a study of the Omaha tribe shows were fundamental to the organization of that tribe were basic also in their close cognates, the Ponca, Osage, Kansa, and Quapaw; and further research may show that these ideas were a common and formative power in other tribes of the Siouan linguistic stock.

## THE HU'THUGA—THE OMAHA TRIBAL FORM

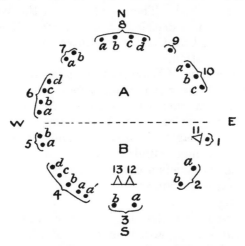

FIG. 20. Diagram of Omaha *hu'thuga* (tribal circle).

A. INSHTA'ÇUNDA DIVISION. B. HON'GASHENU DIVISION. 1. WE'ZHINSHTE. Subgens: None. 2. INKE'ÇABE. Subgentes: (a) Nini'baton; (b) Wathi'gizhe. 3. HON'GA. Subgentes: (a) Waxthe'xeton; (b) Washa'beton. 4. THA'TADA. Subdivisions: (a') Xu'ka; (a) Waça'be itazhi; (b) Wazhin'ga itazhi; (c) Ke'in; (d) Te'pa itazhi. 5. KON'ÇE. Subgentes: (a) Tade'tada; (b) Nini'baton. 6. MON'THINKAGAXE. Subdivisions: (a) Xu'be; (b) Mi'kaçi; (c) Mi'xaçon; (d) Nini'baton. 7. TEÇIN'DE. Subdivisions: (a) Teçin'de; (b) Nini'baton. 8. TAPA'. Subdivisions: (a) Tapa'xte; (b) Thunder rites; (c) Star rites; (d) Nini'baton. 9. INGTHE'ZHIDE. No subdivisions. 10. INSHTA'ÇUNDA. Subgens: (a) Lost gens; (b) Nini'baton; (c) Washe'ton. 11. Sacred Tent of War. 12. Tent of Sacred Pole. 13. Tent of Sacred White Buffalo Hide.

## GENTES OF THE OMAHA TRIBE

### HON'GASHENU DIVISION (A)[a]

#### WE'ZHINSHTE GENS (1)[a]

The We'zhinshte gens camped on the left of the entrance into the *hu'thuga*. The name is descriptive, being composed of *we*, "by whom," and *zhinshte*, an abbreviation of *wazhin'shte*, "to become angry." The meaning of the term We'zhinshte may be defined as those through whom the tribe made known its displeasure or anger, because of some injurious act by another tribe. The Sacred Tent of War(11) was set in front of the line of tents belonging to the We'zhinshte gens and was in the keeping of this gens, together with the paraphernalia of the rites pertaining to war and to Thunder. When any question arose as to the policy to be pursued in dealing with another tribe the members of which had committed acts of hostility, such as killing Omaha or stealing their horses or carrying away by force women of the tribe, it was the duty of the keeper of the Tent of War to call the Seven Chiefs and the leading men of the gens to a council. At this council the We'zhinshte presided. The Sacred Pipe of the Tent of War was filled by the keeper of the Tent and when, after due deliberation on the action to be taken, a decision was reached, the Seven Chiefs smoked this Pipe. This was a religious act and through it the decision became sanctified. Then the herald of the We'zhinshte proclaimed to the tribe the decision of the chiefs. If war was determined upon, the organization of volunteer war parties generally followed this authorization.

The keeper of the Tent of War and the leaders of this gens officiated at the ceremony of Wate'giçtu, when certain prescribed honors were publicly bestowed on successful warriors for acts performed in authorized offensive warfare or in battles fought in defense of the camp or permanent village. It was also the duty of this gens when the tribe was on its annual buffalo hunt, to organize in response to an order from the Seven Chiefs a corps of scouts to spy the country on the discovery of signs of danger.

Rites pertaining to Thunder were also in charge of this gens. These were observed when the first thunder was heard in the spring. This thunder-peal was regarded as a signal of the awakening of certain life-giving forces after the sleep of the winter. In former days a ceremony took place at this time with song and ritual in which the Waça'be itazhi (black bear) subgens of the Tha'tada gens joined with the We'zhinshte gens. It has been impossible to obtain a trustworthy account of this ancient ceremony, owing to the death of the

---

[a] This and similar references throughout this section are to be read in connection with figure 20.

men who knew the rites.    During severe thunder storms, when life
and property were in danger from lightning, sometimes a song said
to have been connected with this lost ceremony was sung by one
who had a right to do so.

The following act of the keeper of the Tent of War (see fig. 22) may
have been a part of this lost ceremony: When the first thunder
sounded, he at once took a small pipe and ascended a hill near by,
where he offered smoke to Wako$^n$'da.    He then planted a small wand
(fig. 21) on the hill so as to point toward the east.    To this wand
were bound with human hair four small bunches of tobacco inclosed
in bits of bladder.    The combination of tobacco, bladder, and human

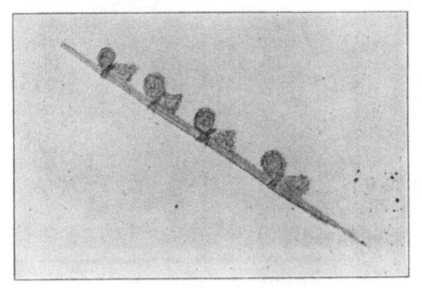

FIG. 21.   Wand used in ceremony when first thunder was heard in the spring.   (Native drawing.)

hair on the wand seems to indicate that this act and lost ceremony
probably related to Thunder as the arbiter of life and death, as is
shown in the ceremony of cutting the lock of hair from the head of the
boy.   (See p. 122.)

The tabu of the We'zhi$^n$shte was the male elk, and the gens was
sometimes spoken of as the Elk gens; this form of speech with reference to the tabu of a gens has already been explained (see p. 136).
Concerning the connection of the male elk with the rites of the gens
the following story is handed down:

When the pipes and the other articles belonging to the rites pertaining to war were
made, the people sought for some skin to be used as a covering in which to keep and
protect these things which were regarded as *waxube*, or sacred; but none could be
found save that of the male elk.   The fact that at that particular time only the skin
of the male elk was obtainable was regarded as an indication that the male elk came
to their aid by direction of Wako$^n$'da.   Therefore, in memory of this act of the male
elk, this animal became tabu to the gens.

No member of the We'zhinshte gens would eat the flesh of the male elk or wear moccasins made of its skin, such acts being considered sacrilegious on account of the service believed to have been rendered the people by that animal. At death moccasins made of the skin of the male elk were put on the feet of the departed We'zhinshte, that he might be recognized by his gentile relatives in the other world. The boy name Nuga'xti, "the real male," refers directly to the tabu of the gens.

FIG. 22. Mon'hinthinge, last keeper of the Tent of War, and his daughter.

Any violation of the tabu of a gens was regarded by the people as a sacrilegious act, the punishment of which took the form of the appearance of sores or white spots on the body of the offender or of the hair turning white.

There were no subdivisions in this gens.

The following are the names- belonging to the We'zhinshte gens. They are classified as *ni'kie*, "dream," "fanciful," and "borrowed" names, and nicknames. The word *ni'kie* has been already translated and explained (see p. 136); as stated, a *ni'kie* name always referred to the rites and tabu of the gens. These names were bestowed on the child at the time the rite of initiation into the tribe was performed. (See p. 121.) The name then given generally clung more or less closely to a man, although later in his career he might take another name, either a *ni'kie* name or one commemorative of a dream, a deed, or an event, or he might have a nickname bestowed

NUGA'XTI

on him. All female names were of the *ni'kie* class and were never dropped or changed, nor did a woman ever have more than one namė.

After the performance of the initiatory rite and bestowal of the *ni'kie* name, the father cut his child's hair in the manner which symbolized the tabu of his gens. This cutting of the hair was repeated every year until the child was about 7 years old, when it was abandoned, never to be resumed.

In the We'zhiⁿshte gens, the symbolic cut of the child's hair was as follows: All the hair on the boy's head was cut close or shaved except a bunch or tuft at the forehead and a long, thick lock left at the nape of the neck (fig. 23). The tuft represented the head of the elk; the lock, its tail.

FIG. 23. Cut of hair, We'-zhiⁿshte gens.

PERSONAL NAMES IN THE WE'ZHIⁿSHTE GENS (1)

*Ni'kie names*

Aⁿe'goⁿtha............ *Aⁿe'*, success; *goⁿ'tha*, desire.

Biⁿçe'tigthe............ *Biⁿçe'*, sound of the elk's voice; *tigthe*, heard at a distance.

Bthoⁿti'................ *Bthoⁿ*, smell, scent; *ti*, comes. Scent borne by wind, discovering game. (In *Nu'xe*, Ponca.)

Çe'çoⁿçnede........... *Çe'çoⁿ*, from *çe'çaça*, trot; *çnede*, long. Refers to elk.

Çiⁿ'dedoⁿpa............ *Çiⁿ'de*, tail; *doⁿpa*, blunt, short. (In *Moⁿkoⁿ'* subdivision, *Poⁿ'caxti*, Ponca.) Refers to the elk.

He'çithiⁿke............. *He'çi*, yellow horn or antler; *thiⁿke*, sitting. Refers to the yellowish color of the velvety skin of the new growth of the antlers of the elk. (In *Ni'kapashna*, Ponca.)

He'çoⁿtoⁿ............. *He*, antler; *çoⁿ*, white; *toⁿ*, standing. Refers to the towering antlers of an elk.

He'shabe............... *He*, antler; *shabe*, dark.

He'shtoⁿga............ *He*, horn, or antlers; *shtoⁿga*, soft. Two of this name. Refers to the new growth of the antlers of the elk.

Iⁿ'gthuⁿhoⁿgasha ...... *Iⁿ'gthuⁿ*, thunder; *hoⁿ*, night; *agasha*, to travel. Refers to Sacred Pipe of War.

Iⁿ'gthuⁿtha............. *Iⁿ'gthuⁿ*, thunder; *tha*, from *the*, to go. Refers to Sacred Pipe of War.

Ki'baxthagthithoⁿ..... *Ki'baxtha*, to face; *gthi*, return; *thoⁿ*, suddenly; to turn and face suddenly (elk). The elk suddenly brought to bay by the hunter.

Ku'kuwiⁿxe........... Turning round and round. Refers to a bewildered elk when surprised.

Ku'wiⁿxaxa........... Turning round in bewilderment (elk).

Moⁿ'geshabe.......... *Moⁿ'ge*, breast; *shabe*, dark. Refers to the dark coloring of the breast of the animal.

Moⁿ'hiⁿthiⁿge (fig. 22).. *Moⁿ'hiⁿ*, stone knife; *thiⁿge*, none.

Noⁿmoⁿ'moⁿtha........ *Noⁿ*, action with the feet; *moⁿatha*, walking with the head thrown back. The repetition of *moⁿ* signifies that the action is repeated. Refers to the peculiar manner in which the elk holds its head in walking.

Nuga'xti (pl. 24)....... *Nuga'*, male; *xti*, real, virile. (In *Poⁿ'caxti*, Ponca.)

Oⁿ'poⁿ................. Elk.

O$^n$'po$^n$çka.............. *O$^n$po$^n$*, elk; *çka*, white. The Ponca have *O$^n$'po$^n$çabe*.
                              (*Hi'çada* gens.)
O$^n$'po$^n$no$^n$zhi$^n$........ *O$^n$'po$^n$*, elk; *no$^n$zhi$^n$*, standing. The Ponca use the Dakota
                              form.
O$^n$'po$^n$to$^n$ga........... *O$^n$'po$^n$*, elk; *to$^n$ga*, big. Appears in Omaha treaties of 1815,
                              1826, 1830, 1836. (In *Thi'xida*, Ponca.)
O$^n$'po$^n$zhi$^n$ga......... Young elk. (In *Po$^n$'caxti*, Ponca.)
Shi'beko$^n$............. *Shi'be*, intestines; *ko$^n$*, a string. Refers to the intestine of
                              the wolf used as a string in the Honor Pack, Tent of War.
Tahe'zho$^n$ka.......... *Ta* refers to deer; *he*, horn; *zho$^n$ka*, forked.
Wako$^n$'dagi............. A mythical being; a monster.
Xaga'mo$^n$thi$^n$.......... *Xaga'*, rough; *mo$^n$thi$^n$*, walking. Refers to the jagged out-
                              line of a herd of elk, their antlers rising like tree branches.

### Borrowed names

Hexa'gato$^n$ga.......... Big male elk. Archaic with Omaha; used by Dakota.
Hi'daha............... Meaning unknown.

### Fanciful names

I$^n$shta'mo$^n$çe.......... Metal eye.
Wa'bado$^n$do$^n$........... Meaning uncertain.
We'btho$^n$aji............ Not satisfied although he has many things.

### Valor name

We'zhi$^n$shtewashushe.. Brave We'zhi$^n$shte.

### Female names

Açe'xube.............. *Açe'*, paint; *xube*, sacred. Three of this name. Refers to
                              the paint used at sacred ceremonies. (In *Wazha'zhe*, Ponca.)
Çi$^n$'dewi$^n$............. *Çi$^n$de*, tail; *wi$^n$*, feminine term. Three of this name.
Ma'zho$^n$wi$^n$........... *Ma'zho$^n$*, fox; *wi$^n$*, feminine term.
Mi'dasho$^n$thi$^n$........ The moon moving.
Mi'gasho$^n$thi$^n$........ The moon moving. (In *Washa'be*, Ponca.)
Ni'dawi$^n$.............. *Ni'da*, mysterious animal; feminine term, *wi$^n$*. Three of
                              this name.
No$^n$çe'i$^n$çe............ Meaning uncertain. (In *Wazha'zhe*, *Thi'xida*, and *Hi'çada*,
                              Ponca.)
O$^n$'po$^n$miga............ Female elk.
Pahi'çi................. *Pahi'*, hair on the head (elk); *çi*, yellow.
Taça'bewi$^n$............ *Ta*, deer; *çabe*, black; *wi$^n$*, feminine term. Five of this
                              name. (In *Wa'zhazhe*, Ponca.)
Wihe'to$^n$ga.............. *Wihe*, younger sister; *to$^n$ga*, big. (In *Washa'be* and *Wazha'-*
                              *zhe*, Ponca.)
Zho$^n$'i$^n$wathe.......... *Zho$^n$i$^n$*, carry wood; *wathe*, to cause. Two of this name. (In
                              *Hi'çada* and *Po$^n$'çaxti*, Ponca.)

## I$^n$KE'ÇABE GENS (2)

The I$^n$ke'çabe camped next to the We'zhi$^n$shte on the left. *I$^n$ke'-*
*çabe* is an archaic word of doubtful meaning. It may refer to the
black shoulder of the buffalo (*i$^n$ke*, an abbreviation of *i$^n$ke'de*,
"shoulder;" *çabe*, "black"). From the myths and traditions it would
seem that the leadership accorded to this gens during certain movements of the people when engaged in the actual pursuit of the buffalo
on the annual tribal hunt began at an early period when the people
took up the custom of following the buffalo. The particular authority

INSHTA'THABI, THE LAST WATHON

and leadership vested in this gens were regarded not only as sacred but as absolutely necessary, so much so that it was said: "If the last Iⁿke'çabe was an infant in its mother's arms it would be carried to lead the people in the *wanoⁿ'çe*" (the surround of the herd). This ancient and hereditary office came to an end at the last buffalo hunt in the winter of 1875–76, with Iⁿshta'thabi, "He who is eyes" (for the people). At that time he served as director or leader of the surround, and was the last *wathoⁿ'* of the *wanoⁿ'çe*. (Pl. 25.)

The following legend is said to have given rise to a series of names in this gens:

The buffalo were underground. A young bull browsing about found his way to the surface of the earth. [This is a figurative expression referring to the birth of the species buffalo from mother earth.] The herd followed him. As they went they came to a river. The water looked shallow, but it was deep. As the buffalo jumped in, the water splashed and looked gray in the air. The herd swam on and over the stream, where on the other side they found good pasture and remained on the earth.

The name Niga'xude refers to this experience of the new-born buffalo; the word is compounded of *ni*, "water;" *ga*, "to strike;" *xude*, "gray." Niga'xude was the name given to the first born son. The second son could be called either Heba'zhu, "knob horns," referring to the protuberances on the head of the calf, or Gthadiⁿ'gthithoⁿ, "the hungry calf running crosswise in front of its mother and stopping her progress." The third son could be named Çikoⁿ'xega, "brown ankles," the color of the ankles of the buffalo calf. When these boys became adults, the eldest could take the name Pe'thoⁿba, "seven;" the second could have Moⁿ'getoⁿga, "big chest;" the third, Noⁿzhi'hatoⁿga, "big hair." When these men became old, they could take the following names: The eldest, He'ubagthoⁿde, "worn horns of the old buffalo bull;" the next, Moⁿe'gahi, "arrow chief;" and the youngest, Moⁿzhoⁿ'wakithe, "land of the buffalo."

The Iⁿke'çabe had two subgentes, Nini'batoⁿ and Wathi'gizhe.

(*a*) Nini'batoⁿ (*nini'ba*, "pipe;" *toⁿ*, "to possess or keep"). The following fragmentary legend is connected with this subgens and its tabu, the red ear of corn:

The Iⁿke'çabe were the first of the Omaha to exist. There were one man and one woman. They lived together and children were born to them. The woman went out one day and found little mounds on the ground. In a few days she went again, and saw that out of the mounds plants were growing not known to her. From time to time she went to look at these plants. They grew tall, and by and by ears grew on them. These she gathered and took to her husband and children. They roasted the ears by the fire and ate them. These were the people to whom the corn was sacred; so to this day they do not eat the red ear of corn.

It was the duty of this subgens to provide the ears of red corn, which were considered the sacred corn, and to give them to the Hoⁿ'gaxti division of the Washa'betoⁿ subgens of the Hoⁿ'ga. When the time for planting arrived, the ceremonial distribution of this sacred corn took place. The Hoⁿ'gaxti sang the ritual of the maize and then gave the sacred kernels to this subgens, who acted as servers and distributed four of the kernels to each family in the tribe.

To a family within this subgens was given the hereditary charge of the Sacred Tribal Pipes. In this connection it is noteworthy that the custodianship of these Sacred Pipes was bestowed on those to whom belonged rites in connection with the cultivation of the maize, whose tabu was the sacred corn. This indicates that the group who controlled the rites of the maize were regarded as the proper persons to have the care of the symbol of tribal authority because of their connection with ancient sacred rites which secured food for the people.

The symbolic cut of the hair of the children of this subgens was peculiar. All hair was cut off the head except two small bunches, one on each side of the crown (fig. 24). This style was observed in all the Nini'bato$^n$ subdivisions of the other gentes of the tribe. These two little tufts of hair may refer to the little mounds, spoken of in the legend, from which the corn grew.

There were two subdivisions of the Nini'bato$^n$ subgens, the No$^n$xthe'-bitube and the I'ekithe. To the first was given the hereditary right

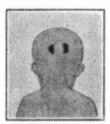

FIG. 24. Cut of hair, Nini'-bato$^n$ subgens.

to prepare the paint for the decoration of the pole used in the He'dewachi ceremony. The name No$^n$-xthe'bitube was descriptive of their duty (*no$^n$xthe*, "charred box elder wood;" *bitu'be*, "to pulverize by rubbing"). This group not only observed the tabu of their subgens, the red ear of corn, but had an additional tabu, the charcoal, which referred to their office of painting the Pole and preparing the paint for the ceremony. As the painting on the Pole was symbolic, it was religious in character.

I'ekithe signifies "he who speaks or proclaims." The hereditary office of tribal herald belonged to this subdivision. The herald had to have a strong, clear voice, as his duty was to proclaim the decisions of the chiefs and to give out orders to the people when the tribe was on its annual hunt. If by any chance the official herald was incapacitated, his substitute had to be chosen from the same subdivision. The I'ekithe observed the tabu of the subgens to which they belonged, the red ear of corn.

(b) Wathi'gizhe. The name of this subgens was also the name of the hoop used in a ceremonial game which, it is said, was formerly played by the chiefs alone, and was connected with the following story, which belongs to the class designated *hi'go$^n$*, a word meaning "the story is not literally true:"

The people were without food, and no game could be found to keep the people from starving. Outside the village lived an orphan boy with his grandmother, and these two consulted together as to how they could help the people to procure food. At last they agreed upon a plan, and the boy set to work and made a hoop. After it was made he gave it to his grandmother, and according to their plan she took it to the top of a hill near by while the boy stationed himself halfway up the hill. When all was ready, the grandmother started the hoop down the hill. As it began to roll she called out: "There goes a young bull with straight horns!" The hoop rolled on and when it reached the place where the boy stood it suddenly turned into a buffalo, which the boy shot and killed. He butchered the animal and gave the flesh to the people to eat. A second time the grandmother took the hoop to the top of the hill and rolled it down and called out to her grandson what kind of buffalo was coming. He was at his station halfway down the hill, and there the hoop turned into a buffalo, which he shot and gave to the people for food. A third and a fourth time the grandmother and the orphan played this game, and after the fourth time great herds of buffalo came and the people had plenty of food. As a mark of their gratitude they made the orphan a Chief.

The office of *watho[n']*, director of the *wano[n']çe*, the surround of the herd, was hereditary in a family of this subgens. The custody of the songs belonging to the He'dewachi ceremony and the singers in this tribal ceremony were taken from this subgens. The bearers of the Sacred Tribal Pipes used on that occasion were of the Nini'bato[n] subgens.

The tabu of the Wathi'gizhe was the tongue and head of the buffalo.

The Wathi'gizhe cut off all the hair from the child's head except a tuft over the forehead, one on each side of the crown, and a short lock at the nape of the neck, to represent respectively the head, horns, and tail of the buffalo (fig. 25).

In the *hu'thuga*, the Nini'bato[n] subgens camped next to the We'zhi[n]shte. The left part of the line of the Nini'bato[n] was occupied by the subdivision of the No[n]xthe'bitube families. On their left camped the Wathi'gizhe subgens, and left of

FIG. 25. Cut of hair, Wa-thi'gizhe subgens.

these and next the Ho[n']ga the subdivision of I'ekithe pitched their tents.

### PERSONAL NAMES IN THE I[N]KE'ÇABE GENS (2)

*Nini'bato[n] subgens (a)*

#### Ni'kie names

Athu'hagemo[n]thi[n]...... *Athu'hage*, last; *mo[n]thi[n]*, walking. Refers to buffalo.

Cho[n']niniba............ *Cho[n]*, said to be *to[n]thi[n]no[n]ba* and to refer to the pipe-bearer at the He'dewachi ceremony; *niniba*, pipe.

Çihi'duba.............. *Çihi'*, feet; *duba*, four.

Edia'ino[n]zhi[n].......... *Edi*, there; *ai* an act; the name given the last ceremonial pause when approaching a herd; *no[n]zhi[n]*, standing.

Edi'to[n]................ From that place; referring to the place of the pipes.

Gahi'ge................ Chief. (In *Waça'be, Hi'çada* subdivision, Ponca.)

Gahi'geçnede......... Tall chief.

Gahi'gexti.............. Real chief.

Gahi'gezhi[n]ga........... Young chief. (In *Wazha'zhe*, Ponca.)

Gaxa'tano[n]zhi[n]........ *Gaxa'ta*, apart from (the herd); *no[n]zhi[n]*, stands.

Gino[n']xthe............. *Gi*, again; *no[n]xthe*, black, like charcoal. Refers to the new hair of the buffalo after shedding.

Gio[n']çethi[n]ge.......... *Gio[n']çe*, to teach; *thi[n]ge*, none. None to teach him.

Gthadi<sup>n</sup>'gthitho<sup>n</sup>....... *Gthadin'*, cross; *gthi*, returns; *thon*, suddenly. The hungry calf runs in front of its mother and stops her progress.

He'akathi<sup>n</sup>ge.......... Meaning uncertain.

Heba'zhu............. *He*, horns; *ba'zhu*, little knobs.

He'benika............. *He'be*, a portion; *nika*, a person.

He'ubagtho<sup>n</sup>de......... The worn horns of an old buffalo.

I<sup>n</sup>shta'pede............. *Inshta'*, eyes; *pede*, fire. (Also in *I'ekithe* subdivision.)

I''uhe................. *I*, from *ie*, speech; *'uhe*, obey. Refers to the performance by the people of the commands of the chiefs, or the submission to their authority.

Ki'ko<sup>n</sup>to<sup>n</sup>ga............ Curlew. (*Numenius longirostris*. Hudsonian.)

Mo<sup>n</sup>e'gahi............. *Mone*, arrow; *gahi*, from *gahi'ge*, chief. (In *Waça'be*, *Hi'çada* subdivision, Ponca.)

Mo<sup>n</sup>'geto<sup>n</sup>ga............ *Mon'ge*, breast; *tonga*, big.

Mo<sup>n</sup>zho<sup>n</sup>'gabtho<sup>n</sup>....... *Monzhon'*, land; *gabthon*, scent remains.

Mo<sup>n</sup>zho<sup>n</sup>'wakithe...... Land of the buffalo.

Na'gu.................. Meaning uncertain.

Ni'ashiga.............. A person. Refers to those who were chiefs in the organization of the tribal government.

Niga'xude............. *Ni*, water; *ga*, to strike; *xude*, gray. Refers to animals stirring up the water.

Niu'bathide............ *Ni*, water; *u'bathide*, overrun, swarm. Refers to masses of buffalo swimming.

No<sup>n</sup>ba't'ewathe........ *Nonba'*, two; *t'e*, dead; *wathe*, to cause.

No<sup>n</sup>i'ça................. Swaying motion, as made by buffalo walking.

No<sup>n</sup>'kaetho<sup>n</sup>be......... *Non'ca*, back; *ethonbe*, appears.

No<sup>n</sup>zhi'hato<sup>n</sup>ga........ *Nonzhi'ha*, hair; *tonga*, great.

Paho<sup>n</sup>'gamo<sup>n</sup>thi<sup>n</sup>....... *Pahon'ga*, first; *monthin*, walking. (In *Waça'be*, Ponca.)

Pe'tho<sup>n</sup>ba............. Seven. Refers to the seven original chiefs.

Sha'geno<sup>n</sup>ba............ *Sha'ge*, hoofs; *nonba*, two: cloven hoofs.

She'thugthito<sup>n</sup>.......... *She'thu*, there; *gthi*, returns; *ton*, stands.

Ta'hesha.............. Meaning lost.

Teço<sup>n</sup>'ho<sup>n</sup>ga............ *Teçon'*, white buffalo; *honga*, leader; used also in the Dakota.

Teço<sup>n</sup>'mo<sup>n</sup>thi<sup>n</sup>......... *Teçon'*, white buffalo; *monthin*, walking.

Tenua'xano<sup>n</sup>zhi<sup>n</sup>....... *Te*, buffalo; *nu*, from *nuga*, bull; *axa*, from *gaxa'ta*, apart from; *nonzhin*, stand.

Ti'zhebegtho<sup>n</sup>.......... Door flap. In Omaha treaty of 1825.

To<sup>n</sup>'thi<sup>n</sup>no<sup>n</sup>ba......... The two who run.

Uga'e.................. Spread out. (The herd as it runs spreads out.)

Ugthi'to<sup>n</sup>.............. Refers to handling the pipes when making them ready for use.

U'nizhabi.............. Meaning uncertain.

Utha'xado<sup>n</sup>gthe......... Meaning uncertain.

Uthi'sho<sup>n</sup>mo<sup>n</sup>thi<sup>n</sup>...... Walking around.

Wada'thi<sup>n</sup>ga............ Refers to the peaceful office of the chief. (In *Thi'xida*, Ponca).

Waki'de.............. *Wa*, action; *ki'de*, to shoot. One who shoots.

Wazhi<sup>n</sup>'texi............ *Wazhin'*, will, disposition; *texi*, difficult. Refers to office of the chiefs. Anger is made difficult because of the Seven Chiefs, who must enforce peace in the tribe.

Xitha'wahi............. *Xitha'*, eagle; *wahi*, bone. Refers to pipe. Not liked, as children of this name are apt to die.

*Borrowed names*

Ish'kadabi............. Borrowed from the Kansa gens in the eighteenth century.

Pude'tha.............. Meaning unknown. (In *Nu'xe*, Ponca.)

*Fanciful names*

Taxie'wathezhi<sup>n</sup>ga..... *Taxi*, knocking sound; *wathe*, to cause; *zhi<sup>n</sup>ga*, little.
U'kiça.................. Empty lodge, or country.
Uko<sup>n</sup>a'digtho<sup>n</sup>......... *Uko<sup>n</sup>a'di*, separate, alone; *gtho<sup>n</sup>*, from *gthi<sup>n</sup>*, sits.

*Female names*

Mi'to<sup>n</sup>i<sup>n</sup>................ New moon.
Po<sup>n</sup>'caço<sup>n</sup>............... Pale Ponca.
Tewa'u................ *Te*, buffalo; *wa'u*, woman.
To<sup>n</sup>'i<sup>n</sup>gi................ New moon coming.

FIG. 26. Du'bamo<sup>n</sup>thi<sup>n</sup>.

*No<sup>n</sup>xthe'bitube subdivision*

*Male names*

Çiçi'kazhi<sup>n</sup>ga.......... Little turkey.
Gashka'wo<sup>n</sup>gthe......... Meaning uncertain.
Tahe'zhi<sup>n</sup>ga........... Little buffalo horns.

*Wathi'gizhe subgens (b)*

*Ni'kie names*

Baço<sup>n</sup>'no<sup>n</sup>ge........... *Baço<sup>n</sup>'*, in the midst of bushes or people; *no<sup>n</sup>ge*, to run.
Çiko<sup>n</sup>'xega ............. *Çiko<sup>n</sup>*, ankles; *xega*, yellowish brown.  Refers to the buffalo calf.  (In *Ni'kapashna*, Ponca).  Two of this name.
Du'bamo<sup>n</sup>thi<sup>n</sup> (fig. 26). *Du'ba*, four; *mo<sup>n</sup>thi<sup>n</sup>*, walking.  (In *Nu'xe*, Ponca)
Gino<sup>n</sup>'zhi<sup>n</sup>wathe....... *Gi*, again; *no<sup>n</sup>zhi<sup>n</sup>*, to rise, to stand; *wathe*, causes them.  He causes them to rise or stand.
Gthedo<sup>n</sup>'mo<sup>n</sup>thi<sup>n</sup>....... *Gthedo<sup>n</sup>'*, hawk; *mo<sup>n</sup>thi<sup>n</sup>*, walking.

Hiⁿçi'zhiⁿga .......... *Hiⁿ*, hair; *çi*, yellow; *zhiⁿga*, little (child's name).

Hiⁿ'xega.............. *Hiⁿ*, hair; *xega*, yellowish brown. Refers to the buffalo.

Iⁿde'ubthiⁿ............. *Iⁿde'*, face; *ubthiⁿ*, twisted.

Iⁿshta'thabi........... *Iⁿshta'*, eye; *tha*, cause; *bi*, he is. Appointed eyes. Refers to the appointed leader of the chase. This name belonged to one who was hereditary leader of the chase.

Moⁿnoⁿ'kuge .......... *Moⁿ*, from *moⁿthiⁿka*, ground; *noⁿ*, action of the foot; *kuge;* hollow sound, like a drum. This name refers to the rumbling sound made by the herds of buffalo with their hoofs when fleeing from the hunters.

Moⁿshtiⁿ'oⁿça .......... *Moⁿshtiⁿ'*, from *moⁿshtiⁿ'ge*, rabbit; *oⁿça*, swift. Refers to the use of rabbit hair on the pipes.

Nioⁿ'bathiⁿ............ *Ni*, water; *oⁿba*, day; *thiⁿ*, from *moⁿthiⁿ*, walk, or travel.

Noⁿke'na.............. *Noⁿ* implies action with the foot; *kena*, an old word signifying good.

Noⁿshki'gthe .......... Tracks of buffalo calf (child's name).

Noⁿzhiⁿ'thia .......... *Noⁿzhiⁿ*, to rise; *thia*, to fail. Unable to rise.

Nuga'................. Male, bull. (In *Poⁿ'caxti*, *Moⁿkoⁿ'* subdivision, Ponca.)

Pa'xehashuga .......... Thick skin of buffalo neck.

Tade'ta................ Modified from *toⁿthiⁿtoⁿ;* refers to the running of the pipe bearers in the He'dewachi ceremony. Two of this name.

Tewa'koⁿnoⁿzhiⁿ...... Sacred buffalo. (Dakota also.)

The'çeçabe............ *The'çe*, tongue; *çabe*, black. Refers to the tip of the buffalo's tongue. (In *Wazha'zhe*, Ponca.)

Ti'zhebegthoⁿ ........ Tent door flap. In Omaha treaty, 1826.

Uthi'shoⁿmoⁿthiⁿ...... To walk around.

U'thixide.............. To look around. Probably refers to the runners. Two of this name. (In *Nu'xe*, Ponca.)

Wanoⁿ'gewathe........ *Wa*, action with purpose; *noⁿge*, to run; *wathe*, one who causes. Causes them to run, or to stampede.

Washu'she............. Brave. (In *Wazha'zhe*, Ponca.)

Wate'xi............... *Wa*, action with purpose; *texe*, difficult.

Wi'thugthoⁿ........... Meaning uncertain.

### Borrowed names

Tewa'koⁿnoⁿzhiⁿ...... *Te*, buffalo; *wakoⁿ*, the Dakota *wakaⁿ*, mysterious; *noⁿzhiⁿ*, standing. Said to be borrowed from the Dakota; equivalent therein to "medicine cow."

### Dream names

Hoⁿ'moⁿthiⁿzhiⁿga..... Little night walk.

### Fanciful names

Giu'ka................. Meaning unknown.

Moⁿthe'gahi............ Refers to arrow.

Moⁿ'thihi.............. Refers to arrow.

### Nicknames

Wa'xupagthoⁿ......... *Wa'xe*, white man; *pa*, head; *ugthoⁿ*, to put in.

### Female names

Ha'wate............... Refers to the child, *Hoⁿ'ga*, in Wa'waⁿ ceremony.

I'nikashabi ........... Refers to tribal pipes—objects by which the tribe is identified as a people.

Mi'gthedoⁿwiⁿ........ Moon hawk, feminine. (In *Ni'kapashna*, *Washa'be*, and *Thi'xida*, Ponca.)

MI'GTHITO''' AND GRANDCHILD

Mi'gthito$^n$i$^n$ (pl. 26) ... Moon returning.

Mi'huça............. Loud voice moon. Two of this name.

Mi'mite............... Meaning uncertain.

Mi'mo$^n$shihathi$^n$....... Moon moving on high.

Mi'texi .............. Sacred moon.

Te'mitexi............. *Te'mi*, buffalo cow; *texi*, sacred. Two of this name.

To$^n$'i$^n$gthihe ......... Sudden apparition of the new moon. (In *Wazha'zhe;* also in *Waça'be, Hi'çada* subgens, Ponca.)

We'to$^n$na.............. Meaning uncertain. (In *Nu'xe*, Ponca.)

### I'ekithe subdivision

#### Ni'kie names

Çiko$^n$'xega............ *Çikon'*, ankles; *xega*, brown. Three of this name. (In *Ni'kapashna*, Ponca.)

Çi$^n$'demuxa........... *Çin'de*, tail; *muxa*, cluster.

Gthadi$^n$'gthitho$^n$....... *Gthadin'*, cross; *gthi*, return; *thon*, suddenly. A wounded buffalo turns sideways on his hunter. Child's name. Refers to a hungry calf crossing its mother's path to nurse.

Heba'zhu............... *He*, horns; *bazhu*, a little lump or knob. Three of this name. (Also in *Nini'baton* subgens.)

Hi$^n$to$^n$'zhi$^n$ga.......... *Hin*, hair; *ton*, possess; *zhinga*, little.

I$^n$shta'pede............ *Inshta*, eyes; *pede*, fire. (Also in *Nini'baton* subgens.)

To$^n$'wa$^n$zhi$^n$ga.......... *Ton'wan*, village; *zhinga*, small.

Wa'baku$^n$ga............ *Wa*, action; *ba*, push; *kunga*, jostling. Buffaloes crowding and pushing each other.

Wazhi$^n$'ho$^n$ga.......... First of birds. Refers to the eagle down put on the head of *Hon'ga* in Wa'wan ceremony.

Xitha'pahi............ *Xitha'*, eagle; *pahi*, neck.

#### Dream names

Xu'ga................ Badger.

#### Nicknames

Ta'thaçapa ............. Wood tick.

#### Female names

Açe'xube.............. *Açe*, paint; *xube*, sacred.

Mi'gasho$^n$thi$^n$........ Traveling or moving moon. (In *Waça'be* and *Thi'xida*, Ponca.)

Mi'gina............... Moon returning.

Mi'gthito$^n$i$^n$........... Return of the new moon.

Mi'o$^n$bathi$^n$........... The moon that travels by day.

Te'mitexi............. *Te'mi*, buffalo cow; *texi*, sacred.

### Ho$^{N}$'GA GENS (3)

The Ho$^n$'ga gens camped next to the I$^n$ke'çabe on the left. Ho$^n$'ga means "leader," or "first," and implies the idea of ancient, or first, people; those who led. The probability of Ho$^n$'ga being the ancient designation of the tribe has been discussed. (See p. 40.) This probability suggests a possible reason for the position of this gens and the duties devolving upon it. The gens occupied the center of the southern half (Ho$^n$'gashenu division) of the *hu'thuga*. The place of the Ho$^n$'ga corresponded to that set apart for the father of the family within the tent and the Ho$^n$'ga filled a directive position toward the gentes within the *hu'thuga*, or dwelling of the tribe, somewhat similar to that of the father toward the members of the family under his care.

Upon the Ho$^n$'ga devolved the leadership in the governing power of the tribe (see p. 201) and in the rites connected with the quest for food.

There were two subgentes, the Waxthe'xeto$^n$ and the Washa'beto$^n$. These had charge of the two Sacred Tents, their contents, and the ceremonies pertaining to the objects kept in them. The tents were pitched in front of the place where the two subgentes came together, and were set about 30 feet in front of the line, toward the center of the *hu'thuga*, about 25 feet apart.

The two tents represented "both sides of the house," the *hu'thuga*. From the rites connected with the White Buffalo Hide, lodged in the tent (13) set in front of the Washa'beto$^n$ subgens, it is probable that this tent represented the Ho$^n$'gashenu division, to which were committed the physical welfare of the people, the rites pertaining to the quest of food, and the control of warfare. The tent (12) pitched in front of the Waxthe'xeto$^n$ subgens contained the Sacred Pole, which was allied to Thunder and the supernatural Powers, and symbolized the authority of the chiefs—an authority believed to be derived from Wako$^n$'da. This tent probably represented the Sky people, the I$^n$shta'çu$^n$da division, which had charge of the rites pertaining to the people's relation to the supernatural.

### Waxthe'xeto$^n$ subgens (a)

Waxthe'xe (*waxthe'xe*, "mottled, as by shadows," "a mottled object"—the name of the Sacred Pole (see pl. 38); *to$^n$*, "to possess or have charge of") implied that the object thus described had the power to confer distinction, as the *xthe'xe*, "the mark of honor." The tabu of this subgens was a double one, the *tezhu'* and the crane. The *tezhu'* was a particular cut of meat from the side of the buffalo (see p. 273), that was brought as an offering to the Sacred Pole at the great tribal ceremony when the Pole was anointed. The feathers of the crane were used on the divining arrows that had a part in this same ceremony.

A group of families belonging to the Waxthe'xeto$^n$ subgens was set apart as servers; these were called *wathi'to$^n$* (from *thito$^{n'}$*, "to work"), "workers". Their duties were connected with ceremonies pertaining to the Sacred Pole. They prepared and distributed the meat brought as offerings by the people at the anointing rites. The tabu of this group was the same as that of the subgens of which they were a part—the *tezhu'* and the crane. This group camped next to the I'ekithe of the I$^n$ke'çabe gens, and at their left camped the remainder of the Waxthe'xeto$^n$ subgens.

### Washa'beto$^n$ subgens (b)

The Washa'beto$^n$ (*washa'be*, "a dark object," the word "dark" referring not to color, but to the general appearance of an object at a distance—the name of a peculiar staff (fig. 27) belonging to the

SACRED TENT OF THE WHITE BUFFALO HIDE

leader of the people when on the annual tribal hunt; $to^n$, to
"possess") had the official duty of making and decorating this staff,
though it did not belong to this subgens to provide the materials
required for the staff. The Washa'beto$^n$ had charge of the Teço$^n$'ha
(*te*, "buffalo;" *ço$^n$*', "pale" or "white;"
*ha*, "skin" or "hide")—White Buffalo
Hide, and its tent. (Pl. 27.) The tabu was
the buffalo tongues which were brought to
the sacred feast. A subdivision of this
subgens, called Ho$^n$'gaxti (*xti*, "original,"
as a parent stock) had charge of the
ceremonies connected with the maize.
They preserved the sacred corn, chanted
its ritual, and fixed the time for planting.
Their tabu was the *hatu'* (the word *hatu'*
is from *ha*, "skin," and *tu*, "green,"
referring to the outer husk of the ear of
corn). In this connection the decoration painted on the Sacred Tent in charge
of the Washa'be subgens, which was the
full grown stalk of corn, becomes significant. It is probable that the Ho$^n$'gaxti
was the original subgens, but when the
people came into the buffalo country,
the rites relating to hunting the buffalo
overshadowed those pertaining to the
maize; hence the subdivision that had
charge of the hunt became the more
important body, the group who possessed the rites of the corn the subordinate. This probability bears out a
tradition of the tribe that the people in

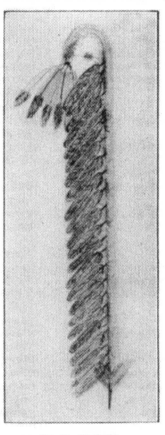

FIG. 27.   Washa'be.

the course of their migrations west and northwest became more strictly
a hunting people and that the cultivation of the maize fell into
abeyance or was temporarily abandoned.

FIG. 28.   Cut of hair,
Ho$^n$'ga gens.

The Washa'beto$^n$ subgens camped to the left
of the Waxthe'xeto$^n$ subgens.

The symbolic cut of the hair of children belonging to the Ho$^n$'ga gens consisted in cutting off all
the hair close to the head except a ridge which
stood up from the forehead to the nape of the
neck (fig. 28). This is said to represent the line
of the buffalo's back as seen against the sky, but
it is equally applicable to the appearance of growing corn viewed in the same way.

PERSONAL NAMES IN THE HO<sup>N</sup>'GA GENS (3)

*Waxthe′xeto<sup>n</sup> subgens (a)*

Ni′kie names

| | |
|---|---|
| A<sup>n</sup>′geda............... | From every direction. (See Ritual of Sacred Buffalo Hide, p. 294.) Two of this name. |
| Bishu′deki............ | Refers to the dust made by the herds as they move. |
| Edi′to<sup>n</sup>................ | *Edi′*, there; *to<sup>n</sup>*, stands. Refers to Sacred Pole. |
| E′tho<sup>n</sup>tho<sup>n</sup>be.......... | To appear repeatedly. (In *Washa′be*, Ponca.) |
| Gai<sup>n</sup>′bazhi............ | Ineffectual striking. |
| Kaxe′giu<sup>n</sup>.............. | *Kaxe*, crow; *giu<sup>n</sup>*, to fly. Flying crow. Two of this name. The crow is used as one of the symbols in making the *washa′be*. (See Ritual of Sacred Buffalo Hide, p. 300.) |
| Kaxe′no<sup>n</sup>ba,........... | *Kaxe*, crows; *no<sup>n</sup>ba*, two. (In *Thi′xida*, Ponca.) (See Ritual of Sacred Buffalo Hide.) |
| Mixa′to<sup>n</sup>............... | *Mi′xa*, swan; *to<sup>n</sup>*, standing. Refers to the down on the Sacred Pole. |
| Mo<sup>n</sup>chu′ha.............. | Grizzly-bear skin. In Omaha treaty, 1836. |
| Mo<sup>n</sup>chu′no<sup>n</sup>tide........ | *Mo<sup>n</sup>chu*, grizzly bear; *no<sup>n</sup>*, action with the feet; *tide*, rumbling sound. |
| Mo<sup>n</sup>chu′pa............. | *Mo<sup>n</sup>chu*, grizzly bear; *pa*, head. |
| Mo<sup>n</sup>′pezhi............. | *Mo<sup>n</sup>*, arrow; *pezhi*, bad. Refers to the divining arrows used in the ceremony of the Sacred Pole. (See Ritual of Sacred Pole, p. 242.) |
| Mo<sup>n</sup>′umizhe............ | On Omaha treaty of 1826. |
| Neka′hano<sup>n</sup>ge......... | *Neka′ha*, edge of a lake; *no<sup>n</sup>ge*, running. |
| Nia′dishtagabi.......... | *Ni*, water; *adi*, there; *shta*, from *i<sup>n</sup>shta*, eye; *gabtha*, to open. (See Legend of Sacred Pole, p. 70), where the name appears without elision. |
| Ni′k′umizhe........... | *Ni′k′umizhe*, resting on a human being. Probably refers to the resting of the Sacred Pole on a scalp. |
| No<sup>n</sup>′gazhi............. | *No<sup>n</sup>′ga*, to run; *zhi*, abbreviated form, not. Not able to run. |
| No<sup>n</sup>′kaetho<sup>n</sup>be ........ | *No<sup>n</sup>′ka*, back; *etho<sup>n</sup>be*, to appear. |
| Nudo<sup>n</sup>′ho<sup>n</sup>ga.......... | Leader, principal. (In *Washa′be*, Ponca.) |
| Sha′beno<sup>n</sup>zhi<sup>n</sup>......... | *Shabe*, dark, as an object; *no<sup>n</sup>zhi<sup>n</sup>*, to stand. Refers to the Sacred Pole. (In *Nu′xe*, Ponca.) |
| Sho<sup>n</sup>′ge ............... | Horse. Old name for wolf. |
| Shu′denaçi_........... | *Shu′de*, smoke; *na*, action by fire; *çi*, yellow. Refers to the smoke stain of the Sacred Pole. |
| Shu′kamo<sup>n</sup>thi<sup>n</sup>........ | *Shu′ka*, groups; *mo<sup>n</sup>thi<sup>n</sup>*, to walk. Walking in groups. Reference uncertain. (In *Washa′be*, *Hi′çada* subdivision, Ponca.) |
| Teba′gizhe............ | *Te*, buffalo; *bagizhe*, crooked, uneven. Refers to the uneven line of a herd of buffalo as seen against the horizon. |
| Teho<sup>n</sup>′mo<sup>n</sup>thi<sup>n</sup>......... | *Te*, buffalo; *ho<sup>n</sup>*, night; *mo<sup>n</sup>thi<sup>n</sup>*, walking. |
| Te′huto<sup>n</sup>bi............ | *Te*, buffalo; *huto<sup>n</sup>bi*, bellowing. Two of this name. (See ritual, p. 298.) |
| Tehu′xthabe.......... | *Te*, buffalo; *hu′xthabe*, the leaf fat. |
| Tenu′ga................ | Buffalo bull. (In *Washa′be*, Ponca.) |
| Tenu′gano<sup>n</sup>pewathe.... | *Tenu′ga*, buffalo bull; *no<sup>n</sup>pewathe*, fear inspiring. Fear-inspiring buffalo bull. |
| Tenu′gawazhi<sup>n</sup>pezhi ... | *Tenu′ga*, buffalo bull; *wazhi<sup>n</sup>*, powerful in will, angry; *pezhi*, bad. |

Tezhe'btho<sup>n</sup>............ *Tezhe'*, buffalo dung; *btho<sup>n</sup>*, smell.

Thiçpo<sup>n</sup>'bi ............ To feel of.  Refers to corn.  (See ritual, p. 266.)

Thigi'çe............... The sound made by corn husks when pulled apart.  (See ritual, p. 266.)

Ushko<sup>n</sup>'bitega......... *Ushko<sup>n</sup>*, wallow; *bitega*, making anew or afresh.

Uthu'shino<sup>n</sup>zhi<sup>n</sup>....... *Uthu'shi*, at the front; *no<sup>n</sup>zhi<sup>n</sup>*, to stand.  Refers to the Sacred Pole.

Wano<sup>n</sup>'shekithabi...... One who is made soldier.

Washi<sup>n</sup>'une............ Refers to the selection of fat for the anointing of the Pole.

Wathi'i<sup>n</sup>ge.............. Braided ears of corn.

We'kushto<sup>n</sup>............ *We'ku*, to give feasts; *shto<sup>n</sup>*, frequent.  Appears in Omaha treaty of 1830.

Xtha'gaxe ............ To blossom.  Refers to corn.  (See ritual, p. 266).

Zho<sup>n</sup>ço<sup>n</sup>'............... White wood.

### Fanciful names

Mo<sup>n</sup>chu'no<sup>n</sup>ba.......... Two grizzly bears.

Shaa<sup>n</sup>'................ Name by which Dakota are designated.

### Female names

I<sup>n</sup>shta'mo<sup>n</sup>çewi<sup>n</sup>........ *I<sup>n</sup>shta*, eye; *mo<sup>n</sup>çe*, metal, iron; *wi<sup>n</sup>*, female term.  Two of this name.

Mi'gasho<sup>n</sup>thi<sup>n</sup>.......... The traveling moon.  Four of this name.

Mi'gthito<sup>n</sup>i<sup>n</sup>.......... Return of the new moon.

Mi'mite............... Meaning uncertain.  Four of this name.

Mi'mo<sup>n</sup>shihathi<sup>n</sup>....... Moon moving on high.

Mi'waço<sup>n</sup>.............. The white moon.  Three of this name.  (In *Po<sup>n</sup>'caxti, Hi'çada* subdivision, Ponca.)

No<sup>n</sup>zhe'gito<sup>n</sup>............ Meaning uncertain.  Two of this name.  (In *Thi'xida* and in *Wazha'zhe*, Ponca.)

To<sup>n</sup>'i<sup>n</sup>thi<sup>n</sup>.............. New moon moving.  Three of this name.  (In *Thi'xida*, Ponca.)

We'to<sup>n</sup>bethi<sup>n</sup>.......... One who gives hope.  (From *uto<sup>n</sup>bethe*, to hope or to wish for.)  (In *Tapa'* gens also.)

### *Wathi'to<sup>n</sup> (hereditary servers) subdivision*

#### Ni'kie names

Gaçu'be............... Appearance of buffalo running against wind.  (In *Wazha'zhe*, Ponca.)

Ha'xigi............... Name of the first man, mythical.

Ho<sup>n</sup>'gaxti.............. *Xti*, real.  Real or original Ho<sup>n</sup>'ga.

I<sup>n</sup>shta'pa.............. Meaning uncertain.

Kage'zhi<sup>n</sup>ga............ *Kage'*, younger brother; *zhi<sup>n</sup>ga*, little.  Child's name.

Ni'kadathi<sup>n</sup>............ *Ni'ka*, man; *dathi<sup>n</sup>*, crazy.

No<sup>n</sup>shto<sup>n</sup>'azhi......... No<sup>n</sup>shto<sup>n</sup>, to stop; *azhi*, not.  He does not stop.

Sho<sup>n</sup>'geho<sup>n</sup>ga.......... Horse leader.  Old meaning, Wolf leader.

Uthu'shino<sup>n</sup>zhi<sup>n</sup>........ *Uthushi*, in front; *no<sup>n</sup>zhi<sup>n</sup>*, stands.  Refers to the Sacred Pole.

#### Fanciful names

I<sup>n</sup>cho<sup>n</sup>'gatha........... Meaning uncertain.

*Female names*

Mi'ako$^n$da............... *Mi*, moon; *ako$^n$da*, part of *Wako$^n$da*.
Mi'mo$^n$shihathi$^n$....... Moon moving on high.   Three of this name.
No$^n$zhe'gito$^n$........... Two of this name.   (In *Wazha'zhe* and *Thi'xida*, Ponca.)
We'ço$^n$kithe............. To come together in an order, as a society or brotherhood.

FIG. 29.  Mo$^n$xe'wathe.

*Washa'beto$^n$ subgens (b)*

*Ni'kie names*

I$^n$sh'a'gewahitha....... *I$^n$sh'a'ge*, old man, venerable; *wahitha'*, lame.   Refers to the
          herald, who leans on a staff as he shouts his message.
I$^n$shta'baçude.......... *I$^n$shta*, eyes; *baçude*, to shed.   Refers to the shedding of
          the hair about the eyes of the buffalo.   (In *Nu'xe*, Ponca.)
Mo$^n$shti$^{n'}$ge............ Rabbit.
O$^{n'}$geda ............... From every direction.   (See ritual, p. 294.)

Pahi′çka................ *Pa*, head; *hi*, hair; *çka*, white.   Refers to the appearance of the shoulder of the buffalo when the hair is shed.

Tenu′gaçka............. *Tenu′ga*, buffalo bull; *çka*, white.

We′no^{n}xitha .......... Meaning uncertain.

*Borrowed names*

Tenu′gagthi^{n}thi^{n}ke .... Sitting buffalo bull.   Said to be Dakota name.

Wako^{n}mo^{n}thi^{n}......... Mysterious walking.   Said to be Dakota name.

*Female names*

A′o^{n}wi^{n}............... Meaning uncertain.   (In *Waça′be*, Ponca.)

Mi′mite................ Meaning uncertain.   Four of this name.

Mi′tena................ Meaning uncertain.   (In *Wazha′zhe*, and *Po^{n′}caxti*, *Hi′çada* subdivision, Ponca.)

Teço^{n′}dabe............. White buffalo.   (In *Waça′be*, Ponca.)   Refers to the Sacred White Buffalo Hide.

Teço^{n′}wi^{n} ............. *Te*, buffalo; *ço^{n}*, white; *wi^{n}*, feminine term.   Two of this name.   (In *Waça′be*, Ponca.)   Refers to the Sacred White Buffalo Hide.

Wihe′zhi^{n}ga........... *Wihe′*, younger sister; *zhi^{n}ga*, little.

*Ho^{n}ga′xti subdivision*

Ho^{n}ga′xti ............. Original Ho^{n′}ga.

Mo^{n}xe′wathe (fig. 29) .. Victorious.

### Tha′tada Gens (4)

The Tha′tada presents points of difference from all other gentes in the tribe.   It has no common rite or symbol.   The rites of three of its subgentes were connected with the growth and care of the maize; the Waça′be shared in rites observed at the awakening of spring; the Wazhi^{n′}ga assisted in the protection of crops from devastation by birds; the Ke′i^{n} rites were connected with rain.   While there was this general association in the purpose of the respective rites of these subgentes, their symbols or tabus and their *ni′kie* names were different.   The Te′pa was the Nini′bato^{n} subgens of the Tha′tada; this subgens seems to indicate the change that had taken place in the principal food supply of the tribe, in a manner somewhat similar to that noted in the case of the Washa′beto^{n} subgens of the Ho^{n′}ga, but reversed.   The tabu and the name of the Te′pa subgens refer to the head of the buffalo, but the symbolic cut of the hair and the *ni′kie* names refer to the eagle, which was probably prominent in rites that were superseded by the buffalo when the people became established in the buffalo country.   The choice of this subgens for the Nini′bato^{n} division and the duty assigned it in connection with the ceremonial use of the Sacred Tribal Pipes seem to indicate that this subgens held an important place in the tribe and its ceremonies prior to the present arrangement of gentes, and that this importance was recognized by the "two old men" of the Sacred Legend.

The Tha'tada gens camped on the left of the Hoⁿ'ga. The word *Tha'tada* is probably a contraction of the phrase *tha'ta tathishoⁿ-thoⁿka* (*tha'ta*, "left hand;" *tathishoⁿ*, "toward;" *thoⁿka*, "those sitting")—that is, "those whose place in the *hu'thuga* was to the left of the Hoⁿ'ga." The name is not an ancient one, probably having been given when the tribe was organized in its present form.

There were four subgentes in the Tha'tada: Waça'be itazhi, Wazhiⁿ'ga itazhi, Ke'iⁿ, and Te'pa itazhi.

### Waça'be itazhi subgens (a)

(*Waça'be*, "black bear;" *itazhi*, "do not touch.") The rites connected with the black bear, which were formerly observed in this subgens, have been lost. Only the memory remains that this subgens used to join with the We'zhiⁿshte gens in rites observed when the first thunder was heard in the spring.

### Xu'ka subdivision (a')

Xu'ka means teacher or instructor in mystic rites. The name was given to a group of families who were designated to act as hereditary prompters to the Hoⁿ'ga gens during the singing of the rituals pertaining to the White Buffalo Hide and to the Sacred Pole, to insure against mistakes when the sacred ritual songs were given.

In the *hu'thuga* the Xu'ka subdivision camped next to the Hoⁿ'ga on the left, and on the left of the Xu'ka camped the remainder of the Waça'be subgens.

The tabu of the Waça'be subgens was the black bear. Its flesh could not be eaten nor its skin touched.

Fig. 30. Cut of hair, Waça'be subgens.

The symbolic cut of the hair of the children of this subgens consisted in the removal of all except a broad lock over the forehead, to represent the head of the bear (fig. 30).

### Wazhiⁿ'ga itazhi subgens (b)

The name of this subgens is derived from *wazhiⁿ'ga*, "bird;" *itazhi*, "do not touch." The rites that once were practised by the subgens pertained to the protection of the crops from the depredation of the birds. These rites have long been disused and are traditional only. It was said that one of the acts was to scatter partially masticated corn over the fields—a symbolic appeal to Wakoⁿ'da to prevent the small birds from attacking the corn and thus depriving the people of food. The rites of this subgens evidently referred to the period when the people depended more on the cultivation of the maize than they did after they entered the buffalo country.

The tabu was all small birds. Even the boys of this subgens, in their games, while they would shoot their arrows or strike with sticks at the birds would never touch one with their hands.

The symbolic cut of the child's hair consisted in the shaving of the head, leaving a fringe of hair around the base of the skull, a short lock in front, and a broad lock behind (fig. 31). The fringe represented the feathered outline of the bird's body, the front lock its head, and the broad lock behind, its tail.

The Wazhiⁿ'ga itazhi camped next on the left of the Waça'be itazhi.

FIG. 31. Cut of hair, Wazhiⁿ'ga itazhi subgens.

### Ke'iⁿ subgens (c)

The name Ke'iⁿ is compounded of *ke*, "turtle;" *iⁿ*, "to carry"—"the turtle carriers or bearers." The rites that were once in the keeping of this subgens have long since fallen into disuse and are known only by tradition. It is said that the form of the turtle was outlined on the ground and the sod cut out so as to make an intaglio of the animal, and that ceremonies were connected with this figure which pertained to the securing of rain and also to the dispelling of storms. The rites of the Turtle-bearers may have been associated with those that belonged to their neighboring subgens, the Wazhiⁿ'ga itazhi, and became obsolete for the same reason, the superseding of agriculture by hunting.

FIG. 32. Cut of hair, Ke'iⁿ subgens.

The tabu was the flesh of the turtle, which could not be eaten.

The symbolic cut of the hair consisted in shaving off all but a short fringe around the head, one small tuft over the forehead, two on each side, and a small lock at the nape of the neck (fig. 32). The short fringe outlined the shell of the turtle, the tuft over the forehead represented its head, the two on each side its feet, and the lock at the nape its tail.

The Ke'iⁿ camped on the left of the Wazhiⁿ'ga itazhi.

### Te'pa itazhi subgens (d)

The derivation of the name of this subgens is: *te*, "buffalo;" *pa*, "head;" *itazhi*, "do not touch." The rites pertaining to the buffalo head, which once belonged to this subgens, have been lost and there remains no trustworthy tradition concerning them. A pipe was given to this subgens to insure to it, as representative of its gens, a place in the tribal Council of Seven Chiefs, when that body was instituted. The names in this subgens which refer to the eagle refer also to this ceremonial pipe. The head of the subgens had an official position as one of the bearers of the Sacred Tribal Pipes when they were ceremonially smoked.

The tabu was the head of the buffalo. No member of this subgens would touch a spoon made from the horn of the buffalo.

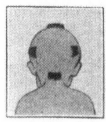

The symbolic cut of the hair of children of this subgens did not refer to the tabu of the gens, but to the eagle, which was connected with the pipe. The hair was cut close to the head except a square tuft over the forehead, a similar one at the nape of the neck, and a broad lock over each ear (fig. 33). The head, tail, and two wings of the eagle were thus represented.

FIG. 33. Cut of hair, Te'pa itazhi subgens.

The pipes used in the Wa'waⁿ ceremony could be painted on the tents of members of this gens, one on each side of the entrance and one at the back of the tent.

This subgens camped next on the left of the Ke'iⁿ.

### PERSONAL NAMES IN THE THA'TADA GENS (4)

#### Waçu'be itazhi subgens (a)

##### Ni'kie names

| | |
|---|---|
| Çida'moⁿthiⁿ | Meaning uncertain. |
| Gada'ka | Meaning uncertain. |
| Giha'zhi | Probable meaning: Unkempt. |
| Gi'thikoⁿbi | He to whom a place is yielded. |
| Iⁿshta'duba | *Iⁿshta*, eyes; *duba*, four. (In *Waça'be*, Ponca.) |
| Kaxe'katithe | *Kaxe'*, crow; *ka*, sound made by the crow; *tithe*, passing. |
| Ku'wiⁿxegthithoⁿ | Whirling around. |
| Moⁿ'shkaaxa | *Moⁿ'shka*, crawfish; *axa*, to cry for. (In *Ni'kapashna*, Ponca.) |
| Moⁿthi'uke | The digger of the ground. (Real name of Xa'debanoⁿ.) |
| Noⁿ'kaxude | *Noⁿka*, back; *xude*, gray. |
| Noⁿ'pabi | One who is feared. (In *Hi'çada*, Ponca.) |
| Pi'çithiⁿge | *Pi'çi*, gall; *thiⁿge*, without, none. Appears in Omaha treaties of 1815, 1836. |
| Shui'na | Meaning uncertain. (In *Waça'be*, Ponca.) |
| Tepa'uthixaga | Meaning uncertain. |
| Te'thiti | Buffalo ribs. In Omaha treaties of 1826, 1845. |
| Toⁿga'gaxe | Pretentions to greatness, self-importance. |
| U'xthetegoⁿ | Meaning uncertain. |
| Waça'apa | Meaning uncertain. (In *Nu'xe*, Ponca.) |
| Waça'be | Black bear. |
| Waça'bezhiⁿga | Black bear; *zhiⁿga*, young, little. (In *Waça'be*, Ponca.) |
| Wawe'xa | To laugh at. He who laughs. |

HU'PETHA

*Dream names*

Ni'daho<sup>n</sup>.................... *Ni'da*, mythical being or animal (see note on this name, p. 194); *ho<sup>n</sup>*, night.

*Fanciful names*

Hu'petha (pl. 28)........ Meaning uncertain.
Niu'gashude............. *Ni*, water; *u'gashude*, to make turbid.  Refers to bears pawing in the water.

*Valor names*

A'gahawashushe......... *A'gaha*, apart from, as outside a crowd; *washushe*, brave. Distinguished for bravery.  (In *Wazha'zhe*, Ponca.)
Pa'thi<sup>n</sup>no<sup>n</sup>pazhi.......... *Pa'thi<sup>n</sup>*, Pawnee; *no<sup>n</sup>pa*, fear; *zhi*, not.  Fears not Pawnee. (In *Thi'xida*, Ponca.)

*Nicknames*

Xa'debano<sup>n</sup>............. Bunch grass.

*Female names*

Do<sup>n</sup>'abi................. Meaning uncertain.  Two of this name.
Do<sup>n</sup>'ama................. Meaning uncertain.
Ma'zho<sup>n</sup>wi<sup>n</sup>.............. *Ma'zho<sup>n</sup>*, *mazho<sup>n</sup>ha*, fox; *wi<sup>n</sup>*, feminine term.  Two of this name.
Mi'bthiwi<sup>n</sup>.............. Meaning uncertain.  (In *Po<sup>n</sup>'caxti*, *Mo<sup>n</sup>ko<sup>n</sup>'* subdivision, Ponca.)
Mi'hupegthi<sup>n</sup>............ Meaning uncertain.
Mi'no<sup>n</sup>dabi.............. The only sun.
Mi'o<sup>n</sup>bathi<sup>n</sup>............. Moon that travels by day.
Mi'to<sup>n</sup>i<sup>n</sup>gi.............. New moon returning.
Ni'dawi<sup>n</sup>................ *Ni'da*, mythical being; *wi<sup>n</sup>*, feminine term.
No<sup>n</sup>çe'i<sup>n</sup>çe.............. Meaning uncertain.
To<sup>n</sup>'i<sup>n</sup>gina.............. Refers to the new moon.  Three of this name.
Wate'wi<sup>n</sup>................ Victory woman.
We'to<sup>n</sup>na................ Meaning uncertain.

*Xu'ka (hereditary prompters) subgens (a')*

*Ni'kie names*

A'gahamo<sup>n</sup>thi<sup>n</sup>........... *A'gaha*, apart from, outside a crowd; *mo<sup>n</sup>thi<sup>n</sup>*, moving, traveling, walking.
Çi'xude................. *Çi*, feet; *xude*, gray.
I<sup>n</sup>gtho<sup>n</sup>'xepa............ Wild cat undersized.
Ka'xepa................. *Ka'xe*, crow; *pa*, head.
Keo<sup>n</sup>'hazhi............. *Ke*, turtle; *o<sup>n</sup>'ha*, to flee; *zhi*, not.  (In *Po<sup>n</sup>'caxti*, Ponca.)
Ke'to<sup>n</sup>gai<sup>n</sup>shage.......... *Keto<sup>n</sup>ga*, great turtle; *inshage*, venerable, also old man.
Mo<sup>n</sup>'gezhide............. *Mo<sup>n</sup>'ge*, breast; *zhide*, red.  Refers to the breast of the turtle.
Mo<sup>n</sup>xpi'axaga............ *Mo<sup>n</sup>xpi*, clouds; *xaga*, rough.

Ni'çtumo<sup>n</sup>thi<sup>n</sup>............ *Ni'çtu*, backwards; *mo<sup>n</sup>thi<sup>n</sup>*, walking. (In *Waça'be*, Ponca.)
Pahe'tape............... Seeking the hills.
Sha'geçka............... *Sha'ge*, claws; *çka*, white.
Watha'wajigthe.......... *Watha'wa*, count; *ji*, then; *gthe*, sits. Refers to the office of prompter, holding the counting sticks of the songs.

### Dream names

Tenu'ga zho<sup>n</sup>thi<sup>n</sup>'ke..... Sleeping buffalo bull.

### Female names

Mi'gthito<sup>n</sup>i<sup>n</sup>............. Return of the new moon.
Mi'hupagthi<sup>n</sup>........... Meaning uncertain.
Mi'to<sup>n</sup>i<sup>n</sup>ge............... Returning new moon.
Tha'tadawi<sup>n</sup>............. *Tha'tada*, name of gens; *wi<sup>n</sup>*, feminine termination.
To<sup>n</sup>'i<sup>n</sup>thi<sup>n</sup>............... New moon moving.

### Wazhi<sup>n</sup>'ga itazhi subgens (b)

#### Ni'kie names

A'bthuzhide............. *A'bthu*, wing, an old word; *zhide*, red. Refers to the red-winged blackbird.
A'hi<sup>n</sup>xega............... *A'hi<sup>n</sup>*, wings; *xega*, brown. Two of this name.
A'hi<sup>n</sup>zhide............. *A'hi<sup>n</sup>*, wings; *zhide*, red—red-winged blackbird.
Axi'abaha............... Meaning uncertain.
Çi'mikaçi............... *Çi*, feet; *mikaçi*, wolf, coyote.
Çi'xude.................. *Çi*, feet; *xude*, gray.
Gamo<sup>n</sup>'xpi............... *Ga*, to strike; *mo<sup>n</sup>'xpi*, clouds. The wind strikes the clouds until it rains. (In *Waça'be*, Ponca.)
Gio<sup>n</sup>'habi.............. *Gi*, from him; *o<sup>n</sup>'ha*, to flee; *bi*, who is. One who is fled from.
Gthedo<sup>n</sup>'no<sup>n</sup>zhi<sup>n</sup>......... *Gthedo<sup>n</sup>*, hawk; *no<sup>n</sup>zhi<sup>n</sup>*, standing. (In *Ni'kapashna*, Ponca.) In Omaha treaty, 1854, 1865.
Gthedo<sup>n</sup>'xude........... *Gthedo<sup>n</sup>*, hawk; *xude*, gray. (In *Ni'kapashna*, Ponca.)
Gthedo<sup>n</sup>'zhi<sup>n</sup>ga........... Little hawk.
I<sup>n</sup>shta'çka............... *I<sup>n</sup>shta'*, eyes; *çka*, white. Refers to blackbirds.
Ke'to<sup>n</sup>ga............... *Ke*, turtle; *to<sup>n</sup>ga*, big. (In *Xu'ka;* also in *Waça'be*, *Hi'çada* subdivision, Ponca.)
Ma'azhi<sup>n</sup>ga............... *Ma'a*, cottonwood; *zhi<sup>n</sup>ga*, little, young. (In *Xu'ka;* also in *Thi'xida*, Ponca.)
Mi<sup>n</sup>ke'shage............. *Mi<sup>n</sup>ke* may be *mika*, raccoon; *shage*, claw.
Mo<sup>n</sup>shti<sup>n</sup>'çka ........... Rabbit; *çka*, white. (In *Wazha'zhe*, Ponca.)
Ni'kuthibtho<sup>n</sup>........... Smelling human being.
No<sup>n</sup>ba'mo<sup>n</sup>thi<sup>n</sup>......... *No<sup>n</sup>ba'*, two; *mo<sup>n</sup>thi<sup>n</sup>*, walking. (In *Waça'be*, Ponca.) In Omaha treaty, 1830.
No<sup>n</sup>be'duba.............. *No<sup>n</sup>be*, hands; *duba*, four. Refers to the bear (?).
No<sup>n</sup>'no<sup>n</sup>de............... *No<sup>n</sup>*, mature; *no<sup>n</sup>de*, heart.
No<sup>n</sup>'pewathe........... One who is feared. (In *Wazha'zhe*, Ponca.)
No<sup>n</sup>zhi<sup>n</sup>'mo<sup>n</sup>thi<sup>n</sup>......... *No<sup>n</sup>zhi<sup>n</sup>*, rain; *mo<sup>n</sup>thi<sup>n</sup>*, walking. Refers to the sand martins which do not retreat before the rain.
Pi'daega................ Meaning unknown. Old name.
Shu'zhi<sup>n</sup>ga............... Little prairie chicken.

Tawa'i$^n$ge................ Meaning uncertain.

Teço$^{n\prime}$ ................... *Te*, buffalo; *ço$^n$*, white.   In Omaha treaties of 1830, 1836, 1865.  (In *Hi'çada*, Ponca.)

U'ho$^n$no$^n$ba.............. *Uho$^n$*, cook, one who prepares a ceremonial repast; *no$^n$ba*, two.  (In *Washa'be*, Ponca.)

U'wethate.............. *U'we*, field; *thate*, eats.   Refers to eating of the corn by blackbirds.

Wa'baçkaha.............. Meaning uncertain.

Washko$^{n\prime}$mo$^n$thi$^n$......... *Washko$^n$*, strength; *mo$^n$thi$^n$*, walking.   In Omaha treaties of 1815, 1826, 1836, 1865.  (In *Washa'be*, Ponca.)

Wa'thidaxe............... Sound as of tearing with claws, as when a bear claws a hollow tree to get at honey.  (In *Wazha'zhe*, Ponca.)

Wato$^{n\prime}$i................. Conspicuous, plainly visible.

Wazhi$^n$'ga............... Bird.  (In *Waça'be*, *Hi'çada* subdivision, Ponca.)

Zhi'do$^n$hathi$^n$............ He who moves in the dew.

### Dream names

Ho$^n$a'kipa................. *Ho$^n$*, night; *akipa*, to meet.

Tenu'gagahi.............. *Tenuga*, male buffalo; *gahi*, chief.  (In *Nu'xe*, Ponca.)

Tenu'gawazhi$^n$.......... Angry buffalo—male.

Uha'hi................... Meaning uncertain.

Wazhi$^n$'agahige.......... Bird chief.  (In *Waça'be* gens, Ponca.)

### Fanciful names

Pe'degahi................ Fire chief.  (In *Waça'be*, Ponca.)   In Omaha treaty of 1865.

Umo$^{n\prime}$ho$^n$to$^n$wo$^n$gtho$^n$.... Omaha village.

### Nicknames

Iti'go$^n$no$^n$pi$^n$............. Medals worn on the neck.

Wabthu'ga............... Hominy.

### Female names

Gixpe'axa................ Meaning uncertain.

Mi'ako$^n$da................ Moon power.

Mi'dasho$^n$thi$^n$.......... Refers to the moon.

Mi'o$^n$bathi$^n$............. Moon travels by day.   Four of this name.

Mi'tena.................. Refers to the sun.

Mo$^{n\prime}$shihathi$^n$............ Moving on high.   Six of this name.

Ni'dawi$^n$................ *Nida*, a mysterious or fabulous being; *wi$^n$*, feminine termination.

Tha'tadawi$^n$.............. *Tha'tada; wi$^n$*, feminine termination.

Tha'taweço$^n$............. White Tha'tada woman.

To$^{n\prime}$i$^n$gthihe............. Sudden return of new moon.

We'to$^n$na ................ Meaning uncertain.

Wihe'to$^n$ga............... Big younger sister.

### Ke'i$^n$ subgens (c)

### Ni'kie names

Ezhno$^{n\prime}$zhuwagthe ...... *Ezhno$^n$*, alone; *zhugthe*, with; *wa*, them.

He'ga................... Buzzard.

Hega'di................ Meaning uncertain.

He'kathon............. *He*, horns; *kathon*, rattle, clatter, as the horns strike the brush. (In *Wazhin'ga* subdivision.)

Inku'shige............. Meaning uncertain.

Ke'chun............. *Ke*, turtle; *chun*, plenty. Two of this name. (Doubtful if *ni'kie*.)

Ke'gaxe............. *Ke*, turtle; *gaxe*, to make. Refers to the drawing of the figure of a turtle on the ground in the ceremony pertaining to the turtle.

Kegthe'çeinshtazhide.. *Ke*, turtle; *gtheçe*, spotted; *inshta*, eye; *zhide*, red. The sand-hill turtle.

Ke'honga............. *Ke*, turtle; *honga*, leader, or ancient.

Ke''inzhinga........... Little *Ke''in*.

Kethi'hi............. *Ke*, turtle; *thihi*, to scare animals. Two of this name.

Kezhin'ga............. *Ke*, turtle; *zhin'ga*, little. (In *Ni'kapashna*, Ponca.)

Mi'xabaku............. *Mi'xa*, goose; *buku*, bent, crooked. (In *Ni'kapashna*, Ponca).

Mon'çedon............. Meaning uncertain.

Na'ethonbe............. *Na*, by heat; *ethonbe*, appear. Refers to the hot days when the turtles rise to the top of the water.

Nia'kibanon............. *Ni*, water; *a*, for; *kibanon*, to run, as in a race. Refers to the flight of the turtle to the water.

Nia'tagigthe........... *Ni*, water; *a*, for; *ta*, towards; *gigthe*, goes home.

Nitha'shtage .......... *Ni*, water; *tha*, action with mouth; *shtage*, tepid.

Non'nonde............. *Non*, mature; *nonde*, heart.

Non'pewathe.......... *Non'pe*, afraid; *wa*, on; *the*, to be. One who is feared. (In *Wazha'zhe*, Ponca.)

Shkonshkon'tithe....... *Shkonshkon*, to move with the body; *tithe*, suddenly.

Shu'zhinga............. Prairie chicken.

Tenu'gawazhin........ *Tenu'ga*, buffalo bull; *wazhin*, means here, anger.

Uga'hatithe........... *Ugaha*, to float; *tithe*, by.

U'namonthin.......... *U'na*, to borrow; *monthin*, walking.

Wanon'çabe...........: The scratcher. This refers to the scratches inflicted by the turtle in his struggles to escape when caught.

Xae'monthin......... *Xae*, rustling sound; *monthin*, moving, walking. Refers to sounds made by birds.

### Dream names

Wathi'shnatigthe...... *Wathi'shna*, plain to the sight; *tigthe*, suddenly.

### Valor names

Ka'xebaha............. *Ka'xe*, crow; *baha*, to exhibit. Refers to the badge of bravery.

Wa'tonnonzhin.......... *Wa'ton*, upon; *nonzhin*, to stand.

### Nicknames

Iti'gonnonp'in........ *Iti'gon*, grandfather; *nonp'in*, to wear around the neck. Refers to wearing medals.

### Female names

Don'ama............... Meaning uncertain. Five of this name.

Mi'akonda............. Moon power.

Mi'gashonthin......... The moon that travels. Four of this name. (In *Washa'be* and *Thi'xida*, Ponca.)

Mi'gthedonwin.......... *Mi*, moon; *gthedon*, hawk; *win*, feminine. Two of this name. (In *Washa'be* and *Thi'xida*, Ponca.)

Mi'monshihathin....... Moon moving on high. Two of this name. (In *Pon'caxti, Monkon'* subdivision, Ponca.)

Mi'tena................. Refers to the moon. Seven of this name. (In *Washa'be*, *Hi'çada* subdivision, and *Wazha'zhe*, Ponca.)

Ni'dawi$^n$............. *Ni'da*, imps, mysterious little beings; *wi$^n$*, feminine. Seven of this name. (See footnote, p. 194.)

No$^n$çe'i$^n$çe............ Meaning uncertain. Eight of this name. (In *Wazha'zhe*, *Thi'xida*, and *Washa'be*, *Hi'çada* subdivision, Ponca.)

To$^{n\prime}$i$^n$gthihe........... Sudden apparition of the new moon.

Wate'wi$^n$............. *Wate*, victory. Three of this name. (In *Thi'xida*, Ponca.)

FIG. 34. Cha'cathi$^n$ge.

*Te'pa itazhi subgens (d)*

Ni'kie names

Agthi$^{n\prime}$duba........ Fourteen.

A'hi$^n$çka............... *A'hi$^n$*, wings; *çka*, white. In Omaha treaty of 1830. (In *Washa'be*, Ponca.)

A'hi$^n$çnede............ *A'hi$^n$*, wings; *çnede*, long. Refers to the eagle.

A'zhido$^n$to$^n$............ *A'zhido$^n$*, bedewed; *to$^n$*, stands. Refers to the eagle upon which the dew has fallen.

Cha'çathi$^n$ge (fig. 34).. *Cha'ça*, unkempt, ruffled; *thi$^n$ge*, not. Refers to an unusual appearance of the tidy eagle.

Çi'çi................. Yellow feet.

Çi'ha................. Soles.

Çi'to$^n$ga............... Big feet.

Ezhno$^n$'ho$^n$ga......... *Ezhno$^n$*, only; *ho$^n$ga*, leader.

Gaha$'$gthi$^n$............ Refers to eagle sitting on tree. Appears in Omaha treaty of 1815.

Gahi$'$ge................ Chief. (In Waça$'$be, Hi$'$çada subdivision, Ponca.)

Gaku$'$wi$^n$xe............ Ga, action by striking; ku$'$wi$^n$xe, to turn. Refers to the soaring of the eagle. (See ritual of hair cutting.) (In Wazha$'$zhe and Thi$'$xida, Ponca.)

Gap$'$o$^{n'}$ditho$^n$......... Eagles jar the branch when alighting.

Hi$^{n'}$xpeagaçnede....... Hi$^n$xpe, downy feather; aga, drooping; çnede, long. Refers to the downy feather taken from the eagle and used as a symbol in the pipe ceremony.

I$'$gachizhe.............. I, with; gachizhe, to fall with a crash on dry leaves or limbs. Refers to the lighting of the eagle.

I$^n$gtho$^{n'}$ga............. Wild cat. (Also in Xu$'$ka.)

Mo$^{n'}$çeguhe............ Meaning uncertain.

Mo$^n$ge$'$çi............... Mo$^n$ge$'$, breast; çi, yellow.

Mo$^n$gthi$'$xta............ Blackbird.

Nini$'$ba................ Pipe. (In Waça$'$be, Ponca.)

Nini$'$bai$^n$sh$'$age........ Nini$'$ba, pipe; i$^n$sh$'$age, old, venerable.

No$^{n'}$no$^n$de............. No$^n$, mature; no$^n$de, heart.

No$^n$zhi$^n'$mo$^n$thi$^n$....... No$^n$zhi$^n$, rain; mo$^n$thi$^n$, walking.

Paço$^{n'}$................. Pa, head; ço$^n$, white or whitish. Bald-headed eagle.

Paço$^{n'}$no$^n$zhi$^n$......... Paço$^{n'}$, bald-headed eagle; no$^n$zhi$^n$, standing.

Pe$'$hi$^n$xte.............. Tuft on the head of the eagle.

Pi$'$daega................ Meaning uncertain.

Sho$^{n'}$to$^n$çabe.......... Black wolf.

Tia$'$gito$^n$.............. Ti, house; a$'$gi, his own; to$^n$, stands. Refers to eagle standing on his nest.

Waça$'$apa.............. Meaning uncertain.

Waje$'$pa............... Old name for the tribal herald.

Wa$'$thishnade (pl. 29) .. One who grasps. Refers to the eagle.

Xitha$'$i$^n$sh$'$age.......... Xitha$'$, eagle; i$^n$sh$'$age, old, aged.

Xitha$'$wahi............. Xitha$'$, eagle; wahi, bone. Probably refers to the eagle-bone whistle used in ceremonies with the pipes.

Xitha$'$xega.............. Xitha$'$, eagle; xega, the color of dried grass, yellowish brown.

Xitha$'$xti............... Xitha$'$, eagle; xti, real. Two of this name.

Xitha$'$zhi$^n$ga............ Xitha$'$, eagle; zhi$^n$ga, little, young. (In Wazha$'$zhe, Ponca.)

### Dream names

Gaki$'$emo$^n$thi$^n$.......... Gaki$'$e, scattered; mo$^n$thi$^n$, traveling. Refers to flocks of birds.

### Female names

Gixpe$'$axa............... Meaning uncertain. Eight of this name.

Mipi$'$.................... Meaning uncertain; probably mi, moon; pi, good.

Mo$^{n'}$shihathi$^n$......... Moving on high. Refers to the eagle. Nine of this name.

Ni$'$dawi$^n$............. Meaning uncertain. Three of this name.

No$^n$çe$'$i$^n$the............ Meaning uncertain. Three of this name.

Tha$'$tadawi$^n$............ Tha$'$tada; wi$^n$, feminine termination.

Tha$'$tawiço$^n$............ Tha$'$ta, tha$'$tada; wi, wi$^n$, feminine termination; ço$^n$, white or pale.

To$^{n'}$i$^n$gthihe............ Sudden apparition of the new moon. Seven of this name.

We$'$to$^n$na............... Meaning uncertain. Eight of this name.

Wihe$'$to$^n$ga ............. Wihe$'$, younger sister; to$^n$ga, big.

WA'THISHNADE  (WAJE'PA)

Ko<sup>N</sup>′çe Gens (5)

The name of this gens is an ancient and untranslatable word. It belongs to one of the tribes (Kansa) of the cognate group of which the Omaha is a member. From this tribe the State of Kansas takes its name.

In the *hu′thuga* the Ko$^n$′çe gens camped on the left of the Tha′tada.

There were two subdivisions in the gens: (*a*) Tade′ata (*tade,* "wind;" *ata,* "in the direction of"—"in the direction of the wind"); the name is said to refer to the clouds. Rites connected with the wind were formerly in charge of this subgens, but they have been lost. In memory of the connection of these people with the wind was the following jesting action: when the mosquitoes were thick, a Ko$^n$′çe man was beaten with robes; this would call up a breeze to drive away the pests. (*b*) Nini′bato$^n$.

The tabu of the entire gens, as well as of its subgentes, was verdigris, which the people were forbidden to touch.

The symbolic cut of the children's hair represents a design which it is said used to be cut upon the earth after the sod had been removed when the ancient rites relating to the wind were practised. All the hair was cut off except a tuft over the forehead, one at the nape of the neck, and one on each side over the ear. From each of these four tufts, representing the four points of the compass, a narrow line of hair extended upward, terminating in a round tuft on the top of the head (fig. 35).

Fig. 35. Cut of hair, Ko$^n$′çe gens.

When the Hethu′shka society formerly was led around the tribal circle by the Ko$^n$′çe the act may have been in recognition of the power of the wind to befriend the warriors, as certain customs practised during warfare suggest. (See p. 39.) The Ko$^n$′çe also had the office of starting the ball game which was played by the two grand divisions of the *hu′thuga.* (See p. 197.)

The Tade′ata subgens camped on the left of the Te′pa itazhi of the Tha′tada, and on the left of the Tade′ata was the Nini′bato$^n$ subdivision.

PERSONAL NAMES IN THE KO<sup>N</sup>′ÇE GENS (5)

*Tade′ata subgens (a)*

*Ni′kie names*

Da′do$^n$thi$^n$ge.......... *Da′do$^n$*, possessions; *thi$^n$ge*, not, nothing. He has nothing. Refers to the invisible nature of the air or wind. (In *Wazha′zhe*, Ponca.)

Ko$^n$′çedathi$^n$........... *dathi$^n$*, crazy—Crazy Ko$^n$′ce.

Kuge′.................... The sound made by a drum.

Ma''axude.............. *Ma''a*, cottonwood; *xude*, gray.

Mu'xano$^n$zhi$^n$ (pl. 30)... Refers to the clouds.

Ni'kagahi.............. Chief.

No$^n$xtha'demo$^n$thi$^n$.... The creeping sensation of a bug crawling.

Taçi'ha................ Old name, meaning uncertain.

Tade'umo$^n$thi$^n$........ *Tade'*, wind; *u*, in; *mo$^n$thi$^n$*, walking. (See ritual of hair cutting.) (In *Wazha'zhe* and *Ni'kapashna*, Ponca.)

Thixthi'gazhi ......... *Thixthiga*, old; *zhi*, not (abbreviated) never old. Two of this name.

Wa'çiçi$^n$de............ Flapping with a quivering motion, as when the wind blows the tent flaps.

### Borrowed names

Cho$^n$'cho$^n$xepa......... Dakota.

Mi'chaxpe............. Omaha.

### Dream names

Waba'hizhi$^n$ga......... *Waba'hi*, to graze; *zhi$^n$ga*, little—little nibbler. (In *Wazha'zhe*, Ponca.)

Zho$^n$çi'mo$^n$de ......... *Zho$^n$*, wood; *çi*, yellow; *mo$^n$de*, bow.

### Female names

Açe'to$^n$ga.............. Meaning uncertain. (In *Po$^n$'caxti. Monko$^n$'* subdivision, Ponca.)

Mi'ako$^n$da............. *Mi*, moon; *ako$^n$da*, power.

Mi'mo$^n$shihathi$^n$....... Moon moving on high.

Mi'texi ................ Sacred moon.

Mi'to$^n$i$^n$ge............ New moon returning.

Mi'xube................ *Mi*, moon; *xube*, sacred.

Mo$^n$'shathi$^n$ke .......... *Mo$^n$'sha*, on high; *thi$^n$ke*, sitting (moon).

Tade'wi$^n$.............. *Tade*, wind; *wi$^n$*, feminine term.

To$^n$'i$^n$thi$^n$............. New moon moving.

Xu'degi................ *Xu'de*, gray; *gi*, returning. Refers to the mist blown by the wind.

### Nini'bato$^n$ subdivision (b)

#### Ni kie names

Ezhno$^n$'githabi ........ *Ezhno$^n$'*, only; *githabi*, who is favored—*gi*, possessive sign; *tha*, favored; *bi*, who is. The favored son (?)

Gahi'zhi$^n$ga (pl. 31).... *Gahi'*, *gahi'ge*, chief; *zhi$^n$ga*, little. (In *Ni'kapashna*, Ponca.)

Micha'xpezhi$^n$ga....... Little star—old name.

Mo$^n$'shewakude........ Meaning uncertain; probably, old man who shoots an arrow.

Mo$^n$zho$^n$'hathi$^n$ ........ *Mo$^n$zho$^n$'*, the earth; *ha*, over; *thi$^n$*, from *mo$^n$thi$^n$*. to walk or travel. Travels over the earth. Refers to the wind. The bearer of this name was a herald.

Mo$^n$'zho$^n$kide.......... Watches over the land. Refers to wind. (In Osage.) Appears in treaties of 1815 and 1826.

Paçi'duba............. Four buffaloes. (In *Washa'be*, Ponca.)

Wami$^n$'................ Blood. (In *Thi'xida*, Ponca.)

Zha'bezhi$^n$ga........... *Zha'be*, beaver; *zhi$^n$ga*, little.

### Female names

Ko$^n$çewi$^n$............... *Ko$^n$çe; wi$^n$*, feminine termination. Five of this name.

MU'XANO‹ZHIᴺ

GAHI'ZHIⁿGA (LITTLE CHIEF)

*Names unclassified as to subgentes*

Ni'kie names

Heba'dizhon............ *Heba'di*, half; *zhon*, sleep.  Sleeps halfway.
Konçegahige........... *Konçe*, Kansa chief.
Kon'çezhinga .......... Little *kon'çe*.
Non'dethinge........... *Nonde*, heart; *thinge*, not any.
Pahi'thagthin.......... Good hair.
Pa'nuhu .............. Owl.
Tade'ta................ To the wind.  Also in *Inke'çabe* ritual of hair cutting.
Tade'unça ............. *Tade'*, wind; *unça*, swift.
Waba'shethon.......... Meaning uncertain.
Wate'wahi............. Meaning uncertain.
Xage'wathe............ One who causes weeping.
Zhega'nonba........... *Zhega*, legs; *nonba*, two.

Female names

Tade'wahage........... Meaning uncertain.

INSHTA'ÇUNDA DIVISION, REPRESENTING THE SKY PEOPLE (A)

MON'THINKAGAXE GENS (6)

The significance of this name (*monthinka*, "earth;" *gaxe*, "to make")
is somewhat obscure, but the rites committed to this gens seem to
have been connected with the rock or stone and with the gray wolf.
What these rites were is not now known.  They have long since fallen
into disuse and become lost.  In myths that deal with the creation of
the earth, with the contention of man against strange monsters that controlled the animals, with the interdependence of various forms of life,
and with the persistent mystery of death we find the idea of perma-
nence, of length of days, of wisdom acquired by age, to be symbolized
by the rock or stone; while man's restlessness, his questionings of fate,
his destructiveness, are frequently symbolized by the wolf.  These
two, the rock or stone and the gray wolf, are in myths represented as
brothers and in the ancient rites belonging to this gens they were
symbolically united, in some way now unknown, a fact that makes it
not unlikely that the name of the gens, "earth makers," preserves the
purpose of the rites once committed to these people—rites that not
only dramatized the myth of Creation, but were believed to insure
the continuance of that which had been created.

According to tradition there were formerly in the keeping of this
gens four sacred stones, which were painted, respectively, white,
black, red, and green or blue.  These stones were ceremonially placed
in a circular hole made in the ground, and over them was spread the
down of the swan (*Cygnus americanus*).  As late as the last century one
of these stones was in existence, in charge of Ton'wongaxe.  It is
said that at the meetings of the Pebble society he would "place it on
the ground and make it walk."  There is a tradition that in the

ancient rites pertaining to the stones water or rain was represented. This tradition is borne out by the use of the down of the swan, a water bird, to cover ceremonially the stones. The connection with water rites is probably also indicated by the statement that the old keeper of the stones could take them to the Pebble society, whose rites pertained to the element water. All four stones are now lost. The last one was probably buried with Ton'wongaxe. The connection of the stones with the water adds to the probability that the lost rites of this gens dealt with the Creation.

There are no subgentes in this gens. Within the last century the groups of families to whom were formerly assigned certain duties connected with the ancient rites have taken names referring to their ancient hereditary office, and as a result these groups have been mistaken for subgentes. The Xu'be (sacred) group had direct charge of the sacred stones. Another group, whose office pertained to that part of the rites which related to the wolf, called themselves the Mi'kaçi (wolf). Still another, to whom belonged the duties relating to the water and the swan, called themselves Mi'xaçon (swan).

All of the above-mentioned groups had the same tabus as the gens, namely: The swan, the clay used for making the colors with which to paint the stones, and the soot from the kettle employed in preparing the black paint used on the stones.

FIG. 36. Cut of hair, Mon'-thinkagaxe gens.

The cut of the hair of the children of these groups was peculiar. The hair on the right side of the head was shaved off, while that on the left side was allowed to grow (fig. 36). It has been impossible to obtain a general explanation of this symbolic style of cutting the hair. Some have said it represented the bare rock and the falling rain.

At the organization of the tribe in its present form a group of families was set apart in the gens as Nini'baton, keepers of the pipes, and a chief from this group was given a place in the Council of.Seven Chiefs. In this group occurs a name found nowhere else in the tribe: Nini'ushi, filler of the pipes; this may refer in some way to the rites which once belonged to this gens, and which, as they probably pertained to the Creation, may have had a significance in the Council of Seven Chiefs, that ruled the tribe.

The cut of the hair of the children belonging to the Nini'baton group was the same as that used by the other Nini'baton subdivisions in the gentes of the tribe.

In camping, the Xu'be (a) pitched their tents immediately on the left of the Kon'çe; then came the Mi'kaçi (b); next, the Mi'xaçon (c); and on their left the Nini'baton subdivision (d).

SHOᴺ'GEÇKA (WHITE HORSE)

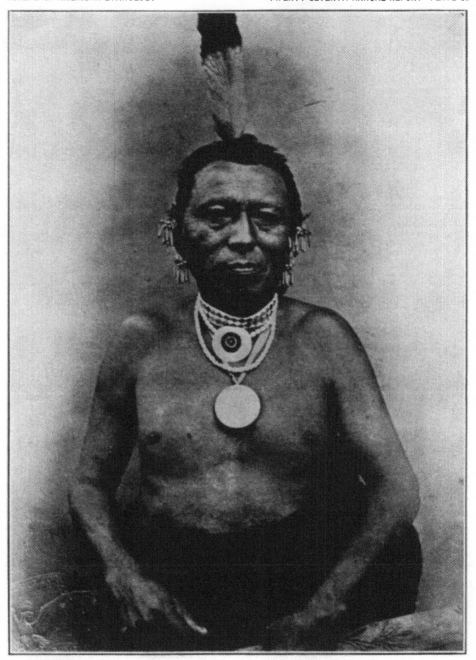

TON'WONGAXEZHINGA (LITTLE VILLAGE MAKER)

## PERSONAL NAMES IN THE MO$^{N'}$THI$^N$KAGAXE GENS (6)

### Xu'be subdivision (a)

#### Ni'kie names

A'xabazhi.............. *A'xa*, to cry for; *ba*, they; *zhi*, not.   One who is not cried for.

Gachi'zhitho$^n$......... *Gachi'zhi*, to fall with a crash; *tho$^n$*, contraction of *itho$^n$*, suddenly.   Refers to the noise made by the eagle when alighting.

I'gasho$^n$.............. Wanderers; refers to wolf.   Two of this name.

Mo$^{n'}$gthitho$^n$.......... Standing up suddenly.   Refers to a little animal that suddenly rises to an upright position.

No$^n$'gemo$^n$thi$^n$........ *No$^n$'ge*, to run; *mo$^n$thi$^n$*, walks or travels.   Travels running. (In *Waça'be*, Ponca.)

No$^n$zhi$^{n'}$mo$^n$thi$^n$...... *Nonzhi$^n$'*, rain; *mo$^n$thi$^n$*, travels.   (In *Washa'be*, Ponca.)

Sho$^{n'}$geçka (pl. 32).... *Sho$^n$'ge*, horse (old name for wolf); *çka*, white.   Appears in treaties of 1826, 1830, 1836, 1854.   (See Sho$^n$ge'çabe, *Tapa'* gens.)   (In *Nu'xe*, Ponca and Osage.)

Uga'sho$^n$zhi$^n$ga........ *Uga'sho$^n$*, traveler; *zhi$^n$ga*, little.   (In *Washa'be*, Ponca.)

Waba'hiçi............. *Waba'hi*, to graze; *çi*, yellow.   Yellow object grazing; refers to yellow wolf.   (In *Po$^n$'caxti*, *Mo$^n$ko$^n$'* subdivision, Ponca.)

Wahu'thabi........... One of whom permission is asked.   Appears in treaty of 1815.

#### Dream names

Çigthe'no$^n$pabi......... *Çigthe*, footprints; *no$^n$pabi*, to fear.   One whose footprints, even, are feared.   (In *Wazha'zhe*, Ponca.)

Waça'beto$^n$ga .......... *Waça'be*, black bear; *to$^n$ga*, big.   (In *Thi'xida*, Ponca.)

Wa'dupa.............. Old dream name.   Two of this name.

Wahe'he.............. Easy to break, tender to the touch.

Wako$^n$'da.............. Power.   Refers to sacred stones.   (In *Wazha'zhe*, Ponca.)

Wako$^n$'daukie ......... Talks to Wako$^n$'da.

Washi'shka............. Shell.   (In *Thi'xida*, Ponca.)

#### Borrowed names

Hexa'gano$^n$zhi$^n$........ *Hexa'ga*, elk (Dakota); *nonzhi$^n$*, to stand.   (In *Washa'be*, Ponca.)

Ko$^n$'çeho$^n$ga .......... *Ko$^n$'çe*, name of gens and tribe, Kansa; *ho$^n$ga*, leader.   (In *Wazha'zhe*, Ponca.)

Mixa'çka.............. White swan.

Wazhi$^n$'gaçabe......... *Wazhi$^n$'ga*, bird; *çabe*, black.   (In *Waça'be*, Ponca.)

#### Fanciful names

To$^{n'}$wo$^n$gaxe........... *To$^n$'wo$^n$*, village; *gaxe*, maker.

To$^{n'}$wo$^n$gaxezhi$^n$ga (pl. *Zhi$^n$ga*, little.   Little village maker.
    33.)

We'thishku........... *We*, to do something for another; *thishku*, from *thishkuda*, to dig with the fingers.

#### Valor names

Mo$^n$ga'azhi.............. *Mo$^n$*, arrow; *ga'azhi*, not afraid.   (In *Waça'be*, Ponca.)

Waçe'athi$^n$............ *Waçe'*, paint; *athi$^n$*, have.   Refers to war parties.

Washi'bino$^n$hi$^n$........ *Washi'bi*, to ask one to work; *no$^n$hi$^n$* from *ino$^n$hi$^n$*, willing.   Willing to serve.

*Female names*

Mi'mitega.............. The new moon. Four of this name.
Mi'moⁿshihathiⁿ....... Moon moving on high.
Mi'texi................ *Mi*, moon; *texi*, sacred. Two of this name.
Mi'toⁿiⁿ............... New moon. Two of this name.
Noⁿzhe'gitoⁿ.......... Meaning uncertain. (In *Wazha'zhe*, Ponca.) Two of this name.
Poⁿ'caçoⁿ............. White Ponka. (In *Poⁿ'caxti*, *Moⁿkoⁿ'* subdivision, Ponca.) Three of this name.
Poⁿ'cawiⁿ............. *Poⁿca* feminine. (In *Waça'be*, Ponca.)
Toⁿ'iⁿgina............ New moon returning. Three of this name.
We'tewiⁿ............. Meaning uncertain. Five of this name.

### Nini'batoⁿ subdivision (d)

*Unclassified names*

Çe'çethiⁿke........... The trotter; indicating the characteristic gait of the wolf.
Çiⁿ'dezhiⁿga.......... Little tail.
Gahi'gewadathiⁿga...... Refers to the peaceful office of the chiefs. This name appears among the Osage, and is sometimes misleadingly translated as Saucy Chief or Crazy Chief.
Gthedoⁿ'noⁿpabi...... Hawk who is feared.
Gthedoⁿ'wiⁿ.......... *Gthedoⁿ*, hawk, *wiⁿ*, feminine termination. Two of this name.
Gu'dahi.............. There-he-goes! An exclamation of hunters who scare up a coyote.
Huti'gthe ........... Voice heard at a distance. Refers to wolves.
Iⁿ'çoⁿ............... White rock. Refers to the sacred stones.
Iⁿke'gaxe............ Refers to pipes.
Iⁿzhi'de............. Red rock. Refers to the sacred stones.
Mi'gthedoⁿwiⁿ......... *Mi*, moon; *gthedoⁿ*, hawk; *wiⁿ*, feminine termination.
Mixa'çka............. *Mixa*, swan; *çka*, white. (In *Thi'xida*, Ponca.) Two of this name.
Moⁿ'gthithoⁿ.......... *Moⁿgthe*, to stand; *ithoⁿ*, suddenly. The last vowel in *moⁿgthi* is dropped. Refers to sudden action of gray wolf. Two of this name.
Ni'kaçtuwathe........ The gatherer. Refers to the Sacred Tribal Pipes and their unification of the people into one social body.
Nini'ushi............ *Nini'*, pipe; *ushi*, to present. Refers to ceremony of pipes.
Shoⁿ'toⁿgaçka......... The white gray wolf.
Shoⁿ'toⁿgamoⁿshiadi ... The tall gray wolf.
Shoⁿ'toⁿgatu......... The blue gray wolf.
Shoⁿ'toⁿgawathihuça... The mad gray wolf.
Shoⁿ'toⁿzhiⁿga........ *Shoⁿtoⁿ*, gray wolf; *zhiⁿga*, little or young.
Thata'xitigthe........ Crunching of bones. Refers to wolf.
The'dewathatha........ Refers to the frequent cautious looking backward of the wolf as he trots along.
Ugaç'iⁿnoⁿ........... The peeper. Refers to the coyote.
Uga'shoⁿnoⁿzhiⁿ....... The wanderer. The restless habit of the coyote.
Uga'shoⁿtoⁿ.......... The wanderer. The restlessness of the wolf.
U'shkadazhi.......... Dauntless, rushing into battle without hesitation. (In *Nu'xe*, Ponca.)
Utha'gabi............ Refers to wolf.

Wa′gawiⁿxe............ The soarer. Refers to the eagle.
Wathi′gthoⁿthiⁿge...... No mind.

### Borrowed names

Ki′shtawagu........... Said to be Pawnee. (In *Waça′be* gens, Ponca.)
Waxua′taiⁿge........... Said to be Oto.

### Dream names

Hoⁿ′hemoⁿthiⁿ......... Night walker.
Moⁿchu′wakoⁿda....... Bear god.

### Valor names

Iⁿke′washushe......... Brave soldier.

### Nicknames

Iⁿshti′thiⁿke.......... Name of a mythical mischievous being.

### Female names

Açe′xube.............. *Açe′*, from *waçe*, paint; *xube*, sacred.
Gixpe′axa.............. Meaning lost. Old name. ·Two of this name.
Mi′ashteshtoⁿ.......... Meaning uncertain. Three of this name.

## TEÇIⁿ′DE GENS (7)

The name of this gens has reference to the buffalo (*te*, "buffalo;" *çiⁿde*, "tail"). There are no subgentes.

The rites anciently committed to the people of this gens have been lost. Nothing but a tradition remains, which states that the ceremony pertained to the crow. In certain myths that speak of the Creation it is said that human beings were at first without bodies; they dwelt in the upper world, in the air, and the crow was instrumental in helping the people to secure bodies so that they could live on the earth and become as men and women.

The tabu of the gens favors the tradition that the rites under its charge referred to the birth of the people in bodily form. They were forbidden to touch the unborn young of an animal. In later days the tabu applied especially to the buffalo young, and also to the lowest rib adhering to the backbone, as the head of the fetus was said to rest against this part of the animal; consequently the meat from this rib could not be eaten.

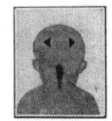

FIG. 37. Cut of hair, Teçiⁿ′de gens.

The symbolic cut of the hair referred to the young of the buffalo. All the hair was cut off except two small tufts on the side of the crown, indicating the coming horns, and a lock at the nape of the neck representing the tail of the calf (fig. 37).

When the tribe was organized in its present form, a Nini′batoⁿ group of families was chosen in this gens and the leader of the group was given a place in the tribal Council of Seven Chiefs.

The tabu of this subdivision was the same as that of the gens itself. The symbolic cut of the hair was like that of all the children belonging to Nini'bato^n subdivisions.

The Teçi^n'de (a) camped on the left of the Mo^n'thi^nkagaxe, the Nini'bato^n subdivision (b) being at the extreme left of the gens.

### PERSONAL NAMES IN THE TEÇI^N'DE GENS (7)

*Teçi^n'de subdivision (a)*

#### Ni'kie names

Heba'zhu............. *He,* horns; *bazhu,* knobby.

He'xude.............. *He,* horns; *xude,* gray.

Hi^nçi'zhi^nga......... *Hi^n,* hair, of an animal; *çi,* yellow; *zhi^nga,* little. Refers to the young buffalo. (In *Washa'be,* Ponca; also in *I^nke'çabe.*)

I'shibazhi............ The name of an old hero whose deeds are preserved in song and story.

Ka'xenumpi^n........ Crow necklace.

Kigtha'zho^nzho^n..... *Kigtha,* himself; *zho^nzho^n,* to shake—shakes himself. Refers to a buffalo. (In *Po^n'caxti, Mo^nko^n'* subdivision, Ponca.)

Tamo^n'xaga......... *Ta,* a corruption of *te,* buffalo; *mo^n,* arrows; *xaga,* bristling. Two of this name.

Uma'abi............. Cut into pieces and spread (scattered?).

Waho^n'thi^nge (pl. 34). *Wa,* a prefix by which a condition is generalized and expressed as a noun; *ho^n,* from *eho^n,* mother (general term); *thi^nge,* none. Hence, *waho^n'thi^nge,* orphan. The loss of the mother makes an orphan, according to the Omaha idea. (In *Wa-sha'be,* Ponca.)

#### Female names

Mi'ako^nda............ *Mi,* moon; *ako^nda, wako^nda.* Four of this name. (In *Po^n'caxti, Mo^nko^n'* subdivision, Ponca.)

Mi'gthito^ni^n........ *Mi,* moon; *gthi,* return; *to^ni^n,* new. The new moon returns. (In *I^nshta'çu^nda* gens.)

Mi'xube............. *Mi,* moon; *xube,* sacred.

Teço^n'wi^n........... White buffalo, feminine term. Three of this name.

To^n'i^ngi............ *To^n'i^n,* new moon, *gi,* coming. (In *I^nshta'çu^nda* gens.)

Umo^n'agthi^n........ Meaning uncertain.

Uthe'amo^nthi^n...... Three of this name.

Uzho^n'geagthi^n...... *Uzho^n'ge,* trail; *agthi^n,* to sit on. Refers to buffalo sitting in the buffalo path.

Wihe'gthedo^n....... *Wihe',* younger sister; *gthedo^n,* hawk. Two of this name.

*Nini'bato^n subdivision (b)*

#### Ni'kie names

Çi^n'dethiho^n........ *Çi^n'de,* tail; *thiho^n,* to lift. The father (now dead) bore same name. (In *Nu'xe,* Ponca.)

I^nshta'shabe........ *I^nshta',* eye; *shabe,* black. Two of this name. (In *Waça'be,* Ponca.)

Mo^na'xaga.......... *Mo^n,* arrow; *a'xaga,* bristling—bristling with arrows.

Mo^n'sho^nho^nga...... Refers to feathers on the pipe leaders.

No^n'dewahi......... Bone heart.

No^n'gethia.......... *No^n'ge,* to run; *thi'a,* not able. Probably refers to the new-born calf. (In *Nu'xe,* Ponca.)

WAHO<sup>N</sup>'THI<sup>N</sup>GE

No$^n$o$^n$'bi............. *No$^n$o$^n$*, to hear; *bi*, who is.  One who is heard.  (In *Wazha'zhe*, Ponca.)

Pe'zhexuta......... Wild sage (artemisia).

Shu'degina.......... *Shu'de*, smoke; *gina*, coming.  Refers to the smoke-like appearance of the cloud of dust raised by the herds of buffalo as they approach.

Ta'mo$^n$ha............ *Ta*, deer; *mo$^n$*, *mo$^n$ge*, breast; *ha*, skin.

Tato$^n$'gashkade....... *Tato$^n$'ga*, *tata$^n$ka*, Dakota for buffalo; *shkade*, to play—Dakota, *ska'ta*.  (In *Wazha'zhe*, Ponca.)

Tenu'gazhi$^n$ga....... *Tenu'ga*, buffalo bull; *zhi$^n$ga*, little.  (In *Wazha'zhe*, Ponca.)

Texe'uno$^n$zhi$^n$....... *Texe*, marsh; *u*, in; *no$^n$zhi$^n$*, to stand.  Standing in buffalo wallow.

Thixa'bazhi.......... *Thixa'*, to chase; *ba*, they; *zhi*, not.  Two of this name.  Refers to the calf that no one chases.

Uzhna'gaxe......... *Uzhna'*, clear space; *gahe*, to make.  Refers to the wallow.  (In *Nu'xe*, Ponca.)

Waba'xe............. The many layers.  Refers to the fat about the stomach of the buffalo.  Two of this name.

Zhu'gthethi$^n$ge ...... *Zhugthe*, companion; *thi$^n$ge*, none.

*Female names*

Mi'çebe............. *Mi*, moon; *çebe*, dark or shadowy.  May refer to the shadowy part of the moon seen when the moon is new.  Two of this name.

Mi'gthito$^n$i$^n$......... *Mi*, moon; *gthi*, return; *to$^n$i$^n$*, new, applied to the new moon.  Three of this name.

Mo$^n$'çepewi$^n$........ Ax; *wi$^n$*, feminine termination.

Teço$^n$'wi$^n$.......... White buffalo, *wi$^n$*, feminine termination.  (In *I$^n$gthe'zhide*.)  Six of this name.  (In *Wazha'zhe*, Ponca.)

Uthe'amo$^n$thi$^n$...... *Uthe*, a route usually taken; *a*, over; *mo$^n$thi$^n$*, walking.  May refer to the migrations of the buffalo.  Six of this name.

*Unclassified names*

Heba'chage ......... *He*, horns; *ba'chage*, crumpled.

No$^n$he'gazhi......... Running hard.

No$^n$'kapai .......... *No$^n$'ka*, back; *pai*, sharp.

Shu'kagthi$^n$......... *Shu'ka*, a group; *gthi$^n$*, *agthi$^n$*, to sit.

*Nicknames*

Wau'xtawathe........ Admirer of women.

*Fanciful names*

Mo$^n$'çepeto$^n$ga....... *Mo$^n$'çepe*, ax; *to$^n$ga*, big.

TAPA' GENS (8)

Tapa', "head of the deer," is the name given to the Pleiades. The rites formerly in charge of this gens are lost, but there are traditions that point to the strong probability that they related to the stars and the night skies.  These rites seem to have been connected with myths dealing with the Creation.  In them the wild-cat skin and the fawn skin were used, their spotted appearance having a symbolic reference to the heavens at night.  The thunder and zigzag lightning were also typified, and were connected with the ceremonies pertaining to the cutting of the child's hair, ceremonies in which this gens formerly took part, and represented the father, the sky. Of the ancient rites only a few vestiges now remain, such as the painting of spots on the child along the sides of its spine, when a few days after birth the child received its baby name. This was done by an old man of the gens, who dipped three fingers into the paint and with them made the symbolic spots on the child. These spots had the double significance of the fawn—the young or newborn of the deer—and the constellation known by the name of "the deer's head." Names in the gens refer to the lightning, and it is said that red lines were sometimes painted on the child's arms, typical of it.

There were no subgentes in the Tapa' gens, but formerly there were groups in charge of certain duties connected with the ancient rites. These groups continued to cling together, although their duties became obsolete with the loss of the rites. They still exist and are known as the group under Mike'nitha or Çin'dexonxon. The members of this group sometimes speak of themselves as Tapa'xti ("the real or original Tapa'"); the group under Pa'thingahige seems to have had charge of that part of the ancient ceremonies which referred to the thunder; to the group under Zhinga'gahige seems to have been committed the symbolic fawn skin. Pa'thingahige and Zhinga'gahige were not chiefs but leading men. These groups have sometimes been mistaken for subgentes.

Tabu: charcoal and verdigris could not be touched by this gens. The verdigris by its color was said to symbolize the sky, and the

FIG. 38. Cut of hair, Tapa' gens.

association of charcoal with the verdigris would indicate that the dark, or night, sky was symbolized in the tabu.

The symbolic cut of the hair consisted in shaving the head, leaving only a tuft over the forehead and a thin lock at the nape of the neck. The significance of this style is uncertain (fig. 38).

At the organization of the tribe in its present form a group of families became the Nini'baton subdivision, and its leader had a seat in the tribal Council of Seven Chiefs. The Nini'baton observed the tabu of the gens, but the hair of the children was cut in the style of all the Nini'baton subdivisions in the tribe.

This gens affords another instance of the change that takes place in the general significance of the name of a gens when the rites intrusted to it have become obsolete and lost. The star cult rites of the gens being no longer practised, the deer's head ceased to be regarded merely as symbolic and took on a literal interpretation.

This is evidenced in the personal names where the stellar significance has been largely lost sight of.

In the *hu'thuga* the group under Çi$^{n'}$dexo$^n$xo$^n$ (*a*), or Mike'nitha, camped on the left of the Teçi$^{n'}$de people; next was the group under Pa'thi$^n$gahige (*b*); on their left the group under Zhi$^n$ga'gahige (*c*); and at the left end of the Tapa' was the Nini'bato$^n$ subdivision (*d*).

### PERSONAL NAMES IN THE TAPA' GENS (8)

*Group under Çin'dexonxon ( Mike'nitha) (a)*

#### Ni'kie names

Bachi'zhithe......... *Bachizhi*, to rush in in spite of obstacles; *the*, to go—as the deer rushing into the bushes. (In *Wazha'zhe*, Ponca.)

Çigthu'no$^n$ge ........ *Çigthu*, trail in; *no$^n$ge*, running.

Çi$^{n'}$deçka .......... *Çi$^n$de*, tail; *çka*, white. (In *Po$^n'$caxti*, *Mo$^n$ko$^n'$* subdivision, Ponca.)

Çi$^{n'}$deço$^n$tigthe...... *Çi$^{n'}$de*, tail; *ço$^n$*, pale; *tigthe*, sudden. Refers to the sudden flash of the white tail of the deer as the animal leaps into the cover. Four of this name.

Çi$^{n'}$degabizhe ...... *Çi$^{n'}$de*, tail; *gabizhe*, wagging. Two of this name.

Çi$^{n'}$dexo$^n$xo$^n$ (fig. 39)_ *Çi$^{n'}$de*, tail; *xo$^n$xo$^n$*, glittering.

Hethi'axe............ *He*, horn; *thiaxe*, rattling. Refers to the rattling sound of the antlers against the bushes as the deer plunges into a thicket.

Hexa'gazhi$^n$ga...... *He*, horn; *xa'ga*, rough; *zhi$^n$ga*, little.

Hezha'ta............ *He*, horn; *zhata*, forked. Two of this name. (In *Thi'xida*, Ponca.)

I'i$^n$gabi............. *I'i$^n$ga*, rejected; *bi*, who is.

Keba'ha............. *Ke*, turtle; *baha*, to show—turtle showing himself. (In *Thi'xida*, Ponca.)

Mika'xage........... *Mika*, raccoon; *xage*, to cry—crying raccoon. (In *Po$^n'$caxti*, *Mo$^n$ko$^n'$* subdivision, Ponca.)

Mike'nitha.......... Old name; meaning uncertain. Four of this name.

Mo$^n$no$^{n'}$xaxa........ *Mo$^n$*, earth; *no$^n$*, action by the feet; *xaxa*, to scrape, to tear up. Refers to the rutting of the deer.

No$^{n'}$ço$^n$dazhi........ *No$^{n'}$ço$^n$da*, to dodge; *zhi*, from *o$^n'$kazhi*, not. (In *Washa'be*, Ponca.)

No$^{n'}$kahega......... *No$^n$ka*, back; *hega*, brown. (In *Wazha'zhe*, Ponca.)

O$^{n'}$hazhi ........... *O$^n'$ha*, to flee; *zhi*, from *o$^n'$kazhi*, not. Makes no attempt to escape.

Pahi'çka............ *Pa*, head; *hi*, hair; *çka*, white.

Shage'duba......... *Shage'*, hoofs; *duba*, four. (In *Waça'be*, Ponca.)

Sha'gezhi$^n$ga........ *Sha'ge*, hoofs; *zhi$^n$ga*, little. Two of this name.

Shko$^{n'}$shko$^n$tithe.... *Shko$^n$*, to move; *shko$^n$shko$^n$*, continually moving; *tithe*, suddenly. Two of this name.

Tato$^{n'}$gamo$^n$thi$^n$..... *Ta*, deer; *to$^n$ga*, big; *mo$^n$thi$^n$*, walking. (In *Ni'kapashna*, Ponca.)

Ta'xtiduba.......... *Ta'xti*, original deer; *duba*, four.

Te'hego$^n$............. *Te*, buffalo; *he*, horn; *go$^n$*, like. Refers to the stage of growth when the antler resembles the horn of the buffalo. Two of this name.

Thiti'bitho$^n$.......... Bounding up.

Tide'moⁿthiⁿ....... *Tide*, noise, rumbling; *moⁿthiⁿ*, walking, moving.
Uwoⁿ'çitithe........ *Uwoⁿ'çi*, to jump up; *tithe*, suddenly.
Wa'xanoⁿzhiⁿ....... *Wa'xa*, in advance; *noⁿzhiⁿ*, standing. (In *Poⁿ'caxti, Moⁿkoⁿ'* subdivision, Ponca.)
Waxpe'sha........... Old name, meaning lost. (In *Wazha'zhe*, Ponca.) Appears in treaty of 1830.
Xitha'nika.......... *Xitha'*, eagle; *nika*, from *nikashiga*, person. (In *Wazha'zhe*, Ponca.)
Zhidetoⁿ'........... *Zhide*, red; *toⁿ*, stands.

FIG. 39. Çiⁿ'dexoⁿxoⁿ (Mike·nitha).

*Female names*

Gthedoⁿ'shtewiⁿ..... Meaning uncertain. Nine of this name.
Hiⁿ'xudewiⁿ........ *Hiⁿ*, hair; *xude*, brown; *wiⁿ*, feminine termination.
Mi'gthedoⁿwiⁿ...... *Mi*, moon; *gthedoⁿ*, hawk; *wiⁿ*, feminine termination. Seven of this name.
Mi'moⁿshihathiⁿ..... *Mi*, moon; moving on high.
Moⁿ'çepewiⁿ........ *Moⁿ'çepe*, axe; *wiⁿ*, feminine termination. Three of this name.

No$^n$çe'i$^n$çe.......... Meaning uncertain.  Four of this name.
Po$^{n\prime}$caço$^n$............ Pale or white Ponca.  Nine of this name.
Po$^n$cawi$^n$............ Ponca woman.
Teço$^{n\prime}$wi$^n$............ *Te*, buffalo; *ço$^n$*, white; *wi$^n$*, feminine.  Belongs also to *I$^n$gthe'zhide* gens.

### Group under Pa'thi$^n$gahige (b)

He'ço$^n$thi$^n$ke......... *He*, horn; *ço$^n$*, white; *thi$^n$ke*, to sit.  Refers to the deer when sitting in the grass so that only his white horns are visible.
Hezho$^{n\prime}$ka............ *He*, horn; *zho$^n$ka*, forked.
Hu'hazhi............. Meaning uncertain.  (In *Washa'be*, Ponca.)
I$^n$chu$^{n\prime}$gaçka......... *I$^n$chu$^{n\prime}$ga*, weasel; *çka*, white.  (In *Ni'kapashna*, Ponca.)
I$^n$shta'basho$^n$sho$^n$.... *I$^n$shta'*, eyes; *basho$^n$sho$^n$*, zigzag.
Kaxe'çabe............ *Kaxe*, crow; *çabe*, black.  (In *Ni'kapashna*, Ponca.)
No$^{n\prime}$kagthezhe...... *No$^n$ka*, back; *gthezhe*, spotted.  Refers to the fawn.  Two of this name.
Ta'shkahiagtho$^n$..... Refers to the oak struck by lightning.
Wapa'de............. One who cuts up the carcass.  (In *Washa'be*, Ponca.)
Weço$^n$githe.......... Old name, an organizer.  Name of Pa'thi$^n$gahige.

#### Borrowed names

A'shkamo$^n$thi$^n$...... *A'shka*, near; *mo$^n$thi$^n$*, walking.  Dakota name.
Pa'thi$^n$gahige........ *Pathi$^n$*, Pawnee; *gahige*, chief.  (In *Wazha'zhe*, Ponca.)

#### Female names,

Ezhno$^{n\prime}$mo$^n$he....... *Ezhno$^n$*, lone, solitary; *mo$^n$he*, one who is dwelling in another's house.  Five of this name.
Gthedo$^{n\prime}$shtewi$^n$..... Refers to hawk difficult to handle.  Three of this name.
Gthedo$^{n\prime}$wi$^n$texi..... *Gthedo$^n$*, hawk; *wi$^n$*, feminine term; *texi*, sacred.  Four of this name.
Mi'huça............ Meaning uncertain.  (In *I$^n$shta'çu$^n$da* gens.)
Po$^{n\prime}$caço$^n$.......... Pale Ponca.  Six of this name.
We'to$^n$bethi$^n$......... Two of this name.

### Group under Zhi$^n$ga'gahige (c)

#### Ni'kie names

Çiha'................ *Çi*, feet; *ha*, skin.  Soles.  (In *Waça'be*, Ponca.)
Te'çehi$^n$çabe........ *Teçe*, belly; *hi$^n$*, hair; *çabe*, black.  (In *Washa'be*, Ponca.)
Tenu'gano$^n$ba....... *Te*, buffalo; *nuga*, bull; *no$^n$ba*, two.  Two of this name.  (In *Thi'xida*, Ponca.)
Thae'githabi......... *Thae*, from *thaethe*, liked or beloved; *gi*, passive; *bi*, who is.  Refers to a calf that is caressed by its mother.  (In *Po$^{n\prime}$caxti*, Ponca.)

#### Female names

He'wegaça.......... *He*, horn: *we*, with; *gaça*, cut.
Mi'giu$^n$the.......... *Mi*, moon; *giu$^n$*, to fly; *the*, to go.
Po$^{n\prime}$caço$^n$.......... Pale or white Ponca.  Three of this name.
To$^{n\prime}$i$^n$gthihe........ Meaning uncertain.
Umo$^{n\prime}$agthi$^n$........ Meaning uncertain.

*Nini'bato<sup>n</sup> subdivision (d)*

*Ni'kie names*

A'kidagahige ........ *A'kida*, to watch over; *gahige*, chief. Chief who watches. (In *Ni'kapashna*, Ponca.)

FIG. 40. Hethi'kuwi<sup>n</sup>xe (son of Sho<sup>n</sup> ge¢abe).

Hethi'kuwi<sup>n</sup>xe (fig. 40). *He*, horn; *thi'kuwi<sup>n</sup>xe*, turning around. Refers to the twisting of the antlers before shedding.

Hexa'ga .............. *He*, horn; *xaga*, rough. Refers to the rough antlers of the deer. Two of this name. (In *Wazha'zhe*, Ponca.)

Shage'dubazhi<sup>n</sup>ga.... *Shage'*, hoofs; *duba*, four; *zhi<sup>n</sup>ga*, little. (It is said that *zhi<sup>n</sup>ga* has been recently added to distinguish this name.)

Sho<sup>n</sup>'geçabe (see fig. 40). *Sho<sup>n</sup>ge*, horse; *çabe*, black. (It is said that this name was originally Shageçabe ("black hoofs") and that it has been changed since the introduction of horses.) (In *Waça'be*, Ponca.)

Tato<sup>n</sup>'ga............. Great Male Deer; old name. (In *Thi'xida*, Ponca.)

Wazhi<sup>n</sup>'kide........ *Wazhi<sup>n</sup>*, will power, anger; *kide*, to shoot. Refers to a challenging male animal.

Xitha'çka............ *Xitha'*, eagle; *çka*, white. (In *Thi'xida*, Ponca.)

Xitha'gahige........ *Xitha'*, eagle; *gahige*, chief. Two of this name. (In *Po<sup>n</sup>'caxti*, *Mo<sup>n</sup>ko<sup>n</sup>'* subdivision, Ponca.)

Xitha'gaxe.......... *Xitha'*, eagle; *gaxe*, maker. Three of this name. (In *Po<sup>n</sup>'caxti*, *Mo<sup>n</sup>ko<sup>n</sup>'* subdivision, Ponca.)

*Borrowed names*

Xitha'giu<sup>n</sup>......... *Xitha'*, eagle; *giu<sup>n</sup>*, to fly. Flying eagle. Dakota name.

*Female names*

Gthedo<sup>n</sup>'wi<sup>n</sup>texi.... *Gthedo<sup>n</sup>*, hawk; *wi<sup>n</sup>*, feminine termination; *texi*, sacred. Five of this name. (In *Waça'be* and in *Po<sup>n</sup>'caxti*, *Mo<sup>n</sup>ko<sup>n</sup>'* subdivision, Ponca.)

Mo<sup>n</sup>'çepewi<sup>n</sup>........ *Mo<sup>n</sup>'çepe*, axe; *wi<sup>n</sup>*, feminine term. Seven of this name.

Po<sup>n</sup>caço<sup>n</sup>............ *Ço<sup>n</sup>*, pale. Pale or white Ponca. Twelve of this name.

We'to<sup>n</sup>beçi<sup>n</sup>......... (In *Ho<sup>n</sup>'ga* gens.) Six of this name.

*Fancy names*

Wani'tawaxa........ Lion. (This name was given by a government official in Washington City when the bearer and other Indians were on a visit.)

*Unclassified names*

Gthedo<sup>n</sup>'thihi....... *Gthedo<sup>n</sup>'*, hawk; *thihi*, to scare by approaching, the bird.

Hexa'gaçka......... *Hexaga, hexaka*, Dakota for elk; *çka*, white.

Hezho<sup>n</sup>'kato<sup>n</sup>ga...... *He*, horns; *zho<sup>n</sup>ka*, forked; *to<sup>n</sup>ga*, big.

I'kuhabi............ *I*, is; *kuhe*, fear of the unknown; *bi*, who is. One who is feared.

Ki'dabazhi.......... *Ki'da*, to shoot; *bazhi*, they not. They do not shoot him.

Mo<sup>n</sup>'çebaha......... *Mo<sup>n</sup>'çe*, metal; *baha*, to show.

Mo<sup>n</sup>'geçka.......... *Mo<sup>n</sup>'ge*, breast; *çka*, white. Refers to the deer.

No<sup>n</sup>zhi<sup>n</sup>'tithe....... *No<sup>n</sup>zhi<sup>n</sup>*, to rise; *tithe*, suddenly.

Pa'thi<sup>n</sup>waça......... Meaning uncertain.

Tano<sup>n</sup>'zhi<sup>n</sup>......... *Ta*, deer; *no<sup>n</sup>'zhi<sup>n</sup>*, to stand.

Wa'bagthazhi....... *Wa'bagtha*, bashful, timid; *zhi*, not, from *o<sup>n</sup>kuzhi*.

Wadu'kishke....... Meaning uncertain.

Wathi'hi........... To startle game.

Xu'bego<sup>n</sup>tha....... *Xu'be*, holy, sacred; *go<sup>n</sup>tha*, want, desire.

*Dream names*

Taçhu'geçka........ *Taçhu'ge*, antelope; *çka*, white.

Ta'xtidathi<sup>n</sup>........ *Ta'xti*, deer; *dathi<sup>n</sup>*, crazy.

## I<sup>n</sup>GTHE'ZHIDE GENS (9)

The name of this gens refers to the reddish excrement of the newly born calf. The rites committed to the keeping of the gens have been lost. Traditions speak of these having been connected with the procreation of the race to insure its continuance through the medium of the sky powers.

The name Iⁿgthe'zhide has given rise to considerable speculation by white observers, and stories are told to account for it,[a] but these stories and explanations are not corroborated by the old and trusty men of the tribe, nor do they accord with what is known of the functions of the gentes of the tribe and the fundamental ideas of the tribal organization.

Tabu: The fetus of an animal must not be touched. As the buffalo was most commonly met with, the tabu came to be confined to the unborn young of the buffalo.

The symbolic cut of the hair consisted in shaving the head, all except a small lock in front, one behind, and one on each side of the head, to represent the head and the tail of the young animal, and the knobs where the horns would grow (fig. 41).

FIG. 41. Cut of hair, Iⁿgthe'zhide gens.

There were no subgentes and no subdivisions or groups, nor was there a representative from this gens in the Council of Seven Chiefs.

The Iⁿgthe'zhide camped on the left of the Nini'batoⁿ subdivision of the Tapa'.

PERSONAL NAMES IN THE IⁿGTHE'ZHIDE GENS (9)

*Ni'kie names*

A'hiⁿwetiⁿ........... *A'hiⁿ*, wings; *wetiⁿ*, to strike.

Çiⁿ'deçiçnu ......... *Çiⁿde*, tail; *çiçnu*, to drag.

Çiⁿ'wanoⁿzhiⁿ ....... Meaning uncertain.

Çni'tithoⁿ........... *Çni*, cold; *tithoⁿ*, to come.

Ihoⁿ'ugine.......... *Ihoⁿ'*, mother (spoken of); *ugine*, seeks for his. Refers to buffalo calf after the slaughter of its mother.

Kaxe'axube.......... *Kaxe'a*, crow; *xube*, sacred. Refers to the symbolic use of the bird.

Koⁿ'çepa............ *Koⁿçe*, name of one of the Omaha gentes; *pa*, head. Old name.

Mika'ezhiⁿga........ *Mika'e*, star; *zhiⁿga*, little.

Sha'nugahi.......... Meaning uncertain. (In *Thi'xida,* Ponca.)

Te'moⁿthiⁿ........... *Te*, buffalo; *moⁿthiⁿ*, walking, traveling. (In *Poⁿ'caxti, Moⁿkoⁿ'* subdivision, Ponca.)

Te'pezhi............ *Te*, buffalo; *pezhi*, from *piazhi*, bad.

Tezhiⁿ'ga........... *Te*, buffalo; *zhiⁿ'ga*, little. (In *Washa'be*, Ponca.)

Ti'shimuxa.......... *Tishi*, tent poles; *muxa*, to spread out. (In *Washa'be*, Ponca.)

Uhoⁿ'gemoⁿthiⁿ..... *Uhoⁿ'ge*, at the end of a single file; *moⁿthiⁿ*, walking. (In *Nu'xe*, Ponca.)

Uhoⁿ'genoⁿzhiⁿ(pl.35) *Uhoⁿge*, at the end of a single file; *noⁿzhiⁿ*, standing. (In *Nu'xe*, Ponca.)

Uki'patoⁿ........... Rolling himself. Two of this name. (In *Poⁿ'caxti, Moⁿkoⁿ'* subdivision, Ponca.)

Wa'baçkaha.......... Meaning uncertain. Two of this name.

---

[a] As in Long, Expedition to the Rocky Mountains, I, 327, Philadelphia, 1823.

UHOᴺ'GENOᴺZHIᴺ

Wa'ino<sup>n</sup>zhi<sup>n</sup>........ *Wa'i*, over them; *no<sup>n</sup>zhi<sup>n</sup>*, standing.  Probably refers to the last halt of the hunters as they ceremonially approach the herd of buffalo.  Two of this name.  (In *Washa'be*, Ponca.)

Wako<sup>n</sup>'ha........... Meaning uncertain.  Two of this name.

Wano<sup>n</sup>'pazhi....... *Wano<sup>n</sup>'pa*, fear; *zhi*, from *o<sup>n</sup>kazhi*, not.  Having no fear.  Two of this name.  (In *Ni'kapashna*, Ponca.)

Wati'thakuge........ Meaning uncertain.

Wazhi<sup>n</sup>'gthedo<sup>n</sup>.... *Wazhi<sup>n</sup>'*, will power; *gthedo<sup>n</sup>*, hawk.  Sometimes translated as Angry Hawk.

*Dream names*

Mo<sup>n</sup>a'zhi<sup>n</sup>ga......... *Mo<sup>n</sup>a'*, bank; *zhi<sup>n</sup>ga*, little.  (In *Thi'xida*, Ponca.)

Mo<sup>n</sup>'çedo<sup>n</sup>.......... *Mo<sup>n</sup>çe*, metal; *do<sup>n</sup>*, to possess.  Two of this name.  (In *Washa'be*, Ponca.)

Mo<sup>n</sup>'sho<sup>n</sup>çka........ *Mo<sup>n</sup>'sho<sup>n</sup>*, feather; *çka*, white.  (In *Ni'kapashna*, Ponca.)

No<sup>n</sup>'katu............. *No<sup>n</sup>'ka*, back; *tu*, blue.  Refers to the sparrow hawk.  (In *Ni'kapashna*, Ponca.)

Waa<sup>n</sup>'.............. *Waa<sup>n</sup>'*, to sing.  (In *Wazha'zhe*, Ponca.)

*Female names*

Gi'do<sup>n</sup>abe........... Meaning uncertain.

Mi'gthedo<sup>n</sup>wi<sup>n</sup>...... *Mi*, moon; *gthedo<sup>n</sup>*, hawk; *wi<sup>n</sup>*, feminine.  Six of this name.

Mi'gthito<sup>n</sup>i<sup>n</sup>........ *Mi*, moon; *gthi*, to return; *to<sup>n</sup>i<sup>n</sup>*, new.  Return of the new moon, or the moon returns new.

Mi'hewi<sup>n</sup>............ *Mi*, moon; *hewi<sup>n</sup>*, the new moon lies horizontal, like a canoe.

Mi'hezhi<sup>n</sup>ga........ Little moon.  Two of this name.

Mo<sup>n</sup>'shihathi<sup>n</sup>...... Moving on high.  Refers to the eagle.

No<sup>n</sup>'gtheçe.......... *No<sup>n</sup>*, action by the foot; *gtheçe*, impressions on the ground in lines.  Refers to the tracks of buffalo calves.  Two of this name.

Teço<sup>n</sup>'wi<sup>n</sup>.......... *Te*, buffalo; *ço<sup>n</sup>'*, pale or white; *wi<sup>n</sup>*, feminine.  Refers to the Sacred White Buffalo Hide.

Ugi'nemo<sup>n</sup>thi<sup>n</sup>...... *Ugi'ne*, seeks for his; *mo<sup>n</sup>thi<sup>n</sup>*, walking.  Wanders seeking for his mother.  The feminine counterpart of *Iho<sup>n</sup>'ugine*.

### I<sup>n</sup>SHTA'ÇU<sup>N</sup>DA GENS (10)

The name of this gens is an ancient term that may be translated as follows: *i<sup>n</sup>shta'*, "eyes;" *çu<sup>n</sup>da*, "flashing."  The word refers to the lightning, and the rites committed to this gens were connected with the thunder and lightning as manifestations of the sky forces which represented the power of Wako<sup>n</sup>'da in controlling man's life and death.  The name of this gens was applied to one-half of the *hu'thuga*—the half that represented the Sky people who, in union with the Earth people, gave birth to the human race.  (See p. 135.)

At present there are in this gens but one subgens and the Nini'bato<sup>n</sup> subdivision.  Formerly there was another subgens, but the ceremonies of which it had charge have long since been lost and the subgens disintegrated.  An example of how such disintegration can come about may be seen to-day in the Nini'bato<sup>n</sup> subdivision.  During the last century the Nini'bato<sup>n</sup> became reduced to one family; of this family there is at the present time but one survivor, who has an only son; if this son should be childless, on his death the subdivision would be extinct. In the past when a subgens lost its distinctive rites and became depleted through death the survivors seem to have joined the nearest related group within the gens. That such a change has taken place in the Iⁿshta'çuⁿda gens is evidenced by the names. Formerly there seems to have been a clear line of demarcation between the subgentes as well as the gentes of the tribe, and each had its set of names that referred directly to the rites belonging to the gens or subgens. Laxity in the use of subgentes' names, owing probably to disintegration, had already set in by 1883, when the names as here given were collected, although each gens still clung with tenacity to its distinctive *ni'kie* names.

Of the two subgentes formerly existing in the Iⁿshta'çuⁿda gens one referred to the earth and the other to the sky. At first glance these two rites appear unrelated, but in fact they were allied and formed an epitome of the basal idea expressed in the tribal organization. The rites which pertained to the earth subgens as well as its name have been lost, and the people who composed this subgens have mingled with the surviving subgens. From the meaning of the name of the latter and the significance of its rites it is possible to identify not only those names which originally belonged to it but also those names which were formerly associated with the rites of the lost earth subgens. In this connection it is interesting to note that the present tabu of the entire gens (worms, insects, etc.) relates to the lost rites of the lost subgens rather than to the rites of the surviving subgens, a fact that throws light on the relation which existed between the rites of the two subgentes. The subgens which survives and the rites which it controls pertain to the sky, to the power which descends to fructify the earth. This power is typified by the rain which falls from the storm clouds, with their thunder and lightning, and causes the earth to bring forth. The response of the earth is typified by the abounding life as seen in the worms, insects, and small burrowing creatures living in the earth. These were the sign, or symbol, of the result of the fructifying power from above. Tradition says that one of the symbols used in the rites of the lost subgens was a mole, painted red (the life color).

The surviving subgens is called Washe'toⁿ. The prefix *wa* denotes action with a purpose; *she* is from *shie*, a generic term for children (as, *shie' athiⁿkithe*, "to beget children," and *shie' githe*, "to adopt children"); *toⁿ* means "to possess" or "become possessed of." The word *washe'toⁿ* therefore means "the act of possessing children." Through the rites pertaining to this subgens the child's life was consecrated to the life-giving power symbolized by the thunder and lightning, and passed out of the simple relation it bore to its parents and was reborn, so to speak, as a member of the tribe.  A detailed account of this ceremony in connection with the consecration of the child and its entrance into the tribe has been given (p. 117).

On the fourth day after the birth of a child a baby name was given to it, and if it was a boy, a belt ornamented with the claws of the wild-cat was put about its body.  The significance and use of the skin of the wild-cat and the skin of the fawn in reference to the stars and the newly born were mentioned in connection with the lost stellar rites of the Tapa' gens which referred to the sky, the masculine (father) element.  If the child was a girl, a girdle of mussel shells strung on a string was put around her.  Here, again, is to be noted the connection of the shell with water and of water as the medium for transmitting power from the Above to the mother earth.  The placing of these symbolic emblems on the infant constituted a prayer for the preservation of the tribe and for the continuation of life through children.

There is a curious tradition concerning the formation of the Nini'-baton subdivision in this gens.  At the time of the organization of the tribe in its present form, when this group of families was selected and the pipe was offered them, they refused, their chief saying: "I am not worthy to keep this pipe that represents all that is good.  I am a wanderer, a bloody man.  I might stain this sacred article with blood.  Take it back."  Three times was the pipe offered and rejected; the fourth time the pipe was left with them and the old men who brought it turned away; but the families returned the pipe, accompanied with many gifts, because they feared to accept the responsibility put upon them by the reception of the pipe.  But again they were remonstrated with, and finally the pipe and the duties connected with it were fully accepted.  These duties consisted in not only furnishing a member of the Council of Seven Chiefs, which governed the tribe, but in the preservation and recital of a ritual to be used when the two Sacred Pipes belonging to the tribe were filled for ceremonial purposes, as at the inauguration of chiefs or some other equally important tribal event.  The recitation of this ritual was essential when the tobacco was placed in the pipes to make them ready for smoking.  This ritual is now irrevocably lost.  Its last keeper was Mon'hinçi.  He died about 1850 without imparting the knowledge of the ritual to anyone.[a]

[a] It is said that he withheld it from his son because of the latter's nervous, energetic temperament.  He thought that, with added years, the young man would be able to become the quiet, sedate person to whom so important an office might be safely trusted; but death overtook the old man before he was satisfied that he ought to put his sacred charge into the keeping of his son.  Since his death the Sacred Tribal Pipes have never been ceremonially filled.  The son developed into a fine, trustworthy man, with a remarkably well-poised mind but with a great fund of humor.

It has been impossible to learn the exact nature of this ritual, but from the little information that could be gleaned it would seem to have been a history of the development of the Sacred Pipes and their ceremonies.  The old chiefs who had heard it regarded it as too sacred to talk about.

The Nini'bato[n] subdivision bids fair soon to follow the lost ritual, as only one person survives.

When the growing corn was infested by grasshoppers or other destructive insects the owner of the troubled field applied to the I[n]shta'çu[n]da gens for help.  A feast was made, to which those were invited who had the hereditary right to make the ceremonial appeal for the preservation of the crop.  A young man was dispatched to the threatened field of corn with instructions to catch one of the grasshoppers or beetles.  On his return he handed the captured insect to the leader, who removed one of its wings and broke off a bit from the tip, which he dropped into the vessel containing the food about to be eaten.

The whole ceremony was a dramatic form of prayer.  The feast symbolized the appeal for a plentiful supply of food; breaking the

FIG. 42. Cut of hair, I[n]shta'çu[n]da gens.

wing and putting a piece of its tip into the pot of food set forth the wish that the destructive creatures might lose their power to be active and thus to destroy the corn.  This latter act exemplified the belief in the living connection of a part with its whole; consequently, the bit of wing was thought to have a vital relation to all the insects that were feeding on the maize, and its severance and destruction to have a like effect on all its kind.

This ceremony, which is probably the survival of a rite pertaining to the lost subgens, has been inaccurately reported and misunderstood.  Only a bit of the wing was cast into the food for the ceremonial feast.  No other creature, nor any other part of the insect, was used.

In the hu'thuga, the place of the lost gens (a) was left of the I[n]gthe'zhide; next came the Nini'bato[n] subdivision (b); then the Washe'to[n] (c); this last-named subgens formed the eastern end of the line of the I[n]shta'çu[n]da division of the tribe.

Tabu: The entire gens was forbidden to touch all manner of creeping insects, bugs, worms,[a] and similar creatures.

The symbolic cut of the hair consisted in removing all hair from the crown, leaving a number of little locks around the base of the skull (fig. 42), said to represent the many legs of insects.

---

a Lightning is said to feed on the gum weed, mo[n]ko[n]  to[n]ga ("big mocasin"), and to leave a worm at the root.

PERSONAL NAMES IN THE I<sup>N</sup>SHTA'ÇU<sup>N</sup>DA GENS

*Nini'bato<sup>n</sup> subdivision (b)*

*Ni'kie names*

Gahi'petho<sup>n</sup>ba............ *Gahi*, from *gahige*, chief; *pe'tho<sup>n</sup>ba*, seven.   Refers to the
                         seven original chiefs when the Omaha reorganized.

FIG. 43. Teu'ko<sup>n</sup>ha.

Ho<sup>n</sup>'gashenu............. *Ho<sup>n</sup>'ga*, leader; *shenu*, young man (full brother of Kawa'ha;
                         now lives with the Pawnee tribe).  (In *Wazha'zhe*,
                         Ponca.)
Kawa'ha................ Meaning uncertain.
Mo<sup>n</sup>hi<sup>n</sup>çi................ *Mo<sup>n</sup>hi<sup>n</sup>*, stone knife; *çi*, yellow.
U'kiça.................. Deserted, as a dwelling.

### Dream names

Moⁿchu'waxe............ *Moⁿchu'*, grizzly bear; *waxe*, maker.
Teu'koⁿha (fig. 43)....... *Te*, buffalo; *u'koⁿha*, alone; refers to the male buffalo in the winter season, when its habit was to remain alone.

### Borrowed names

Ushka'dewakoⁿ........... Dakota name.

### Derisive names

Wazhe'thiⁿge............. *Wazhe'*, gratitude; *thiⁿge*, none.　(In *Wazha'zhe*, Ponca.)

### Female names

Mi'gthitoⁿiⁿ............. Return of the new moon.
Mi'moⁿshihathiⁿ........ Moon moving above.
Mi'moⁿthiⁿ.............. *Mi*, moon; *moⁿthiⁿ*, walking, traveling; refers to the moving of the moon across the heavens.　Two of this name.
Mi'texiçi................ *Mi*, moon; *texi*, sacred; *çi*, yellow.　Three of this name.
Moⁿ'shadithiⁿ........... One moving on high.
Toⁿ'iⁿgi ................. *Toⁿiⁿ*, new; *gi*, coming.　Refers to moon.　Two of this name.
We'toⁿna............... Meaning uncertain.　Two of this name.　(In *Thi'xida*, Ponca.)

## Washe'toⁿ (*owners of the children*) *subgens* (c)

### Ni'kie names

A'thiude................ Left alone, abandoned.
Athu'hage.............. The last, in a file of men or animals.　(In *Wazha'zhe*, Ponca.)
Chuⁿgthi'shkamoⁿthiⁿ.... *Chuⁿ*, meaning uncertain, perhaps wood; *wagthi'shka*, bug; *moⁿthiⁿ*, walking.　Two of this name.
Edi'toⁿ.................. *Edi*, there; *toⁿ*, stands.
Ga'gigthethiⁿ............ *Ga*, at a distance; *gigthe*, passing toward home; *thiⁿ*, moving.　Refers to thunder.　Two of this name.
Gahi'iⁿshage............ *Gahi*, chief; *iⁿshage*, old.
Ha'shimoⁿthiⁿ .......... Walking last in a file.　Two of this name.　(In *Thi'xida*, Ponca.)
Heba''a................ *He*, horn; *ba'a*, worn down.
Heba'çabazhi........... *He*, horn; *baçabe*, splinter; *zhi*, *oⁿkazhi*, not.　Refers to a horn not yet jagged from age.
Heçoⁿ'nida............. *He*, horn; *çoⁿ*, white or pale; *nida*, a mythical animal.　(See note on *nida*, p. 194.)
He'shathage............ *He*, horn; *shathage*, branching.　Refers to the elk.　(In *Thi'xida*, Ponca.)
Hoⁿ'doⁿmoⁿthiⁿ.......... *Hoⁿ*, night; *doⁿ*, when or at; *moⁿthiⁿ*, walking.　Refers to thunder.
Hu'toⁿtoⁿ............... *Hu'toⁿ*, noise; *toⁿ*, stands.　Roars as he stands (referring to thunder).　Two of this name.
I'bahoⁿbi.............. *I'bahoⁿ*, to know; *bi*, he is.　He is known.　Refers to a chief's son.　(In *Ni'kapashna*, Ponca.)
I'gadoⁿne............... Same as preceding.
I'gadoⁿtha.............. Probably refers to clouds driven by the wind.
Iⁿke'toⁿga.............. *Iⁿke'*, shoulder; *toⁿga*, big.　Two of this name.　(In *Poⁿ'caxti*, *Moⁿkoⁿ'* subdivision, Ponca.)
Iⁿsha'gemoⁿthiⁿ ........ *Iⁿsha'ge*, old man; *moⁿthiⁿ*, walking.　Refers to thunder.　(In *Nu'xe* gens, Ponca.)

I<sup>n</sup>shta′xi.................. *I<sup>n</sup>shta′*, eye; *xi*, yellowish. Refers to lightning,. "the yellow eye of the thunder."

Ka′etha.................. *Ketha*, clear sky, after a storm.

Ki′mo<sup>n</sup>ho<sup>n</sup>.............. Against or facing the wind. Two of this name. (In *Wazha′zhe*, Ponca.)

Ku′zhiwate.............. *Ku′zhi*, afar; *wate*, a valorous deed. Victory widespread.

Ma′çikide................. *Ma′çi*, cedar; *kide*, to shoot. Refers to the myth of the thunder striking the cedar tree. (In *Wazha′zhe*, Ponca.)

Mo<sup>n</sup>a′gata............... *Mo<sup>n</sup>*, arrow; *a′gata*, to aim.

Mo<sup>n</sup>′hi<sup>n</sup>duba............ *Mo<sup>n</sup>′hi<sup>n</sup>*, stone knife; *duba*, four. One of the names of the keeper of the ritual used in cutting the hair and consecrating the child to the thunder. The bearer of this name died in 1884.

Mo<sup>n</sup>shi′ahamo<sup>n</sup>thi<sup>n</sup>...... *Mo<sup>n</sup>shi′aha*, above; *mo<sup>n</sup>thi<sup>n</sup>*, moving. (In' *Thi′xida*, Ponca.)

Mo<sup>n</sup>xpi′................. Clouds. Two of this name.

Mo<sup>n</sup>xpi′mo<sup>n</sup>thi<sup>n</sup>......... *Mo<sup>n</sup>xpi′*, clouds; *mo<sup>n</sup>thi<sup>n</sup>*, walking. This name appears in the treaties of 1826 and 1836, signed by Omaha chiefs.

Paga′sho<sup>n</sup>................ *Pa*, head; *ga′sho<sup>n</sup>*, to nod. Refers to bugs nodding the head as they walk.

Sheda′mo<sup>n</sup>thi<sup>n</sup>.......... *Sheda*, meaning uncertain; *mo<sup>n</sup>thi<sup>n</sup>*, walking. Appears in treaty of 1826.

Shugi′shugi.............. Meaning uncertain.

Te′bi′a.................. Frog.

Thigthi′çemo<sup>n</sup>thi<sup>n</sup>........ *Thigthiçe*, zigzag lightning; *mo<sup>n</sup>thi<sup>n</sup>*, walking. (In *Washa′be*, Ponca.)

Thio<sup>n</sup>′bagigthe.......... *Thio<sup>n</sup>′ba*, general term for lightning; *gigthe*, going by, on the way home. (In *Washa′be*, *Hi′çada* subdivision, Ponca.)

Thio<sup>n</sup>′bagina............. *Thio<sup>n</sup>′ba*, lightning; *gina*, coming. Two of this name.

Thio<sup>n</sup>′batigthe........... *Thio<sup>n</sup>′ba*, lightning; *tigthe*, sudden. (In *Washa′be*, *Hi′çada* subdivision, Ponca.)

Ti′gaxa.................. *Ti*, tent or village; *gaxa*, to approach by stealth. Refers to the thunder under the guise of a warrior approaching the village by stealth.

Ti′uthio<sup>n</sup>ba.............. *Ti*, tent; *u*, in; *thio<sup>n</sup>ba*, lightning. Lightning flashes into the lodge. (In *Waça′be*, *Hi′çada* subdivision, Ponca.)

U′bani<sup>n</sup>................. *U*, in; *ba*, to push; *ni<sup>n</sup>*, digging. Digging in the earth. Said to refer to a small reptile that disappears in the earth when the thunder comes. Two of this name; one in *I<sup>n</sup>shta′çu<sup>n</sup>daxti* subdivision.

Uçu′gaxe................ *Uçu′*, path; *gaxe*, to make. Refers to one who leads. (The name of a subdivision of *Wazha′zheçka* gens, Osage. Occurs in *Wazha′zhe* gens, Ponca.) Appears in Omaha treaty of 1815. Two of this name.

Uha′mo<sup>n</sup>thi<sup>n</sup>............. *Uha′*, in a hollow; *mo<sup>n</sup>thi<sup>n</sup>*, walking. Refers to the thunder storms following the valleys and river courses.

Ushu′demo<sup>n</sup>thi<sup>n</sup>......... *U*, in; *shu′de*, mist; *mo<sup>n</sup>thi<sup>n</sup>*, walking.

Wagi′asha............... Meaning lost. (In *Wazha′zhe*, Ponca.)

Waha′xi................. *Waha*, skin; *xi*, yellowish. (In *Washa′be*, Ponca.) Two of this name.

Wa′huto<sup>n</sup>to<sup>n</sup>............. *Wa*, prefix denoting action with a purpose; *huto<sup>n</sup>*, noise; *to<sup>n</sup>*, stands. (See *Hu′to<sup>n</sup>to<sup>n</sup>*.)

Wano<sup>n</sup>′kuge (fig. 44)...... *Wa*, purpose in action; *no<sup>n</sup>*, action with the feet; *kuge*, sound of a drum. Refers to the resounding footsteps of the thunder. Appears in the Omaha treaties of 1854 and 1865.

Washa'ge ............... Claw. Refers to the wild-cat claw, an hereditary possession, and used in ceremonies conducted by this gens.

Washe'to$^n$zhi$^n$ga.......... *Washe'to$^n$*, the name of this subdivision; *zhi$^n$ga*, little.

Washe'zhi$^n$ga............. *Washe'*, an abbreviation of *washe'to$^n$*; *zhi$^n$ga*, little.

Washko$^n$'hi............... *Washko$^n$*, strength. Refers to the power of thunder. (In
*Wazha'zhe*, Ponca.)

FIG. 44. Wano$^n$'kuge.

Wazhi$^n$'çka............... *Wazhi$^n$'*, will, mind; *çka*, white. Wisdom. (In *Thi'xida*,
Ponca.)

Wazhi$^n$'o$^n$ba............. *Wazhi$^n$'*, will power, energy; *o$^n$ba*, day. Sometimes translated as "angry or turbulent day," a day of storms of
thunder and lightning.

We'ç'a ................... Snake.  (In *Wazha'zhe*, Ponca.)
We'ç'aho<sup>n</sup>ga ............. *We'ç'a*, snake; *ho<sup>n</sup>ga*, leader.  (In *Wazha'zhe*, Ponca.)
We'ç'azhi<sup>n</sup>ga ............. *We'ç'a*, snake; *zhi<sup>n</sup>ga*, little.  Two of this name.  (In *Wazha'zhe*, Ponca.)
Wi'ukipae ............... Meaning uncertain.

### Valor names

Ku'e'the ................ Rushing forward suddenly.  This name was bestowed on the man because he rushed suddenly on a large party of Sioux, armed only with a hatchet.
Waba'açe ................ *Wa, waa<sup>n</sup>*, a valorous deed; a successful war party is also called *waa<sup>n</sup>; baaçe*, to put to flight, to scare.  This name was won by a man who, although partially paralyzed, killed his adversary in single combat during a fight with the Dakota.  (In *Wazha'zhe*, Ponca.)
Wai<sup>n</sup>'washi ................ *Wai<sup>n</sup>*, to carry; *washi*, to ask another to do something for one.
Wano<sup>n</sup>'shezhi<sup>n</sup>ga ........ *Wano<sup>n</sup>she*, soldier; *zhi<sup>n</sup>ga*, little.  (In *Wazha'zhe*, Ponca.)  Two of this name—one in *Nini'bato<sup>n</sup>* subdivision.

### Dream names

O<sup>n</sup>'po<sup>n</sup>wahi .............. *O<sup>n</sup>'po<sup>n</sup>*, elk; *wahi*, bone.
Sho<sup>n</sup>'geo<sup>n</sup>ça .............. *Sho<sup>n</sup>ge*, horse; *u<sup>n</sup>ça*, from *u<sup>n</sup>çagi*, swift.
Wa'shi<sup>n</sup>nixa ............. The layers of fat about the stomach of an animal—the buffalo.

### Names taken from incidents or historic experiences

Çithe'dezhi<sup>n</sup>ga ......... *Çithe'de*, heel; *zhi<sup>n</sup>ga*, little.  (In *Waça'be*, Ponca.)
Nibtha'çka .............. *Ni*, water; *bthaçka*, flat.  The name by which the Omaha call the Platte river.  Nebraska is a corruption of *Nibtha-çka*.
Tahe'gaxe ................ *Ta*, deer; *he*, horn; *gaxe*, branch.
To<sup>n</sup>'wo<sup>n</sup>pezhe ........... *To<sup>n</sup>'wo<sup>n</sup>*, village; *pezhe*, bad.  Said to be a nickname given to a man who had poisoned several persons.  It is said also that the name refers to the Thunder village, whence the Thunder issues to kill men.
U'ho<sup>n</sup>zhi<sup>n</sup>ga .............. *U'ho<sup>n</sup>*, cook; *zhi<sup>n</sup>ga*, little.  Two of this name—one in *Nini'bato<sup>n</sup>* subdivision.  Appears in Omaha treaty of 1826.  (In *Washa'be*, Ponca.)
Une'çezhi<sup>n</sup>ga ........... *Une'çe*, fireplace; *zhi<sup>n</sup>ga*, little.

### Names borrowed from cognate tribes, modified or unmodified

No<sup>n</sup>xe'wanida ........... Dakota name.
Thio<sup>n</sup>'baçka ............ *Thio<sup>n</sup>'ba*, lightning; *çka*, white.  This is said to be taken from the Dakota name *Wakiya<sup>n</sup>ska*, meaning White Thunder.
Waxtha'thuto<sup>n</sup> ......... Oto name.

*Female names*

Çiçi'kawate............... *Çiçi'ka*, turkey; *wate*, victory.

Hu'to$^n$wi$^n$................ *Hu'to$^n$*, noise; *wi$^n$*, feminine termination. Refers to thunder.

I$^n$shta'ço$^n$wi$^n$........... *I$^n$shta'*, eye; *ço$^n$*, white or pale; *wi$^n$*, feminine termination. Two of this name.

Mi'asheto$^n$ .............. *Mi*, moon; *asheto$^n$*, the end. The waning moon.

Mi'gthito$^n$i$^n$............. *Mi*, moon; *gthi*, to return; *to$^n$i$^n$*, new. The return of the new moon. Four of this name—one in *Nini'bato$^n$* subdivision. (In *Washa'be* and *Thi'xida*, Ponca.)

Mi'huça................. *Mi*, moon; *huça*, loud voice.

Mi'mo$^n$shihathi$^n$........ *Mi*, moon; *mo$^n$shiha*, above; *thi$^n$*, moving. Five of this name—one in *Nini'bato$^n$* subdivision.

Mi'o$^n$bathi$^n$............. *Mi*, moon; *o$^n$ba*, day; *thi$^n$*, moving. Three of this name. (In *Thi'xida*, Ponca.)

Mo$^n$'shadithi$^n$............ One moving on high. Refers to thunder. Six of this name—one in *Nini'bato$^n$* subdivision. (In *Washa'be* and *Ni'kapashna*, Ponca.)

Ni'dawi$^n$................. *Ni'da*, a mythical being; *wi$^n$*, feminine. Six of this name.[a]

Ni'kano$^n$zhiha.......... *Ni'ka*, person; *no$^n$zhiha*, human hair. Three of this name.

No$^n$'xtiçewi$^n$............ Meaning uncertain.

O$^n$'bathagthi$^n$........... *O$^n$'ba*, day; *thagthi$^n$*, fine. Two of this name.

To$^n$'i$^n$gina................ *To$^n$'i$^n$*, new; *gi*, coming; *na*, who does. Refers to the moon symbolically. Three of this name. (In *Ni'kapashna*, Ponca.)

To$^n$'i$^n$gthihe ............. *To$^n$'i$^n$*, new; *gthihe*, to return suddenly. The sudden apparition of the new moon. Three of this name.

To$^n$'i$^n$thi$^n$............... *To$^n$'i$^n$*, new; *thi$^n$*, moving. Refers to the new moon moving in the heavens. Three of this name.

---

After the preceding detailed account of the Omaha gentes it may be of service to the reader to recapitulate briefly the salient features of the tribal organization.

Five gentes composed the southern half of the *hu'thuga* or tribal circle. These had charge of the physical welfare of the people. The We'zhi$^n$shte gens had charge of the Sacred Tent of War and its duties, and also of rites connected with the first thunder of the spring. These rites, which were fragmentary, probably once formed part of ancient ceremonies connected with surviving articles no longer ceremonially used—the Sacred Shell and the Cedar Pole. The elk was tabu to the We'zhi$^n$shte gens, and it is to be noted that elk rites were associated with war in the Osage tribe. (See Ceremony of Adoption, p. 61.) The other four gentes were charged with duties and rites connected with the food supply and were under the direction of the Ho$^n$'ga gens. This gens was leader, as its name implies, and had the care of the two Sacred Tents; one contained the White

---

[a] The Nida was a mythical creature, in one conception a sort of elf that crept in and out of the earth. The word was applied also to the bones of large extinct animals, as the mastodon. When the elephant was first seen it was called Nida, and that name is still applied to it by the Omaha, Ponca, and Osage.

Buffalo Hide.    Its keeper conducted the rites attending the planting
of maize and the hunting of the buffalo.    The other tent held the
Sacred Pole.    Its keepers were the custodians of the rites concerned
with the maintaining of the authority of the chiefs in the government of the tribe.    Protection from without, the preservation of
peace within the tribe, the obtaining of food and clothing, devolved
upon the rites in charge of the gentes composing the Ho$^n$'gashenu
half of the *hu'thuga*.

The five gentes on the north half of the tribal circle were custodians
of rites that related to the creation, the stars, the manifestation of
the cosmic forces that pertain to life.    Nearly all of these rites have
become obsolete, except those of the last-named class, in charge of
the I$^n$shta'çu$^n$da gens.    These constituted the ritual by which the
child was introduced to the Cosmos (see p. 115), the ceremony through
which the child was inducted into its place and duty in the tribe
(see p. 117), and the ritual required when the two Sacred Tribal
Pipes were filled for use on solemn tribal occasions.

In view of what has been discerned of the practical character of
the Omaha, it is interesting to note that only those rites directly
concerned with the maintenance of the tribal organization and government were kept active and vital, while other rites, kindred but
not so closely connected with the tribal organization, were suffered
to fall into neglect.

### The Omaha Gens not a Political Organization

From the foregoing account of the gentes of the tribe, it is apparent
that the Omaha gens was not a political organization.    It differed
from the Latin gens in that the people composing it did not claim to
be descended from a common ancestor from whom the group took
its name and crest.    There was, however, one point of resemblance,
and because of this one point of resemblance the name gens is applied
to the Omaha group; namely, the practice of a common rite the
title to share in which descended solely through the father.    Beyond
this one point all resemblance ends.    The rights and duties of the
Omaha father in no way corresponded to those devolving on the
head of a Roman family.    Nor was the Omaha group a clan, for the
bond between the people was not because of a common ancestor
whose name and crest were the clan designation and from whom were
descended the hereditary rulers of the clan.    The Omaha gens was a
group of exogamous kindred who practised a particular rite, the
child's birthright to which descended solely through the father; and
the symbol characteristic of that rite became the symbol, crest, or
"totem," of the gens.    There was no political or governing chief of
an Omaha gens or subgens, but there were persons to whom belonged

the hereditary right to be keepers, or "priests," in the ceremonies that were in charge of the gens. The Omaha gens, the two grand divisions composing the tribe, and the tribe as a whole, were each and all expressive and representative of certain fundamental religious ideas and beliefs that were dramatized in rites.

Later, when the tribe was reorganized into its present form, the political government of the people was vested in certain chiefs, but these did not derive their position from their gentes as representatives of political organizations.

## INTERRELATION OF THE TWO GRAND DIVISIONS

Looking at the *hu'thuga*, we observe that the rites and duties belonging to the gentes composing the Hon'gashenu division bear out their designation as "the Earth people." All the rites and all the duties intrusted to these gentes have a direct relation to the physical welfare of the people. The ceremonies connected with the warrior as the protector of the life and property of the tribe were in charge of the We'zhinshte gens, whose place was at the eastern end of this division and at the southern side of the opening, or "door," of the *hu'thuga*, viewed as when oriented. The rites pertaining to the people's food supply—the hunting of the buffalo, the planting of the maize, the protection of the growing crops from the depredations of birds, and the fostering help of wind and rain—were in charge of the other four gentes of this division, each gens having its special share in these ceremonies. Besides these rites which bore directly upon the food supply, there were other duties which were concerned with the governing power and the maintenance of peace within the tribe. When the governing power was vested in a Council of Seven Chiefs, the right to convene this council became the duty of the Hon'ga gens, and the custody of the two Sacred Tribal Pipes was given to the Inke'çabe gens. The presence and use of these pipes were essential to any authoritative proceeding but the preparation of the pipes for use could not be undertaken by any member of the Hon'gashenu division. This preparation belonged solely to the Inshta'çunda gens. Therefore the pipes when in use became tribal, and represented both of the divisions of the tribe.

The Inshta'çunda division, spoken of as "the Sky people," had charge of those rites by which supernatural aid was sought and secured. The rites committed to the gentes composing this division were all connected with the creation and the maintenance on the earth of all living forms. To the Inshta'çunda gens belonged the rites which enforced the belief that the life and the death of each person was in the keeping of a supernatural power—a power that could punish an offender and that alone could give authority to the

words and acts of the council of chiefs.   Although the rites and duties
of the Iⁿshta'çuⁿda division pertained distinctively to the supernatural, to the creative and directive forces as related to man's social
and individual life, yet they were necessary and essential to the rites
and duties of the Hoⁿ'gashenu division, in whose charge was the
physical well-being of the people.   The former gave a supernatural
sanction and authority to the latter, and made them effective not
only over the animals and the fruits of the earth, but exercised an
equally potent control over the governing power and the life of every
member of the tribe.   Thus the belief that by union of the Sky people
and the Earth people the human race and all other living forms
were created and perpetuated was not only symbolized in the organization of the tribe, but this
belief was kept vital and continually present to the
minds of the people by the rites, the grouping and
interrelation of the gentes, and the share given
the two great divisions in tribal affairs and
ceremonies.   No tribal ceremony, negotiation, or
consultation could take place without both divisions being represented; no council could act
unless there were present one chief from the
Iⁿshta'çuⁿda division and two from the Hoⁿ'-
gashenu.   In this connection, the saying of an
old Omaha man may throw light on how this
representation from the two divisions was regarded by the people.   He said: "The Iⁿshta'-
çuⁿda represented the great power, so that one
chief from that side was enough, while two were
necessary from the Hoⁿ'gashenu."   This native
estimate of the reason for the unequal representation of chiefs is the reverse of what a member
of the white race would naturally conclude—that
the more important division should be represented
by the two chiefs.

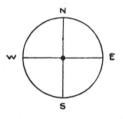

FIG. 45.   Diagram of ball
game.

   In former times a ball game used to be ceremonially played between
the young men of the two divisions.   At such times it was the duty
of a member of the Tade'ata, or Wind, subgens of the Koⁿ'çe gens, to
start the ball.   A circle with two lines crossing each other at right
angles was drawn on the cleared ground, and the ball placed in the
center (fig. 45).   The ball was first rolled toward the north along the
line drawn to the edge of the circle, and then back on the same line to
the center.   It was then rolled on the line toward the east to the
edge of the circle and back to the center.   Next it was rolled to the
south and returned on the same line to the center.   Finally it was
rolled to the west on its line, and back to the center, and then it was

tossed into the air and the game proper began.   The game is said to have had a cosmic significance and the initial movements of the ball referred to the winds, the bringers of life.   It was played by the two divisions of the *hu'thuga* as representatives of the earth and the sky.

The demarcation between the two divisions of the *hu'thuga* was well known to the boys of the tribe, and no boy dared to go alone across this line.   When for any purpose a boy was sent on an errand from the Hon'gashenu side to the Inshta'çunda side, he was obliged to go attended by his friends from the gentes belonging to his own side, for a fight was always the result of an attempt to cross the line. It is an interesting fact that while the old men of the tribe generally punished boys for fighting together, these juvenile combats over the line were not objected to by the parents and elders.   This custom seems to have come into practice to serve a purpose similar to that of the symbolic cutting of the hair.   The cutting of the hair was done, it was said, in order to impress on the mind of a child, as in an object lesson, the gentes to which his playmates belonged.   That it served its purpose has been observed by the writers.   Frequently when a man has been asked to what gens a certain person belonged, he would pause and then say: "I remember, his hair used to be cut thus and so when we were boys, so he must be ———," mentioning the gens that used this symbolic cut of the hair.   The line that marked the two divisions of the *hu'thuga*, although invisible, was well known to the boys as the fighting line, where they could have a scrimmage without being interfered with, and each boy knew his own half of the *hu'thuga* and the boundary, where he was at liberty to attack and where he must stand on the defensive.   This custom of one division standing by its members in a fight as against outsiders throws a side light on the word for tribe already referred to.

# V

## TRIBAL GOVERNMENT

From an examination by the light of tribal traditions of the rites, duties, and interrelations of the gentes, one discerns in the tribal organization of the Omaha and cognates, as it stood in the early part of the nineteenth century, the evidences of past vicissitudes, all of which show that a tendency had existed toward disintegration because of a lack of close political organization, and that various expedients for holding the people together had been tried. This weakness seems to have been specially felt when the people were in the buffalo country; while there groups would wander away, following the game, and become lost. Occasionally they were discovered and would rejoin the main body, as has been shown in the case of the Hon'ga utanatsi of the Osage tribe. The environment of the people did not foster sedentary habits, such as would have tended toward a close political union; therefore the nature of the country in which these cognates dwelt added to rather than lessened the danger of disintegration. This danger was further increased by the number of religious rites among the people, each one of which was more or less complete in itself and was in the keeping of a group of exogamous kindred. The fact that the group was exogamous indicates that some form of organization had long existed among the people, but the frequent separations that took place emphasized the importance of maintaining the unity of the tribe, and the problem of devising means to secure this essential result was a matter of serious concern to the thinking and constructive minds among the people. The Sacred Legend, already quoted, says: "And the people thought, How can we better ourselves?"

As has been stated, the ideas fundamental to the tribal organization of the Omaha and their cognates related to the creation and perpetuation of living creatures. The expression of these ideas in the dramatic form of rites seems to have been early achieved and those which symbolically present the connection of cosmic forces with the birth and well-being of mankind seem to have persisted in whole or in part throughout the various experiences of the five cognate tribes, and to have kept an important place in tribal life. These rites constitute what may be regarded as the lower stratum of religious ceremonies—for example, in the recognition of the vital relation of the Wind, as shown in the ceremony of Turning the Child, performed when it entered on its tribal life (see p. 117); in the names bestowed on females, which generally refer to natural phenomena or objects rather than to religious observances; in the ceremonies connected with Thunder as the god of war and arbiter of the life and death of man.   There are indications that other rites relating to cosmic forces have been lost in the passage of years.   Among the Omaha certain articles still survive rites long since disused, as the Cedar Pole and the Sacred Shell, both of which were preserved until recently in the Sacred Tent of War in charge of the We'zhiⁿshte gens. It is probable that the rites connected with the Sacred Shell were the older and that they once held an important place and exercised a widespread influence in the tribe, as indicated by the reverence and fear with which this object was regarded by the people of every Omaha gens.   Other Omaha rites, as has been shown, have ceased to be observed—those connected with the thunder (p. 142), the stars (p. 177), and the winds (p. 169).   The disappearance of former rites may indicate physiographic changes experienced by the people, which affected their food supply, avocations, and other phases of life, thereby causing certain rites to be superseded by others more in harmony with a changed environment.   Thus life in the buffalo country naturally resulted in rites which pertained to hunting the buffalo finally taking precedence over those which pertained to the cultivation of the maize (see pp. 147, 155).

There are indications that under these and other disturbing and disintegrating influences certain ceremonies were instituted to counteract these tendencies by fostering tribal consciousness in order to help to bind the people together.   The Hede'wachi ceremony is of this character and seems to date far back in the history of the Omaha tribe.   It is impossible to trace as in a sequence the growth of the idea of the desirability of political unity, for there were many influences, religious and secular, at work to bring about modifications of customs and actual changes in government.   The efforts to regulate warfare and to place it under greater control and at the same time to enhance the honor with which the warrior was to be regarded seem to have been among the first steps taken toward developing a definite governing power within the tribe.   The act of placing the rites pertaining to war in charge of one gens was probably the result of combined influences.   When this modification of earlier forms was accomplished a new name seems to have been given to the gens holding this office, and thus the present term We'zhiⁿshte (see p. 142) came into use.   The former name of this kinship group is not known, but judging from analogy it probably had reference to one or the other of the lost ceremonies connected with the sacred articles left in its care.   While the segregation of the war power may have tended to stay some of the disintegrating tendencies it did not have the positive unifying force that was desired. If other devices were tried to bring about this result nothing is known of them.

The Sacred Legend and other accounts tell the story of the way in which a central governing body was finally formed and all agree that it was devised for the purpose of "holding the people together." One version speaks of seven old men who, while visitors to the tribe, inaugurated the governing council. The Sacred Legend declares that the council was the outcome of "thought" and "consultation among the wise old men," their purpose taking form in the plan to establish a Nini'bato[n] [a] subdivision in some of the gentes, each subdivision to furnish one member to the council, which was to be the governing authority, exercising control over the people, maintaining peace in the tribe, but having no relation to offensive warfare. According to the Legend account of the formation of the Nini'bato[n], "two old men," one from the Ho[n]'ga gens and the other from the I[n]ke'çabe gens, were commissioned to carry out the plan of the "wise old men." The term "old" is one of respect and indicates that these men had gained wisdom from experience, and that their plan was the result of knowledge and thought concerning actual conditions in the past and in the present, rather than one based on speculative notions. The "two old men" were entrusted with the two Sacred Tribal Pipes; as they passed around the *hu'thuga* they would stop at a certain gens, designating a family which was to become a Nini'bato[n] and making this choice official by the presentation of a pipe. For some unknown reason in this circuit of the tribe the "old men" passed by the I[n]gthe'-zhide gens and did not give them a pipe. Nor was a pipe given to the We'zhi[n]shte gens or to the Ho[n]'ga gens. It was explained concerning these latter omissions that the We'zhi[n]shte had already been given the control of the war rites of the tribe, while the duties of the council formed from the Nini'bato[n] subdivisions were to be solely in the interests of peace, and to the Ho[n]'ga gens was to belong the duty of calling together this governing council.

The two Sacred Pipes carried by the "two old men" were their credentials. The authority of these two pipes must have been of long standing and undisputed by the people in order to have made it possible for their bearers to inaugurate such an innovation as setting apart a certain family within a gens and giving to it a new class of duties—duties that were to be civil and not connected with the established rights of the gentes. These new duties did not conflict,

---

[a] The word *nini'bato[n]* means "to possess a pipe." The origin of the significant use of the pipe lies in a remote past. Among the Omaha and cognate tribes the pipe was regarded as a medium by which the breath of man ascended to Wako[n]'da through the fragrant smoke and conveyed the prayer or aspiration of the person smoking; the act also partook of the nature of an oath, an affirmation to attest sincerity and responsibility. The pipe was a credential known and respected by all.

however, with any of such rites, nor did they deprive the Nini'bato$^n$ families from participating in them. A new class of obligations to Wako$^{n\prime}$da and to all persons composing the tribe were laid upon the Nini'bato$^n$ and the new council.

## CHIEFTAINSHIP

The earliest tradition among the Omaha as to the establishment of chiefs is contained in the story already recounted concerning the formation of the Nini'bato$^n$ and governing council, which was to be composed of hereditary chiefs. How long the hereditary character was maintained and what had previously constituted leadership in the tribe are not known, nor is there any knowledge as to how the change from hereditary to competitive membership in the council came about. It may be that the change was the result of increasing recognition of the importance of strengthening the power of the governing council by making it both the source and the goal of tribal honors, thus enhancing its authority and at the same time emphasizing the desirability of tribal unity. All that the writers have been able to ascertain concerning the change in the composition of the council from hereditary to competitive membership has been that it took place several generations ago, how many could not be learned.

### Orders of Chiefs

The period of the establishment of these orders is lost in the past, but internal evidence seems to point to their formation after the council with its Nini'bato$^n$ membership had been fully established and accepted by the people.

There were two orders of chiefs, the Ni'kagahi xu'de and the Ni'kagahi sha'be. The name of the first (*ni'kagahi*, "chief;" *xu'de*, "brown") has reference to a uniform color, as of the brown earth, where all are practically alike, of one hue or rank. The Ni'kagahi xu'de order was unlimited as to membership, but admittance into it depended upon the consent of the Ni'kagahi sha'be (*ni'kagahi*, "chief," *sha'be*, "dark"). The word *sha'be* does not refer to color, but to the appearance of an object raised above the uniform level and seen against the horizon as a dark object. Men who had risen from the Ni'kagahi xu'de into the limited order of the Ni'kagahi sha'be were regarded as elevated before the people.

#### WATHI$^{N\prime}$ETHE

Entrance into this order was possible only when a vacancy occurred, and then only to a member of the order of Ni'kagahi xu'de after the performance of certain acts known as *wathi$^{n\prime}$ethe* (from *wa*, "thing having power;" *thi$^n$*, from *thi$^n\prime$ge*, "nothing;" *the*, "to make" or "to cause," the word meaning something done or given for which there is no material return but through which honor is received). *Wathin'ethe* stands for acts and gifts which do not directly add to the comfort and wealth of the actor or donor, but which have relation to the welfare of the tribe by promoting internal order and peace, by providing for the chiefs and keepers (see p. 212), by assuring friendly relations with other tribes; they partook therefore of a public rather than a private character, and while they opened a man's way to tribal honors and position, they did so by serving the welfare of all the people. Entrance into the order of Ni'kagahi xu'de was through the performance of certain *wathin'ethe;* in this instance the gifts of the aspirant were made solely to the Seven Chiefs.

The election of members to the order of Ni'kagahi xu'de took place at a meeting of the Ni'kagahi sha'be called by the leaders of the Hon'ga gens for this purpose. After the tribal pipes had been smoked the name of a candidate was mentioned, and his record and the number and value of his gifts were canvassed. The prescribed articles used in making these gifts were eagles, eagle war bonnets, quivers (including bows and arrows), catlinite pipes with ornamented stems, tobacco pouches, otter skins, buffalo robes, ornamented shirts, and leggings. In olden times, burden-bearing dogs, tents, and pottery were given; in recent times these have been replaced by horses, guns, blankets, blue and red cloth, silver medals, and copper kettles. It is noteworthy that all the raw materials used in construction, as well as the unmanufactured articles of the early native type, were such as required of the candidate prowess as a hunter, care in accumulating, and skilled industry. A man often had to travel far to acquire some of these articles, and be exposed to danger from enemies in securing and bringing them home, so that they represented, besides industry as a hunter, bravery and skill as a warrior. Moreover, as upon the men devolved the arduous task of procuring all the meat for food and the pelts used to make clothing, bedding, and tents, and as there was no common medium of exchange for labor in the tribe, such as money affords, each household had to provide from the very foundation, so to speak, every article it used or consumed. It will therefore be seen that persistent work on the part of a man aspiring to enter the order of chief was necessary, as he must not only provide food and clothing for the daily use of his family, but accumulate a surplus so as to obtain leisure for the construction of the articles to be counted as *wathin'ethe.* The men made the bows and arrows, the war bonnets, and the pipes; the ornamentation was the woman's task. Her deft fingers prepared the porcupine quills after her husband or brother had caught the wary little animals. For the slow task of dyeing the quills and embroidering with them she needed a house well stocked with food and defended from lurking war parties, in order to have time and security for her work. A lazy fellow or an impulsive, improvident man could not acquire the property represented by these gifts. There was no prescribed number of gifts demanded for entrance into the Xu′de order but they had to be sufficient to warrant the chiefs in admitting him, for the man once in the order could, by persistent industry and care, rise so as to become a candidate for the order of Sha′be when a vacancy occurred.

When a favorable decision as to the candidate was reached the chiefs arose and followed the Sacred Pipes, borne reverently, with the stems elevated, by the two leading chiefs. Thus led, the company walked slowly about the camp to the lodge of the man who had been elected a Xu′de and paused before the door. At this point the man had the option to refuse or to accept the honor. If he should say: "I do not wish to become a chief," and wave away the tribal pipes offered him to smoke, thus refusing permission to the chiefs to enter his lodge, they would pass on, leaving him as though he had not been elected. When the man accepted the position he smoked the pipes as they were offered, whereupon the chiefs entered his lodge, bearing the pipes before them, and slowly passed around his fireplace. This act signified to all the tribe that the man was thenceforth a chief, a member of the order of Ni′kagahi xu′de. He was now eligible to other honors—all of which, however, depended upon further efforts on his part. (For portrait of Omaha chiefs, see pls. 36, 37.)

Eligibility to enter the order of Ni′kagahi sha′be depended upon the performance of certain graded *wathiⁿ′ethe*. Vacancies occurred only by death or by the resignation of very old men. A vacancy was filled by the one in the Xu′de order who could "count" the most *wathiⁿ′ethe* given to the chiefs or who had performed the graded acts of the *wathiⁿ′ethe*. The order and value of these graded acts were not generally known to the people, nor even to all the chiefs of the Xu′de. Those who became possessed of this knowledge were apt to keep it for the benefit of their aspiring kinsmen. The lack of this knowledge, it is said, occasionally cost a man the loss of an advantage which he would otherwise have had.

There were seven grades of *wathiⁿ′ethe* the performance of which made a man eligible to a place in the order of Ni′kagahi sha′be. They ranked as follows:

First. Washa′be ga′xe (*washa′be*, "an official staff;" *ga′xe*, "to make"). This grade consisted in procuring the materials necessary to make the *washa′be*, an ornamented staff carried by the leader of the annual buffalo hunt. (See p. 155.) These materials were a dressed buffalo skin, a crow, two eagles, a shell disk, sinew, a pipe with an ornamented stem, and, in olden times, a cooking vessel of pottery, replaced in modern times by a copper kettle. The money

GAHI'GE, AN OLD OMAHA CHIEF

GȻHEDOⁿNOⁿZHIⁿ (STANDING HAWK) AND WIFE

value of these articles, rated by ordinary trading terms, was not less than \$100 to \$130. The performance of the first grade four times would constitute the highest act possible for a man. No Omaha has ever accomplished this act so many times.

Second. Bon'wakithe ("I caused the herald to call"). The aspirant requested the tribal herald to summon the Ni'kagahi sha'be together with the keeper of the ritual used in filling the Sacred Pipes, from the Inshta'çunda gens, to a feast. Besides providing for the feast, gifts of leggings, robes, bows and arrows, and tobacco were required as gifts for the guests. If it chanced that the aspirant for honors was not on friendly terms with the keeper of the ritual, or if from any other motive the keeper desired to check the man's ambition, it lay in his power to thwart it by allowing the pipes to remain unfilled, in which case the gifts and feast went for nothing.

Third. U'gashkegthon ("to tether a horse"). A man would make a feast for the Ni'kagahi sha'be and tie at the door of his tent a horse with a new robe thrown over it. The horse and the robe were gifts to his guests. A man once gained renown by "counting" seven acts of this grade, performing four in one day.

Fourth. Gaçi'ge nonshton wakithe (gaçi'ge, "marching abreast;" nonshton, "to halt;" wakithe, "to make or cause"), "causing the people to halt." This act was possible only during the annual hunt. As the people were moving, the Sacred Pole and the governing chiefs in advance, a man would bring a horse or a new robe and present it to the Pole. The gift was appropriated by the Waxthe'-xeton subgens of the Hon'ga, who had charge of the Pole. During this act the entire tribe halted, while the herald proclaimed the name of the giver. This act should be repeated four times in one day.

Fifth. Te thishke' wakithe (te, "buffalo;" thishke', "to untie;" wakithe, "to make or cause"), "causing the Sacred White Buffalo Hide to be opened and shown." During this ceremony of exhibiting the White Buffalo Hide a shell disk or some other article of value was presented to the Hide, the gifts becoming the property of the Waxthe'beton subgens of the Hon'ga, who had charge of this sacred object. This act had to be repeated four times in one day.

Sixth. Wa't'edonbe (wa, "things having power and purpose;" t'e, "dead;" donbe, "to see"). This act consisted in taking gifts to the family of a chief when a death occurred. The costliest donation remembered to have been made under this class was on the occasion of the death of the son of old Big Elk, who died of smallpox in the early part of the nineteenth century, when a fine horse on which was spread a bearskin was offered in honor of the dead.

Seventh. When a person had been killed accidentally or in anger the chiefs took the Sacred Tribal Pipes to the kindred of the man, accompanied by gifts, in order to prevent any revengeful act. All those who contributed toward these gifts could "count" them as belonging to the seventh grade. If the aggrieved party smoked the pipe and accepted the gifts, bloodshed was averted and peace maintained in the tribe.

All of the gifts constituting these seven grades were made to the chiefs of the governing council in recognition of their authority. They were for a definite purpose—to enable the giver to secure entrance into the order of Ni'kagahi sha'be whenever a vacancy should occur in that body.

It will be noticed that the act constituting the first grade differed from the other six in that it was not a direct gift made to the chiefs, but was connected with the ceremonial staff of the leader of the annual buffalo hunt. It was, however, a recognition of authority, an authority which held the people in order and made it possible for each family to secure its supply of food and clothing. It was therefore, in its intrinsic character, in harmony with the purpose of the other six graded *wathin'ethe*.

*Waba'hon*, designated an act not belonging to the regular *wathin'ethe*, but esteemed as a generous deed that redounded to the credit of the doer. The term means "to raise or push up," and refers to placing a deer, buffalo, or elk on its breast and putting bits of tobacco along its back, all of which signified that the hunter had dedicated the animal as a gift to the chiefs. A chief could not receive such a gift, however, unless he had performed the act of *waba'hon* four times. If he had not performed the acts and desired to receive the gift he could call on his near of kin to help him to "count." If he was thus able to receive the gift, it became his duty to divide the game with those who had helped him by lending their "count." If he was able to "count" four *waba'hon* himself, he could then keep the entire animal for his own use.

In admitting a man to either order of chiefs his personal character was always taken into consideration. If he was of a disputatious or quarrelsome nature no amount of gifts would secure his election to the order of Ni'kagahi xu'de or make possible a place for him in the Ni'kagahi sha'be. The maxim was: "A chief must be a man who can govern himself."

### The Council of Seven Chiefs

The origin of this governing council as given in the Sacred Legend and elsewhere has been recounted and the change from the early form of hereditary membership mentioned. The institution of a small body representing the entire tribe, to have full control of the people, to settle all contentions, and to subordinate all factions to a central authority, was an important governmental movement. The credential of this authority both for the act of its creation and for the exercise of its functions was the presence and ceremonial use of the two Sacred Tribal Pipes.   The two stood for the fundamental idea in the dual organization of the $hu'thuga$ (see p. 137).   This was recognized also in the ceremonial custody and preparation of the Pipes.   The keeping of them belonged to the $I^nke'çabe$ gens of the southern (earth) side of the $hu'thuga;$ the office of ceremonially filling the Pipes, making them ready for use, was vested in the $I^nshta'çu^nda$ gens of the northern (upper) realm of the $hu'thuga$, representative of the abode of the supernatural forces to which man must appeal for help. Through the ceremonies and use of the two Sacred Pipes the halves of the $hu'thuga$ were welded, as it were, the Pipes thus becoming representative of the tribe as a whole.   The prominence given to the Pipes, as the credential of the "old men," as their authority in the creation of chiefs and the governing council, seems to indicate that the institution of the Nini'bato$^n$ and the establishment of the  ouncil, although a progressive movement, was a growth, a development of earlier forms, rather than an invention or arbitrary arrangement of the "old men."   The retaining of the two Pipes as the supreme or confirmatory authority within the council rather than giving that power to a head chief was consonant with the fundamental idea embodied in the tribal organization!   The number of the council (seven) probably had its origin in the significance of the number which represented the whole of man's environment—the four quarters where were the four paths down which the Above came to the Below, where stood man.   The ancient ideas and beliefs of the people concerning man's relation to the cosmos were thus interwoven with their latest social achievement, the establishment of a representative governing body.

Whether the ornamentation of the two Tribal Pipes was authorized at this time is not known; but it is probable that in this as in every other arrangement there was the adaptation or modification of some old and accepted form of expression to meet the needs of newer conditions.   It is said that the seven woodpecker heads on one of the Tribal Pipes stood for the seven chiefs that composed the governing council, while the use of but one woodpecker head on the other pipe represented the unity of authority of the chiefs.   This explanation explains only in part.   The reason for the choice of the woodpecker as a symbol lies far back in the history of the people, and it may be that it did not originate in this linguistic group.   In myths found throughout a wide region this bird was connected with the sun. It was used on the calumet pipes, which had a wide range, covering almost the whole of the Mississippi drainage.   It is not improbable that the woodpecker symbol was accepted at the time the calumet ceremony became known to the Omaha and adopted as a symbol of peaceful authority, but a definite statement on the subject at present is impossible.

The seven members of the council belonged to the order of Ni'kagahi sha'be, in fact they may be said to have represented that order in which each man held his place until death or voluntary resignation. Five other persons were entitled to attend the meetings of the council, being of an ex officio class: The keeper of the Sacred Pole; the keeper of the Sacred Buffalo Hide; the keeper of the two Sacred Tribal Pipes; the keeper of the ritual used when filling them; and the keeper of the Sacred Tent of War. None of these five keepers had a voice in the decisions of the council, the responsibility of deciding devolving solely on the Seven Chiefs who composed the council proper.

At council meetings the men sat in a semicircle. The two chiefs who could count the greatest number of $wathi^{n'}ethe$ were called Ni'kagahi u'zhu ($u'zhu$ "principal"); these chiefs sat side by side back of the fireplace, facing the east and the entrance of the lodge. They represented the two halves of the $hu'thuga$, the one who sat on the right (toward the south) representing the Ho$^{n'}$gashenu, the one who sat on the left (toward the north), the I$^{n}$shta'çu$^{n}$da. The other members sat in the order of their "counts" on each side of the principal chiefs, the highest next to those chiefs and so on to the end of the line. The position assigned each member on entrance into the council remained unchanged until a death or resignation took place. In the case of a vacancy in the $u'zhu$, the place was taken by whoever could count the most $wathi^{n'}ethe;$ he might be an old member of the council or a new man from the order of Ni'kagahi xu'de. Any vacancy occurring was likely to cause a change in the places of the members, according to the "count" of the new member, but the place and position of $u'zhu$ were affected only by death or resignation. An $u'zhu$ held his rank against all claimants.

The manner of deliberating and coming to a decision in the Council of Seven is said to have been as follows: A question or plan of operation was presented by a member; it was then referred to the chief sitting next, who took it under consideration and then passed it on to the next person and so on around the circle until it reached the man who first presented it. The matter would pass again and again around the circle until all came to agreement. All day was frequently spent in deliberation. No one person would dare to take the responsibility of the act. All must accept it and then carry it through as one man. This unity of decision was regarded as having a supernatural power and authority. Old men explained to the writers that the members of the council had been made chiefs by the Sacred Tribal Pipes, which were from Wako$^{n'}$da; therefore, "when the chiefs had deliberated on a matter and had smoked, the decision was as the word of Wako$^{n'}$da."

The ceremonial manner of smoking the Sacred Pipes was as follows:

After the members of the council were in their places the keeper of the Sacred Pipes laid them before the two principal chiefs, who called on the keeper of the ritual to prepare the Pipes for use. As he filled them with native tobacco he intoned in a low voice the ritual which belonged to that act. He had to be careful not to let either of the Pipes fall. Should this happen, that meeting of the council would be at an end, and the life of the keeper would be in danger from the supernatural powers. After the Pipes were filled they were again laid before the two principal chiefs. When the time came to smoke the Pipes in order to give authority to a decision, the $I^n$ke'çabe keeper arose, took up one of the Pipes, and held it for the principal chief sitting toward the north, to smoke. The assistant from the Te'pa subgens of the Tha'tada gens (see p. 159) followed, taking up the other Pipe and holding it for the principal chief sitting toward the south, to smoke. The Pipes were then passed around the council, the $I^n$ke'çabe keeper leading and carefully holding the Pipe for each member to smoke, the assistant following and serving the other Pipe in the same manner. The principal chief sitting toward the south was the last to smoke from the Pipe borne by the $I^n$ke'çabe keeper, who then laid the Pipe in the place from which he had taken it. When the Te'pa assistant reached the chief to whom he had first offered the Pipe he laid it down beside the other. The keeper of the ritual from the $I^n$shta'çu$^n$da gens then arose and cleaned the Pipes, after which he laid them back before the two chiefs, who then called the keeper from the $I^n$ke'çabe gens to take them in charge.[a]

"The seven must have but one heart and speak as with one mouth," said the old men who explained these things to the writers, adding: "It is because these decisions come from Wako$^n$'da that a chief is slow to speak. No word can be without meaning and every one must be uttered in soberness. That is why when a chief speaks the others listen, for the words of a chief must be few." When a conclusion was reached by the council the herald was summoned, and he went about the camp circle and proclaimed the decision. No one dared to dispute, for it was said: "This is the voice of the chiefs."

Among the duties of the Council of Seven besides that of maintaining peace and order within the tribe were making peace with other tribes, securing allies, determining the time of the annual buffalo hunt, and confirming the man who was to act as leader, on whom rested the responsibility of that important movement. While on the hunt the Seven Chiefs were in a sense subordinate to the leader, their duties being advisory rather than governing in character; they were always regarded, however, as directly responsible to Wako$^n$'da for the welfare of the tribe. The council appointed officers called

---

[a] All the other sacred articles used in tribal ceremonies have been turned over to the writers for safekeeping, but no arguments could induce the leading men to part with the two Sacred Pipes. The answer was always, "They must remain." And they are still with the people.

*wano*<sup>n</sup>*'she* ("soldiers") to carry out their commands. These officers were chosen from the order of Ni'kagahi xu'de and were always men who had won honors, and whose character commanded the respect of the tribe. (Fig. 46.) Frequently they were appointed for some special service, as when an unauthorized war party committed depredations on a neighboring tribe; if the chiefs ordered the stolen

Fig. 46. Kaxe'no<sup>n</sup>ba, who frequently served as a "soldier."

property returned, the booty would then be sent back under "soldiers" selected for the task. "Soldiers" were appointed by the council to preserve order during the annual hunt, the office expiring with the hunt. Men who had once filled the office of "soldier" were apt to be called on to assist the council in the preservation of order within the tribe.

Should a sudden attack be made on the tribe the Seven Chiefs would then join in the defense and if need be lead the people against the enemy. The council cooperated with the keeper of the Tent of War in sending out scouts during the annual tribal hunt (see p. 279). The punishment of men who slipped away on unauthorized warfare devolved on these chiefs (see p. 404). On one notable occasion the Council of Seven temporarily resigned, and placed the entire tribe under the control of one man, Wa'baçka, who led the people against the Pawnee. This exception to all tribal rule has been preserved in both story and song (see p. 406). When a man desired to perform the Wa'wa$^n$ ceremony (see p. 376) and carry the pipes to another tribe or to a man within the tribe, permission from the chiefs had first to be obtained. The consent of the Seven Chiefs was also necessary to the admission of a candidate to the Ho$^n$'hewachi.

There were no other governing chiefs in the tribe besides those of the council. No gens had a chief possessing authority over it, nor was there any council of a gens, nor could a gens act by itself. There was one possible exception; sometimes a gens went on a hunt under the leadership of its chiefs, for there were chiefs in every gens, men who belonged to the order of Ni'kagahi xu'de or who had entered the ranks of the Ni'kagahi sha'be; but none of these men could individually exercise governing power within a gens or in the tribe. The gens, as has been shown, was not a political organization, but a group of kindred, united through a common rite. The leading men of a gens were those who had charge of its rites; those who could count many *wathi$^n$'ethe*, and those who had been designated to act as "soldiers." Such men were invited on various occasions to sit with the Council of Seven, as in the communal tent when the ceremony of anointing the Sacred Pole took place. There was no tribal assembly or tribal council. All power for both decision and action was lodged in the Council of Seven.

The old Omaha men, who are the authority for the interpretations of tribal rites and customs contained in this memoir, have earnestly sought to impress upon the writers that peace and order within the tribe were of prime importance; without these it was declared neither the people nor the tribe as an organization could exist. War was secondary; its true function was protective—to guard the people from outside enemies. Aggressive warfare was to be discouraged; any gains made by it were more than offset by the troubles entailed. It was recognized that it was difficult to restrain young men; therefore restrictions were thrown about predatory warfare (see p. 404), that all who went on the warpath should first secure permission, while the special honors accorded to those whose brave acts were performed in defense of the tribe tended to make war secondary to peace.

"Plentiful food and peace," it was said, "are necessary to the prosperity of the tribe."

In later years, under the influence of traders and of United States Government officials, the old order of chieftainship lost much of its power. Men who were pliant were enriched by traders and became unduly important, and the same was frequently true of the men who were made "chiefs" by United States Government officials. Some of these have been men who had no rightful claim according to tribal usage to that office. Chiefs made by the Government were called "paper chiefs." These men sometimes exercised considerable influence, as they were supposed by the people to be supported by the Government, but their influence was that born of expediency rather than that growing out of the ancient belief that the chief was one who was favored by Wako$^{n}$'da and who represented before the people certain aspects of that mysterious power.

### EMOLUMENTS OF CHIEFS AND KEEPERS

Entrance into the order of chieftainship was secured through certain prescribed acts and gifts called *wathi$^{n}$'ethe* (see p. 202). All of the gifts, except those belonging to the first and second grades (see p. 204), were made to the Seven Chiefs. The two exceptions were contributions to ceremonies connected with the maintenance of order and the consequent welfare of the tribe. While all the *wathi$^{n}$'ethe* were in a sense voluntary, they were obligatory on the man who desired to rise to a position of prominence in the tribe. It was explained that "the gifts made to the chiefs were not only in recognition of their high office and authority as the governing power of the tribe but to supply them with the means to meet the demands made upon them because of their official position." It was further explained that—

Chiefs were expected to entertain all visitors from other tribes, also the leading men within the tribe and to make adequate gifts to their visitors. Both Chiefs and Keepers were often deterred from hunting by their official duties and thus were prevented from securing a large supply of food or of the raw material needed for the manufacture of articles suitable to present as gifts to visitors. The gifts made by aspirants to tribal office therefore partook of the nature of payment to the Chiefs and Keepers for the services they rendered to the people.

Not only did the *wathi$^{n}$'ethe* accomplish the purpose as explained above, but the custom stimulated industry and enterprise among the men and women, and thus indirectly served the cause of peace within the tribe.

Beside their use as stated above, gifts were demanded as entrance fees to the various societies. Those requisite for admission to the Ho$^{n}$'hewachi were particularly costly (see p. 493). Moreover, the meetings of the societies made demands on the accumulated wealth, so to speak, of the family. Food was required for the "feasts" of the members, and gifts were expected as a part of some of the ceremonies. All these had to be drawn from the surplus store, a store that had to be created by the skill of the man as a hunter and by the industry of the woman. No one gave feasts or made gifts which left the family in want of food or of clothing.

At the anointing of the Sacred Pole a supply of meats of the cut called *tezhu'* (see p. 273) was expected from every family in the tribe except from those of the Ho$^n$'ga subgens, that had charge of the Pole and its ceremonies. While there was no penalty attached to the non-fulfillment of this tribal duty, as it was considered, yet from a series of coincidences a belief had grown up that a refusal would be. punished supernaturally.

These customs in reference to gifts made as *wathi$^{n'}$ethe* show that the people had progressed to the recognition that something more was required of a man than merely to supply his own physical needs; that he had social and public duties to perform and must give of his labor to support the chiefs and keepers, officers who served and promoted the general welfare of the people.

### OFFENSES AND PUNISHMENTS

The authority of the chiefs and social order were safeguarded by the following punishment:

Within the Tent Sacred to War was kept a staff of ironwood, one end of which was rough, as if broken. On this splinted end poison was put when the staff was to be used officially for punishment. In the pack kept in this tent was found a bladder, within which were four rattlesnake heads, and with them in a separate bundle the poison fangs (fig. 47; Peabody Museum nos. 48262–3). These were probably used to compound the poison put on the staff. As men's bodies were usually naked, it was not difficult when near a person in a crowd to prod him with the staff, making a wound and introducing the deadly poison, which is said always to have. resulted in death. This form of punishment was applied to a man who made light of the authority of the chiefs or of the *wain'waxube*, the packs which could authorize a war party, such a person being a disturber of the peace and order of the tribe. The punishment was decided on by the Council of Seven Chiefs, which designated a trustworthy man to apply the staff to the offender. Sometimes the man was given a chance for his life by having his horses struck and poisoned. If, however, he did not take this warning, he paid the forfeit of his life, for he would be struck by the poisoned staff end and killed.

Thieving (*wamo$^n$'tho$^n$*) was uncommon. Restitution was the only punishment. Assaults were not frequent. When they occurred they were settled privately between the parties and their relatives.

In all offenses the relatives stood as one.   Each could be held responsible for the acts of another—a custom that sometimes worked injus-
tice, but on the whole was conducive to social order.

Running off with a man's wife or committing adultery was severely
punished.   In this class of offenses the husband or his near relatives
administered punishment.   The woman might be whipped, but the
heavy punishment fell on the guilty man.   Generally his property
was taken from him, and if the man offered resistance he was either

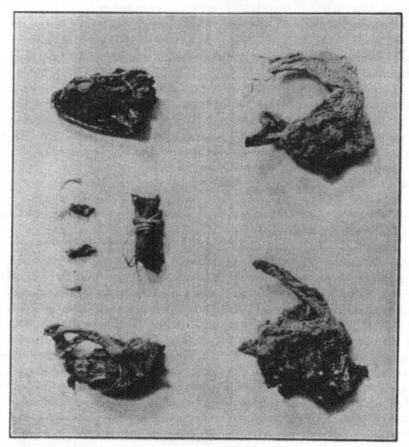

FIG. 47.  Rattlesnake heads and fangs.

slashed with a knife or beaten with a bludgeon.   The revenge taken by
a husband on a man making advances to his wife was called *miwa'da*.

A wife jealous of another woman who was attentive to her husband was apt to attack her with a knife.   An assault of this kind,
called *non'won̥çi*, was seldom interfered with.   If a man's wife died
and left children, custom required that he marry his wife's sister.
Should he fail to do so, the woman's relatives sometimes took up the
matter and threatened the man with punishment.

The term *wano^n'kathe* was used in reference to murder, or to any act which caused personal injury to another, even if it was unpremeditated. In the latter case the act would be condoned by gifts made to the injured party or his relatives. Deliberate murder was punished by banishment. When the knowledge of such a deed was brought to the notice of the chiefs, banishment was ordered, the offender was told of the decision and he obeyed. Banishment was four years, unless the man was sooner forgiven by the relatives of the murdered man. During this period the man had to camp outside the village and could hold no communication with anyone except his nearest kindred, who were permitted to see him. He was obliged to wear night and day a close-fitting garment of skin, covering his body and legs, and was not allowed to remove this covering during his punishment. His wife could carry him food but he was obliged to live apart from his family and to be entirely alone during the period of his exile.

It was believed that the spirit of a murdered man was inclined to come back to his village to punish the people. To prevent a murdered man from haunting his village he was turned face downward, and to impede his steps the soles of his feet were slit lengthwise. The return of a spirit to haunt people was called *wathi'hide*, "disturbance." Such a haunting spirit was supposed to bring famine. To avert this disaster, when a murdered man was buried, besides the precautions already mentioned, a piece of fat was put in his right hand, so that if he should come to the village he would bring plenty rather than famine, fat being the symbol of plenty. Even the relatives of the murdered man would treat the body of their kinsman in the manner described.

The sentence being passed on a murderer, the chiefs at once took the Tribal Pipes to the family of the murdered man and by gifts besought them to forego any further punishment upon the family of the murderer. If they accepted the gifts and smoked the pipe, there was no further disturbance connected with the crime. (See seventh grade, p. 205.)

The offense of *wathi'hi*, that of scaring off game while the tribe was on the buffalo hunt, could take place only by a man slipping away and hunting for himself. By this act, while he might secure food for his own use, he imperiled the food supply of the entire tribe by frightening away the herd. Such a deed was punished by flogging. Soldiers were appointed by the chiefs to go to the offender's tent and administer this punishment. Should the man dare to resist their authority he was doubly flogged because of his second offense. Such a flogging sometimes caused death. Besides this flogging, the man's tent was destroyed, his horses and other property were confiscated, and his tent poles burned; in short, he was reduced to beggary.

The punishment of a disturber of the peace of the tribe, by the exercise of *wazhiⁿ'agthe*, the placing of will power on the offender by the chiefs, was a peculiar form of chastisement by which the person was put out of friendly relations with men and animals. (See p. 497.) For a similar placing of the mind on an offender, see Ponca custom, page 48.

White Eagle (Ponca) narrated the following as showing the Ponca treatment of a murderer, even if the killing was an accident:

A Ponca killed a man. It was not intentional, but nevertheless he was, by the consent of the people, punished by the father of the man who was killed. The father cut all the edges of the man's robe, so that nothing about him could flutter should the wind blow. The spirit of a murdered person will haunt the people, and when the tribe is on the hunt, will cause the wind to blow in such a direction as to betray the hunters to the game and cause the herd to scatter, making it impossible for the people to get food. [The Omaha have the same belief about ghosts scattering the herds by raising the wind.] After the man's robe was cut it was sewed together in front, but space was left for his arm to have freedom. He was then bade to say, as he drew the arrow from the wound and rubbed it over the dead man, "I did not kill a man, but an animal." Then his hair was cut short for fear it might blow and cause the winds to become restless. The covering about the heart of a buffalo was taken and put over the man's head, and he was banished from the tribe for four years. The man obeyed strictly all the directions given him, and, further than that, he wept every day for the man he had slain. This action so moved the relatives of the dead, it is said, that in one year they pardoned him, gave him his liberty, and he returned to the tribe and his family.

# VI

## THE SACRED POLE

### ORIGIN.

In the process of governmental development it became expedient to have something which should symbolize the unity of the tribe and of its governing power—something which should appeal to the people, an object they could all behold and around which they could gather to manifest their loyalty to the idea it represented. The two Tribal Pipes, which hitherto had been the only representative of the governing authority, were not only complex in their symbolism, but they were not easily visible to the entire tribe and did not meet the need for a central object at great tribal gatherings. The ceremony of the He′dewachi had familiarized the people with the symbol of the tree as a type of unity. A similar idea would seem to have been expressed in the ancient Cedar Pole, which is said to have stood as a cosmic symbol representative of supernatural authority; its name was taken and the ceremonies formerly connected with it seem to have been preserved in part, at least, in those of the Sacred Pole.

Tradition states that the Sacred Pole was cut before the "Ponca gens broke away [from the Omaha] and became the Ponca tribe." Other evidence indicates that the tribes had already become more or less distinct when the Sacred Pole was cut.

There are two versions of the story of the finding of the Sacred Pole. Both have points in common. One runs as follows:

A great council was being held to devise some means by which the bands of the tribe might be kept together and the tribe itself saved from extinction. This council lasted many days. Meanwhile the son of one of the ruling men was off on a hunt. On his way home he came to a great forest and in the night lost his way. He walked and walked until he was exhausted with pushing his way through the underbrush. He stopped to rest and to find the "motionless star" for his guide when he was suddenly attracted by a light. Believing that it came from a tent the young hunter went toward it, but on coming to the place whence the welcome light came he was amazed to find that it was a tree that sent forth the light. He went up to it and found that the whole tree, its trunk, branches, and leaves, were alight, yet remained unconsumed. He touched the tree but no heat came from it. This mystified him and he stood watching the strange tree, for how long he did not know. At last day approached, the brightness of the tree began to fade, until with the rising of the sun the tree with its foliage resumed its natural appearance. The man remained there in order to watch the tree another night. As twilight came on it began to be luminous and continued so until the sun again arose. When the young man returned home he told his father of the wonder. Together they went to see the tree; they saw it all alight as it was before but the father observed something that had escaped the notice of the young man; this was that four animal paths led to it. These paths were well beaten and as the two men examined the paths and the tree it was clear to them that the animals came to the tree and had rubbed against it and polished its bark by so doing. This was full of significance to the elder man and on his return he told the leading men of the mysterious tree. It was agreed by all that the tree was a gift from Wako<sup>n</sup>'da and that it would be the thing that would help to keep the people together. With great ceremony they cut the tree down and hewed it to portable size.

Both Omaha and Ponca legends concerning the Pole say that the people were living in a village near a lake, and that the tree grew near a lake at some distance from where the people were dwelling. The finding of the Pole is said to have occurred while a council was in progress between the Cheyenne, Arikara, Omaha, Ponca, and Iowa, to reach an agreement on terms of peace and rules of war and hunting, and to adopt a peace ceremony.[a]  (See p. 74.)

The account in the Omaha Sacred Legend is as follows:

During this time a young man who had been wandering came back to his village. When he reached his home he said. "Father, I have seen a wonderful tree!" And he described it. The old man listened but he kept silent, for all was not yet settled between the tribes.

After a little while the young man went again to visit the tree. On his return home he repeated his former tale to his father about the wonderful tree. The old man kept silent, for the chiefs were still conferring. At last, when everything was agreed upon between the tribes, the old man sent for the chiefs and said: "My son has seen a wonderful tree. The Thunder birds come and go upon this tree, making a trail of fire that leaves four paths on the burnt grass that stretch toward the Four Winds. When the Thunder birds alight upon the tree it bursts into flame and the fire mounts to the top. The tree stands burning, but no one can see the fire except at night."

When the chiefs heard this tale they sent runners to see what this tree might be. The runners came back and told the same story—how in the night they saw the tree standing and burning as it stood. Then all the people held a council as to what this might mean, and the chiefs said: "We shall run for it; put on your ornaments and prepare as for battle." So the men stripped, painted themselves, put on their ornaments, and set out for the tree, which stood near a lake. They ran as in a race to attack the tree as if it were a warrior enemy. All the men ran. A Ponca was the first to reach the tree, and he struck it as he would an enemy. [Note the resemblance to the charge upon the He'dewachi tree; also in the manner of felling and bringing the tree into camp. (See p. 253.)]

Then they cut the tree down and four men, walking in line, carried it on their shoulders to the village. The chiefs sang four nights the songs that had been composed for the tree while they held a council and deliberated concerning the tree. A tent was made for the tree and set up within the circle of lodges. The chiefs worked upon the tree; they trimmed it and called it a human being. They made a basket-work receptacle of twigs and feathers and tied it about the middle. Then they said: "It has no hair!" So they sent out to get a large scalp lock and they put it on the top of the Pole for hair. Afterward the chiefs bade the herald tell the people that when all was completed they should see the Pole.

Then they painted the Pole and set it up before the tent, leaning it on a crotched stick, which they called imo<sup>n</sup>gthe (a staff). They summoned the people, and all the

a See the Hako, in the *Twenty-second Annual Report of the Bureau of American Ethnology*, part 2.

TATTOOED  OSAGE

people came—men, women, and children. When they were gathered the chiefs stood up and said: "You now see before you a mystery. Whenever we meet with troubles we shall bring all our troubles to him [the Pole]. We shall make offerings and requests. All our prayers must be accompanied by gifts. This [the Pole] belongs to all the people, but it shall be in the keeping of one family (in the Ho$^n$ga gens), and the leadership shall be with them. If anyone desires to lead (to become a chief) and to take responsibility in governing the people, he shall make presents to the Keepers [of the Pole] and they shall give him authority." When all was finished the people said: "Let us appoint a time when we shall again paint him [the Pole] and act before him the battles we have fought." The time was fixed; it was to take place in "the moon when the buffaloes bellow" (July). This was the beginning of the ceremony of Waxthe'xe  xigithe (see p. 230), and it was agreed that this ceremony should be kept up.

## MARK OF HONOR

Waxthe'xe, the name given to the Pole, was the name of the ancient Cedar Pole preserved in the Tent of War. The word is difficult to translate. The prefix *wa* indicates that the object spoken of had power, the power of motion, of life; *xthexe* means "mottled as by shadows;" the word has also the idea of bringing into prominence to be seen by all the people as something distinctive. *Xthexe'* was the name of the "mark of honor" put on a girl by her father or near of kin who had won, through certain acts, entrance into the Ho$^n$'hewachi, and so secured the right to have this mark tattooed on the girl. (See fig. 105.) The name of the Pole, Waxthe'xe, signifies that the power to give the right to possess this "mark of honor" was vested in the Pole. The mark placed on the girl was not a mark of her own achievements, but of her father's, as no girl or woman could by herself win it. The designs tattooed on the girl were all cosmic symbols. While the "mark of honor," as its name shows, was directly connected with the Cedar Pole, which was related to Thunder and war, the tattooed "mark of honor" among the Omaha was not connected with war, but with achievements that related to hunting and to the maintenance of peace within the tribe.

It was the custom among the Osage to tattoo the "mark of honor" on the warrior and on the hereditary keeper of the Honor Packs of War. The description of the Osage practice, which appears below, may relate to a time antedating the separation of the cognate tribes when the Cedar Pole may have been common property. The photograph from which the accompanying illustration (pl. 37a) was made, was taken in 1897. The design tattooed on the neck and chest (fig. 48) comes to a point about 2 inches above the waist line and extends over the shoulders to the back. The central part of the design, extending from under the chin downward to the lowest point, represents the stone knife. Two bands on each side of this central figure extend up to the hair an inch or two behind the ear, terminating in a knob solidly tattooed. This figure is called *i'bashabe* (meaning unknown); the name and significance of these bands were not given.   A pipe is tattooed on each side of the central figure, the bowl pointing upward.   At the root of the neck, on each side of the stone knife, a triangle is traced; a line from the hypotenuse extends to the top of the shoulder.   These represent tents.   The design means that "the Sacred Pipe has descended."   "All its keepers must be marked in this way."   If a keeper had cut off heads in battle, skulls would be represented between the pointed ends of the bands which fall over the shoulders.   It was explained that the

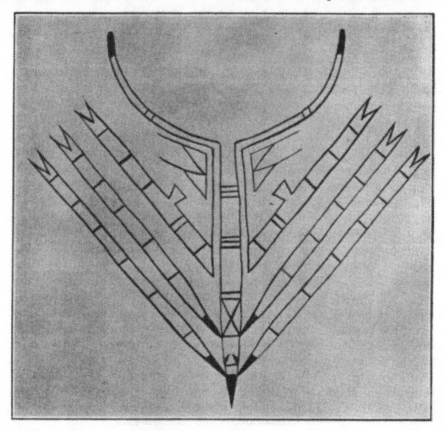

FIG. 48.   Tattooed design, "mark of honor" (Osage).

pictured skulls would draw to the tattooed man the strength of the men he had killed, so that his life would be prolonged by virtue of their unexpended days.

The man here shown was about 17 years old when he was tattooed. He said that the tattooing was done "to make him faithful in keeping the rites;" that he had tried to have visions by the Pipes, which he had always respected and "had never laid on the ground;" and that he had sought these visions and had been thus careful of the Pipes in order that his children might have long life.

A warrior who had won honors in battles was entitled to the privilege of tattooing his body or that of his wife or daughter as a mark of distinction. The lowest mark of such honors was three narrow lines beginning at the top of each shoulder and meeting at an angle at the lower part of the chest. The next higher mark had in addition to the lines on the chest three narrow lines running down the outer surface of the arms to the wrists. The highest mark had in addition to the lines on the chest and arms three narrow lines that continued from the shoulders, where the lines of the first mark began, meeting at an angle in the middle of the back. The tattooing was done by a man who was learned in the rituals connected with the ceremony. The needles used were tipped with the rattles of the rattlesnake.

## The Sacred Tents

The tent set apart for the Sacred Pole was pitched in front of the Waxthe'xeto$^{na}$ subgens of the Ho$^n$'ga gens, who, as their name implies, were given charge of the Pole. The tent was decorated with round red spots, which probably referred to the sun. Some have said they represented the buffalo wallow, but this seems improbable, judging from other evidence and the character of the Pole. The three Sacred Tents of the Omaha tribe were all objects of fear to the people because of the character of their contents. No one unbidden went near them or touched them; nor could any one borrow fire from any of the Sacred Tents; nor could holes be made about the fireplace. Should any person, animal, or object, as a tent pole, accidentally come in contact with any of these Sacred Tents, the offending person, animal, or thing had to be taken to the keeper of the tent that had been touched and be cleansed ceremonially in order to prevent the evil believed to follow such sacrilege. A piece of meat that chanced to drop into the fire while being roasted in one of the Sacred Tents could not be taken out but was left to be entirely consumed.

The contents of two of the Sacred Tents of the Omaha tribe have been placed for safe keeping in the Peabody Museum of Harvard University—those of the Sacred Tent of War in 1884 and the Sacred Pole with its belongings, in 1888. (See p. 411.) All these relics are unique and of ethnologic value. The disposition to be made of these sacred objects, which for generations had been essential in the tribal ceremonies and expressive of the authority of the chiefs, was a serious problem for the leading men of the tribe. To destroy these sacred relics was not to be thought of, and it was finally decided that they should be buried with their keepers.

For many years the writers had been engaged in a serious study of the tribe and it seemed a grave misfortune that these venerable

---

a *Waxthe'xe,* the name of the Sacred Pole; *to$^n$,* "to possess" or "to keep and care for."

objects should be buried and the full story of the tribe be forever lost, for that story was as yet but imperfectly known, and until these sacred articles; so carefully hidden from inspection, could be examined it was impossible to gain a point of view whence to study, as from the center, the ceremonies connected with these articles and their relation to the autonomy of the tribe. The importance of

FIG. 49.   Joseph La Flesche.

securing the objects became more and more apparent, and influences were brought to bear on the chiefs and their keepers to prevent the carrying out of the plan for burial. After years of labor, for which great credit must be given to the late Inshta'maza (Joseph La Flesche, fig. 49), former principal chief of the tribe, the sacred articles were finally secured.

### Legend and Description of the Sacred Pole

When the Pole was finally in safe keeping it seemed very important to secure its legend, which was known only to a chief of the Hon'ga. The fear inspired by the Pole was such that it seemed as though it

Fig. 50. Monchu'nonbe (Shu'denaçi).

would be impossible to gain this information, but the desired result was finally brought about, and one summer day in September, 1888, old Shu'denaçi (Smoked Yellow; refers to the Sacred Tent of the Hon'ga gens), figure 50, came to the house of Joseph La Flesche to tell the legend of his people treasured with the Sacred Pole. Extracts from this Sacred Legend have already been given.

It was a memorable day.  The harvest was ended, and tall sheafs
of wheat cast their shadows over the stubble fields that were once
covered with buffalo grass.  The past was irrevocably gone.  The
old man had consented to speak but not without misgivings until
his former principal chief said that he would "cheerfully accept for
himself any penalty that might follow the revealing of these sacred
traditions," an act formerly held to be a profanation and punish-
able by the supernatural.  While the old chief talked he continually
tapped the floor with a little stick he held in his hand, marking with
it the rhythm peculiar to the drumming of a man who is invoking
the unseen powers during the performance of certain rites.  His
eyes were cast down, his speech was deliberate, and his voice low, as
if speaking to himself alone.  The scene in that little room where
sat the four actors in this human drama was solemn, as at the obse-
quies of a past once so full of human activity and hope.  The fear
inspired by the Pole was strengthened in its passing away, for by a
singular coïncidence the touch of fatal disease fell upon Joseph
La Flesche almost at the close of this interview, which lasted three
days, and in a fortnight he lay dead in the very room in which had
been revealed the Sacred Legend connected with the Pole.

The Sacred Pole (pl. 38 and fig. 51) is of cotton wood, 2½ m. in length,
and bears marks of great age.  It has been subjected to manipulation;
the bark has been removed, and the pole shaved and shaped at both
ends, the top, or "head," rounded into a cone-shaped knob, and the
lower end trimmed to a dull point.  Its circumference near the head
is 15 cm. 2 mm.  The circumference increases in the middle to 19 cm.
and diminishes toward the foot to 14 cm. 6 mm.  To the lower end is
fastened by strips of tanned hide a piece of harder wood, probably
ash, 55 cm. 2½ mm. in length, rounded at the top, with a groove cut
to prevent the straps from slipping, and with the lower end sharpened
so as to be easily driven into the ground.  There is a crack in the
Pole extending several centimeters above this foot piece, which has
probably given rise to a modern idea that the piece was added to
strengthen or mend the Pole when it had become worn with long
usage.  But the Pole itself shows no indication of ever having been
in the ground; there is no decay apparent, as is shown on the foot
piece, the flattened top of which proves that it was driven into the
ground.  Moreover, the name of this piece of wood is *zhi'be*, "leg;" as
the Pole itself represents a man and as the name *zhi'be* is not applied
to a piece of wood spliced on to lengthen a pole, it is probable that
this foot or leg was originally attached to the Pole.

Upon this *zhi'be* the Pole rested; it was never placed upright but
inclined forward at an angle of about 45°, being held in position by
a stick tied to it 1 m. 46 cm. from the "head."  The native name of
this support is *i'monᵍthe*, meaning a staff such as old men lean upon.

THE SACRED POLE

Upon the top, or "head," of the Pole was tied a large scalp, *ni'ka no*nzhiha*. About one end, 14 cm. 5 mm. from the "head" is a piece of hide bound to the Pole by bands of tanned skin. This wrapping covers a basketwork of twigs, now shriveled with age, which is lightly filled with feathers and the down of the crane. The length of this bundle of hide is 44 cm. 5 mm., and its circumference about 50 cm. In 1875 the last ceremony was performed and the wrapping put on as it remains to-day.

Fig. 51. A section of the Sacred Pole showing incrustation from ancient anointings. (The Pole is here represented in its usual position, supported by the *i'mo*ngthe*, or staff.)

The name of this receptacle, *a'xo*ndepa*, is the word used to designate the leather shield worn on the wrist of an Indian to protect it from the bowstring. This name affords unmistakable evidence that the Pole was intended to symbolize a man, as no other creature could wear the bowstring shield. It indicates also that the man thus symbolized was one who was both a provider for and a protector of his people.

## Sacred Packs and Contents

The pack (fig. 52; Peabody Museum no. 47834) accompanying the Pole contained a number of articles which were used in the ceremonies of the Sacred Pole. It is an oblong piece of buffalo hide which, when wrapped around its contents, makes a round bundle about 80 cm. long and 60 cm. in circumference, bound together by bands of rawhide. The pack was called *wathi'xabe*, meaning literally "things flayed," referring to the scalps stored within the pack. Nine scalps were found in it when opened at the Museum. Some show signs of considerable wear; they are all very large and on one are the remains of a feather, worn away all but the quill.

The pipe belonging to the Pole and used in its rites was kept in this pack (fig. 53; Peabody Museum no. 47838). The stem is round and 89 cm. in length. It is probably of ash and shows marks of long usage. The bowl is of red catlinite, 12 cm. 5 mm. at its greatest

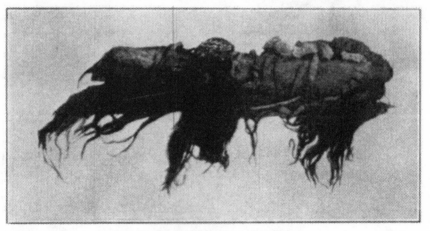

FIG. 52. Pack belonging to Sacred Pole.

length, and 7 cm. 2 mm. in height. The bowl proper rises 4 cm. 5 mm. from the base. Upon the sides and bottom of the stone certain figures are incised, which are difficult to identify; they may represent a conventionalized bird grasping the pipe. The lines of the figures are filled with a semilustrous black substance composed of vegetable matter, which brings the design into full relief; this substance is also painted on the front and back of the bowl, leaving a band of red showing at the sides. The effect is that of a black and red inlaid pipe. When this pipe was smoked the stone end rested on the ground; it was not lifted but dragged by the stem as it passed from man to man while they sat in the Sacred Tent or inclosure. To prevent the bowl falling off, a mishap which would be disastrous, a hole was drilled through a little flange at the end of the stone pipe where it is fitted to the wooden stem, and through this hole one end of a sinew cord was passed and fastened, the other end being securely tied about the pipestem 13 cm. above its entrance into the bowl.

The stick used to clean this pipe, *niniu'thubaçki* (fig. 54), was kept in a case or sheath of reed wound round with a fine rope of human hair,

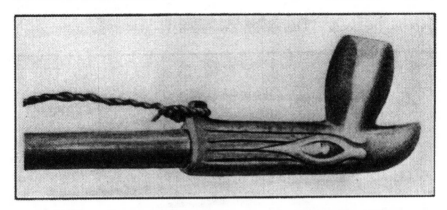

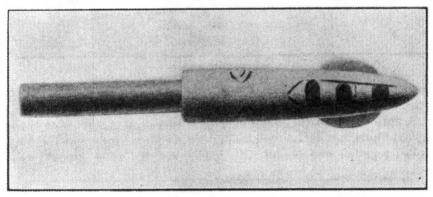

FIG. 53.  Pipe belonging to Sacred Pole.

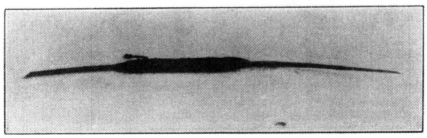

FIG. 54.  Pipe-cleaner.

fastened with sinew; a feather, said to be from the crane, was bound to the lower end of this sheath.  Only part of the quill remains.

Sweet grass (*pe'zheço^nçta*) and cedar (*ma'çi*), broken up and tied in bundles, were in the pack.  Bits of the grass and cedar were spread on the top of the tobacco when the pipe was filled, so that when it was lighted these were first consumed, making an offering of savory smoke. Sweet grass and cedar were used also in consecrating the seven arrows for ceremonial use.

Seven arrows, *mo^n'petho^nba* (fig. 55; Peabody Museum no. 47835) were in the pack. The shafts are much broken; they were origi-

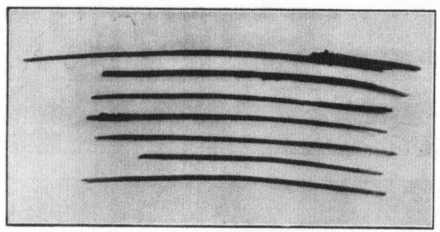

FIG. 55.  Divining arrows.

nally 45 cm. 6 mm. long, feathered from the crane, with stone heads. Part of the quills of the feathers remain but the arrowheads are lost.

A curious brush (fig. 56; Peabody Museum no. 47837) made of a piece of hide, having one edge cut into a coarse fringe and the hide rolled together and bound with bands, was the rude utensil with

FIG. 56.  Brush used in painting Sacred Pole.

which the paint, mixed with buffalo fat, was put on the Pole. A bundle of sinew cord, and of red paint (*waçe'zhide*), used in painting the Pole, complete the contents of the pack.

The ancient Cedar Pole (fig. 57; Peabody Museum no. 37561) preserved in the Tent of War was the prototype of the Sacred Pole. The two had features in common; both simulated something more than a pole, and did not typify a tree, as did the pole in the He'dewachi ceremony, but represented a being; both had the *zhi'be*, or leg; on the body of one was bound a stick like a club, on the other a device called a bow shield. Both poles were associated with Thunder, and any profanation of either was supernaturally punished by death. The cedar tree was a favorite place for the Thunder birds to alight and according to the Legend attention was called to the tree from which the Sacred Pole was shaped by the Thunder birds coming to it from the four directions and the mysterious burning which followed, all of which caused the Sacred Pole to stand in the minds of the people as endowed with supernatural power by the ancient Thunder gods. "As a result," the Legend says, "the people began to pray to the Pole for courage and for trophies in war and their prayers were answered."

Associated with the Pole was the White Buffalo Hide. Its tent stood beside that of the Pole. The ritual and ceremonies relating to the Hide (given on p. 286) show that it was directly connected with hunting the buffalo. The Pole, on the other hand, was a political symbol representative of the authority of the chiefs, and mysteriously associated with Thunder, as cited above; it was related to defensive warfare as a means of protecting the tribe and was also connected with the hunt, the means by which food, clothing, and shelter were secured by the people.

The Pole had its keeper, who was one of the subgens having its rites in charge. When the tribe moved out on the annual hunt the Pole was carried on the back of the keeper by means of a strap passed over his shoulders, the ends of which were fastened near the head and foot of the Pole. As he walked carrying the Pole the keeper had to wear his robe ceremonially, the hair outside. The food, tent, and personal belongings of the keeper could be transported on a horse; the Pole had always to be carried on the back of the man. The presence of the Pole was regarded at all times as of vital importance. "It held the tribe together; without it the people might scatter," was the common expression as to the purpose and needed presence of the Pole.

FIG. 57. Ancient Cedar Pole.

The following incident occurred during the early part of the last century:

The keeper of the Pole had become a very old man, but he still clung to his duties. Misfortune had come to him, and he had no horse when the time came for the tribe to move out on the annual hunt. The old man and his aged wife had no one to help them to carry their tent and provisions, which, added to the Sacred Pole, made a heavy load for the old people. The old man struggled on for some days, his strength gradually failing. At last the time came when he had to choose between carrying food or carrying the Pole. The tribe had started on; he hesitated, then self-preservation decided in favor of the food, so leaving the Pole as it stood the old man slowly walked away. As he neared the tribal camp a young man saw him and asked what had happened that he was without the Pole. The old man told his story. The young man was poor and had only the horse he was riding, but he at once turned back to the deserted camp to rescue the Pole. The ride was a dangerous one, for there were enemies near. He risked his life to save the Pole by turning back. He found it where it had been left by the old man; then mounting his horse with it he made haste to rejoin the tribe. When he came near to where the people were camped he dismounted, took the Pole on his back, and leading his horse made his way to the old keeper, delivered to him the Pole, and at the same time presented his horse to the old man. This was the only time the Pole was ever carried on horseback. The act of the young man was at once known, and he was publicly thanked by the Hoⁿ′ga subgens that had charge of the Pole and its ceremonies. A few days later the Seven Chiefs were called to a council, and they sent for the young man, bidding him to come to them and to wear his robe in the ceremonial manner. He hesitated at what seemed to him must be a mistake in the summons, but he was told he must obey. When he entered the tent where the chiefs were sitting he was motioned to a vacant place beside one of the principal chiefs. The young man was thus made an honorary chief because of his generous act toward the Pole; he could sit with the chiefs, but he had no voice in their deliberations.

## ANOINTING THE SACRED POLE

The name of this ceremony was Waxthe′xe xigithe ( *Waxthe′xe*, "the Sacred Pole;" *xigithe*, "to tinge with red"). The ceremony of Anointing the Pole was commemorative of the original presentation of the Pole to the people, and the season set for this ceremony made it also a ceremony of thanksgiving for the gifts received through the hunt. The ceremony took place after the fourth tribal chase and the four ceremonies connected with the buffalo tongues and hearts had taken place. Then the Waxthe′xetoⁿ subgens of the Hoⁿ′ga gens, which had charge of the Pole, called the Seven Chiefs, the governing council, to the Sacred Tent to transact the preliminary business. They sat there with the tent closed tight, clad in their buffalo robes, worn ceremonially, the hair outside and the head falling on the left arm; in a crouching attitude, without a knife or spoon, in imitation of the buffalo's feeding, they ate the food provided and took care not to drop any of it. Should a morsel fall on the ground, however, it was carefully pushed toward the fire; such a morsel was said to be desired by the Pole, and as the Legend says, "No one must take anything claimed by the Pole."

When the council had agreed on the day for the ceremony they smoked the pipe belonging to the Pole, and the herald announced the decision to the tribe. Runners were sent out to search for a herd of buffalo, and if one was found within four days it was accounted a sacred herd, and the chase that took place provided fresh meat for the coming ceremony. If within four days the runners failed to discover a herd, dried meat was used.

In this preliminary council the number of men to be called on to secure poles for the communal tent was determined; then each chief took a reed from a bundle kept in the Sacred Tent, which constituted the tally of the men of the tribe, and mentioned the name of a man of valorous exploits. When the names of the number of men agreed on had been mentioned, the leader of the subgens gave the representative reeds to the tribal herald to distribute to these designated men. On receiving the reed each man proceeded to the Sacred Tent, and by the act of returning his reed to the leader of the subgens accepted the distinction that had been conferred on him. It was now the duty of these men to visit the lodges of the tribe and select from each tent a pole to be used in the construction of a lodge for the coming ceremonies. This they did by entering the tent and striking a chosen pole, while they recounted the valiant deeds of their past life. These men were followed by other men from the Waxthe'-xeto$^n$ subgens, who, with their wives, withdrew the selected poles and carried them to the vicinity of the Sacred Tent, where they were set up and covered so as to form a semicircular lodge (fig. 58).[a] This lodge was erected on the site of the Sacred Tents, which were incorporated in it. The lodge opened toward the center of the tribal circle; as the poles used in its construction were taken from the tents of the tribe the lodge represented all the people and was called *waxu'be*, "holy" or "sacred," because it was erected for a religious ceremony.

Up to this time the tribe may have been moving and camping every day, but now a halt was called until the close of the ceremony. From this time to the close of the rites all the horses had to be kept outside the *hu'thuga*, and the people were not allowed to loiter about or pass to and fro across the entrance. To enforce this regulation two men were stationed as guards at the opening of the tribal circle.

All being in readiness, the leader of the subgens of the Ho$^n$'ga having charge of the Pole summoned the Seven Chiefs and the headmen of the gentes, who, wearing buffalo robes in the ceremonial manner, sedately walked to the communal tent and took their seats.

The Xu'ka, a group belonging to the Tha'tada gens, which in the *hu'thuga* camped next to the Ho$^n$'ga on the left, and whose duty it was to act as prompters in the ceremonies performed by the Ho$^n$'ga, took their places toward the end of the great communal tent on the left. The Xu'ka followed closely the singing of the ritual songs. To aid them in their duty as prompters they used counters—little sticks

---

[a] The four figures in front were made of grass; later in the ceremony these represented enemies.

about 6 inches long.  As soon as a song was sung, its counter was laid at one side.  If the Ho$^n$'ga had any doubt as to the proper song in the sequence of the ritual, they consulted the Xu'ka.

If by any chance a mistake occurred during the ceremonies connected with the Sacred Pole, and one of the songs was sung out of sequence, then the following ceremony became obligatory: All the Waxthe'xeto$^n$ subgens of the Ho$^n$'ga, they who had charge of the Sacred Pole and its rites, arose, lifted their arms, held their hands with the palms upward, and, standing thus in the attitude of supplication, wept.  After a few moments one of the official servers came forward, passed in front of the line of standing singers. and wiped the

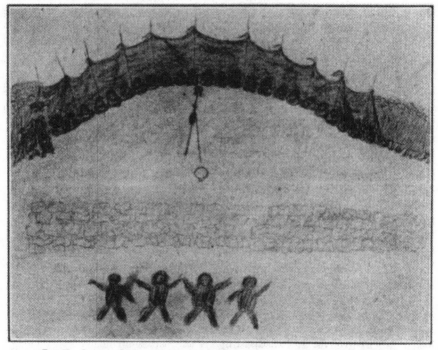

FIG. 58.  Communal ceremonial structure—grass figures in foreground (native drawing).

tears from each man's face.  Then the singers resumed their places, and the ceremony began again from the beginning as though for the first time.  This ceremony of contrition took place only when by accident the sequence of the songs of the Sacred Pole was broken.

The Xu'ka also acted as prompters when the Washa'beto$^n$ subgens of the Ho$^n$'ga sang the ritual of the Sacred White Buffalo Hide. If a song of that ritual was sung out of its order the entire ritual had to be begun again, for there must be no break in the parts of the ritual— its course "must be straight."

On the ceremonial occasion here described the herald wore a band of matted buffalo wool about his head, with a downy eagle feather standing in it.

The Sacred Pole was carried by the wife of the keeper of the Pole to the edge of the communal lodge, where the keeper arranged it so as to lean on its "staff" (a crotched stick) toward the center of the *hu'thuga*.

The pipe belonging to the Sacred Pole was first smoked; then the bundle of reeds was brought, which served as a count of the men of the tribe who were able to serve as warriors. Each chief as he drew a reed mentioned the name of a man. He must be one who lived in his own lodge as the head of a family (what we would term a householder), not a man dependent on relatives. As the chief spoke the name, the herald advanced to the Pole and shouted the name so as to be heard by the whole tribe. Should the name given be that of a chief, the herald substituted that of his son. The man called was expected to send by the hand of one of his children his finest and fattest piece of buffalo meat, of a peculiar cut known as the *tezhu'*. (See p. 273.) If the meat was heavy, one of the parents helped to carry it to the communal tent. The little ones were full of dread, fearing particularly the fat which was to be used on the Pole. So they often stopped to wipe their greasy fingers on the grass so as to escape any blame or possible guilt of sacrilege. Anyone refusing to make this offering to the Pole would be struck by lightning, wounded in battle, or lose a limb by a splinter running into his foot. There are well-known instances of such results having followed refusal.

### RITUAL SONGS

All the ritual songs relating to the ceremonies of the Sacred Pole were the property of the Waxthe'xeton subgens of the Hon'ga gens, and were sung by them during the performance of the rites.

This song accompanied the placing of the Pole and the cutting of the symbolic design on the ground in front of it:

### FIRST SONG

1

Thea'ma wagthitonbi tho ho! gthitonba
Wagthitonbi, wagthitonbi, tho ho
Te'xi ehe gthitonba
Wagthitonbi, wagthitonbi te'xi ehe gthitonba

Literal translation: *Theama*, here are they (the people); *wagthi-to^n bi*—the prefix *wa* indicates that the object has power, *gthito^n bi*, touching what is theirs ("touching" here means the touching that is necessary for a preparation of the objects); *tho ho!* is an exclamation here used in the sense of a call to Wako^n'da, to arrest attention, to announce that something is in progress relating to serious matters; *te'xi*, that which is of the most precious or sacred nature; *ehe*, I say.

*Free translation*

The people cry aloud—tho ho! before thee.
Here they prepare for sacred rites—tho ho!
Their Sacred, Sacred Pole.
With reverent hands, I say, they touch the Sacred Pole before thee.

After the Pole was in place, the one who officiated and represented the keepers of the Pole, the Waxthe'xeto^n subgens of the Ho^n'ga, advanced toward the Pole to untie the skin which concealed the wickerwork object bound to the middle of the Pole. As this was being done, the Ho^n'ga keepers sang the next stanza:

2

Wagthishkabi, wagthishkabi tho ho! gthishkaba
Wagthishkabi, wagthishkabi tho ho
Te'xi ehe gthishkaba
Wagthishkabi, wagthishkabi, te'xi ehe gthishkaba

Literal translation: *Wagthishkabi*—the prefix *wa* indicates that the object has power; *gthishkabi*, undoing, so as to expose to view that which is covered or encased. The rest of the words have been translated in the first stanza.

*Free translation*

We now unloose and bring to view, tho ho! before thee,
We bring to view for sacred rites, tho ho!
This sacred, sacred thing,
These sacred rites, this sacred thing comes to view before thee.

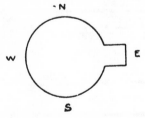

FIG. 59. Uzhi^n'eti.

In front of the Pole the symbolic figure, called *uzhi^n' eti*, figure 59 (see p. 241), was then cut on the ground, the sod removed, and the earth loosened, after which the following song was sung:

SECOND SONG

E - he   the   he   gthi - toⁿ - bi   tha   ha   ha   gthi -

toⁿ - bi   E - he   the   he   the   wa   gthi - toⁿ - bi

tha   ha   ha   gthi   toⁿ - bi   E - he   the   he

the   wa   gthi - toⁿ - bi   tha   ha   ha   gthi - toⁿ - bi

Ehe the he gthitoⁿbi thaha ha
    Gthitoⁿbi
Ehe the he the wagthitoⁿbi tha ha ha
    Gthitoⁿbi
Ehe the he the wagthitoⁿbi tha ha ha
    Gthitoⁿbi

Literal translation: *Ehe,* I say; *the,* this; *he,* vowel prolongation of preceding word; *gthitoⁿbi,* preparing what is theirs; *tha,* a punctuation word indicating the end of the sentence, used in oratory and dignified speech; *ha,* vowel prolongation of preceding word.

*Free translation*

I here declare our work to be completed,
    Done our task!
I here declare that all our work is now completed,
    Done our task!
I here declare that all our work is now completed,
    Fully completed!

On the following day the culminating rites of the ceremony took place. In these the wife of the officiating priest had a share. He was clothed in his gala shirt and leggings, and red bands were painted across his cheeks from the mouth to the ear. The woman wore over her gala costume a buffalo robe girded about her waist, the skin side out, which was painted red. Across her cheeks and her glossy black hair red bands were painted and to the heel of each moccasin was attached a strip of buffalo hair like a tail.

Early in the morning the following song was sung as the wicker-work object containing the down of the crane, which bore the name *a'xoⁿdepa* (wrist shield) was fully opened, to be ready for the ceremonies of the day:

THIRD SONG

Axoⁿdepa ha ha! wiⁿ the thoⁿ
Axoⁿdepa ha ha! wiⁿ the thoⁿ
Axoⁿdepa ha ha! wiⁿ the thoⁿ
Axoⁿdepa ha ha! wiⁿ the thoⁿ
Axoⁿdepa ha ha! wiⁿ the thoⁿ

Literal translation: *Axoⁿdepa*, the wrist shield worn on the left wrist of a man to prevent it being cut by the bowstring when the latter rebounds from being drawn; *ha ha*, exclamation, behold!; *wiⁿ*, one; *the*, here this; *thoⁿ*, round, referring to the shape of the wrist shield.

The reiteration of the words makes it difficult to present a translation of the song literally, for to the Indian mind the repeated words brought up the varied aspects of the Pole. It represented the unity of the tribe; the unity of the Council of Seven Chiefs, which made them "as one heart, as one voice;" the authority of the Thunder. It was a being—a man; it was a bow, the weapon of a man which was used for the defense of life and to secure the game that gave food, shelter, and clothing. As this song (which referred to the shield—the article that protected the wrist of the man when he pulled the bow string) was sung, the wickerwork containing the down was fully opened, preparatory to the ceremonies in which it had a part. The full meaning of the lines of the song does not appear from the literal words, but must be found in the symbolism of the ceremonial acts connected with this "round object."

The fourth song was sung as the officiating priest arranged on the ground in front of the Pole, side by side, four of the best *tezhu'* pieces of buffalo meat. These represented four buffaloes, also the four hunts and the four ceremonial offerings of hearts and tongues which had preceded this ceremony. The other pieces were laid along the front of the communal tent. Sometimes there were four parallel rows of this meat. From these offerings the officiating priest was later to cut ceremonially the fat that was to be mixed with the paint and used to anoint the Pole. As this action was a preparatory one, it was accompanied by the same song as when the Sacred Pole was put in place and prepared for the ceremony. The song was repeated eight times.

### Fourth Song—Same as the First

When the meat was finally arranged, the completion of the task was announced by again singing the second ritual song.

### Fifth Song—Same as the Second

The next song embodied the command of the Ho$^n$'ga in charge of these ceremonies to the officiating priest, bidding him to advance toward the meat with his knife and hold the latter aloft preparatory to the movements which accompanied the ceremonial cutting of the meat.

### Sixth Song

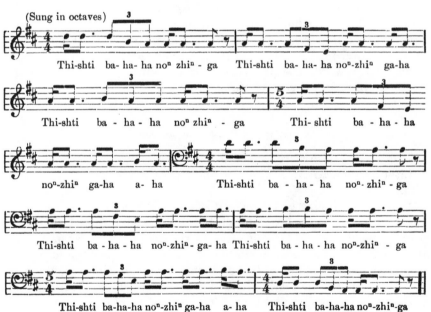

Thishti bahaha no$^n$zhi$^n$ga

These words were repeated nine times.

Literal translation: *Thishti*, thou, too—addressed to the officiating priest; *bahaha*, to show, meaning that the priest shall grasp the knife with which he is to cut the fat and hold it up to view; *no$^n$zhi$^n$*, to stand; *ga*, word of command. "Do thou show thy knife, standing there!"

SEVENTH SONG

1

Abaha kithe, abaha kithe hehe

These words were repeated four times.

Literal translation: *Abaha,* to hold toward or over; *kithe,* I make him (the Hon'ga, who have charge of the rites speak, authorizing the action of the priest, who is their representative); *hehe,* vocables used as vowel prolongations. At the conclusion of the fourth repetition of the words the priest lowered the knife preparatory to the act authorized in the second stanza, and then sang:

2

Ma'xon akithe, Ma'xon akithe, hehe

These words also were repeated four times.

Literal translation: *Ma'xon,* to cut; *akithe,* I make or authorize him.

During the singing of the second stanza the priest cut the fat from the four *tezhu'* lying in front of thé Pole, and dropped it into a wooden bowl held by his wife for its reception. The fat cut from the meat offerings was pounded to a sort of paste and mixed with red paint. While this was being done the pipe belonging to the Pole was ceremonially smoked by the chiefs and leading men gathered in the communal tent. The act of smoking was a prayer of consecration and the asking of a blessing on the anointing of the Pole about to take place. When the ceremony of smoking was completed and the fat and paint were made ready, the eighth ritual song was sung.

EIGHTH SONG

1

Abahe he the abahe he the
Te ehe the
Abahe he the abahe he the

Literal translation: *Abahe*, to hold toward; *he*, vowel prolongation; *the*, this; *te*, buffalo; *ehe*, I say; *the*, this.

During the singing of this song the priest took the brush (see p. 228) with which he was to anoint the Pole and made a ceremonial approach toward the Pole, holding the brush near it, while the woman at the same time presented the bowl. Fat was the emblem of abundance; red, the color of life. The mixture therefore symbolized abundant life. The line *Te ehe the* was explained to mean that the buffalo was here declared to be a life-giving gift from Wakon'da, and that the buffalo yielded itself to man for his abundant food and also to provide him with shelter and clothing. The ceremony of anointing was one of recognition of the gift by Wakon'da of the buffalo and of thanksgiving for it.

The second stanza of this song was now sung. The words are:

2

Ite he ehe the ite he ehe the
Te ehe the
Ite he ehe the ite he ehe!

Literal translation: *Ite*, to touch; *he*, vowel prolongation; *ehe*, I say; *the*, this; *te*, buffalo; *ehe*, I say; *the*, this.

The brush, on which was some of the sacred paint, was then brought close to the Pole and permitted to touch it. As all of the movements related to the care of Wakon'da for man, they were religious in character and consequently were very deliberate. The brush ceremonially touched the Pole and four lines were made down its length. The anointing followed as the next song was sung.

## NINTH SONG

(Sung in octaves)　Harmonized by John C. Fillmore for interpretation on the piano

1

Athaha kithe, athaha kithe he he

These words were repeated four times.

Translation: *Athaha,* to adhere; *kithe,* I make or cause; *he he,* vowel prolongation. "I cause [the paint] to adhere."

More than one application of the paint was made. As the Pole began to assume a ruddy hue the second stanza was sung.

2

Zhide akithe, zhide akithe he he

These words were repeated four times.

Translation: *Zhide,* red; *akithe,* I make or cause it; *he he,* vowel prolongation. "I make it to be red."

By the end of the fourth repetition of the second stanza the anointing was completed. Then the third stanza was sung.

3

Ko$^n$pi akithe, Ko$^n$ akithe he he

Translation: *Ko$^n$pi,* an abbreviation of *uthuko$^n$pi,* comely or handsome to look upon; *akithe,* I cause or make it; *he he,* vowel prolongation. "I make it beautiful." The word *ko$^n$pi,* it was explained, here refers to man, the most comely of all creatures endowed with life, to whom Wako$^n$'da has given the promise of abundance. The people, who had gathered from their tents and were watching the ceremony and listening to these sacred songs, as this stanza was sung nudged one another and laughed, enjoying the complimentary reference to themselves and the promise given.

When the anointing was completed that part of the ceremony began in which the woman officiated.

In this portion of the ceremonial the Pole lost something of its political significance and became the representative of man as the protector and provider of the family. The figure cut in the ground in front of the Pole then had a share in the rites. This figure (see p. 234) was called *uzhi$^n$'eti* (*uzhi$^n$,* the wistfulness of a child, as when it stands before its parent waiting to share in some good thing; *ti,* house). The design was said to signify the wistful attitude of the people, looking for the good that Wako$^n$'da was to send to them in the house, the dwelling of the family, and in a larger sense, the *hu'thuga,* the dwelling of the tribe; it also brought to mind the fathers who established these ceremonies that opened the way for the reception of good gifts from Wako$^n$'da. An old man said, "As I stand before the *uzhi$^n$'eti* I seem to be listening for the words of the venerable ones who gave us these rites." It was a prayer symbol. In the center of this symbolic figure, where the fireplace would be in the lodge, a buffalo chip was placed; when it was kindled, sweet grass used in peaceful ceremonies and sprays of cedar sacred to thunder were laid on it and through the aromatic smoke arising therefrom the seven arrows were passed. These represented the Seven Chiefs, who held the tribe together in peaceful unity, and also the means by which man secured for his family Wako$^n$'da's gift of the buffalo, whence came food and clothing. The woman stood for the mother of the race and her share in the rites was a prayer for its continuance and prosperity.

As the woman, in her representative capacity, held the arrows over the consecrating smoke which arose from the burning of fragrant offerings sacred to war and to peace, the following song was sung:

### Tenth Song

Music the same as for the eighth song (p. 239) and the words the same as those of the first stanza of the song.

After consecrating the arrows by passing them through the smoke, the woman advanced toward the Pole and stood holding an arrow aloft while the following song was sung:

### Eleventh Song

The same as the sixth song (p. 237). The words of the song were repeated nine times. A number multiplied by itself, as 3 times 3 or 4 times 4, as not infrequently occurs in ceremonials, indicates completed action.

### Twelfth Song

The music of the twelfth song, which accompanied the shooting by the woman of the arrows through the basketwork, is the same as that of the ninth ritual song (p. 240), sung when the Pole was painted; the words are as follows:

Baxo$^n$ akithe, baxo$^n$ akithe, he he

Literal translation: *Baxo$^n$*, to thrust; *akithe*, I cause it.

These words were repeated four times to fill out the measure of the song that was sung seven times, once to each of the arrows.

In this act the Pole became the bow, and the basketwork the wrist shield on the arm of the man who grasped the bow. The woman shot the arrow along the bow, simulating the shooting of the buffalo, to secure the gift of abundance. When the arrow was not checked by the wickerwork or down, but passed clear through the bundle with sufficient force to stand in the ground on the other side, a shout of joy arose from the people, for this was an augury of victory over enemies and of success in hunting. After this divination ceremony with the arrows the wickerwork on the Pole was folded together and tied in its skin covering until the next year, when the ceremony would be repeated.

## Ceremony of the Sacred Pole—Conclusion

It will be noted that the ceremony of the Sacred Pole is divided into two parts and that the significance of the Pole is twofold. In the first part the Pole stands for the authority that governed the tribe, an authority granted and guarded by the supernatural powers; in the second part the Pole stands for the men of the tribe, the defenders and the providers of the home. The same songs are used for both parts, but in the first part the ceremonial acts are performed by a man; in the second part the ceremonial acts are performed by a woman. In this two-part ceremony and its performance are reflected the fundamental ideas on which the tribal organization is based, the union of the masculine and the feminine.

All the buffalo meat laid before the Pole was now gathered up and laid away and four images made of grass and hair were set up before the Pole. These represented enemies of the tribe. The tribal herald then went forth and shouted: "Pity me [an expression of courtesy], my young men, and let me [he speaks for the keepers of the Pole] complete my ceremonies!" In response to this summons all those men who had won honors in defensive warfare put on the regalia that represented those honors and made ready to act their part in the drama about to be performed; for only men whose honors had been gained in defensive warfare could have a share in this drama. Meanwhile all the young men of the tribe mounted their horses and rode off outside the camp. Suddenly some one of them turned, and crying, "They have come! they have come!" the whole company charged on the camp. (This was once done in so realistic a manner as to deceive the people into the belief of an actual onslaught of an enemy, to the temporary confusion of the whole tribe.) After this charge the young men dismounted, turned loose their horses, and mingled with the spectators, who gathered at both ends of the communal tent as a vantage point whence to view the spectacle. The warriors acted out their warlike experiences in defending the tribe and charged on the grass images, while the chiefs and leaders remained in the "holy" tent, in front of which stood the Pole. In later days guns were shot off, adding to the noise and commotion. Those who had been wounded in defensive battles rolled about as if struck; those who had speared or scalped enemies thrust their spears into an image or scalped it. Four of these charges were made on the images, which were finally captured and treated as if conquered, and this ended the scene called "shooting the Pole," an act intended to do public honor to the defenders of the home and the tribe.

On the day following, preparations for the He'dewachi ceremony (see p. 251) began, at the close of which the ceremonial camp broke up and each family followed its own inclination, either to return to the village or to continue to hunt. All rules and regulations as to hunting the buffalo were now at an end for the season.

The visitor to the Peabody Museum, Harvard University, will notice upon the upper portion of the Pole an encrustation resembling pieces of thick bark; this is the dried paint that remains from the numerous anointings of the Pole. (Fig. 51.) The old chief told the writers in 1888 that long ago, beyond the memory of the eldest, it was the custom to anoint the Pole twice a year—after the summer hunt and after the winter hunt; but within his own memory and that of his father the anointing had taken place only in the summer.

The rapid destruction of the herds of buffalo in the decade following 1870 caused the Indian not only sore physical discomfort but also great mental distress. His religious ceremonies needed the buffalo for their observance, and its disappearance, which in its suddenness seemed to him supernatural, had done much to demoralize him morally as well as socially.

After several unsuccessful buffalo hunts poverty took the place of former plenty and in distress of mind and of body, seeing no other way of relief, the people urged on the Ho$^n$'ga the performance of the ceremony of Anointing the Pole, although misfortune in hunting through the diminution of the buffalo made it impossible to perform this act in its integrity. A plan was suggested by which the ceremony could be accomplished and, as they fondly hoped, the blessing of plenty be restored to the people. The tribe had certain moneys due from the United States in payment for ceded lands, and through their Agent they asked that such a sum as was needful to purchase 30 head of cattle should be paid them. Little understanding the trouble of mind among the Indians under his charge or the motive of their request, the Agent wrote to the Interior Department, at Washington, that "The Omahas have a tradition that when they do not go on the buffalo hunt they should at least once a year take the lives of some cattle and make a feast." This interpretation of the Indian's desire to spend his money for the purchase of the means by which he hoped to perform rites that might bring back the buffalo and save him from an unknown and dreaded future is a significant gauge of the extent to which the Indian's real life had been comprehended by those appointed to lead him along new lines of living and thinking. The cattle were bought at a cost of about a thousand dollars. The ceremony took place; but, alas! conditions did not change. A second third time the tribe spent its money, but to no avail. New ces and interests grew stronger every year. The old customs be made to bend to the new ways forced on the people. to further outlay for cattle to hold the old ceremony Government and also from some of the tribe; so years passed while the Pole stood untouched in its tent, dreaded as a thing that was powerful for harm but seemingly powerless to bring back the old-time prosperity to the people.

The following is the boy memory of these ancient ceremonies of the Sacred Pole, now forever gone, by one of the present writers, the only living witness who is able to picture in English those far-away scenes:

One bright summer afternoon the Omahas were traveling along the valley of one of the streams of western Kansas on their annual buffalo hunt. The mass of moving people and horses extended for nearly half a mile in width and some 2 miles in length. There was an old man walking in a space in the midst of this moving host. The day was sultry and everybody around me was in the lightest clothing possible; but the solitary old man wore a heavy buffalo robe wrapped about his body. Around his shoulders was a leather strap the width of my hand, to the ends of which was attached a dark object that looked like a long black pole. From one end hung a thing resembling a scalp with long hair. One of my playmates was with me, and we talked in low tones about the old man and the curious burden on his back. He looked weary, and the perspiration dropped in profusion from his face, as with measured steps he kept apace with the cavalcade.

The horses that I was driving stopped to nibble the grass, when, partly from impatience and partly out of mischief, I jerked the lariat I was dragging with all the force I could muster in the direction of the horses, and the end of it came with a resounding whack against the sleek side of the gray. Startled at the sound, all of the five horses broke into a swift gallop through the open space, and the gray and the black, one after the other, ran against the old man, nearly knocking him over. My friend turned pale; suddenly he became anxious to leave me, but I finally persuaded him to remain with me until camp was pitched. He stayed to help me to water the horses and drive them to pasture and I invited him to dinner, which he seemed to expect.

While we were eating, the boy asked me if he should tell my father of the incident. I consented, for I thought that would relieve him from any fears of the consequences. As he was telling of what happened I watched the expression of my father's face with some trepidation, and felt greatly relieved when he smiled. We finished our dinner, but as we started to go out my father stopped us and said: "Now, boys, you must go to the Sacred Tent. Take both horses with you, the gray and the black, and this piece of scarlet cloth; when you reach the entrance you must say, 'Venerable man! we have, without any intention of disrespect, touched you and we have come to ask to be cleansed from the wrong that we have done.'"

We did as we were instructed and appeared before the Sacred Tent in which was kept the "Venerable Man," as the Sacred Pole was called, and repeated our prayer. The old man who had been so rudely jostled by our horses came out in response to our entreaty. He took from me the scarlet cloth, said a few words of thanks, and reentered the tent; soon he returned carrying in his hand a wooden bowl filled with warm water. He lifted his right hand to the sky and wept, then sprinkled us and the horses with the water, using a spray of artemisia. This act washed away the anger of the "Venerable Man," which we had brought down upon ourselves.

A few weeks later we were moving from the high hills down to the valley of the Platte river, returning from the hunt, our horses heavily laden with buffalo skins and dried meat. A beautiful spot was selected for our camp, and the crier gave in a loud voice the order of the chiefs that the camp be pitched in ceremonial form. This was done.

In the evening my playmate came and we ate fried bread and drank black coffee together. When we had finished the little boy snapped his black eyes at me and said: "Friend, let us go and play in the Holy (communal) Tent; the boys will be there and we will have fun." We went, and there was the Holy Tent, 60 or 70 feet in length. The two Sacred Tents of the Ho<sup>n</sup>'ga gens had been united and a dozen or more other skin tents were added to them on either side, making a tent that could easily hold two or three hundred people. No grown people were there, so we youngsters had no end of fun playing hide and seek in the folds of the great tent, while the serious sages were taking the census of the people elsewhere, using small sticks to count with, preparatory to calling upon each family to contribute to the coming ceremony.

The next night we youngsters had again our fun in the Holy Tent. On the third night, when we went to play as usual, we found at the Tent two officers with whips, who told us that boys would not be permitted to play in the Tent that night. Still we lingered around and saw that even older persons were not allowed to come near, but were told to make a wide detour in passing, so as not to disturb the fresh grass in front of the Tent. Dogs were fired at with shotguns if they approached too near. The ceremony was to begin the next day, so the chiefs and priests, through the crier, requested the people to conduct themselves in such manner as the dignity of the occasion required.

Early in the morning I was wakened by my mother and told to sit up and listen. I did so and soon heard the voice of an old man calling the names of boys. Most of them I recognized as my playmates. Suddenly I heard my own name distinctly called. I arose to make answer but was held back by my mother, who put in my arms a large piece of meat, with no wrapping whatever, regardless of my clean calico shirt, while she bade me go to where I was called. When I emerged from the tent with my burden the crier stopped calling my name, and called the boy in the next tent. As I neared the Holy Tent to which I had been summoned, an old man, wearing a band of buffalo skin around his head and a buffalo robe about his body, came forward to meet me. He put both his hands on my head and passed them down my sides; then he took from me the meat and laid it down on the grass in front of a dark pole standing aslant in the middle of the Holy Tent, a scalp dangling on the end of it. I recognized this pole as the one that was carried by the old man whom my horses ran against only a few weeks before. The calling of the names still went on; a man sat immediately back of the pole with two piles of small sticks before him; he would pick up a stick from one pile and give a name to the crier, who, leaning on a staff, called it out at the top of his voice; when this was done the stick was placed on the other pile.

When every family in the tribe excepting those of the Ho<sup>n</sup>'ga gens had thus been called upon to make an offering, the priests began to sing the songs pertaining to this peculiar ceremony. I was now very much interested and watched every movement of the men who officiated. Four of the fattest pieces of meat were selected and placed just at the foot of the Sacred Pole. A song was sung and a man stood ready with a knife near the meat; when the last note died out the man made a feint at cutting and then resumed his position. Three times the song was repeated with its accompanying act, when on the fourth time the man in great haste carved out all of the fat from the four pieces of choice meat and put it in a wooden bowl. After the fat had been mixed with burnt red clay and kneaded into a paste, another song was sung, and the same priest stood ready with bowl and brush in hand beside the Pole. At the close of the song he made a feint at the Pole with the brush and resumed his former position. Four times this song was sung, each time followed by a feint. Then a new stanza was sung, at the end of which the priest touched the Pole lightly with his brush the entire length. This song and act were repeated four times. Then a different song was sung, the words of which I can remember even to this day: "I make him beautiful! I make him beautiful!'' Then the priest with great haste dipped his brush into the bowl and daubed the Pole with the paste while the singing was going on. Four times the song was sung, the anointing was finished, and the Pole stood shining in fresh paint. Then many of the people cried: '' Oh! how beautiful he is!'' and then laughed, but the priests never for an instant changed the expression of their faces. I did not know whether to join in the merriment or to imitate the priests and maintain a serious countenance; but while I stood thus puzzled the ceremony went on.

A woman dressed in a peculiar fashion took the place of the priest who had painted the Pole. She wore on her head a band of buffalo skin and the down of the eagle, around her body a buffalo robe with the fur outside and to her ankles were tied strips of buffalo skin with the hair on. In her left hand she held six arrows and stood ready with one poised in her right. A song was sung and at the close she made a feint with the arrow at the bundle of feathers in the middle of the Pole. Four times this was done; then other songs were sung and at the close of each song, with a quick movement the woman thrust an arrow through the bundle containing down tied to the middle of the Pole with such force that it passed entirely through and as it dropped stuck in the ground, and the people shouted as with great joy. I joined in the shouting, although at the time I did not know why the people cheered. There were seven arrows in all; on this occasion every one of the arrows went successfully through the downy bundle. It is said that if an arrow failed to go through and bounded back, the gens which it represented would meet with misfortune; some member would be slain by the enemy.

After the singing of the songs and the anointing of the Pole, the meat was distributed among the families of the Ho$^n$ʹga gens, the keepers of the Sacred Pole. The moment that this was done a man was seen coming over the hill running at full speed, waving his blanket in the air in an excited manner, and shouting the cry of alarm: ''The enemy are upon us!'' The horses were familiar with this cry and the moment they heard it they stampeded into the camp circle, making a noise like thunder. Men rushed to their tents for their bows and arrows and guns and were soon mounted on their best horses. Warriors sang the death song, and women sang songs to give the men courage. The excitement in camp was at its height, but the singing of the priests in the Holy Tent went on. Instead of going out to meet the enemy, the warriors gathered at one side of the camp circle opposite the Holy Tent and at the firing of a gun came charging toward it. It was a grand sight—four or five hundred warriors rushing on us at full speed. There was no enemy; the man who gave the alarm was only acting his part of a great drama to be performed before the Sacred Pole. The warriors fired their guns and shot their arrows at a number of figures made of bundles of tall grass and arranged before the Holy Tent. Shouts of defiance went from the tent and were returned by the charging warriors. This play of battles lasted nearly the whole day.

Years passed, and with them passed many of the brave men who told the tale of their battles before the Sacred Pole. So also passed the buffalo, the game upon which the life of this and other tribes depended. During these years I was placed in school, where I learned to speak the English language and to read and write.

Through a curious chain of circumstances, which I need not here relate, I found myself employed in the Indian Bureau at Washington. The Omaha had given up the chase and were putting all their energies into agriculture. They had abandoned their villages and were scattered over their reservation upon separate farms, knowing that their former mode of living was a thing of the past and that henceforth their livelihood must come from the tilling of the soil. To secure themselves in the individual ownership of the farms they had opened, the people petitioned the Government to survey their reservation and to allot the land to them in severalty. Their petition was granted by an act of Congress and the work of apportioning the lands was assigned to a lady who is now known among the scientists of this and other countries. I was detailed to assist her in this work, and together we went to the reservation to complete the task.

While driving over the reservation one day we came to a small frame house with a porch in front. Around this dwelling were patches of corn and other vegetables and near by was an orchard of apple trees with ripening fruit. In strange contrast with all this there stood in the back yard an Indian tent, carefully pitched, and the ground around it scrupulously clean. My companion asked, "What is that?" "It is the Holy Tent of the Omahas," I replied. "What is inside of it?" "The Sacred Pole," I answered. "I want to see it." "You can not enter the Tent unless you get permission from the Keeper." The Keeper was not at home, but his wife kindly conducted us to the entrance of the Tent, and we entered. There in the place of honor stood my friend, the "Venerable Man," leaning aslant as I saw him years before when I carried to him the large offering of choice meat. He had served a great purpose; although lacking the power of speech, or any of the faculties with which man is gifted, he had kept closely cemented the Seven Chiefs and the gentes of the tribe for hundreds of years. He was the object of reverence of young and old. When the United States Government became indebted to the tribe for lands sold, he, too, was accounted as one of the creditors and was paid the same as a man of flesh and blood. He now stood before us, abandoned by all save his last Keeper, who was now bowed with age. The Keeper seemed even to be a part of him, bearing the name "Smoked Yellow," a name referring both to the age and to the accumulation of smoke upon the Pole. Silently we stood gazing upon him, we three, the white woman in the middle. Almost in a whisper, and with a sigh, the Keeper's wife said, "I am the only one now who takes care of him. When it rains I come to close the flaps of the Tent, at all hours of the night. Many were the offerings once brought to him, but now he is left all alone. The end has come!" [For portrait of the wife of the keeper of the Pole, see pl. 26.]

A few years later I went to the house of Smoked Yellow and was hospitably entertained by him and his kind wife. After dinner, as we sat smoking in the shade of the trees, we spoke of the past life of the tribe and from time to time in our conversation I pleasantly reminded him of important events within my own knowledge, and of others of which I had heard, where his knowledge guided the actions of the people. This seemed to please him very much and he spoke more freely of the peculiar customs of the Omaha. He was an important man in his younger days and quite an orator. I have heard him deliver an address on the spur of the moment that would have done credit to almost any speaker in either branch of our Congress. He was one of the signers of the treaty entered into between the Omaha and the United States.

As my visit was drawing to a close, without any remarks leading thereto, I suddenly swooped down upon the old chief with the audacious question: "Why don't you send the 'Venerable Man' to some eastern city where he could dwell in a great brick house instead of a ragged tent?" A smile crept over the face of the chieftain as he softly whistled a tune and tapped the ground with his pipe stick before he replied, while I sat breathlessly awaiting the answer, for I greatly desired the preservation of this ancient and unique relic. The pipe had cooled and he proceeded to clean it. He blew through it now and then as he gave me this answer: "My son, I have thought about this myself but no one whom I could trust has hitherto approached me upon this subject. I shall think about it, and will give you a definite answer when I see you again."

The next time I was at his house he conducted me to the Sacred Tent and delivered to me the Pole and its belongings. [See fig. 50 for portrait of the last keeper of the Sacred Pole.] This was the first time that it was purposely touched by anyone outside of its hereditary Keepers.  It had always been regarded with superstitious awe and anyone touching even its Tent must at once be cleansed by the priest.  Even little children shared in this feeling and left unclaimed a ball or other plaything that chanced to touch the Tent made sacred by its presence.

Thus it was that the Sacred Pole of the Omaha found its way into the Peabody Museum in 1888 but leaving its ritual songs behind.  During these years I have searched for men in the Hoⁿ′ga gens who would be likely to know these songs but without success.  The old priest, Tenu′ga, whose office it was to sing them, died before I came in touch with him.

By the use of the graphophone I was enabled in 1897 to secure the ritual songs of the Sacred White Buffalo from Wakoⁿ′moⁿthiⁿ, the last keeper; and when the record was finished I said to him: "Grandfather, years ago I saw you officiating at the ceremonies of the Sacred Pole and from this I judge that you are familiar with its songs.  May I ask if you would be willing to sing them for me?"  The old priest shook his head and replied: "Eldest son, I am forced to deny your request.  These songs belong to the opposite side of the house and are not mine to give.  You are right as to my knowledge of them and you did see me officiating at the ceremony you referred to; but I was acting as a substitute.  The man whose place I took was newly inducted into his office and was not familiar with its various forms; he feared the results of any mistakes he might make, on account of his children, for it meant the loss of one of them by death should an error occur.  You must consult the keepers of the Pole."

Knowing that it would be useless even with bribes to attempt to persuade the priest to become a plagiarist, I refrained from pushing the matter further, trusting that circumstances in the future might take such a turn as to relieve him from his obligations to recognize any individual's ownership in the ritual songs.

In the latter part of June, 1898, I happened to be on the Omaha reservation, and while there I drove over to Wakoⁿ′moⁿthiⁿ's house.  (Figs. 60, 61.)  He was at home and after the exchange of greetings I addressed him as follows:

"Grandfather, last summer, after you had taught me the songs connected with the ceremony of the Sacred Buffalo, I asked you to teach me the songs of the Sacred Pole.  You replied that you knew the songs, but could not sing them for me, because they belonged to the other side of the house and were not yours to give.  I respected your purpose to keep inviolate your obligations to maintain the respective rights and offices of the two houses that were so closely allied in the preservation of order among our people, so I did not press my quest for the knowledge of the songs at that time, believing that you would soon see that the object for which that Sacred Tree and its accompanying rites were instituted had vanished, never to return.  Our people no longer flock to these sacred houses as in times past, bringing their children laden with offerings that they might receive a blessing from hallowed hands; new conditions have arisen, and from force of circumstances they have had to accede to them and to abandon the old.  I have been here and there among the members of the opposite side of the house, to which you referred, to find some one who knew the songs of the Sacred Pole, so that I might preserve them before they were utterly lost; but to my inquiries the invariable answer was: 'I do not know them.  Wakoⁿ′moⁿthiⁿ is the only man who has a full knowledge of them.'  Therefore I have made bold to come to you again."

After holding the pipe he had been filling during my speech, up to the sky, and muttering a few words of prayer, the old man lit the pipe and smoked in silence for a time, then passed the pipe to me and made his reply, speaking in low tones:

"My eldest son, all the words that you have just spoken are true.  Customs that governed and suited the life of our people have undergone a radical change and the new generation has entered a new life utterly unlike the old.  The men with whom I have associated in the keeping and teaching of the two sacred houses have turned into spirits and have departed, leaving me to dwell in solitude the rest of my life. All that gave me comfort in this lonely travel was the possession and care of the Sacred Buffalo, one of the consecrated objects that once kept our people firmly

Fig. 60  Wakon'monthin.

Fig. 61.  Wakon'monthin's house.

united; but, as though to add to my sadness, rude hands have taken from me, by stealth, this one solace, and I now sit empty handed, awaiting the call of those who have gone before me. For a while I wept for this loss, morning and evening, as though for the death of a relative dear to me, but as time passed by tears ceased to flow and I can now speak of it with some composure."

At this point I passed the pipe back to the priest and he smoked, keeping his eyes fixed upon the ground as if in deep meditation. When he had finished smoking, he resumed his address, cleaning the pipe as he spoke:

"I have been thinking of the change that has come over our people and their departure from the time-honored customs, and have abandoned all hope of their ever returning to the two sacred houses. No one can now with reason take offense at my giving you the songs of the Sacred Pole, and I am prepared to give them to you. As I sit speaking with you, my eldest son, it seems as though the spirits of the old men have returned and are hovering about me. I feel their courage and strength in me, and the memory of the songs revives. Make ready, and I shall once more sing the songs of my fathers."

It took but a few moments to adjust the graphophone to record the songs for which I had waited so long. As I listened to the old priest his voice seemed as full and resonant as when I heard him years ago, in the days when the singing of these very songs in the Holy Tent meant so much to each gens and to every man, woman, and child in the tribe. Now, the old man sang with his eyes closed and watching him there was like watching the last embers of the religious rites of a vanishing people.

## The He′dewachi

In speaking of the development of political unity, attention has been called to the dangers arising from groups parting company when the people were hunting and the enfeebled separated bands becoming a prey to active enemies. These dangers were sometimes fomented by the rivalry of ambitious leaders. To quote from the old Sacred Legend: "The wise old men thought how they might devise some plans by which all might live and move together and there be no danger of quarrels." It seems probable that the He′dewachi ceremony may have grown out of such experiences and was one of the plans of the "wise old men" by which they sought to avert these dangers and to hold the tribe together. There are indications that the He′dewachi ceremony is older than the Sacred Pole; it is said to have been instituted at a time when the people depended on the maize for their food supply and were not dominated by ideas definitely connected with hunting the buffalo. It may be significant to this contention that this ceremony was the only rite in which the two Sacred Tribal Pipes appeared as leader; these pipes were antecedent in authority to the Sacred Pole, and, on the occasion of the He′dewachi, they led the people in their rhythmic advance by gentes toward the central symbolic tree or pole.

The He′dewachi took place in the summer, "when the plum and cherry trees were full of fruit" and "all creatures were awake and out." Abundant life and food to sustain that life were typified in the season. The choice of the tree from which the pole, the central object of the ceremony, was cut, was significant and allied to the same thought. It was either the cottonwood or the willow, both of which are remarkably tenacious of life. It is said that this ceremony "grew up with the corn." It was under the charge of the subgens of the Iⁿke'çabe gens that had as tabu the red ear of corn. This fact and the symbolism of the ceremony indicate that the He'dewachi was connected with the cultivation of corn and that the influence of the care of the fields tended to develop an appreciation of peace and tribal unity. The duties of this Iⁿke'çabe subgens in reference to the distribution of the sacred corn to the tribe have already been mentioned (p. 147). In later days the He'dewachi took place at the conclusion of the ceremony of Anointing the Sacred Pole but was distinct from it in every respect except that permission for its performance had to be obtained from the Hoⁿ'ga gens as a matter of courtesy.

The He'dewachi was related to the cosmic forces, as revealed in the succession of night and day and the life and growth of living things. When the time came for the ceremony, some man, ambitious to have the honor and to "count" it, went to the hereditary keepers of this rite in the Nini'batoⁿ subgens of the Iⁿke'çabe, and said: "Let the people waken themselves by dancing." This form of speech used when making the request for the performance of the ceremony referred to the passing of night into day. On receiving this formal request, which was accompanied by a gift, the keepers returned their thanks. That night those who had hereditary charge of the He'dewachi held a council and chose a man of their gens who had won many war honors to go and select a tree to be cut for the ceremony. Early the next morning he went forth, picked out a tall, straight cottonwood tree and then came back, returning as would a victorious warrior. If he represented one who had secured booty, he dragged a rope, and carried a long stick with which he ran from side to side as though he were driving horses; or he carried a pole having a bunch of grass tied at the top, to picture a return with the scalp of an enemy. On entering the *hu'thuga* he went at once to the lodge in which the hereditary keepers sat awaiting him. At the door he thrust his stick into the ground, and said, "I have found the enemy." The keepers then arose, put on their robes in the ceremonial manner—the hair outside—and prepared to make their ceremonial thanks to the people and to indicate to the tribe that the ceremony would take place in two days. They were accompanied by a woman, who had to be of the Iⁿke'çabe gens and who bore on her the tattooed "mark of honor." She also wore her robe with the hair side out, carried an ax and a burden strap, and followed the men as they passed around the *hu'thuga* and publicly proclaimed their thanks for the request to have the ceremony take place.

Meanwhile the warrior who had selected the tree gathered the men of the gens together to await the return of the hereditary keepers.

At this time those women of the gens who had recently lost children or other dear ones wailed, being reminded of their loss by the contrast afforded by this ceremony, which was typical of abounding life. Other women brought forth gifts, which were to benefit their husbands or brothers by adding to their "count." All gifts made during this ceremony could be "counted" by a man who was seeking eligibility to membership in the Ho$^n$'hewachi. The words of one of the songs sung at the dance refer to these gifts, which were not only exchanged between members of the tribe but were bestowed on the keepers of the ceremony—a custom resulting in a common feeling of pleasure. Moreover, these acts, being remembered and "counted" as steps toward a man's attaining tribal honors, tended to foster in the minds of the people the value of tribal unity. The symbolism of the ceremony was illustrative of this idea. Four young men were chosen to cut willow wands, strip them of all leaves except a bunch at the end, and paint the stem red. These wands were distributed to the leading men of each gens in the tribe. After the wands had been received, the men and boys of each gens went out to cut similar wands, for at the coming ceremony every man, woman, and child must carry one of these painted wands, which symbolized the people of the tribe.

After making the round of the *hu'thuga* the keepers and the "honor" woman entered their tent, in which was smoked the pipe belonging to the ceremony. It was passed around four times. At the close of the smoking they arose as before and, led by the warrior who had selected the tree, went to the place where the tree stood. Meanwhile young men had been dispatched to simulate scouts, guarding against the danger of a surprise. When the tree was in sight the warriors charged on it and struck it as an enemy. Then the men counted their war honors, standing before the tree, while the keepers sat in a circle around it and smoked, passing the pipe four times. Then the woman bearing the "mark of honor," taking her ax, made four feints, one on each side of the tree toward one of the four directions, after which she gave four strokes, one on each of the four sides of the tree. Then the young men cut it down. As it was about to fall it was caught and held so that it would incline and fall toward the east.

In this ceremony in which war was so simulated the recognition of the authority of Thunder was manifest, for no man could become a warrior or count his honors except through his consecration to Thunder and the approval of his acts by that god of war. Moreover, it was believed that no man fell in battle through human agency alone; he fell because Thunder had designated him to fall, as is shown in the ritual songs of cutting the hair and in the songs of the warrior societies. So the tree that had been struck as a warrior foe fell because Thunder had so decreed.

The leader now approached the fallen tree and said: "I have come for you that you may see the people, who are beautiful to behold!" The young men cut the branches from the trees, leaving a tuft of twigs and leaves at the top, stripped off the bark, then tied the tuft at the top together with a black covering. Latterly a black silk handkerchief was used, but formerly a piece of soft dressed skin, dyed black, was employed. All the branches, bark, and chips were made into a pile and deposited at the stump of the tree.

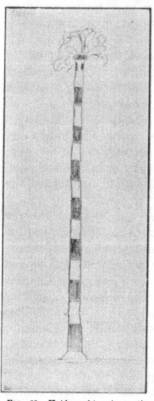

FIG. 62. He'dewachi pole (native drawing).

In early days it was the duty of the woman to carry the pole; but in recent times she walked, with her burden strap, beside the young men, who bore it on their left shoulders, care being taken to choose men of equal height so that the pole would be carried in a level position. Four halts were made on the way to the hu'thuga. On reaching the camp, the pole was taken to the tent of the leader and the butt end was thrust in the door until it reached the fireplace.

Two men from the Nonxthe'bitube subdivision now performed their hereditary duty of mixing the red and black paint with which they were to decorate the pole. This group had, besides the red corn, a tabu of charcoal, as this substance was used in making the black paint. The painting was done in bands of red and black; one man painted the black bands, the other the red. (Fig. 62.) These bands signified night and day; they also referred to thunder and death and to the earth and sky, the vivifying and conserving powers.

Young men dug the hole for the pole, which had to be in the center of a level place. Sometimes the hole was made in the center of the hu'thuga; at other times it was outside the camp. The dirt taken from the excavation was heaped at the east, and between this heap and the hole the symbolic figure (uzhin'eti; see fig. 59) was incised on the earth.

The keepers sat in a circle around the hole and again smoked the pipe, passing it four times. Down of swan, a water bird (the significance of water as connecting the Above and the Below has been given), and tobacco, the offering to Wakon'da, were sprinkled in the hole, which was thus made ready to receive the symbolically decorated pole. The leader said, "It is finished; raise him, that your grandfather may see him!" And the pole was set in the hole and made steady by tamping the earth about it.

These preparatory ceremonies occupied three days. The dance and public festival took place on the fourth day.

The pole simulated a man; the black covering on the top, his head. The decorations referred to the cosmic forces which gave and maintained life. As a tree it symbolized the tribe; the wands of the people were its branches, parts of the whole. Thus was the idea of unity symbolically set forth.

It was explained that seven kinds of wood were sacred to this ceremony—the hard and the soft willow, the birch, the box elder, the ironwood, the ash, and the cottonwood. Of these the cottonwood furnished the pole; the elder, the charcoal for the black paint; the ash, the stem of the pipe; the seeds of the ironwood were used for the rattles; and the willow for the wands distributed to the people. The birch seems to have dropped out, though its former use survives in a personal name belonging to the subgens having the rite in charge. The significance of this lies in the fact that male personal names always referred to rites and their paraphernalia. The omission of the birch may refer to a change in environment. It will be recalled that the Sacred Legend states that the Omaha once used birch-bark canoes.

On the day of the ceremony the people were astir early. The women put on their gala costume; the men were barefoot and naked except for the breechcloth. They wore the decoration of their war honors, and depicted their war experiences by the manner of painting their faces and bodies. The place of a wound was painted red; if a man had been struck a hand was painted on his body or face (fig. 63). Some painted black bands on their arms and legs, indicating that they had been in danger of death; others bore white spots scattered over their bodies, to show that they had been where the birds of prey dropped their excrement on the bodies of the slain enemies. The man who had cut the neck of an enemy drew an inflated bladder by a string, to set forth his act. Those warriors who had taken scalps tied to the wands they carried in the dance bits of buffalo hide with the hair on:

Meanwhile, the keepers of the ceremony selected from their gens the young men who were to sing. These men received pay for their

services.   Four rattles, struck on pillows, and two drums were used
to accompany the singers, who took their places at the foot of the pole.
The men who were going to give away horses were the only riders.
They dashed about among the people, who became more and more

FIG. 63.   Painting on warrior's face.

impatient waiting for the signal—four strokes on the drums—to
announce the beginning of the ceremony.   After the four drum
beats had been given, the following "call" was sung:[a]

---

[a] The upper music staff gives simply the aria; the two lower staves translate the same aria for the
piano by harmonization, giving the tremolo of the drum, the echoing cadences, the dying away of the
voices of the singers, and their rising again with the call to "Rejoice."

## HE′DEWACHI CALL

(Aria as sung)   Harmonized by John C. Fillmore for interpretation on the piano

Zhawa iba iba ha ehe
Zhawa iba iba ha ehe

Translation: *Zhawa*, from *uzhawa*, to rejoice; *iba*, to come; *ha*, musical prolongation of the vowel; *ehe*, I bid or command. "I bid ye come, and rejoice!"

The people of each gens gathered, standing before their tents, the men and boys in front, each holding his wand; behind them the women and girls, with their wands. Two men from the Nini′bato$^n$ subdivision[a] then stepped forth and took their place in front of the rest of the I$^n$ke′çabe gens, and held aloft the Sacred Tribal Pipes as the singers at the foot of the pole sang the following:

---

[a] There is a personal name in the Nini′bato$^n$ which refers to the bearers of the two Pipes in this ceremony—*Ton′thinnonba*, "the two who run."

There are no words to this song—only vocables. The song is a prayer expressed not by words but in musical phrases. The tribe presented a spectacle that must have been impressive—the great circle of people, with their branches, standing like a living grove on the prairie, as the singers voiced their prayer to Wako$^n$'da.

At the conclusion of the song the warriors who had charged the tree sounded the war cry, and all the people standing in their places, gave an answering shout and waved their branches in the air. Then the two bearers of the Sacred Tribal Pipes moved forward rapidly a few steps toward the pole and the people by gentes moved forward in the same way while the song given below was sung. At its conclusion a halt was made. Four times there was a forward movement as the song was sung and a halt made at its close.

Ya du-da    e-a    ha    e-he he!

Ya duda ea ha ehe tha ehe he
Shethi$^n$ duda a ea ha ehe tha
Ehe he ehe he tha ea ha ehe tha
Ehe he ehe he tha ea ha ehe tha

Literal translation: *Ya*, come; *duda*, hither; *ea*, come; *ha*, vowel prolongation; *ehe*, I bid; *shethi$^n$*, ye walking yonder; *duda*, hither; *a*, vowel prolongation; *ea*, come; *e*, vocable; *ehe*, I bid; *he*, vocable; *tha*, end of sentence.

*Free translation*

Come hither, I bid you!
Ye who walk yonder, come hither!
I bid you, I bid you to come!
I bid you, I bid you, come hither!

At the conclusion of the fourth repetition the people had moved up toward the pole, the men being the nearer and the women behind. There they all halted for the fourth and last time.

As the singers struck up the next song (the fourth) the two pipe bearers turned to the left, having their right side to the pole, and all the men of the different gentes turned also; the I$^n$ke'çabe followed the pipe bearers, next came the We'zhi$^n$shte, then the I$^n$shta'çu$^n$da, and so on, around to the Ho<sup>n</sup>'ga, who were last, and all began to dance around the pole. The women also turned, but to the right, their left side being next to the circle of men and the pole, and danced in the opposite direction from the men. The tribe thus divided into two concentric circles, revolved in opposite directions about the pole while the choir at its foot sang the following song:

### HE'DEWACHI DANCE

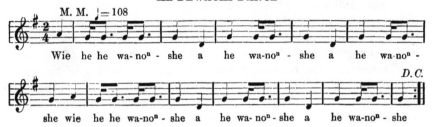

Wie he he wano<sup>n</sup>she a he
Wano<sup>n</sup>she a he wano<sup>n</sup>she
Wie he he wano<sup>n</sup>she a he
Wano<sup>n</sup>she a he wano<sup>n</sup>she

Literal translation: *Wie*, I; *he he*, vocables; *wano<sup>n</sup>she*, take from them. The meaning of this song can not be gathered from a literal translation of the few words used. It has been explained to mean that the pole here speaks as embodying the meaning and spirit of the ceremony and refers to the gifts made, which are an important part of the ceremony. They not only contribute to happiness and good feeling in the tribe but they redound to the credit of the giver. It was during this song that the people danced in the two concentric circles around the pole, everyone carrying his branch, with its leaves. When at any time a person made a gift the dancers halted while the gift was proclaimed. At each halt, if any of the gentes became mixed up, the person out of place returned to his proper gens before the dance was resumed. The song was repeated four times, or four times four.

Finally, the last song was given. During the singing of this rapid song the people continued to dance in the two circles. The young people made merry as they danced and the warrior acted out dramatic scenes in his career. It was a hilarious time for all.

There are no words to this song, only vocables. The song was repeated an indefinite number of times. At the conclusion of this song everyone threw his branch at the foot of the tree, as though it were returned to the parent stem from which it had been broken. The small boy, however, sometimes amused himself by aiming his wand at the singers rather than at the tree. These pranks were all taken in good part. The branches carried by the people were tied to the pole and left for the sun and wind to dispose of.

The manner in which the tree was cut and also the approach to the pole by the people in their tribal order, with war cry and charge, were in recognition of the victories gained by the favor of the war god, Thunder. The ceremony was a dramatic teaching of the vital force in union not only for defense but for the maintenance of internal peace and order. The He'dewachi [a] was a festival of joy consonant with the words of the opening song, "Come and rejoice." The whole scene vibrated with color and cheer around the Thunder-selected tree as a symbol of life and tribal unity.

---

[a] Years ago the Osage had a somewhat similar ceremony long since abandoned.

# VII

## THE QUEST OF FOOD

### THE RITUAL OF THE MAIZE

The various environments in which the Omaha people lingered as they moved westward left their impress on the ceremonials of the tribe. Some of these, as has been shown, were lost and the relation of others to the welfare of the people suffered change. Among the latter were the ceremonies connected with the maize.

The facts that the tabu of the subgens of the I$^n$ke'çabe, which had charge of the two Sacred Tribal Pipes, was the red ear of corn and that it was the duty of this subgens to provide the sacred corn for distribution at the time of planting, indicate that the rites of the maize and those of the Pipes were once closely connected. In the political development of the tribe the Pipes, through their significance, kept an important place; while, owing to the environment of the people, the maize, as the sustainer of life, became subordinated to the buffalo, which yielded not only food but also raiment. Nevertheless, it is noteworthy that the maize did not wholly lose prestige but continued to be treated ceremonially.

The ancient Sacred Legend already cited, besides speaking of the discovery of maize, adds later on, evidently referring to the ceremony and ritual observed when distributing the grain for planting:

The maize being one of the greatest of means to give us life, in honor of it we sing. We sing even of the growth of its roots, of its clinging to the earth, of its shooting forth from the ground, of its springing from joint to joint, of its sending forth the ear, of its putting a covering on its head, of its ornamenting its head with a feather, of its invitation to men to come and feel of it, to open and see its fruit, of its invitation to man to taste of the fruit.

When maize was discovered the grain was distributed among the people that they might plant and eat of the fruit of their labor, and from that time on it has been the custom to sing the song of the maize and to repeat the distribution of the corn every year at the time of planting.

The songs [stanzas] are many. They begin with the gathering of the kernels. The people talk of where they shall plant. Then the men select the land and wherever each man selects he thrusts a pole in the ground to show that now the corn shall be planted.

The stanzas last referred to have been lost, as well as the ceremony of selecting the planting plot and the thrusting of the pole into the ground. It is also impossible to give an accurate account of the ceremonies attending the distribution of the sacred corn for planting. The rites have long been disused, their abandonment being largely due to the influence of the Government. It is said that formerly when spring came the Hoⁿ'ga subgens, whose duty it was to keep the sacred ears of red corn, met with the subgens of the Iⁿke'çabe, whose right it was to provide them, and after the prescribed rites had been performed and the ritual sung, the Iⁿke'çabe men acted as servers to the Hoⁿ'ga and distributed four kernels to each family. The women received the sacred corn and mixed it' with their seed corn, which they preserved from year to year. It was believed that the sacred corn was able to vivify the seed and cause it to fructify and yield a good harvest. Only the red corn was used for this sacred purpose. Its color was indicative of its office.

Even after the discontinuance of these rites of distributing the maize its ritual was still sung just before the ritual of the White Buffalo Hide was given in connection with the hunting ceremonies. (See p. 286.)

MAIZE RITUAL SONG

Yo ko ho the he he    wi - aⁿ - doⁿ - ba    ga!

Koⁿ    du - ba    ha - noⁿ-zhiⁿ    hi, wi - aⁿ - doⁿ - ba    ga!

1

1  Yo ko ho the he he
2  Wi aⁿdoⁿba ga
3  Koⁿ duba ha noⁿzhiⁿ hi
4  Wi aⁿdoⁿba ga

2

5  Yo ko ho the he he
6  Wi aⁿdoⁿba ga
7  Abe he wiⁿ'axchi ha noⁿzhiⁿ hi
8  Wi aⁿdoⁿba ga

3

9  Yo ko ho the he he
10  Wi aⁿdoⁿba ga
11  Abe he noⁿ'ba ha noⁿzhiⁿ hi
12  Wi aⁿdoⁿba ga

4

13  Yo ko ho the he he
14  Wi aⁿdoⁿba ga
15  Abe he tha'bthiⁿ ha noⁿzhiⁿ hi
16  Wi aⁿdoⁿba ga

5

17   Yo ko ho the he he
18   Wi a$^n$do$^n$ba ga
19   Abe he duba ha no$^n$zhi$^n$ hi
20   Wi a$^n$do$^n$ba ga

6

21   Yo ko ho the he he
22   Wi a$^n$do$^n$ba ga
23   Abe he ça'to$^n$ ha no$^n$zhi$^n$ hi
24   Wi a$^n$do$^n$ba ga

7

25   Yo ko ho the he he
26   Wi a$^n$do$^n$ba ga
27   Abe he sha'pe ha no$^n$zhi$^n$ hi
28   Wi a$^n$do$^n$ba ga

8

29   Yo ko ho the he he
30   Wi a$^n$do$^n$ba ga
31   Abe he pe'tho$^n$ba ha no$^n$zhi$^n$ hi
32   Wi a$^n$do$^n$ba ga

9

33   Yo ko ho the he he
34   Wi a$^n$do$^n$ba ga
35   'Kite he wi$^n$axchi ha no$^n$zhi$^n$ hi
36   Wi a$^n$do$^n$ba ga

10

37   Yo ko ho the he he
38   Wi a$^n$do$^n$ba ga
39   'Kite he no$^n$'ba ha no$^n$zhi$^n$ hi
40   Wi a$^n$do$^n$ba ga

11

41   Yo ko ho the he he
42   Wi a$^n$do$^n$ba ga
43   'Kite he tha'bthi$^n$ ha no$^n$zhi$^n$ hi
44   Wi a$^n$do$^n$ba ga

12

45   Yo ko ho the he he
46   Wi a$^n$do$^n$ba ga
47   'Kite he duba ha no$^n$zhi$^n$ hi
48   Wi a$^n$do$^n$ba ga

13

49   Yo ko ho the he he
50   Wi a$^n$do$^n$ba ga
51   'Kite he ça'to$^n$ ha no$^n$zhi$^n$ hi
52   Wi a$^n$do$^n$ba ga

14

53  Yo ko ho the he he
54  Wi a$^n$do$^n$ba ga
55  'Kite he shape ha no$^n$zhi$^n$ hi
56  Wi a$^n$do$^n$ba ga

15

57  Yo ko ho the he he
58  Wi a$^n$do$^n$ba ga
59  'Kite he pe'tho$^n$ba ha no$^n$zhi$^n$ hi
60  Wi a$^n$do$^n$ba ga

16

61  Yo ko ho the he he
62  Wi a$^n$do$^n$ba ga
63  Hathe he to$^n$ ha no$^n$zhi$^n$ hi
64  Wi a$^n$do$^n$ba ga

17

65  Yo ko ho the he he
66  Wi a$^n$do$^n$ba ga
67  Pahi hi kugthi ha no$^n$zhi$^n$ hi
68  Wi a$^n$do$^n$ba ga

18

69  Yo ko ho the he he
70  Wi a$^n$do$^n$ba ga
71  Pahi hi zi ha no$^n$zhi$^n$ hi
72  Wi a$^n$do$^n$ba ga

19

73  Yo ko ho the he he
74  Wi a$^n$do$^n$ba ga
75  Pahi hi shabe ha no$^n$zhi$^n$ hi
76  Wi a$^n$do$^n$ba ga

20

77  Yo ko ho the he he
78  Wi a$^n$do$^n$ba ga
79  Xtha kugthi ha no$^n$zhi$^n$ hi
80  Wi a$^n$do$^n$ba ga

21

81  Yo ko ho the he he
82  Wi a$^n$do$^n$ba ga
83  Xtha çka ha no$^n$zhi$^n$ hi
84  W ia$^n$do$^n$ba ga

22

85  Yo ko ho the he he
86  Wi a$^n$do$^n$ba ga
87  Xtha ziha no$^n$zhi$^n$ hi
88  Wi a$^n$do$^n$ba ga

23

89  Yo ko ho the he he
90  Wi aⁿdoⁿba ga
91  Zhu 'toⁿha noⁿzhiⁿ hi
92  Wi aⁿdoⁿba ga

24

93  Yo ko ho the he he
94  Wi aⁿthiçpoⁿ a
95  Zhu 'toⁿha noⁿzhiⁿ hi
96  Wi aⁿthizha

25

97  Yo ko ho the he he
98  Wi aⁿbaçnoⁿ a
99  Zhu 'toⁿha noⁿzhiⁿ hi
100  Wi aⁿbaçnoⁿ a

26

101  Yo ko ho the he he
102  Wi aⁿthigtha
103  Zhu 'toⁿha noⁿzhiⁿ hi
104  Wi aⁿthata

*Literal translation*

*First stanza.*  1. *yo ko ho the he he* is probably a corruption of
*thikuthe*, meaning "to hasten." The process of change in singing
the word was from *thikuthe* to *thekothe*, and then on to *yokothe*, the
first syllable being dropped to give the free vowel sound of the *o* in
beginning the song. In view of this probable change the line would
read: *'yokohothe he he*, *yokoho* representing the vowel sound of the
second syllable of the word *thekuthe*, and the syllables *he he* the
vowel prolongation of the last syllable, *the*. The line would thus
mean "Hasten!"

2. *wi*, I. In this song it is the Maize that speaks. *aⁿdoⁿba*,
behold me (*aⁿ*, me; *doⁿba*, see or behold); *ga*, the sign of a command.
3. *koⁿ*, root; *duba*, four; *ha noⁿzhiⁿ*, I stand (the "*h*" is added to
the *a* in singing); *hi*, vowel prolongation.

*Second stanza.*  7. *abe*, leaves—a general term; *he*, vowel continued; *wiⁿaxchi*, one.

*Third stanza.*  11. *noⁿba*, two.
*Fourth stanza.*  15. *tha'bthiⁿ*, three.
*Fifth stanza.*  19. *du'ba*, four.
*Sixth stanza.*  23. *ça'toⁿ*, five.
*Seventh stanza.*  27. *sha'pe*, six.
*Eighth stanza.*  31. *pe'thoⁿba*, seven.
*Ninth stanza.*  35. *'kite*, *u'kite*, the joint of the stalk, the node—
a general term for joint, in an animal or vegetable growth; *he*, vowel
prolongation.

*Sixteenth stanza.* 63. *hathe*, clothing—a general term (the word here refers to the husk around the ear of the maize); *'to^n, ato^n*, I have, or possess.

*Seventeenth stanza.* 67. *'pahi*, hair (*'pa*, head; *hi*, hair); *hi*, vowel continued; *kugthi*, light, shining.

*Eighteenth stanza.* 71. *zi*, yellow.

*Nineteenth stanza.* 75. *sha'ba, sha'be*, dark colored.

*Twentieth stanza.* 79. *xtha*, the tassel of the maize.

*Twenty-first stanza.* 83. *çka*, white.

*Twenty-third stanza.* 91. *zhu*, flesh, as of fruit; *to^n*, to possess.

*Twenty-fourth stanza.* 94. *a^nthiçpo^n*, feels me (*a^n*, me; *thiçpo^n*, to feel of); *a, ha*, the end of the sentence. 96. *a^nthizha*, to pull or push apart, to pluck, as the ear from the stalk.

*Twenty-fifth stanza.* 98. *a^nbaçno^n*, roasts (*a^n*, me; *baçno^n*, to thrust on a stick and roast before the fire).

*Twenty-sixth stanza.* 102. *a^nthigtha, a^nthi gtha*, to push off with a stick, to shell. 104. *a^nthata* (*thata*, to eat; *a^n*, me).

*Free translation*

### 1

O hasten!
Behold,
With four roots I stand.
Behold me!

### 2

O hasten!
Behold,
With one leaf I stand.
Behold me!

### 3

O hasten!
Behold,
With two leaves I stand.
Behold me!

### 4

O hasten!
Behold,
With three leaves I stand.
Behold me!

### 5

O hasten!
Behold,
With four leaves I stand.
Behold me!

### 6

O hasten!
Behold,
With five leaves I stand.
Behold me!

7

O hasten!
  Behold,
With six leaves I stand.
  Behold me!

8

O hasten!
  Behold,
With seven leaves I stand.
  Behold me!

9

O hasten!
  Behold,
With one joint I stand.
  Behold me!

10

O hasten!
  Behold,
With two joints I stand.
  Behold me!

11

O hasten!
  Behold,
With three joints I stand.
  Behold me!

12

O hasten!
  Behold,
With four joints I stand.
  Behold me!

13

O hasten!
  Behold,
With five joints I stand.
  Behold me!

14

O hasten!
  Behold,
With six joints I stand.
  Behold me!

15

O hasten!
  Behold,
With seven joints I stand.
  Behold me!

16

O hasten!
  Behold,
With clothing I stand.
  Behold me!

17

O hasten!
  Behold,
With light, glossy hair I stand.
  Behold me!

18

O hasten!
  Behold,
With yellow hair I stand.
  Behold me!

19

O hasten!
  Behold,
With dark hair I stand.
  Behold me!

20

O hasten!
  Behold,
With light, glossy tassel I stand.
  Behold me!

21

O hasten!
  Behold,
With pale tassel I stand.
  Behold me!

22

O hasten!
  Behold!
With yellow tassel I stand.
  Behold me!

23

O hasten!
  Behold,
With fruit possessed I stand.
  Behold me!

24

O hasten!
  Grasp ye,
My fruit as I stand.
  Pluck me!

25

O hasten!
  Roast by a fire
My fruit as I stand.
  Even roast me!

26

O hasten!
  Rip from its cob
My fruit as I stand,
    And eat me!

In this ritual the maize is anthropomorphized and is conscious of its mission. The poetic feeling of the ritual lies in the call of the maize to man to behold its up-springing life, its increasing growth, and its fruitage. Its final abnegation is almost hidden under the rather matter-of-fact directions of the last stanzas. Still, it is there.

## CULTIVATION OF MAIZE

Garden patches were located on the borders of streams. Occupancy constituted ownership and as long as a tract was cultivated by a family no one molested the crops or intruded on the ground; but if a garden patch was abandoned for a season then the ground was considered free for anyone to utilize. Men and women worked together on the garden plots, which ranged from half an acre to two or three acres in extent. Occasionally a good worker had even a larger tract under cultivation. These gardens were mounded in a peculiar manner: The earth was heaped into oblong mounds, their tops flat, about 18 by 24 inches, and so arranged as to slant toward the south. The height on the north side was about 18 inches; on the south the plot was level with the surface of the ground. These mounds were 2 or 3 feet apart on all sides. In one mound seven kernels of corn were scattered; in the next mound squash seeds were placed, and so on alternately. If the family had under cultivation a large garden tract the beans were put into mounds by themselves and willow poles were provided for the vines to climb upon; but if ground space was limited the beans were planted with the corn, the stalk serving the same purpose as poles. Squash and corn were not planted together, nor were corn, beans, and squash grown in the same mound. After the planting the ground was kept free of weeds and when the corn was well sprouted it was hoed with an implement made from the shoulder blade of the elk. The second hoeing took place when the corn was a foot or more high. Up to this time the mounds were carefully weeded by hand and the earth was kept free and loose. After the second hoeing the corn was left to grow and ripen without further cultivation. The mounds containing the squash and those in which the melons were planted were weeded and cared for until the second hoeing of the corn, when they, too, were left, as about this time the tribe started out on the annual buffalo hunt.

## NAMES OF PARTS AND OF PREPARATIONS OF MAIZE

The following names refer to the maize or corn and the preparations made of it:

*Waton'zi:* corn growing in the field; also shelled corn.
*Waton'zihi:* corn stalk or stalks.
*Waha'ba:* an ear of corn.
*Waha'bahi:* a corn cob or cobs.

*Wa'xanha:* corn husk.

*Hatu:* the green husk.

*Wathi'inge:* braided corn. The husks were braided, leaving the ear hanging.

*Wami'de:* seed corn. This word is applied to any seed used for reproduction. Other seed, such as apple seeds, are called *çi.*

*Washon'ge:* pounded corn. A stick, *nonxpe,* was thrust into the cob and the corn roasted before a fire; then it was shelled and the chaff blown off; finally it was pounded in a mortar (*uhe*) with a pestle (*wehe*).

*Wa'çke:* pounded corn mixed with honey and buffalo marrow.

*Wani'de:* mush or gruel—pounded corn mixed with water.

*Um'bagthe:* corn boiled with beans, set over night to cool and harden, then served cut in slices. Considered a delicacy.

*Wana'xe:* parched corn—used by travelers, and carried in skin bags.

*Wabi'shnude:* corn boiled with ashes and hulled—a sort of coarse hominy.

*Wabthu'ga: wabi'shnude* boiled with meat.

*Watonziçkithe:* sweet corn roasted in the milk, cut off the cob, and dried.

## HUNTING

There were various ways of going hunting, each of which had its distinctive name:

*Eshnon' monthin,* "walking alone," was used to indicate that a single family had gone hunting or trapping.

*A'bae,* an old, untranslatable term, meaning that a single man, or a man accompanied by a few male companions, leaving their families in camp, had started out on foot in search of game. This word was applied to this form of hunting even after horses had come into use.

*U'zhon,* "to sleep with them," referring to the game. This term was applied only to the hunting of deer by a small party of men, or to a single person going out and bivouacking among the game.

*Shkon'the,* "to make to move." The word refers to starting up the game. It was applied to a party of men going to a given locality to hunt deer. Young brothers and sons of the hunters formed this kind of hunting party. The hunters scattered out and advanced abreast, while the lads rushed into the woods, started up the game, and, if they could, secured a shot on their own account.

*Tathie'une* (*ta,* a part of *taxti,* "deer;" *thie,* a peculiar cut of the deer meat; *une,* "to seek"). A man who was not a good hunter frequently joined a *shkon'the* party and strove to be the first to reach the slain deer and so secure the right to be the first butcher. For his services he was entitled to the cut called *tathie.*

The *eshnon' monthin,* the *a'bae,* and the *shkon'the* hunting parties went out only in the fall and winter; these were the only parties that were not organized and under the direction of a leader. The buffalo and the elk moved in herds and were hunted differently from the deer, antelope, and bear. The latter were sought for by individuals or by small parties, as already described.

During the summer months the annual tribal buffalo hunt took place. At this time the main supply of meat was secured. This hunt was attended with much ceremony and was participated in by the entire tribe; it was called *te'une* (from *te,* "buffalo," and *une,* "to seek"). The summer buffalo hunt was more generally spoken of as *wae'gaxthon* (*wae,* "cultivating the soil;" *gaxthon',* "moving after"—"going on the hunt after the cultivation of the corn is done") or *nuge'teune* (*nuge*, "summer;" *te*, "buffalo;" *une*, "to seek"). *Ma'theteune* was the name of the winter buffalo hunt (*ma'the*, "winter;" *te'une*, "buffalo hunt"). The buffalo was hunted in winter for pelts. When the herd was found, the act of chasing it was called *wano$^{n'}$çe*, the literal meaning of the word being "to intercept." In surrounding a herd the animals were intercepted by the hunters at every turn; this was the usual mode of attacking a herd of any kind. If among a party going out to hunt the buffalo in winter there was a man from the I$^n$ke'çabe gens, the right to be the leader of the company was his by virtue of his gens, and his authority was obeyed by all the hunters of the party. The leadership accorded to this gens applied only to chasing the buffalo. The life of the people depended on this animal, as it afforded the principal supply of meat and pelts; therefore the buffalo hunt was inaugurated and conducted with religious rites, which not only recognized a dependence on Wako$^{n'}$da, but enforced the observance by the people of certain formalities which secured to each member of the tribe an opportunity to obtain a share in the game.

As neither the elk nor the deer stood in a similar vital relation to the people, hunting these animals was attended with less ceremony. A party going to find elk was spoken of as *o$^{n'}$po$^n$ ano$^n$çe* (*umpo$^n$*, "elk;" *ano$^n$çe* has the same meaning as *wano$^{n'}$çe*). In such a party an I$^n$ke'çabe enjoyed no special privileges but was on the same footing as all the other hunters. There was a leader, however, generally the man who initiated the hunting party. Winter was the season for elk hunting. Deer also were hunted in the winter, as during that season the animals were fat and in good condition. When a man went alone for still hunting he used a whistle that simulated the cry of the fawn, and thus attracted the male and female deer. When a party went out they camped near a place where deer were plentiful; the hunters then went off and returned to the camp. On such expeditions boys were sometimes sent into the brush to beat up the game for the hunters.

While the animals were alive, and in connection with the hunt, each had its distinctive name, but when they were butchered their flesh bore the common name of *ta*. If the meat was fresh it was spoken of as *tanuka*, "wet meat;" when dried it was simply *ta*.

### RULES OBSERVED IN BUTCHERING

The following customs were observed in cutting up the carcasses of the deer, antelope, elk, and buffalo:

After a chase anyone could help in butchering the game. The first person to arrive had to set to work at once in order to secure the rights of the first helper. Every animal was cut up into certain portions.

These were graded and assigned by custom to the helpers in the order of their beginning work on the carcass. The man who shot the animal might find, on reaching it, men already engaged in cutting it up. In that case he would go to work on some other man's game. He did not, however, lose his rights in the animal he had shot. As every man's arrows bore the owner's peculiar mark, there could be no dispute as to who fired the fatal shot and so owned the killer's share.

All animals were made ready for butchering by being rolled on the back with the head pulled around backward by the beard until the face lay on the ground; next, the head was pushed under the edge of the side to serve as a support to the body as it lay on its back with feet upward. First, the skin was removed in this way: An incision was made at the lower end of the dewlap and the knife run up to the middle of the underlip; the knife was then again inserted at the starting point and a straight cut was made down to the vent; again the knife was inserted at the starting point and a straight cut made down the inside of each fore leg to the ankle. A straight cut was made down the inner side of each hind leg to the ankle. A cut was then made around the mouth and up the line of the nose to the base of the horns and around the horns, leaving the hide, when taken from the deer, antelope, elk, or buffalo, in one piece. The hide was called *ha;* this belonged to the man who killed the animal. The summer hide of the buffalo was called *teshna'ha,* meaning · "hide without hair." From the *teshna'ha* clothing, moccasins, and tent covers were made, as these hides were easily tanned on both sides. The hides taken in winter were called *meha;* these were used for robes and bedding and were tanned on one side only. The hide of an old bull was preferred for bedding. In flaying the animal for this purpose the usual incisions were made on the breast; after this was flayed it was turned thereon, the hind legs were stretched out backward, the fore legs doubled under the body, and a straight cut was made down the back; then the skin was drawn off on each side. Skill was required to make straight cuts and was the result of much practice. One of the most difficult cuts to make was to follow the dewlap. A true outline was the pride of the hunter and added to the value of a skin, as well as to its beauty, particularly when it was to be used as a robe.

After flaying a buffalo, one of the hind legs was disjointed at the hip and cut off. The flesh of the leg was cut lengthwise, following the natural folds of the muscle, and the bone extracted; this portion was called *tezhe'ga.* The next act was to open the body sufficiently to remove the intestines. The large intestine, the stomach, and the bladder were removed and laid to one side. The fore leg was then unjointed and cut off at the shoulder and the bone extracted; this portion was called *tea'.* The breast was next cut; this portion was called *temo<sup>n</sup>'ge*. The meat between the ends of ribs and the breast was called *tezhu'*. There were two portions of this cut, which were considered very choice. These were the pieces that were offered at the ceremony of Anointing the Sacred Pole and were tabu to the Waxthe'xeto<sup>n</sup> subgens of the Ho<sup>n</sup>'ga, who had charge of these rites. Next, the ribs were severed from the backbone; the ribs from both sides made one portion, which was called *tethi'ti*. The tongue was last to be taken out; this was secured by making an incision in the middle of the underjaw, pulling the tongue through the slit and then cutting it off at the roots. If it was late in the day, or the hunters were in haste, the tongue was left untouched. When one of the writers commented on the loss of so dainty a part, she was answered: "Men do not pay attention to these little delicacies but when their children ask for them, the men remember."

The following are the portions of the buffalo and their graded values:

1. Tezhu'—side meat; 2 portions.
2. Tezhe'ga—hind quarters; 2 portions.
3. Tethi'ti—ribs; 2 portions.
4. U'gaxetha—includes the stomach, beef tallow, and intestines; 1 portion.
5. Teno<sup>n</sup>'xahi—back; includes muscles and sinew; 1 portion.
6. Temo<sup>n</sup>ge—the breast; 1 portion.
7. Tea'—forequarters; 2 portions.

To the man who killed the animal belonged the hide and one portion of *tezhu'* and the brains. Whether he had more or not depended on the number of men who were helping. If there were only three helpers, their portions were as follows: To the first helper to arrive, one of the *tezhu'* and a hind-quarter; to the second comer, the *u'gaxetha;* to the third, the ribs. The various portions were adjusted by the owner of the animal. Each helper received something for his services. It sometimes happened that eight or ten men helped, in which case all the cuts were required. If two or more men butchered an animal in the absence of the hunter, when they finished the work each man took his proper portions and left those belonging to the man who had killed the game. When, therefore, the hunter returned to the animal he had shot, he might find it flayed and cut up and his portions lying on the hide awaiting him. Prominent men did not do the butchering. This work was performed by the poor or by young men, who thus secured food or choice bits. Should a chief or the son of a chief appear on the scene when butchering was in progress, he would be allowed the choice of any portion of the animal.

The large intestine was disentangled by the men, stripped between the fingers, and its contents were thrown away. Then it was handed over to the women to be prepared for cooking. They turned it inside out, washed it, and turned it back, being careful not to disturb the fat that adhered to the outside. A narrow strip of tender meat from the side of the backbone was then cut; one end of the intestine bearing fat on it was turned in and the strip of meat was inserted at this end. As the meat was pushed along, the intestine became reversed—the fatty outside became the inside. After the meat was in, both ends of the intestine were securely tied; it was then boiled, or roasted on coals. This was called $ta^{n'}he$ and was esteemed a great delicacy. The meat thus cooked was very tender and all the juice was preserved within its close covering. The stomach was turned inside out, carefully washed, and the inner coating removed and thrown away; the remainder was used for food. The heart and lungs were usually left in the carcass. The small intestines of the sucking calf were braided and roasted over coals; these were regarded as a delicacy. Meat was generally boiled, the water, or soup, being taken after the meat had been eaten.

The bones, used for their marrow after roasting, were: *wazhi'be*, "leg bones;" *teno^{n'}xahi*, "backbone." The *waba'çno^{n}*, "shoulder blades," were valuable as implements, particularly those of the elk, used as hoes. The other bones were called: *te'pa*, "skull;" *he*, "horns;" *u'gaxo^{n}*, "hip bone;" *wazhi'beuto^{n'}ga*, "upper leg bone;" *zhi'beuçni*, "lower leg bone;" *te sha'ge*, "hoofs."

The buffalo meat was brought into camp on ponies. Boys drove these animals out to the hunting field for the purpose of packing the meat on them. The running horses used in hunting were not permitted to carry burdens. Sometimes women went out to help in butchering, particularly widows or childless women, or they drove the pack ponies. It was the woman's part to cut the meat into thin sheets and hang it on the racks for drying. The rib meat was cut into strips, braided, and dried.

The rules for butchering an elk and dividing the meat among the helpers were the same as for the buffalo.

After being flayed a deer was cut in half, one side being cut close to the backbone; this half was called the *tathie'*. This cut became the property of the first man to reach the deer and to begin to butcher the game. The other half of the deer, that to which the backbone and the neck adhered, was divided through the ribs, making two portions. The hind part of this cut belonged to the second person who arrived on the scene and took part in the butchering. To the man who shot the deer belonged the skin and the portion to which the neck was attached. Sometimes a man was alone when he killed a deer. In that case, after he had flayed the animal he cut all the meat from the bones and left the skeleton. If after he had finished a person should come up, the hunter would say, *Bthe'uthi shnude* (*bthe*, "all;" *uthishnude*, "stripped"), that is, "the meat is stripped from the bones."

making but one piece without divisions. Under such circumstances no portion would be given to the newcomer nor would any be demanded. This manner of taking home the deer saved labor to the women, as the meat was nearly ready to hang on the *wa'mo^n shiha*, or "rack," for jerking.

The rules for butchering and dividing the flesh of the antelope and bear were the same as observed with the deer.

### TE'UNE, OR ANNUAL BUFFALO HUNT

When the crops were well advanced and the corn, beans, and melons had been cultivated for the second time, the season was at hand for the tribe to start on its annual buffalo hunt. Preparations for this great event occupied several weeks, as everyone—men, women, and children—moved out on what was often a journey of several hundred miles. Only the very old and the sick and the few who stayed to care for and protect these, remained in the otherwise deserted village. All articles not needed were cached and the entrances to these receptacles concealed for fear of marauding enemies. The earth lodges were left empty, and tent covers and poles were taken along, as during the hunt these portable dwellings were used exclusively. For a century ponies have superseded dogs as burden bearers. The tent poles were fastened to each side of the pony by one end; the other trailed on the ground. The parfleche cases containing clothing, regalia, the food supplies, and the cooking utensils, were packed on the animal. Travoix were used, supporting a comfortable nest for the children, some of whom, however, often found places among the household goods on the pony's back. Men and women walked or rode according to the family supply of horses. Between the trailing tent poles, which were fastened to a steady old horse, here and there rode a boy mounted on his own unbroken pony, for the first time given a chance to win his place as an independent rider in the great cavalcade. Many were the droll experiences recounted by older men to their children of adventures when breaking in their pony colts as the tribe moved over the prairies on the hunt. Much bustling activity occupied the households in anticipation of the start. Meanwhile a very different kind of preparation had been going on for months in the thought and actions of the man who had determined to seek the office of *watho^n'*, or director of the hunt. He had been gathering together the materials to make the *washa'be*, or staff of that office. These consisted of an ash sapling, two eagles (one black, one golden), a crow, a swan skin, a dressed buffalo skin, two pieces of sinew, a shell disk, a copper kettle (formerly a pottery cooking vessel), and a pipestem. These articles were all more or less difficult to obtain, and represented a determined purpose and labor on the part of the man and his family.

## THE WATHOⁿ

The office of *wathoⁿ'*, or director of the hunt, was one of grave responsibility and high honor. The man who aspired to fill it needed to possess courage and ability to lead men and command their respect and obedience. During the term of his office the entire tribe was placed under his direction and control; the Council of Seven Chiefs acted only as his counselors and, together with the people, obeyed his instructions. He directed the march of the tribe, selected its camping places, chose and dispatched the runners in search of buffalo herds, and directed the hunt when the game had been found. He became responsible for all occurrences, from the pursuit of the buffalo and the health and welfare of the people down to the quarreling of children and dogs.

When the time drew near for the tribe to go forth on the hunt, the aspirant to the office of *wathoⁿ'* took or sent the prescribed articles he had secured for making the *washa'be*, or ceremonial staff of the director, to the Washa'be subgens of the Hoⁿ'ga gens, to which belonged the hereditary right to make the staff. It was a pole of ash more than 8 feet high, the end bent like a shepherd's crook. The buffalo skin furnished by the aspirant was cut and a case made from it for covering the pole. All the coarse feathers were removed from the swan skin, leaving only the down; the skin was cut in strips and wound about the staff, making it a white object. On one side of the staff was fastened a row of eagle feathers, and a cluster of golden eagle feathers hung at the end of the crook. Crow feathers were arranged at the base about 10 inches from the end of the pole, which was sharpened. (For picture of the *washa'be*, see fig. 27.) To the pipestem which must accompany the *washa'be* was fastened a shell disk. This stem was probably used when smoking the peculiar pipe belonging to the White Buffalo Hide.

After the *washa'be* was made, the Hoⁿ'ga subgens in charge of the White Buffalo Hide called a council composed of the governing tribal council (p. 208) and the Washa'be subgens, to which was invited the man who desired to be the *wathoⁿ'*. This action of the Hoⁿ'ga subgens constituted the appointment of the man to the office of *wathoⁿ'*. This council had also to determine the direction in which the people were to go and the day on which they were to start. This decision was considered one of the most important acts in the welfare of the people; on it depended the food supply and also safety from enemies while securing it. The food eaten at this council was either dried buffalo meat or maize, which had to be cooked before sunrise. At this council the two Sacred Tribal Pipes were ceremonially filled while their ritual was chanted. This was done as the sun rose. Everyone present wore the buffalo robe with the hair outside, the head on the left arm and the tail on the right, and sat with head bowed and arms crossed on the breast so as to bring the robe around the head like a hood. No feathers or ornaments or any articles pertaining to war could be worn or could be present in the Sacred Tent. The Pipes were smoked in the formal manner; the I$^n$ke'çabe and Tha'tada servers passed them to the members. The smoking was in silence. After the Pipes had been cleaned by the officers appointed for this duty and returned to their keeper, one of the principal chiefs opened the proceedings by mentioning the terms of relationship between himself and the others present. Each one responded as he was designated. The chief then spoke of the great importance of the subject before them and called on those present to express their opinions. If since the last similar council any chief or member present had given way to violence in word or act, he must not speak. So long as he took no part in these official proceedings the evil consequences of his words or actions remained with himself, but should he act officially the consequences of his misdeed would be transferred to the people. After all who could rightfully take part in the discussion had spoken with due deliberation, the newly chosen *watho$^{n\prime}$* was called on. He generally summed up the views that were acceptable to the majority of those present. If there were differences of opinion, then the men had to remain in council until they came to an agreement. At this council the general route the tribe was to take was laid out. In planning the route two necessary features were always considered—wood and a plentiful supply of water. It was also important to lead the people where they could gather the wild turnip in great quantities. These turnips were peeled, sliced, dried, and sewed up in skin bags for winter use. Only the general direction was determined at this council. The daily camps were selected by the *watho$^{n\prime}$* as the people went along. These were usually from 10 to 15 miles apart, wood and water again being important factors in the choice of the camping place. If, owing to the lack of wood or water, the distance between two camping places was greater than could conveniently be made in one journey, the *watho$^{n\prime}$* directed the tribal herald to consult the women, on whom devolved much of the labor of the camp as well as the care of the children, and to ascertain their decision in the matter. The herald then reported the wishes of the majority and the *watho$^{n\prime}$* issued his order accordingly.

When, at the initial council held by the Washa'be subgens, the governing tribal council, and the *watho$^{n\prime}$*, a decision was reached, the official herald was sent to proclaim to the people the day fixed for departure. Meanwhile the council sat in the bowed attitude and the sacred feast was served in seven wooden bowls. These were passed four times around the council, each person taking a mouthful from a black horn spoon. This food could not be touched with the fingers or any other utensil.   The sun must have set before the chiefs could lift their heads and the council break up, and the members return to their homes.   The day for the start once fixed, no change could be made, as that would be breaking faith with Wako<sup>n'</sup>da, in whose presence the decision had been reached.

No prescribed order was observed in making the start.   Those who were ready moved first, but all kept fairly well together.   For four days prior to the start the man who was to act as *watho<sup>n'</sup>* fasted, and when all were departing he remained behind.   After every-one had gone he took off his moccasins and, carrying no weapons, followed slowly with bare feet.   He reached the camp after the peo-ple had eaten their supper, went to his own tent, and as he entered everyone withdrew and left him alone.   The fast, the barefoot march, and the lonely vigil were explained to be "a prayer to Wako<sup>n'</sup>da to give courage to the man to direct wisely and to lead successfully the people as they went forth to seek for food and clothing."   The old men went on to state that "during all the time the man is *watho<sup>n'</sup>* he must be abstemious, eat but little, and live apart from his family; he must continually pray, for on him all the people are depending." This manner of life by the director was called *no<sup>n'</sup>zhi<sup>n</sup>zho<sup>n</sup>*—the same word that was applied to the fast observed by the youth when he went alone to pray to Wako<sup>n'</sup>da.   (See p. 128.)   The idea expressed in this word was explained to be that "the man stands oblivious to the nat-ural world and is in communication only with the unseen and super-natural world which environs him and in which he receives power and direction from Wako<sup>n'</sup>da, the great unseen power."   Every effort was made by the chiefs and leading men to prevent or to con-trol petty contentions, for if everyone was to secure a share in the products of the chase, there had to be harmony, obedience to author-ity, and good order throughout the tribe.   If, however, disturbances frequently occurred, or if the winds continually blew toward the game, thus revealing the approach of the people and frightening away the buffalo, such ill fortune might necessitate the resignation of the *watho<sup>n'</sup>*.   To avoid this necessity on the part of the director, a man was appointed by the chiefs who took the name *watho<sup>n'</sup>* and was to assume all the blame of quarrels and other mishaps.   This official scapegoat took his office good-naturedly and in this humorous way served the tribal director.

On the march the contents of the three Sacred Tents were in charge of their keepers.   In late years the White Buffalo Hide was packed on a pony; in early days it was carried on the back of its keeper.   The *washa'be* (fig. 27) was carried by a virgin, and as it belonged to the White Buffalo Hide she walked near that sacred article.   When in camp this staff of office was kept in the Sacred Tent containing the Hide. The Sacred Pole was carried by its keeper.   When the camping place

was reached, each woman knew exactly where to place her tent in the
*hu'thuga*, or tribal circle.  The Sacred Tents were set up in their
respective places and the sacred articles put at once under cover.
After the camp was made the daily life went on as usual; the ponies
were tethered or hobbled and put where they could feed; wood and
water were secured, and soon the smoke betrayed that preparations
for the evening meal were going forward.

The beauty of an Indian camp at night deserves a passing word.
It can never be forgotten by one who has seen it and it can hardly
be pictured to one who has not.  The top of each conical tent,
stained with smoke, was lost in shadow, but the lower part was aglow
from the central fire and on it the moving life inside was pictured in
silhouette, while the sound of rippling waters beside which the camp
stood accentuated the silence of the overhanging stars.

The signal to move in the morning was the dropping of the cover
from the tent of the director.  When the poles of his tent were visible
every woman began to unfasten her tent cover, and in a short time
the camp was a memory and the people were once more on the march,
stretched out as a motley colored mass over the green waste.

As the buffalo country was reached—that is, when signs of game
were discerned—then the chiefs, the *watho*$^{n'}$, and the Washa'be subgens
of the Ho$^{n'}$ga gens met in council and appointed a number of men who
were to act as "soldiers" or marshals.  These men were chosen from
among the bravest and most trusty warriors of the tribe, those who
had won the right to wear "the Crow" (see p. 441).  They were
summoned to the Sacred Tent of the White Buffalo Hide, where they
were informed of their duty.  It is said that these officers were told:
"You are to recognize no relations in performing your duty—neither
fathers, brothers, nor sons."  Their services began when the
camp was within hearing distance of the herd selected for the coming
surround.  The marshals were to prevent noises, as loud calls and
the barking of dogs, and to see that no one slipped away privately.
Few, however, ever attempted to act independently, as it meant death
to a man to stampede a herd by going out privately to secure game.
During the surround the marshals held the hunters back until the
signal was given for the attack on the herd.  It was in the exercise
of this duty that the marshals were sometimes put to the test of keeping true to the obligations of their office.

The *watho*$^{n'}$ chose some twenty young men to act as runners to
search for a herd suitable for the tribe to surround.  If the region
was one in which there was danger of encountering enemies, the runners went out in groups; otherwise they might scatter and go singly
in search of game.  When the runners had been selected the tribal
herald stood in front of the Sacred Tent containing the White Buffalo
Hide, and intoned the following summons.  First he called the name

of a young man and then added: *Mo<sup>n</sup>zho<sup>n</sup> i<sup>n</sup>thegaço<sup>n</sup>ga tea ia thi<sup>n</sup> ho!* (*mo<sup>n</sup>zho<sup>n</sup>*, "land;" *i<sup>n</sup>thegaço<sup>n</sup>ga*, "explore for me;" *tea*, "may;" *ia*, "come;" *thi<sup>n</sup>*, "action;" *ho*, "calling attention")—"Come! that you may go and secure knowledge of the land for me."

When the runners (the *wado<sup>n</sup>'be*, "those who look") had found a suitable herd, they made a speedy run back to where the tribe was camped; when they were near they paused on some prominent point where they could be seen and signaled their report by running from side to side; if there were two young men, both ran, one from right to left and the other from left to right, thus crossing each other as they ran. (See picture of I'shibazhi, pl. 39, a runner on the last tribal buffalo hunt.) This signal was called *waba'ha*. As soon as they were seen, word was taken to the Sacred Tents and to the *watho<sup>n</sup>'*. The Sacred Pole and the pack containing the White Buffalo Hide were carried to the edge of the camp in the direction of the returning runners, followed by the Seven Chiefs. There a halt was made while the runners approached to deliver their message. The White Buffalo Hide was taken out and arranged over a frame so as to resemble somewhat a buffalo lying down. The Sacred Pole was set up, leaning on its staff, the crotched stick. The chiefs, the keepers, and the herald were grouped in the rear of these sacred objects. The first runner approached and in a low tone delivered his message, telling of the whereabouts and the size of the herd, being careful not to exaggerate its numbers. He was followed by the second runner, who repeated the same message. The herald was then dispatched by the chiefs to notify the people. He returned to the camp and shouted: "It is reported that smoke (dust) is rising from the earth as far as the eye can reach!"

Meanwhile, as soon as signs of the returning runners were seen the director went to his own tent and remained alone until he heard the voice of the herald shouting to the people. Then he went at once to the Sacred Tent of the White Buffalo, where were the Seven Chiefs and the subgens of the Ho<sup>n</sup>'ga, who had charge of the tent and its belongings. The *watho<sup>n</sup>'* now became the leader of the council, and gave commands to the herald. Two men were selected by him to lead in the surround, one to carry the *washa'be* and the other the pipestem. Two boys were also selected to secure the twenty tongues and one heart for the sacred feast. Then the herald went out, and turning to the left passed around the tribal circle, calling as he went the command in the name of the director:

You are to go upon the chase, bring in your horses.
Braves of the I<sup>n</sup>shta'çu<sup>n</sup>da, Ho<sup>n</sup>'gashenu, pity me who belong to you!
Soldiers of the I<sup>n</sup>shta'çu<sup>n</sup>da, Ho<sup>n</sup>'gashenu, pity me who belong to you!
Women of the I<sup>n</sup>shta'çu<sup>n</sup>da, Ho<sup>n</sup>'gashenu, pity me who belong to you!

The tribe was always addressed by the names of its two divisions, and the words "Pity me who belong to you" constituted an appeal by

I'SHIBAZHI

the *watho<sup>n</sup>'* to the honor and the compassion of the people to avoid all dissensions and imprudence which might bring about trouble or misfortune, since any misdeed or mishap would fall heavily on the director, who was responsible for every action, fortunate or unfortunate, and who must suffer for the acts of the tribe, as through his office he belonged to them, was in a sense a part of them, "as," an Omaha explained "a man's hand belongs to his body."

If the herd was at such a distance that the tribe must move on and camp again before the chase took place then the Pole and the Hide remained where the message of the runners had been received, until the people were ready to go to the new camping place. On that journey the two sacred objects, with the Seven Chiefs, led the advance, while the marshals rode on the sides of the great cavalcade and kept the people in order. Once arrived at the camping place, the camp was made silently, for fear of any sound frightening the herd, and strict silence was maintained until the hunters were ready to start. If, however, the herd was discovered near the camp, then after the message from the runners had been delivered the two sacred objects, the Sacred Pole and the White Buffalo Hide, were returned to their tents and the marshals at once enforced silence, killing any barking dogs if necessary. All preparations were made as quietly as possible. Each hunter was attended by one or two mounted boys who led the fast running horses to be used in the chase: later his own mount would be used to bring in the meat from the field. Once again the herald circled the camp. His return to the tent of the White Buffalo Hide was the signal for the hunters to move. The two young men bearing the *washa'be* and the pipestem were the first to start; these led the procession of hunters, headed by the *watho<sup>n</sup>'* and the Seven Chiefs. The advance to the herd was by four stages. At the close of each stage the chiefs and the director sat and smoked. This slow approach to the herd was for definite purposes: First, to afford opportunity to make prayer offerings of smoke to Wako<sup>n</sup>'da, to secure success; second, to check haste and excitement among the hunters; third, to insure an orderly progress toward the buffalo so that each person might take part in the chase and obtain his share of the food supply. As the four stops partook of a religious character they could not be disregarded with impunity. The following incident occurred during a tribal hunt early in the last century: At the third halt a man galloped up to where the *watho<sup>n</sup>'* and the chiefs sat smoking and spoke impatiently of the slow progress, declaring that the herd was moving and might escape because of the delay. The *watho<sup>n</sup>'* said quietly, "If your way is the better, follow it!" The man dashed off, followed by the hunters, who rushed on the herd; in the confusion several of the hunters were injured and the man who led the people to disobey the rites was crippled for life by his horse falling on him. This disaster was regarded as a supernatural punishment of his irreverent action in interrupting the prescribed order of procedure.

When the designated place for the attack was reached the two youths paused while the hunters divided into two parties. One was to follow the youth with the *washa'be*; the other the youth with the pipestem. At the command of the *wathon'* the two young men started and ran at full speed to circle the entire herd, followed by the horsemen. The marshals with their whips held the riders back and in order, for no one was allowed to break into the herd or advance beyond the *washa'be* or the pipestem. Whosoever attempted to do so or who failed to control his horse and keep in line was flogged, the rawhide thong of the marshal falling on the bare body of the hunter with all the force of the strong arm of the officer. These officers were the only men to wear ornaments on the hunts. They were decorated with the highly prized insignia, " the Crow." All of the hunters were nude except for moccasins and breechcloths. When the two youths bearing the *washa'be* and the pipestem met, the *washa'be* was thrust into the ground and the pipestem tied to it. This was the signal at which the marshals gave the word of command to charge on the herd. The hunters responded with shouts and yells, driving the bewildered buffalo in confused circles toward the camp. When the two youths started with the emblems of authority to circle the herd their places were immediately taken by the two boys who had been selected to secure the tongues and heart for the sacred feast. As soon as the hunters rushed on the herd and a buffalo was seen to fall, these boys pushed in, dodging in and out among the animals and hunters, for they must take the tongue from a buffalo before it had been touched with a knife. They carried their bows unstrung and thrust the tongues on them. They had been instructed as to the manner in which the tongues must be taken. An opening was made in the throat of the buffalo and the tongue pulled through and taken out; then the end of the tongue was bent over and the fold cut. It was thought that if a knife was thrust through the tongue to make a hole, it would bring bad luck. Through the slit thus made the unstrung bow was thrust. Ten tongues were carried on one bow. When the twenty tongues and the heart were secured, the boys returned with these articles to the Sacred Tent of the White Buffalo Hide. Meanwhile the slaughter of the game went on. The Omaha were expert hunters and many a man could boast of sending his arrow clear through a buffalo and wounding a second one beyond with the same missile. (Pl. 40.) At the conclusion of the hunt the *washa'be* and the pipestem were brought back and delivered to the *wathon'*. The meat was packed on the horses and taken to camp, where it was jerked by the women. On the night of the surround the feast of tongues and heart was held in the

ARROW RELEASE

Tent of the White Buffalo Hide. The Seven Chiefs, the *watho$^{n\prime}$*, the Washa'be subgens of the Ho$^{n\prime}$ga, and sometimes a few of the leading men, were present. All wore the buffalo robe in ceremonial fashion. On this occasion, though the subgens prepared the food they could not partake of it—the buffalo tongue was their tabu. Their position was that of host; they were acting for the White Buffalo, of which they were the keepers, and tribal etiquette demanded that at a feast the host should not eat any of the food offered his guests. Those who were permitted to eat at this feast took their food in the crouching attitude observed at the initial council when the *watho$^{n\prime}$* was authorized and the route to be taken on the hunt determined. Sometimes the boys gathered more than the twenty tongues required and if the supply was more than sufficient for the feast they received a portion, as did other persons. The feast being a sacred one, the consecrated food was prized, as it was believed to bring health and long life. A share was sometimes begged and the portion received was divided among a number of people, who ate of it in the hope that they might thereby secure to themselves the promised benefits. The tongues and heart were boiled; only the chiefs and the *watho$^{n\prime}$* were present during the cooking.

After the feast the Washa'beto$^{n}$ subgens of the Ho$^{n\prime}$ga sang the ritual of the White Buffalo Hide. The Hide was mounted on its frame and occupied the place of honor in the back of the tent facing the east, while the chiefs and the *watho$^{n\prime}$* muffled in their robes sat with bowed heads and smoked the peculiarly shaped pipe belonging to the Hide.

### THE WHITE BUFFALO HIDE

The manner in which the ritual of the White Buffalo Hide was obtained, as well as that of the Sacred Pole, has been recounted (pp. 247–250). When the old man Wako$^{n\prime}$mo$^{n}$thi$^{n}$ (fig. 60) had completed the rituals, he agreed to deliver the White Buffalo Hide to the writers the following spring or summer. He desired to have this sacred object, which had been so long his care, with him during one more winter and until "the grass should grow again." He kept the Hide in a tent set apart for its use that was pitched near his little cabin. He used to go and sit near it as it hung on a pole tied up as a bundle. There he would muse on the memory of the days when it presided over the hunt and its ritual was sung by him and his companions while the chiefs smoked its sacred pipe and the people feasted on the product of the chase, enjoying peace and plenty. It was hard for the old man to adjust himself to the great changes that had taken place. He realized that his years were few, that the other sacred articles belonging to the tribe were in safe keeping, and he said: "It is right that the Hide should go and be with the Pole, as it always used to be, and it shall go there when the grass comes again." Pitying the old man, the writers acceded to his request, although a large sum of money had been given him for the Hide, and they left it with him. In February, 1898, came the tidings that while the old man was at the Agency (whither he had been called to transact some business), thieves had broken into his tent and had stolen the White Buffalo Hide. The grief of the old keeper was most pathetic. For months every morning he went out and while yet the morning star hung in the eastern sky he wailed as for the dead. His sorrow shortened his days, for he survived only a season or two. He bitterly lamented not putting the Hide where no irreverent hands could reach it—but it was too late. After months of search the writers traced the Hide, which had been sold to a man in Chicago, and learned the name of the thief. Efforts were made to buy back the stolen relic and place it where the old keeper had wished it to go, beside the Sacred Pole, but the purchaser would not accede to any plan looking to that end. The Hide is now deposited with the Academy of Sciences, Lincoln Park, Chicago.

It is the skin of a small, whitish[a] buffalo, with hoofs and horns intact. A row of shell disks are fastened down the back. (Pl. 41.) The exact measurements the writers have been unable to obtain. The pipe is peculiar. It is of red catlinite, nearly circular in shape, and represents the hoof of the buffalo. (Fig. 64). The significance of this pipe is indicated in the last stanza of the first song of Part II of the ritual belonging to the Hide. (See p. 290.)

According to Mo$^n$xe'wathe, who was hereditarily one of the keepers of the Tent of the Sacred Hide, there were formerly two Sacred White Buffalo Hides, one male, the other female. The male hide was buried with its keeper many years ago, so that it was the female that was in the charge of Wako$^n$'mo$^n$thi$^n$. The same authority stated that on the first or second camp, when the tribe was on the annual buffalo hunt, any man who desired to make a present to the Sacred Tent, so as to "count" the gifts, could do so in the following manner: He would send to the keeper and ask him to "untie the buffalo." The keeper made a sort of frame of withes and spread over it the Hide, so as to give it the appearance of a live buffalo. The man who wished to make gifts, took them and with a little girl stood before the tent but at a distance from it. Then he sent his presents one by one by the hand of the little girl to the keeper, who received them. When he had finished, some other ambitious man would advance with presents and send them by a little girl in the same manner. These presents

---

[a] The albino buffalo was sacred among all the close cognates of the Omaha and also among the Dakota tribes. Catlin mentions that the Mandan gave the Blackfeet the value of eight horses for a white buffalo skin, wh...... placed with great ceremony in their medicine lodge. Personal names referring to the white buffalo occur in all the cognates. (For an account of a "White Buffalo Ceremony" among the Dakota, see Peabody Museum Reports, III, 260–275, 1880–86, Cambridge, 1887.)

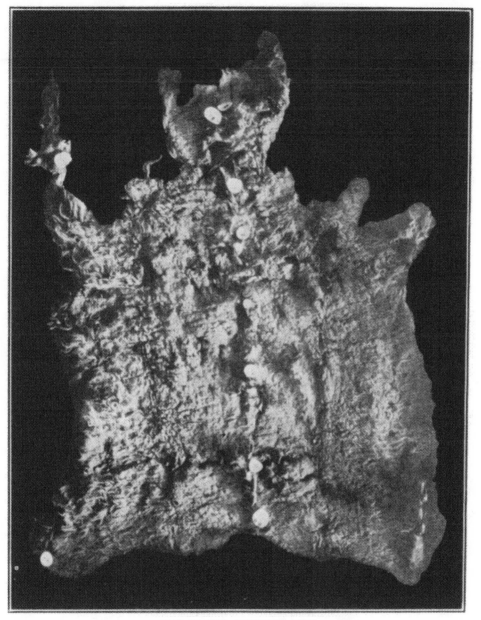

THE WHITE BUFFALO HIDE

could all be "counted" toward the one hundred which would entitle
a man to entrance into the Ho<sup>n'</sup>hewachi and to put the "mark of
honor" on his daughter.   The reason the presents were sent one at a

Upper surface

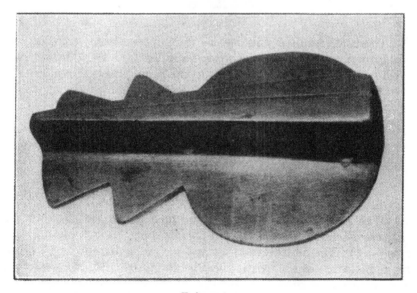

Under surface
FIG. 64.   Pipe belonging to White Buffalo Hide.

time was to give the man the ability to say, "I have been to the
Sacred Tent so many times."   If he had sent all his presents at once,
they would have counted as only one gift.

When the tribe was near the buffalo herds the people moved abreast and not in a file.  As the Sacred Tent was then always in advance, when the Tent stopped and the buffalo was untied all the people had to stop, so the man was then seen by all the tribe as he made his presents to the Sacred Hide.

### THE RITUAL OF THE WHITE BUFFALO HIDE

The ritual of the White Buffalo Hide is dramatic in character but hardly a drama in form.  It is composed of nineteen songs, divided into four groups.  The ritual deals with the gift of the buffalo to man and although it pictures in a realistic way man's efforts to secure this gift provided for him, yet a supernatural presence more or less pervades the ritual from its opening song to the close.  The belief in the supernatural presence was emphasized by the muffled figures of the chiefs and the *watho$^{n\prime}$* as they sat with bowed heads and smoked the peculiar pipe sacred to the Hide while the ritual was sung.

The argument of the ritual is briefly as follows:

#### Part I.—The Pipe
(TWO SONGS)

(1) The pipe "appears."  (2) Man is commanded to take it, that he may supplicate Wako$^{n\prime}$da.

#### Part II.—The Supplication
(FOUR SONGS)

(1) Creation recalled; the species buffalo created.  (2) The buffalo's growth and its perpetuation are provided for.  (3) The buffaloes converge toward man.  (4) They come from every direction and cover the face of the earth.

#### Part III.—Assurance of Wako$^{n\prime}$da
(ONE SONG)

(1) The animals are to grow and perpetuate themselves that they may benefit man.

#### Part IV.—The Hunt
(TWELVE SONGS)

(1) The chiefs' song; refers to the council when the route for the hunt was decided upon.  (2) The people start "toward the lowing herds."  (3) The herds retreat but are seen at a distance.  (4) Runners go in search of the herds, aided by the birds.  (5) Return of the runners; joyful murmurs among the people at the good news.  (6) The herald tells of the council's decision to move on the herd and repeats the director's admonition.  (7) The herald proclaims the signal for the start.  (8) Depicts the field of the hunt; the men seek the animals they have shot.  (9) Refers to the custom of cutting up the meat.  (10) The song of plenty and teaching of economy.  (11) Re-

turn to camp of the hunters, when the boys carry the meat for the sacred feast.   (12) The plentifulness of the game causes some hunters to camp on the field.

Each song was repeated four times.   There was a pause after each part, for all ceremonials had to be performed with deliberation.   The singing of this ritual occupied the greater part of the night.   And the same rule applied to these songs as to those belonging to the Sacred Pole.   An error made it necessary to begin at the first song again, for the ritual must go straight through without any break in the order of the songs.

It is a question with the writers whether the ritual as here given is entire.   The old keeper-priest gave the songs as a whole and the few old men who remembered them declared them correct and complete. Still, there may be unintentional omissions.   To sing these songs into a graphophone was very different for the old man from giving them in their order during the ceremonial, when any omission would have been rectified at once by aid of the *xu'ka*, or prompters.   The ritual as it here stands is at least fairly complete, and if any songs are lacking they would seem to be unimportant to the general outline.

*Part I.—The Pipe*

First Song

**WHITE BUFFALO HIDE**

(Sung in octaves)

Tha - ni - ba - ha!.........   Xu - be   he - he.................

Tha ni - ba- ha   e - thoⁿ be   tha - ni - ba - ha,   Doⁿ - ba?

1. Thani'baha
2. Xu'be hehe
3. Thani'ba ha, e'thoⁿbe
4. Thani'ba ha.   Doⁿ'ba

*Literal translation*

1. *Thani'ba*, an old form of *nini'ba*, pipe.   The Osage use this form in daily speech.   *Ha*, vowel prolongation of preceding syllable.

2. *Xu'be*, part of *waxu'be*, an object set apart from ordinary usage and made holy; some consecrated thing that is used as a medium of communication with the supernatural, with Wakoⁿ'da.   *Hehe, ehe*, I say; the added *h* is for euphony in singing.

3. *E'thoⁿbe*, appears, comes into view, of its own volition, from a covered place, so as to be seen by all.

4. *Do^n'ba*, to see; the word as here used is a part of the phrase *do^n'ba iga* (*do^nba*, to see; *i*, plural sign, a number addressed; *ga*, command).   The phrase is equivalent to "Behold ye!"

*Free translation*

The holy Pipe!
Holy, I say.
Now it appears before you,
The holy Pipe, behold ye!

In this song the pipe is not addressed, but speaks through its keeper-priest, first by its proper name, then by a term indicative of its function; it is then asserted that it "appears" not by any agency of man, but by its own power, and commands men to behold.   The use of the word *etho^nbe* gives the key to the meaning of the song—the Pipe acts, "appears;" it is not acted upon or made to appear.   Although so simple and concrete, this song throws more light on the native thought and belief in the use of the pipe than any single song the writers have found.   The pipe is here represented as infused with "movement," that special attribute of life, and "appears" to become the bearer of man's supplication to Wako^n'da.   The music fittingly clothes the thought expressed in the words and makes a majestic opening to the ritual.

SECOND SONG

1. Niniba, xuba, he tho^ntho^nba ha hetho^nbe
2. Ha ehe the
3. Iugthe, he tho^ntho^nba ha he tho^nbe
4. Thaniniba ha, he tho^ntho^nba ha he tha
5. Ha ehe the
6. Iugthe he tho^ntho^nba ha, he tho^nbe
7. Thaniniba ha he'tho^ntho^nba ha, he tha

*Literal translation*

1. *Nini'ba,* pipe; *xuba,* part of *waxu'be,* holy object.   The change of the final vowel to *a* is for euphony in singing; *hethontho*n*ba,* the same as *e'tho*n*be*—prefixing of *h,* doubling of syllable *tho*n, and change of final vowel to *a* are for euphony and to bend the word to the music, and to convey the sound of the breath; *ha,* vowel prolongation.

2. *Ha,* modified form of *ho,* now, at this time; *ehe,* I say; *the,* this.

3. *Iugthe—i,* mouth; *ugthe,* to insert.

4. *He,* a part of *ehe,* I say; *tha,* an oratorical sign at the close of the sentence, implying something of a command.

*Free translation*

Holy Pipe, most holy, appears; it appears before you.
  Now I bid ye
Within your lips take this holy Pipe, holy Pipe.
The Pipe, it appears, appears before you, I say.
  Now I bid ye
Within your lips take this holy Pipe, holy Pipe.
The Pipe it appears, appears before you, I say.

In this song the chiefs, the representatives of the people, are bidden to accept the holy Pipe, take it within their lips, that the fragrant smoke may carry upward their supplication.   This song precedes the actual smoking of the Pipe.   The music is interesting, as in it the motive of the first song is echoed, but it is treated in a way to suggest the movement toward the Pipe, which in the first song stood apart, clothed with mysterious power.   It now comes near and in touch with the supplicants and lends itself to service.   These two songs complement each other and show both dramatic and musical form.

*Part II.—The Supplication*

FIRST SONG

1. Kinon shkon ha, I bahadon ha, ehe ehe, thishton, adon Pa te shkon, ehe a ha
2. Kinon shkon ha, I bahadon ha, ehe ehe, thishton adon, Inde shkon, ehe a ha
3. Kinon shkon ha, I bahadon ha, ehe ehe, thishton adon, Inshta shkon, ehe a ha
4. Kinon shkon ha, I bahadon ha, ehe ehe, thishton adon, He te shkon, ehe a ha
5. Kinon shkon ha, I bahadon ha, ehe ehe, thishton adon, Nitateshkon, ehe a ha
6. Kinon shkon ha, I bahadon ha, ehe ehe, thishton adon, Nonshki shkon, ehe a ha
7. Kinon shkon ha, I bahadon ha, ehe ehe, thishton adon, Nonka shkon, ehe a ha

8. Kinⁿshkoⁿ ha, I bahadoⁿ ha, ehe ehe, thishtoⁿ adoⁿ, Tea shkoⁿ, ehe a ha
9. Kinⁿshkoⁿ ha, I bahadoⁿ ha, ehe ehe, thishtoⁿ adoⁿ, Moⁿge shkoⁿ, ehe a ha
10. Kinⁿshkoⁿ ha, I bahadoⁿ ha, ehe ehe, thishtoⁿ adoⁿ, Thiti shkoⁿ, ehe a ha
11. Kinⁿshkoⁿ ha, I bahadoⁿ ha, ehe ehe, thishtoⁿ adoⁿ, Zhuga shkoⁿ, ehe a ha
12. Kinⁿshkoⁿ ha, I bahadoⁿ ha, ehe ehe, thishtoⁿ adoⁿ, Nixa shkoⁿ, ehe a ha
13. Kinⁿshkoⁿ ha, I bahadoⁿ ha, ehe ehe, thishtoⁿ adoⁿ, Çiⁿde shkoⁿ, ehe a ha
14. Kinⁿshkoⁿ ha, I bahadoⁿ ha, ehe ehe, thishtoⁿ adoⁿ, Imbe shkoⁿ, ehe a ha
15. Kinⁿshkoⁿ ha, I bahadoⁿ ha, ehe ehe, thishtoⁿ adoⁿ, Zhiⁿga shkoⁿ, ehe a ha
16. Kinⁿshkoⁿ ha, I bahadoⁿ ha, ehe ehe, thishtoⁿ adoⁿ, Çite shkoⁿ, ehe a ha, Çi gthe

*Literal translation*

1. *Ki*, himself or itself; *noⁿshkoⁿ*, movement, action—it moves itself; *ha*, end of the sentence; *I bahadoⁿ*, conscious, having knowledge; *ha*, behold; *ehe*, I say; *thishtoⁿ*, it is done, it is finished, accomplished; *adoⁿ, badoⁿ*, because; *pa te*, nose (*te*, suffix, standing); *shkoⁿ*, moves; *a ha*, behold.

2. *Iⁿde'*, face.

3. *Iⁿshta'*, eyes.

4. *He*, horns; *te* (suffix), standing.

5. *Nita'*, ears; *te*, standing.

6. *Noⁿshki'*, head.

7. *Noⁿ'ka*, back.

8. *Tea'*, arm (buffalo arm).

9. *Moⁿ'ge*, breast.

10. *Thi'ti*, ribs.

11. *Zhu'ga*, body.

12. *Ni'xa*, stomach.

13. *Çiⁿ'de*, tail.

14. *Im'be*, hind quarters.

15. *Zhiⁿ'ga*, little one, the calf.

16. *Çite*, feet; *Çi gthe*, tracks, footprints.

In this song the creation of the buffalo is depicted. "Movement" is synonymous with life. The living embryo moves of itself. According to native reasoning it moves because it is endowed with consciousness. As breath is the sign of life, the nose, whence the breath issues, is the first to "move." Next the face moves, then the eyes, and so on until all the parts of the body "move" because of conscious life. Then the little one, the calf, is born. Finally as the feet move they leave on the earth a sign of life—"tracks."[a]

The music is recitative and in a minor key. The emphasis on the keynote, of the last word, *Çigthe*, "tracks," indicates the finality of the creation.

---

[a] Observe in this connection the peculiar pipe belonging to the Hide (fig. 64), in the shape of a track of a buffalo hoof.

SECOND SONG

(Recitative in octaves)

Nu-ga ha du-di ha    i-thi$^n$ he - he    Nu-ga- ha du-di ha...

i-thi$^n$ he    Nu-ga ha du-di ha    i thi$^n$    he    he

1

Nu′ga ha! du′di ha i thi$^n$! he he
Nu′ga ha! du′di ha i thi$^n$! he
Nu′ga ha! du′di ha i thi$^n$! he he

2

Zha′wa ha! du′di ha i thi$^n$! he he
Zha′wa ha! du′di ha i thi$^n$! he
Zha′wa ha! du′di ha i thi$^n$! he he

3

Mi′ga ha! du′di ha i thi$^n$! he he
Mi′ga ha! du′di ha i thi$^n$! he
Mi′ga ha! du′di ha i thi$^n$! he he

4

Zhi$^n$′ga ha! du′di ha i thi$^n$! he he
Zhi$^n$′ga ha! du′di ha i thi$^n$! he
Zhi$^n$′ga ha! du′di ha i thi$^n$! he he

5

Texi he du′di ha i thi$^n$! he he
Texi he du′di ha i thi$^n$! he
Texi he du′di ha i thi$^n$! he he

*Literal translation*

1. *Nu′ga*, male, bull. The word is here used in a generic sense. *Ha*, sign showing that the male is addressed; *du′di ha*, nearer this way; *i*, come; *thi$^n$*, sign showing that the object spoken of is moving; *he he, ehe*, I say—the *h* is added for euphony in singing.

2. *Zha′wa*, large, majestic, imposing; *zha′wa ha!*, O majestic one!

3. *Mi′ga*, cow, female. The word is here generic and not specific. *Mi′ga ha!*, O mother one!

4. *Zhi$^n$′ga*, little—the word refers to the young of the buffalo; *zhi$^n$′ga ha!*, O little one!

5. *Texi*, difficult to accomplish; *he, ha*, the sign of address.

This song is closely related to the preceding. In the first stanza of this supplicating song the newborn male moving yonder is addressed and asked to come nearer this way—that is, toward man, for whose benefit he was created. In the second stanza the male has grown, has reached maturity, and presents the imposing appearance of the buffalo bull. He is asked to come nearer with all his powers, that man may be helped to live. In the third stanza, the female, the mother with all her potency, is addressed, and bidden to come nearer toward waiting mankind to yield him food. The fourth stanza addresses the calf, with its promise of growth and of a future supply of food. The calf is bidden, as were its progenitors, to come nearer and give food to man. In the fifth stanza the word *texi* is used as a trope. It refers to the great power of Wako$^n$'da as shown in the vast herds brought about by the multiplication of single pairs. These moving herds are asked, supplicated, to come nearer to man, to yield him food and life.

The music is the five-tone scale of F major. Although divided into three phases it is recitative in character and the motive is similar to the preceding song, to which it is related.

THIRD SONG

(Sung in octaves)

In-to$^n$ a-i    ba-do$^n$ ha - i   bi   hi   the zho$^n$-ge he she-no$^n$-ha    ge tho$^n$

In - to$^n$   a - i      ba - do$^n$   ha - i   bi   hi    the

to$^n$ - a - i    ba-do$^n$ ha - i - bi   hi   the    Yo    yo    du - da!

1. I $^n$to$^n$ ai bado$^n$ ha ibi'hi the, zho$^n$ge he sheno$^n$ha ge tho$^n$
2.· I $^n$to$^n$ ai bado$^n$ ha ibi'hi the, 'to$^n$ ai bado$^n$ ha ibi'hi the
3. Yo, yo, duda

*Literal translation*

1. *I$^n$to$^n$*, now, at the present time; *ai bado$^n$*, they coming; *ha*, end of sentence; *ibi'he*, they are coming; *the, tha*, oratorical close of sentence; *zho$^n$ge, uzho$^n$'ge*, path or paths; *he*, vowel prolongation; *she'no$^n$ha*, all; *ge*, many; *tho$^n$*, the.

2. *'To$^n$, i$^n$'to$^n$*, now.

3. *Yo*, come—a form of call; *duda*, this way.

In this supplicatory song the "moving herds" spoken of in the previous song are now drawing near, converging by many paths toward man. Such was the motive of their birth, to benefit man, to respond to his supplications and yield their life when he reverently calls them: *Yo, yo, duda!*—"this way, hither come!" The music is in the five-tone scale of F sharp minor. The call is on the keynote an octave and a fifth below the opening of the song, which is recitative in form, and follows the motive of the two preceding songs, to which it is related.

FOURTH SONG

(Sung in octaves)

Wi-ax-chi ha ha-i bi hi the wi-ax-chi ha ha a - i bi hi the

Wi - ax-chi-ha ha - i bi hi the wi - ax - chi - ha ha-i bi hi

wi-ax-chi ha- ha - i bi-hi the wi - ax - chi ha - i bi hi

1

Wiaxchi ha, hai bi 'hi the
Wiaxchi ha, hai bi 'hi the
Wiaxchi ha, hai bi 'hi the
Wiaxchi ha, hai bi 'hi the

2

Non̄ba ha, hai bi 'hi the
Non̄ba ha, hai bi 'hi the
Non̄ba ha, hai bi 'hi the
Non̄ba ha, hai bi 'hi

3

Thabthin̄ ha, hai bi 'hi the
Thabthin̄ ha, hai bi 'hi the
Thabthin̄ ha, hai bi 'hi the
Thabthin̄ ha, hai bi 'hi

4

Duba ha, hai bi 'hi the
Duba ha, hai bi 'hi the
Duba ha, hai bi 'hi the
Duba ha, hai bi 'hi

5

Çaton̄ ha, hai bi 'hi the
Çaton̄ ha, hai bi 'hi the
Çaton̄ ha, hai bi 'hi the
Çaton̄ ha, hai bi 'hi

6

Shape ha, hai bi 'hi the
Shape ha, hai bi 'hi the
Shape ha, hai bi 'hi the
Shape ha, hai bi 'hi

7

Petho$^n$ba ha, 'i bi 'hi the
Petho$^n$ba ha, 'i bi 'hi the
Petho$^n$ba ha, 'i bi 'hi the
Petho$^n$ba ha, 'i bi 'hi

8

Pethabthi$^n$ ha, 'i bi 'hi the
Pethabthi$^n$ ha, 'i bi 'hi the
Pethabthi$^n$ ha, 'i bi 'hi the
Pethabthi$^n$ ha, 'i bi 'hi

9

Sho$^n$ka ha, hai bi 'hi the
Sho$^n$ka ha, hai bi 'hi the
Sho$^n$ka ha, hai bi 'hi the
Sho$^n$ka ha, hai bi 'hi

10

Gthebo$^n$ ha, hai bi 'hi the
Gthebo$^n$ ha, hai bi 'hi the
Gthebo$^n$ ha, hai bi 'hi the
Gthebo$^n$ ha, hai bi 'hi

11

O$^n$geda ha, 'i bi 'hi the
O$^n$geda ha, 'i bi 'hi the
O$^n$geda ha, 'i bi 'hi the
O$^n$geda ha, 'i bi 'hi

*Literal translation*

1. *Wiaxchi,* one; *ha* added to the word makes it to mean "in one direction;" *hai, ai,* they are coming—the *h* is added for euphony in singing; *bi,* are; *'hi,* a part of *ehe,* I say—the final vowel is changed for euphony; *the,* the same as *tha,* the oratorical end of the sentence.

2. *No$^n$ba ha,* two directions.

3. *Thabthi$^n$ ha,* three directions.

4. *Duba ha,* four directions.

5. *Çato$^n$ ha,* five directions.

6. *Shape ha,* six directions.

7. *Petho$^n$ba ha,* seven directions; *'i,* contraction of *ai,* they are coming.

8. *Pethabthi$^n$ ha,* eight directions.

9. *Sho$^n$ka ha,* nine directions.

10. *Gthebo$^n$ ha,* ten directions.

11. *O$^n$geda ha,* from every direction.

In this song the "moving herds" are depicted as coming wherever man can turn; they cover the face of the earth; they approach him from every direction. O$^n$'geda is one of the *ni'kie* names in the Ho$^n$'ga gens and was taken from this ritual. The old priest shook his head as he sang this stanza and in a broken voice he repeated the word *on'geda*, meaning the buffalo are coming from everywhere, and added: "Not now! not now!" Wako^n'da's promises seemed to him to have been swept away. He could not face what appeared to be a fact nor could he understand it.

The music follows the five-tone scale of E major; the movement of the phrase is dignified and lends itself well to unison singing.

*Part III.—Assurance of Wako^n'da*

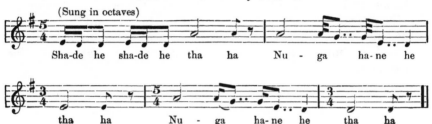

(Sung in octaves)

Sha-de  he  sha-de  he  tha  ha  Nu - ga  ha-ne  he

tha  ha  Nu - ga  ha- ne  he  tha  ha

1

Shade he shade he tha ha
Nuga hane 'he tha ha
Nuga hane 'he tha ha

2

Shade he shade 'he tha ha
Zhawa hane 'he tha ha
Zhawa hane 'he tha ha

3

Shade he shade he tha ha
Miga hane 'he tha ha
Miga hane 'he tha ha

4

Shade he shade he tha ha
Zhi^nga hane 'he tha ha
Zhi^nga hane 'he tha ha

5

Shade he shade he tha ha
Texi hane 'he tha ha
Texi hane 'he tha ha

*Literal translation*

1. *Shade*, it is done—a declaration of something accomplished; *he*, part of *ehe*, I say; *tha ha*, oratorical close of the sentence, calling attention to an important declaration; *nuga*, male; *hane*, you have; *'he, ehe*, I say.

2. *Zhawa*, majestic one.

3. *Miga*, female, mother one.

4. *Zhi^nga*, little one, calf.

5. *Texi*, difficult to accomplish.

In this song Wako<sup>n</sup>′da gives assurance that man's supplication for the animals desired for his food has been heard. In it the form of the second song of Part II is repeated, both as to words and music, with the difference that the act supplicated by man in the first song is here stated authoritatively as accomplished. The change in the motive of the music after the second *he* in the first measure is marked and emphasizes the meaning of the words of the entire song, which was explained to be the emphatic assertion, *ehe*, "I say," of Wako<sup>n</sup>′da that the provision for the perpetuation of the buffalo and the creation of the "moving herds" was because of the needs of man, and to give him food in abundance. The music is in D minor and is recitative in character.

### Part IV.—The Hunt

#### First Song—The Chiefs and the Council.

1. 'Be to<sup>n</sup>thi<sup>n</sup> hi ie te do<sup>n</sup>
2. 'Be 'to<sup>n</sup>thi<sup>n</sup> hi ie te do<sup>n</sup>
3. Mo<sup>n</sup>zho<sup>n</sup> ho<sup>n</sup>' thoe' thoe te do<sup>n</sup>
4. Wi eto<sup>n</sup>thi<sup>n</sup> hithae te do<sup>n</sup> ame, to<sup>n</sup>thi<sup>n</sup> hi te ṭe do<sup>n</sup>
5. 'Be 'to<sup>n</sup>thi<sup>n</sup> hi ie te do<sup>n</sup>
6. Mo<sup>n</sup>zho<sup>n</sup> ho<sup>n</sup> 'thoe'thoe te do<sup>n</sup>
7. Wi eto<sup>n</sup>thi<sup>n</sup> hithae te do<sup>n</sup> ame, to<sup>n</sup>thi<sup>n</sup> hi ie te do<sup>n</sup>

*Literal translation*

1. '*Be, ebe,* who; '*to$^n$thi$^n$, eto$^n$thi$^n$*, first; *hi*, the prolongation of the last vowel sound; *ie*, speak; *te*, must; *do$^n$*, a terminal word or syllable to indicate a question.

3. *Mo$^n$zho$^n$*, land or country; *ho$^n$*, prolongation of vowel sound; '*thoe, uthue*, to speak of.

4. *Wi*, I (the chiefs); *eto$^n$thi$^n$*, first; *hithae*, I speak—the chiefs must speak with one mind and voice; *ame*, they say (the people).

The above song refers to the preliminary council held by the Seven Chiefs with the Washa'beto$^n$ subgens of the Ho$^n$'ga, which had charge of the hunt, at which the route to be taken by the tribe when going after the buffalo was determined. The responsibility thrown on this council was regarded as very grave. This responsibility is indicated by the question in the first line: "Who must be the first to speak," speak of the land (the route to be taken)? The fourth line gives the answer: "I" (the chiefs), "I speak" (the chiefs must speak as with one mind, as one person); *ame*, they say (i. e. the people, the words implying the authority placed on the chiefs by the people; see definition of *ni'kagahi*, p. 136). The song not only refers to the council and its deliberations in reference to the hunt but it voices the loyalty of the people to their chiefs and also the recognition by the chiefs of their responsibility for the welfare of the tribe. While the words refer only to the "land," the route to be traveled by the tribe, the music fills out the picture of the purpose of the journey. The motive is similar to that of the second song of Part II, that deals with the perpetuation of the buffalo and the moving herds, and also recalls the Song of Assurance in Part III. The song is divided into seven phrases and is in the five-tone scale of D major.

SECOND SONG—THE PEOPLE MOVE TOWARD THE LOWING HERDS

(Sung in octaves)

1

Huton'ma 'di wapi, ehe tha
Huton'ma 'di wapi, ehe tha
Huton'ma 'di wapi, ehe tha
Huton'ma 'di wapi, ehe tha
Huton'ma 'di wapi, ehe tha
Huton'ma 'di wapi, ehe tha
Huton'ma 'di wapi, ehe tha

2

Xthazhe ama 'di wapi, ehe tha
Xthazhe ama 'di wapi, ehe tha
Xthazhe ama 'di wapi, ehe tha
Xthazhe ama 'di wapi, ehe tha
Xthazhe ama 'di wapi, ehe tha
Xthazhe ama 'di wapi, ehe tha
Xthazhe ama 'di wapi, ehe tha

*Literal translation*

1. *Huton*, the noise—of the animals, as the lowing of the herds;
*ma, ama,* they; *'di,* a part of the word *edi,* there; *wapi,* to bring (*bthe,*
I go, is understood, although the word *bthe* is not present in the
song)—"I go to the lowing herds to bring back the product of the
hunt," is the meaning of the line; *ehe,* I say; *tha,* the oratorical close
of the sentence.

2. *Xthazhe,* the bellowing of the bulls.

The music of this song is spirited and suggests movement, not merely the moving of the lowing herds but the orderly progression of the people going over the prairies to bring back the spoils of the hunting field. It is in the five-tone scale of F minor, and is divided into seven phrases.

### THIRD SONG—THE HERDS RETREAT

Shu'de aki ama 'di bthe na, hehe the he tha
Shu'de aki ama 'di bthe na, hehe the he tha
Shu'de aki ama 'di bthe na, hehe the he tha
Hehe he bthe na, hehe the he na
Shu'de aki ama 'di bthe na, hehe the he tha
Shu'de aki ama 'di bthe na, hehe the he tha

*Literal translation*

*Shu'de*, smoke; *aki*, retreating; *ama*, they; *'di*, a part of *edi*, there; *bthe*, I go; *na*, a vocable introduced to accommodate the music; *hehe, ehe*, I say; *the* and *he*, vowel prolongations; *tha*, the oratorical termination of the sentence. "Where yonder retreating herds enveloped as in smoke, there I go."

The song recounts the vicissitudes of the hunt; herds sometimes scent the people and scatter; they are seen in the distance, the dust raised by their trampling rising and covering them as if enveloped in smoke.

The music, in B flat major, is rather rapid and partakes of the recitative character.

FOURTH SONG—THE RUNNERS GO FORTH

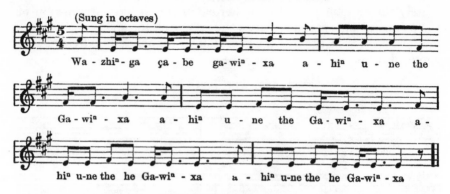

Wazhi ⁿga çabe gawi ⁿxa
Ahiⁿ une the he gawiⁿxa
Ahiⁿ une the he gawiⁿxa
Ahiⁿ une the he gawiⁿxa
Ahiⁿ une the he gawiⁿxa

*Literal translation*

*Wazhiⁿ'ga*, bird; *çabe*, black—the word is used as a trope and means the crow; *gawiⁿxe*, soaring; *ahiⁿ*, wings; *une*, to search; *the*, to go, or goes; *he*, vowel prolongation.

The crow follows the herds—"He is a buffalo hunter," the old man explained. "He watches to find his chance for carrion." So, when the runners go out to search for herds, they scan the sky to catch sight of the crow and other birds of prey, that they may direct their steps in the direction of the soaring birds. When the herds are found, credit is given to the guiding birds who thus lend their assistance to man when searching for the game. (Note the ritual in which the crow promises to help man, p. 311.)

The music, in A major, is recitative in form, but resembles the motive of the buffalo songs already referred to in Part II.

FIFTH SONG—RETURN OF THE RUNNERS

**Recitative**
( Sung in octaves )

E- thon-be   a - ke - da ha   ha ha   ça - e   ti - the   a-wa-the

E- thon-be   a - ke - da ha   ha ha   ça - e   ti - the   a-wa-the

E- thon-be   a - ke - da ha   ha ha   ça - e   ti the   a-wa-the

E- thon-be   a - ke - da ha   ha ha   ça - e   ti the   a-wa-the

E- thon-be   a - ke - da ha   ha ha   ça - e   ti the   a-wa-the

**1**

Ethonbe ake da ha ha ha, çae tithe awa the
Ethonbe ake da ha ha ha, çae tithe awa the
Ethonbe ake da ha ha ha, çae tithe awa the
Ethonbe ake da ha ha ha, çae tithe awa the
Ethonbe ake da ha ha ha, çae tithe awa the

**2**

Ethonbe ake da ha ha ha, wezhnon tithe awathe
Ethonbe ake da ha ha ha, wezhnon tithe awathe
Ethonbe ake da ha ha ha, wezhnon tithe awathe
Ethonbe ake da ha ha ha, wezhnon tithe awathe
Ethonbe ake da ha ha ha, wezhnon tithe awathe

**3**

Ethonbe ake da ha ha ha, gthongthon tithe awathe
Ethonbe ake da ha ha ha, gthongthon tithe awathe
Ethonbe ake da ha ha ha, gthongthon tithe awathe
Ethonbe ake da ha ha ha, gthongthon tithe awathe
Ethonbe ake da ha ha ha, gthongthon tithe awathe

*Literal translation*

1. *Ethonbe*, appear; *ake, aki*, I return; *e*, vowel prolonged; *da, don*, when; *ha*, end of sentence; *ha ha*, vowel prolonged; *çae*, noise, as made by voices; *tithe*, suddenly; *awathe*, I make them.

2. *Wezhnon*, grateful.

3. *Gthongthon*, murmur, as many people talking in low tones.

The runner speaks in the song, telling that when he appears on the eminence near the camp and signals his tidings, then suddenly the sound of many voices is heard, the people talking of the good news he brings. The second stanza speaks of the gratitude voiced by the people over the word he brings to them. The third stanza refers to the restraint that is put on the camp—no loud talking permitted, nor any noise, for fear of frightening the herd.

The music is in E major and is recitative and subdued in character. Even the song is repressed in conformity with the scene to which it is related.

SIXTH SONG—THE HERALD TELLS OF THE DECREE AND ADMONITIONS OF THE COUNCIL

1

Wanita a′noⁿçe e ta ama ha, edi shne te ea thoⁿka a tha ha edi shne te ea thoⁿka a tha ha

Watoⁿ 'thohe tha ha; edi shne te ea thoⁿka a tha ha, edi shne te ea thoⁿka a tha ha wani ta a′noⁿçe e ta ama ha edi shne te ea thoⁿka a tha ha

2

Wanita a′noⁿçe e ta ama ha, edi shne te ea thoⁿka a tha ha, edi shne te ea thoⁿka a tha ha

Çabe uthohe tha ha; edi shne te ea thoⁿka a tha ha, edi shne te ea thoⁿka a tha ha wani′ta a′noⁿçe e ta ama ha, edi shne t′e ea thoⁿka a tha ha

3

Wani'ta a'noⁿçe e ta ama ha, edi shne te ea thoⁿka a tha ha, edi shne te ea thoⁿka a
tha ha
Gthezhe uthohe tha ha; edi shne te ea thoⁿka a tha ha, edi shne te ea thoⁿka a tha ha
wani'ta a'noⁿçe e ta ama ha, edi shne te ea thoⁿka a tha ha

4

Wani'ta a'noⁿçe e ta ama ha, edi shne te ea thoⁿka a tha ha, edi shne te ea thoⁿka a
tha ha
Gani uthohe tha ha; edi shne te ea thoⁿka a tha ha, edi shne te ea thoⁿka a tha ha
wani'ta a'nonçe e ta ama ha, edi shne te ea thoⁿka a tha ha

5

Wani'ta a'noⁿçe e ta ama ha, edi shne te ea thoⁿka a tha ha, edi shne te ea thoⁿka a
tha ha
Gashpe uthuhe tha ha; edi shne te ea thoⁿka a tha ha, edi shne te ea thoⁿka a tha ha
wani'ta a'noⁿçe e ta ama ha, edi shne te ea thoⁿka a tha ha

6

Wani'ta a noⁿçe e ta ama ha, edi shne te ea thoⁿka a tha ha, edi shne te ea thoⁿka a
tha ha
Texi uthohe tha ha; edi shne te ea thoⁿka a tha ha, edi shne te ea thoⁿka a tha ha
wani'ta a 'noⁿçe e ta ama ha, edi shne te ea thoⁿka a tha ha

7

Wani'ta a'noⁿçe e ta ama ha, edi shne te ea thoⁿka a tha ha, edi shne te ea thoⁿka a
tha ha
Çani uthuhe tha ha; edi shne te ea thoⁿka a tha ha, edi shne te ea thoⁿka a tha ha
wani'ta a'noⁿçe e ta ama ha, edi shne te ea thoⁿka a tha ha

*Literal translation*

1. *Wani'ta*, animals, game; *anoⁿçe*, surround, inclose; *e*, vowel prolongation; *ta*, will, intention; *ama*, they; *ha*, the sign of the end of the sentence; *edi*, there; *shne*, you go; *te*, must; *ea thoⁿka*, say they, who are sitting (refers to council in the White Buffalo Tent); *a*, vowel prolongation; *ha*, modification of *tha*, the oratorical close of a sentence; *watoⁿ*, possessions; *'thohe*, part of *uthohe*, a collection of sacred articles (refers particularly to all the materials used in making the *washa'be*, the staff or badge of the office of the leader of the hunt).

2. *Çabe*, black (used as a trope, meaning the crow, one of the birds used in making the *washa'be*).

3. *Gthezhe*, spotted or brown eagle (used in making the *washa'be*).

4. *Gani*, the golden eagle (the feathers are tied on the *washa'be*).

5. *Gashpe*, broken (a trope, meaning the shell disk fastened on the pipestem. These disks were presented to the White Buffalo Hide and fastened in a row down the back).

6. *Texi*, difficult to perform (the word refers to the labor involved in securing the materials used in making the *washa'be*).

7. *Çani*, all—that is, not only the "possessions," but what they in their collective form stand for officially.

In this song of the herald the people are notified that the council has ordered the hunters to make ready to surround the herd. They are to follow the *washa'be*, and to remember all that it signifies and the help given by the birds—the crow, the eagle—and the elements, represented by the shell. All these things, difficult to bring together, are now united to lead the people toward the herd and to help them in securing food wherewith to sustain the life of the people, both young and old.

The music, in E flat major, is recitative.

SEVENTH SONG—THE HERALD PROCLAIMS THE TIME TO START

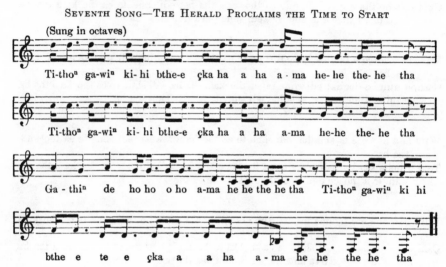

Titho$^n$ gawi$^n$' ki hi bthe e çka ha a a ha ama hehe the he tha
Titho$^n$ gawi$^n$' ki hi bthe e çka ha a a ha ama hehe the he tha
Gathi$^n$ 'deho' ho o ho ama hehe the he tha
Titho$^n$ gawi$^n$' ki hi bthe e te e çka a a ha ama hehe the he tha

*Literal translation*

1. *Titho$^n$*, village, camp; *gawi$^n$*, part of *gawi$^n$xe*, to circle, as a bird soars; *ki*, when; *hi*, vowel prolongation; *bthe*, I go; *e*, vowel prolongation; *çka*, may; *ha a ha*, vowel prolongation; *ama*, they; *hehe*, *ehe*, I say; *e he*, vowel prolongation; *tha*, oratorical close of the sentence.

3. *Gathi$^n$*, yonder walking; *'deho, edea*, what does he say? (the final vowel changed); *ho o ho*, vowel prolongation.

4. *Te*, must.

In this song the figure of speech, which likens the herald going around the camp to the soaring and circling of a bird, recalls the song of the runner when the birds by their soaring guided to the game. The herald left the Sacred Tent of the White Buffalo Hide and passed around the tribal circle by the left; the completion of his round by his return to the Sacred Tent was the signal that the tribe had been notified and the people were to start. The song refers to the questioning of the people as he walked giving the order of the leader.

The music, in G minor, is recitative.

### EIGHTH SONG—THE HUNTING FIELD

(Sung in octaves)　Harmonized by John C. Fillmore for interpretation on the piano

*Spirited, with marked rhythm*

Wiⁿa-u the thiⁿ ga thu hi-thiⁿ he Wiⁿa-u the thiⁿ ga thu hi thiⁿ

he he Wiⁿa-u the i wa mi hi-thiⁿ he Wiⁿa-u

the-thiⁿ ga thu hi thiⁿ he he wiⁿa-u the thiⁿ ga thu hi thiⁿ he he

1

Wiⁿ au the thiⁿ gathu hi thiⁿ he
Wiⁿ au the thiⁿ gathu hi thiⁿ he he
Wiⁿ au the i wami hi thiⁿ he
Wiⁿ au the thiⁿ gathu hi thiⁿ he he
Wiⁿ au the thiⁿ gathu hi thiⁿ he

2

Wiⁿ au the thiⁿ gathu hi thiⁿ he
Wiⁿ au the thiⁿ gathu hi thiⁿ he he
Wiⁿ au the takikiⁿ hi thiⁿ he
Wiⁿ au the thiⁿ gathu hi thiⁿ he
Wiⁿ au the thiⁿ gathu hi thiⁿ he

3

Wiⁿ au the ke gathu hi ke he
Wiⁿ au the ke gathu hi ke he he
Wiⁿ au the xiatha hi ke he
Wiⁿ au the ke gathu hi ke he he
Wiⁿ au the ke gathu hi ke he

*Literal translation*

1. *Wiⁿ*, one; *au*, I wounded; *the*, there; *thiⁿ*, moving; *gathu*, yonder, in a definite place; *hi*, has reached or arrived at; *thiⁿ*, moving; *he, ha*, the end of the sentence; *i*, mouth; *wami*, blood or bleeding.

2. *Takikiⁿ*, staggering.

3. *Ke*, lying; *xiatha*, fallen.

In this song, the wounded, bleeding, staggering, and fallen game is referred to.

The music, in C major, is vigorous, virile, and suggestive of action.

NINTH SONG—CUTTING UP THE GAME

1

Iⁿ thiⁿ woⁿthoⁿ ga iⁿgthoⁿ hoⁿ çiihi iⁿ thiⁿ woⁿthoⁿ ga ha
Iⁿ thiⁿ woⁿthoⁿ ga iⁿgthoⁿ hoⁿ çiihi iⁿ thiⁿ woⁿthoⁿ ga ha
Iⁿ thiⁿ woⁿthoⁿ ga iⁿgthoⁿ hoⁿ çiihi iⁿ thiⁿ woⁿthoⁿ ga ha

2

Iⁿ thiⁿ bahoⁿ ga iⁿgthoⁿ hoⁿ pa thoⁿ hoⁿ iⁿ thiⁿ bahoⁿ ga ha
Iⁿ thiⁿ bahoⁿ ga iⁿgthoⁿ hoⁿ-pa thoⁿ hoⁿ iⁿ thiⁿ bahoⁿ ga ha
Iⁿ thiⁿ bahoⁿ ga iⁿgthoⁿ hoⁿ pa thoⁿ hoⁿ iⁿ thiⁿ bahoⁿ ga ha

3

Iⁿ thiⁿ woⁿthoⁿ ga iⁿgthoⁿ hoⁿ çiⁿde he iⁿ thiⁿ woⁿthoⁿ ga ha
Iⁿ thiⁿ woⁿthoⁿ ga iⁿgthoⁿ hoⁿ çiⁿde he iⁿ thiⁿ woⁿthoⁿ ga ha
Iⁿ thiⁿ woⁿthoⁿ ga iⁿgthoⁿ hoⁿ çiⁿde he iⁿ thiⁿ woⁿthoⁿ ga ha

*Literal translation*

1. *Iⁿ*, mine; *thiⁿ*, you; *woⁿthoⁿ*, hold; *ga*, the sign of command; *iⁿgthoⁿ*, eldest son; *hoⁿ*, prolongation of the vowel sound; *çiihi, çihi*, ankle (the middle *i* is to prolong the vowel).

2. *Bahoⁿ*, to push up, to boost; *pa*, head; *thoⁿ*, the roundish shape of the head; *hoⁿ*, vowel prolongation.

3. *Çiⁿde*, tail; *he*, vowel prolongation.

The customs relating to cutting up the game have been given (p. 271). The first stanza of this song refers to the hunter directing his assistants during the butchering, placing the animal on its back; the second stanza, putting the head so as to hold the body in position; the third speaks of the tail, used to lift the carcase in order that the task may be completed.

The music, in E flat, is recitative rather than melodic in character.

### TENTH SONG—OF PLENTY AND ECONOMY

Te - a mi-ke tha  te - a-a-a Te-a - a-a  mi-ke he tha thi$^n$ he  he

Tea miketha, tea a, tea a, mikehetha thi$^n$ he

#### *Literal translation*

*Tea*, buffalo arm, the fore quarter; *a*, vowel prolongation; *miketha mikihethe*, to put on the hip; *thi$^n$*, moving (equivalent in this instance to walking); *he*, end of sentence.

Teaching economy: The fore quarter, being tough, was the least desirable part of the animal for food, and was frequently thrown away. When the hunter took it, he did not carry it with the rest of his load, but on his hip, so he could drop it if it became too burdensome. The meaning of the song could hardly be gathered from the words. It was explained that the song indicated a plentiful supply of meat; but the good hunter, unwilling that anything should be lost, took the fore quarter, the most undesirable piece, and, being heavily laden, he had to carry it on his hip. The song, the old priest said, was one to instill the teaching that even when there is abundance there should never be wastefulness.

The music, in C major, is recitative.

### ELEVENTH SONG—RETURN TO THE CAMP

**Recitative**
(Sung in octaves)

She a - ki  a - ma - ha - ki  a-ma - ha   do$^n$  wa - i$^n$

ki  a - ma-ha wa - no$^n$ xthi$^n$ a - hagthe a - ma-ha do$^n$   wa - i$^n$

gthe  a - ma ha   She a - ki - a-ma-ha  ki - a - ma-ha

She aki ama, haki ama ha Wai$^n$ 'ki ama ha, wano$^n$xthi$^n$ ahagthe ama ha do$^n$, wai$^n$
'gthe ama ha
She aki ama, haki ama ha

*Literal translation*

*She*, yonder; *aki*, a point on the return (to camp); *ama*, one moving; *haki, aki*, returning to camp; *ha*, vowel prolongation; *wai*$^n$, carrying a burden; *'ki, aki*, returning; *wano*$^n$*xthi*$^n$, hurrying; *ahagthe, agthe*, going home; *'gthe, agthe*, going home.

The hunters hasten back to camp, and, as they go, see one hurrying with a burden. This is one of the boys, who is carrying the tongues and heart for the sacred feast. All are going home.

The music is recitative.

TWELFTH SONG—THE BELATED HUNTERS

1

Texi ehe bimo$^{n'}$ aha, a
Bimo$^{n'}$ aha a e tha
He ehe bimo$^{n'}$ ha ha
Bizi a ha ha bimo$^{n'}$
Bizi aha ha bimo$^{n'}$

2

Texi ehe bimo$^{n'}$ aha, a
Bimo$^{n'}$ aha a e tha
He ehe bimo$^{n'}$ ha ha
Shude eha bimo$^{n'}$
Shude eha bimo$^{n'}$

3

Texi ehe bimo$^{n'}$ aha, a
Bimo$^{n'}$ aha a e tha
He ehe bimo$^{n'}$ ha ha
Zia ha ha bimo$^{n'}$
Zia ha ha ha naxthi$^n$

*Literal translation*

1. *Texi*, difficult; *ehe*, I say; *bimo*$^{n'}$, rubbing (*bi*, to press; *mo*$^n$, rubbing, as between the hands); *aha, ehe*, I say (the vowel modified in singing); *a, ha, tha*, syllables indicating prolonged effort; *bizi—bi*, part of *bimo*$^{n'}$, to rub, *zi*, yellow (the word describes the appearance of the wood when it begins to glow, and is used only to indicate the act of making fire by rubbing).

2. *Shude*, smoke.

3. *Zia*, yellow glow; *naxthi*$^n$, flames

This song refers to *edi'nethe*, building a fire on the hunting field by hunters who have killed so much game they can not get through in time to carry all the meat back to camp.   The words mark the progress of kindling fire by friction, twirling one stick in another stick prepared to receive it, by rubbing between the hands—first the glow, then the smoke, and at last the yellow flames.   The rhythm of the rubbing can be brought out in the singing of the song, as well as the efforts used in kindling the fire.   While this song is realistic, yet the making of fire by friction was always an act more or less fraught with religious sentiment and it probably was esteemed a fitting close to the ritual sacred to the buffalo.

In hunting the buffalo no songs invoking magical help were sung or decoy calls used or disguises worn, success being believed to come through the strict observance of the ritual by the leader, the obedience of the tribe to the prescribed rites, and the skill of the individual hunter. From the detailed description of the Omaha tribal hunt here given, as it was told the writers by those who had taken part in it both as officials and as ordinary hunters, it is evident that the Omaha's hunting was not a sporting adventure but a task undertaken with solemnity and with a recognition of the control of all life by Wako$^n$'da.   The Indian's attitude of mind when slaying animals for food was foreign to that of the white race with which he came into contact and perhaps no one thing has led to greater misunderstandings between the races than the slaughter of game.   The bewilderment of the Indian resulting from the destruction of the buffalo will probably never be fully appreciated.   His social and religious customs, the outgrowth of centuries, were destroyed almost as with a single blow.   The past may have witnessed similar tragedies but of them we have no record.

### THE PONCA FEAST OF THE SOLDIERS

An old man, a leader among the Ponca, who died some fifteen years ago, related the following:

When I was a young man I used to see a very old man perform this ceremony and recite the ritual of the Feast of the Soldiers.   This feast took place when many buffalo had been killed, when food was plenty, and everyone was happy.   The *hu'thuga* was made complete and a large tent pitched, where were gathered all those who were entitled to be present.   When the feast was ready, a bowl containing soup and bits of meat was placed near the door of the lodge and the leader said, as the bowl was set down, "It is done!"   When the leader said this the old man went to the bowl and took it up and held it as he sat and began to recite the ritual.   The ritual is in four parts. There are two names mentioned in the ritual.   The name mentioned after the first part was A'thi$^n$washe.   This name belonged to the Wazha'zhe gens.   The name mentioned after the second part I can not recall; it belonged to the Mako$^n$ gens.   When the first name was mentioned the old man made a depression in the ground near the edge of the fire with the knuckle of his first finger and into this depression he dropped four drops from the tip of the little spoon which was in the bowl.   The offering was to the spirit of this man.   At the end of the second part, when he mentioned the name of the second man, he again dropped four drops from the tip of the spoon.   At the end of the third part, which referred to the wolf, he dropped four more drops and at the close of the fourth part, in which the crow is spoken of, he dropped four drops, making four times four—sixteen drops in all.

After this ceremony was completed the servant approached the one who presided and fed him from the bowl. He took the food deliberately and solemnly. He was fed all that was in the bowl. When he finished, those present could begin to eat. Each person who had his bowl could take only four spoonfuls and must then pass his bowl to his next neighbor, who took four spoonfuls and passed the bowl on. In this manner the bowl was kept moving until the feast was consumed.

The following is the ritual recited on this occasion. Of line 2 the old man said: "The teaching implied in these words is that thus the chiefs had spoken, and there is never any variation or change in these words." And of line 9 he said: "It is said that the club as the badge or mark of the chief or leader was older than the pipe." The red clubs mentioned in the ritual represented the chiefs, the black clubs the officers of the hunt. Concerning the dropping of the broth he remarked: "The chiefs, although long dead, are still living and still exercise a care over the people and seek to promote their welfare; so we make the offering of food, the support of our life, in recognition of them as still our chiefs and caring for us."

RITUAL

1

1. He! Ni′kagahi eçka
2. Esha bi a bado$^n$
3. He! Ni′kagahi eçka
4. Ni′to$^n$ga athite uthishi ke tho$^n$
5. He! ni uwitha ati thagthi$^n$ bado$^n$
6. He! Ni′kagahi eçka

2

7. E no$^n$ atho$^n$ka bi abado$^n$ eçka
8. He! Ni′kagahi
9. He! weti$^n$ duba ça′be tha bado$^n$
10. Duba zhide tha bado$^n$
11. Çabe the te tho$^n$
12. Thuda the thi$^n$ge xti abthi$^n$ ta athi$^n$ he esha biabado$^n$ ni′kawaça
13. Shi$^n$gazhi$^n$ga wiwita xti thi$^n$ke shti wa$^n$
14. Thuda agitha mo$^n$zhi ta mike esha bi abado$^n$ eçka

3

15. He! ugaxe thi$^n$ge xti ni′kawaça
16. Wani′ta to$^n$ga duba utha agthi bado$^n$
17. Edi aino$^n$zhi bado$^n$
18. Ni′kawaça eçka
19. Wani′ta shukato$^n$ wi$^n$
20. Ushte′ thi$^n$ge xti gaxa bado$^n$
21. U′zhawa xti agtha bado$^n$
22. Wai$^{n\prime}$gi uzho$^n$ge ke washi$^n$ uno$^n$bubude xti mo$^n$thi$^n$ bado$^n$
23. Sho$^{n\prime}$to$^n$ga nuga thathi$^n$she tho$^n$
24. Çi$^n$de ke gaathiko$^n$
25. Kigthi′ho$^n$ho$^n$ xti mo$^n$bthi$^n$ ta athi$^n$ he edi eshe abado$^n$

4

26. He! ni′kawaça eçka
27. Ka′xe nuga thathi$^n$she tho$^n$
28. Ugaxe thi$^n$ge xti edi uwehe ta athi$^n$he eshe abado$^n$
29. Xu′ka edi uwehe ta athi$^n$he eshe abado$^n$
30. He! nikashiga aho! ethabi wathe ego$^n$ mo$^n$thi$^{n′}$ aho$^n$
31. Baxu wi$^n$ thaçtube ego$^n$ ithe ado$^n$
32. Go$^n$te zhi$^n$ga ego$^n$ mo$^n$thi$^n$ ki
33. Baxu ke ibiu xti ethu$^n$be gthi abado$^n$
34. He! nikashiga aho! etha bi wathe ego$^n$ ethu$^n$be gthia do$^n$
35. Baxu ke tho$^n$ ethu$^n$be gthi ki
36. Wani′ta shuka to$^n$ wi$^n$ te wiki the xti mo$^n$iyatha ethi$^n$ abado$^n$
37. Xu′ka edi uwihe abado$^n$
38. Ni′kawaça eçka

*Free translation*

1

1. O! Chiefs, eçka [eçka, I desire]
2. Thus you have spoken, it is said
3. O! Chiefs, eçka
4. The great water that lay impossible to cross
5. O! you crossed, nevertheless, and sat upon the banks
6. O! Chiefs, eçka

2

7. Thus have you ever spoken, it is said, eçka
8. O! Chiefs
9. Four clubs you have blackened
10. Four you have reddened
11. Those that are black
12. Verily, my people, without fear I shall carry, you have said, so it is said
13. Not even my own child
14. Shall stay my hand, you have said, so it is said, eçka

3

15. Without overconfidence, my people
16. Word has been brought back that great animals have been found
17. Near to them they (the people) approached, and stood
18. My people, eçka
19. A great herd of animals
20. Verily they (the people) shall cause none of them to remain
21. Verily they (the people) shall go toward home rejoicing
22. Along a trail strewn with fat.
23. I, the male gray wolf, shall move
24. With tail blown to one side
25. I shall gallop along the trail, you have said, so it is said

4

26. O! my people, eçka
27. I, the male crow
28. Verily, without overconfidence I shall join (in giving help), you have said, so it is said
29. As instructor I shall join, you have said, so it is said
30. The people, astonished at your coming, cry O-ho!
31. Beyond the ridge you disappear as though piercing the hill
32. After a little you return
33. Sweeping closely the hill
34. The people, astonished at your coming, cry O-ho!
35. As you appear on the ridge
36. Verily, one herd of animals I have killed for you, you have said, so it is said
37. Thus you have instructed, it is said
38. My people, eçka

## FISHING

The streams and lakes accessible to the Omaha abounded in fish, which were much liked as food. Men, women, and children engaged in the pursuit of catching fish; while greatly enjoyed, it could hardly be called sport, for it was engaged in for a very practical purpose. The names of fish known to the tribe are given on page 106.

So far as can be learned there were no fishhooks of native manufacture, but small fish were caught by means of a device called *takon'hon-tha çni'de*, made as follows: Three or four strings having bait tied at one end were fastened by the other end, about 6 inches apart, to a slender but tough stick; a cord of twisted hair tied to the middle of this stick was attached to a stout pole. This was thrown into the stream, and often as many fish as there were lines were caught and landed. This style of fishing was called *huga'çi*, a name now applied to fishing with hook and line. As the name implies, the bait usually consisted of bits of meat (*hu'tazhu*).

Fish were sometimes shot or speared. The former method of taking them was termed *huki'de* (*hu*, "fish;" *ki'de*, "to shoot"); spearing fish was termed *huzha'he*. Another mode of fishing was by means of a kind of movable weir of willows tied together, taken into deep water by a company of men or women, some holding the ends upright and others the center; all would walk up the stream pushing this fence of willows before them and so drive the fish into shallow water where they were shot, speared, or caught by the hand. The willow weir was called *hu'bigide*, and this manner of fishing, *hu'kontha*.

CPSIA information can be obtained
at www.ICGtesting.com
Printed in the USA
LVHW040157150723
752404LV00001B/93

9 780803 268760